Jay Cooke's Gamble

Jay Cooke (1821–1905), ca. 1875. Courtesy Baker Library, Harvard Business School.

Jay Cooke's Gamble

The Northern Pacific Railroad, the Sioux,
and the Panic of 1873

M. John Lubetkin

UNIVERSITY OF OKLAHOMA PRESS : NORMAN

Library of Congress Cataloging-in-Publication Data

Lubetkin, M. John.
   Jay Cooke's gamble : the Northern Pacific Railroad, the Sioux, and the Panic of 1873 / M. John
Lubetkin.
      p.   cm.
   Includes bibliographical references and index.
   ISBN 0-8061-3740-1 (alk. paper)
   1. Northern Pacific Railroad Company. 2. Cooke, Jay, 1821–1905. 3. Indian Wars / Custer, George
Armstrong, 1839–1876. 4. Financial crises—United States—History—19th century. I. Title.

HE2791.NL83 2006
330.973'082—dc22

                                                                                              2005051241

Five people made this book truly possible. This is to my wife, Linda, whose love, common sense, good humor, and support have always been indispensable. It is also to the memory of my parents, Alice and Jacques Lubetkin, and two outstanding teachers, Tom Donovan ("T. D.") of the Northfield–Mount Hermon School and Joseph David ("D-Minus") Doty of Union College. These teachers practiced old-fashioned tough love, set high standards, and always made you push just a little harder.

CONTENTS

ILLUSTRATIONS

FIGURES

Sitting Bull
View of Big Hill
Pompey's Pillar, 1873
White Bull
Rain-in-the-Face
Army Scientific Corps, 1873
NP advertisement in *Philadelphia Inquirer,* August 16, 1873
Luther P. Bradley
Location of Custer's charge, August 11, 1873
Sketch of Custer's camp, September 9, 1873, by Montgomery Meigs
Charles H. Fahnestock
J. Pierpont Morgan
Newspaper sketch, September 18, 1873
Surveyors' reunion, January 1906
Thomas Rosser at about 70
Gall's grave
Jay Cooke at 80

MAPS

TABLES

PREFACE

Acknowledging petty larceny might seem out of place; but, as numerous people have asked how an easterner with a cable TV background ever got to write this book, an honest answer is needed. A long time ago, in what now seems like a far-away galaxy, during the late 1950s, I joined a fraternity at Union College (Alpha Delta Phi). The fraternity's solid, 1898 building, since commandeered by the college in a wave of political correctness, had over the course of decades acquired hundreds of dated and seldom—if ever—read books.

Although happily susceptible to the immoderation, self-indulgence, and licentiousness associated with fraternities, I also liked to browse through the books and ran across the slim *Union College, Record of Class [of] 1868, 50th Year Reunion*. I was fascinated by the profiles of George Westinghouse (who resigned, rather than flunk out, after four months) and numerous Civil War veterans. One was a Congressional Medal of Honor winner; and another, after surviving the Little Round Top and Wilderness battles (and Andersonville prison), became a minister. There was also a civil engineer, Edward Jordan, who was hired by the Central Pacific Railroad and was at Promontory Point in 1869 when the golden spike completing the transcontinental railroad was driven. But what caught my eye was something else Jordan had written about himself:

> [I]n 1870 on engineering corps of Northern Pacific [Railroad] then [surveying] from Lake Superior to Puget Sound, had charge of location and construction of about 100 miles of road; was on locating expeditions from Missouri River to Yellowstone Valley under military escort to protect from Sitting Bull's band, *a hazardous but interesting time*. [emphasis added]

The "hazardous but interesting" hooked me; and, before I graduated, I left a sheet of paper in the book. Now to the larcenous part: on my tenth college reunion I returned, respectively, to my alma mater, the fraternity, its bookcases, the book, and—Eureka!—the untouched book mark.

Jay Cooke's Gamble really began in the spring of 1994. While working on my *Union College's Class of 1868: The Unique Experiences of Some Average Americans,* I was attempting to track down information about Jordan, who had died childless in 1935. After a half-dozen phone calls I reached a Mark Jordan of Gorham, Maine, at his office. Somewhat sheepishly, and after profuse apologies for taking his time, I asked him if he had ever heard of an Edward C. Jordan who had attended Union College in the 1860s. After what seemed ages and instead of hanging up on me— as I'm sure he now regrets—he replied, "Oh, you mean Uncle Ned?"

Over the next few years, with consistent good humor and promptness, Mark sent me Ned Jordan's handful of surviving letters and remembrances and suggested various books about the Jordan family to read. Mark also found letters on Northern Pacific stationery from Tom Rosser and Ira Spaulding, both Civil War generals. Through Ned Jordan I "discovered" the all-but-forgotten, and never comprehensively described, Yellowstone Surveying Expeditions. All the surveys had one unique feature: they cut through Sioux Indian country in Montana and North Dakota. In fact, Ned Jordan and his fellow surveyors very much needed protection from Sitting Bull (and Crazy Horse, Gall, Rain-in-the-Face, Hump, Spotted Eagle, White Bull, and others). And who protected them in 1873? None other than George Armstrong Custer. But that was *what* happened. *Why* Ned Jordan was surveying along the Yellowstone traced back to a forgotten American, the "financier of the Civil War," Jay Cooke.

INTRODUCTION

The Panic of 1873 began shortly before 11 A.M. on Thursday, September 18, when the Wall Street branch of the nation's most prestigious private banking house, Jay Cooke & Associates, the financiers of the Northern Pacific Railroad, unexpectedly ushered its customers out and then literally closed its doors, thereby signaling that it was bankrupt. Before the day ended, scores of private banking firms in large cities and an untold number in medium-sized and smaller communities had shut their doors for lack of cash. The Panic lasted some five years, and its economic damage was second only to the past century's Great Depression.

That afternoon one of America's richest and most prominent businessmen, Cornelius Vanderbilt, gave a rare interview to a reporter for the *New York Herald*. Referring to the Northern Pacific Railroad, he commented that "you can't build a railroad from nowhere to nowhere." What Vanderbilt meant was that railroads had to make economic sense by either serving existing communities or meeting a national political need, as in the case of the transcontinental railroad, which was largely financed with government funds and guarantees.

Just thirteen years earlier, in 1860, there was limited American settlement from St. Cloud, Minnesota, to the Pacific Ocean for some 250 miles south of the Canadian border, except for a handful of trappers, traders, and soldiers. The census of 1860 did not include Idaho, Montana, or Wyoming. There were 4,837 souls in Dakota (mostly along the Missouri River near Iowa) and 11,494 in Washington, near the Columbia River or Puget Sound. On the route that the Northern Pacific's engineers were to survey, past St. Cloud and Duluth through Fargo, Bismarck, Billings, Helena, Missoula, Spokane, and Walla Walla, the Euro-American population was perhaps 5,000 (including soldiers) in an area encompassing some half-million square miles.[1]

Before 1860 ended, census figures were useless: gold was discovered in Idaho and two years later in Montana. Despite the Civil War, or perhaps because of it (entrepreneurial Southerners also being well represented), the area from central Montana west quickly grew to over 30,000 in 1870. Yet settlement east of the Bozeman Pass—Billings, Fargo-Moorhead, and Brainerd—did not exist at that time. While the total Euro-American population between Duluth and Bozeman (975 miles) was perhaps 2,500 (mainly soldiers) the area remained the home to tens of thousands of Native Americans, mostly west of the Missouri River.

By planning to build a railroad through this area, the Northern Pacific appeared to violate an underlying economic tenet of railroad construction: to connect existing communities or large regions. That the NP raised tens of millions of dollars is due to the action of one man who wanted to follow Meriwether Lewis and William

Clark's pioneering efforts, a man who felt he had been "chosen" to save the Union financially during the Civil War and to build a northern transcontinental railroad. If classic Greek tragedy involves the fall of a great or noble person who is brought down by his own flaws and mistakes, Jay Cooke fills the role as well as any nineteenth-century American.

But Cooke's gamble is more than a story of the American frontier. It is also a cautionary story of American business that could have been lifted from the front pages of newspapers over the past ten years. Investors in high-tech stocks or related funds during the "dot.com" bubble or those for whom names like Adelphia, Enron, Tyco, or Worldcom have resonance can find numerous parallels with the Northern Pacific. Certainly the management failings and insider manipulations of the railroad's forgotten president J. Gregory Smith and his "Vermont clique"—including his brother, congressman Worthington C. Smith—will seem familiar.

This is a post–Civil War book, peopled by those who, with few exceptions, earned their reputations during the war. Commentators describing office seekers today often use words like "handlers" and "actors" on the political stage. Similarly, many historians regard nineteenth-century individuals as one-dimensional stick figures— identified by name only—bobbing up and down in the economic, social, or military currents of their era. In writing this narrative history, however, I have attempted to portray these individuals in flesh-and-blood terms; their actions were motivated by various forces, including, among others, idealism, greed, fear, ethical standards, revenge, ego, alcoholism, and, sometimes, plain old laziness and stupidity. One must also carefully distinguish between errors of commission and omission, as there would be plenty of both in the conduct of the Yellowstone surveys of 1871, 1872, and 1873 and the construction of the Northern Pacific Railroad.

But the keystone of the Yellowstone surveys was Jay Cooke: Ohio born, a Philadelphia banker, financial promoter, devout Christian, Union loyalist, and American visionary. Cooke was not just inspired by Lewis and Clark; he had worked in St. Louis when the aged Clark lived nearby, in an era when people pointed to the Missouri and the Rockies as they spoke of the country's future. By the time the Civil War ended, Cooke had become so financially successful that there is a tendency today to assume dishonesty on his part and to label him an early Robber Baron. Certainly he had more raw power than any other banker in America, including J. P. Morgan; was assisted in his rise by Abraham Lincoln (who did not like him); and bribed elected officials on an unprecedented scale. Yet, while Cooke delighted in cheating cheaters and selling war bonds to Quakers, if anything, he was cursed by not understanding that others did not share his optimistic vision of America and his sense of fiduciary responsibility.

Cooke's great gamble—through which he changed western American and Canadian history—was his attempt to finance and build a second transcontinental railroad, the Northern Pacific.

Cooke's gamble resulted in track built to the Missouri at Bismarck, the creation of Yellowstone National Park, and the rescue of George Armstrong Custer from obscurity. The gamble reignited the Great Sioux War, forced the Canadian-British governments to build their own transcontinental railroad (the Canadian Pacific), and ushered in a flood of northern European immigration. It also triggered the Panic of 1873 and set in motion the forces that ended the last large vestige of Native American independence. And the gamble continues to be felt; for better or worse, the largest private landholder in the United States today is the Burlington Northern Santa Fe Railroad, the successor to the Northern Pacific.

In the end, Cooke's gamble failed not because of his inability to sell bonds or because of national economic conditions but because of the resistance of Sitting Bull's "militant" followers, at most a thousand warriors taking the field at any one time. Ironically, in the fighting that developed in 1872 and 1873, Sitting Bull was defeated time and again in open battle.

As will be seen, the impact of newspaper stories concerning fighting between army units protecting Northern Pacific surveyors and Native Americans led by Sitting Bull badly damaged Cooke's bond sales in 1872. Yet these stories were nothing compared with the extensive coverage by a half-dozen of what we call today "embedded" reporters who were on the 1873 Yellowstone Surveying Expedition. This coverage, given newspaper space equal to that of major Civil War battles, reached its apex with a florid report of the fighting written by a participant, George Armstrong Custer.

Although less than a dozen soldiers and civilians died on surveys in the Yellowstone Valley, by mid-morning on September 18, 1873, a national panic had begun: hundreds of banks and businesses and tens of thousands of individuals went bankrupt, and Cooke's role in American history ended.

In March 1869, as president-elect Ulysses S. Grant decided on the composition of his cabinet, Cooke was considered a leading candidate to be treasury secretary. No other aspirant matched his standing or contribution to the war effort. Cooke's brother Henry was a card-playing crony of the president-elect, and Cooke himself had taken a lead role in ensuring Grant's financial peace of mind, both publicly and very privately.

Had Grant appointed Cooke treasury secretary that March, Sitting Bull and his followers might have lived in relative peace for another decade, or at least until their ecological world collapsed; western Canada would have continued drifting into the economic orbit of the United States, with British and Canadian officials increasingly befuddled as their colony continued to fill with Americans; Custer might be remembered as the Civil War's best Northern cavalry general, rehabilitated by Philip H. Sheridan after Grant left office and perhaps huffing and puffing to a noble death at San Juan Hill; and J. P. Morgan would be recalled as the founder of the Metropolitan Museum of Art and possibly as an associate of the powerful Charles H. Fahnestock, Cooke's New York partner. But Cooke was not appointed by Grant—and thus our story begins.

Jay Cooke's Gamble

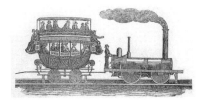

CHAPTER 1

"God's Chosen Instrument"

Philadelphia, Thursday, September 18, 1873: like most businessmen, Jay Cooke was concerned about the "stringency" (shortage) of cash, Wednesday's sharp stock decline, and the failure of Kenyon Cox & Co., a respected medium-sized banking house, the previous week. Three days earlier, when President Grant had spent the evening at Cooke's 53-room mansion, the two men likely touched on Wall Street's condition. As he had for the past few days, Cooke came to his offices early Thursday morning to keep abreast of the news through his private telegraph system.

Jay Cooke & Co., if not the nation's largest banking house, was clearly its most powerful. Decades later, people who knew both men would compare J. Pierpont Morgan with Cooke, the man regarded as one of the Union's saviors, *the* "financier of the Civil War," who had conceived and managed the sale of over $1.6 billion in federal bonds to hundreds of thousands of investors, all without a whiff of scandal. The public and the military, aware of George Washington's monetary travails during the Revolution, were grateful for Cooke's effectiveness and honesty. After the war, as mid-twentieth-century business historian John T. Flynn noted, Cooke bought members of Congress, bribed two vice presidents, built churches, gave vacations to penniless ministers, and combined the qualities of money getting, corruption, farsightedness, and piety in such successful proportion that he was venerated by the public, feared by politicians, and considered by all the country's leading banker.[1]

In the past days, despite Wall Street's failures, sell-offs, rumors, and melodramatic accounts of Indian fighting along the Yellowstone, Cooke's Northern Pacific Railroad had held firm, buttressed not so much by logic as by his support. In the two years since the death of his wife, he had become increasingly reclusive—his life more rigid, his dress outdated and almost bizarre, his vacations varying only by the number of fish he caught. Cooke was not a gifted speaker, read little other than the Bible and religious tracts, and had no interest in the arts; but he was an insightful businessman and brilliant listener, instinctively understanding others—only he would have thought to have a magician entertain a visiting Sioux delegation.

At 52, Cooke was absorbed by the Northern Pacific. His interest in the Northwest had begun as a teenager in St. Louis, watching steamships leave for and arrive from the Upper Missouri. In 1873 he firmly believed, as he had during the war, that he was again acting as "God's chosen instrument" by building the NP. Cooke *was* the NP to tens of thousands of investors. After thirty months of inept, dishonest management, he had stepped in and taken charge; for the first time the NP would take in more cash than it spent, complete its transcontinental surveying, and let bids for 205 miles of track between Bismarck and the Yellowstone River.

About 11 A.M. there was a discreet knock on Cooke's door. However rigid he was in dress and decorum, he wanted news instantly. At first glance, the telegram's contents may not have registered; but then, upon rereading it, stoical as he was, he probably had to fight an involuntary gasp. Other telegrams quickly arrived. Glancing up and walking toward the front of his bank, Cooke gave an order and attempted to regain his composure.

Any understanding of the Northern Pacific must begin with Cooke, a descendant of Henry Cooke, who arrived in Salem, Massachusetts, about 1638. "I never paid much attention to this matter," Cooke wrote, but "I believe fully in *good* ancestry" (Cooke's emphasis). While he professed little interest, Cooke knew that the family's story was an honorable one. His grandfather Asaph Cooke may have lined up on the village green at Lexington, Massachusetts, on April 18, 1775; more documentably, his maternal grandfather, David Carswell, marched with Richard Montgomery into Canada and helped capture Montreal. Carswell was taken prisoner at Quebec, but he survived both wounds and scurvy and, after Saratoga, was exchanged and freed.[2]

Meanwhile Asaph Cooke and his wife settled near Glen Falls, New York. Jay's father was born in 1787 and given the name of an obscure second-century saint and bishop of Rome, Eleutheros. According to family history, he attended Union College (Schenectady) and studied law in Albany under Chancellor Kent. In 1812 he married Carswell's daughter Martha and in 1816 set out for the West. It took them over a month following the Mohawk (by canoe), Allegheny (by log raft), and Ohio (by flatboat) until they stopped at Madison, Indiana. Two years later Eleutheros, briefly returning to New York, "discovered" Sandusky Bay and moved his family there.[3]

Jay Cooke was born in Sandusky on August 10, 1821. Eleutheros, hating his own name, kept his son's short and simple: Jay, after John Jay, without even a middle name. The land was still comparatively wild, with bears and wolves, and the fishing, which Jay loved, was spectacular. When Wyandot Indians, decimated by defeat, disease, and alcohol, came to receive their annual government payments, it was a time of high excitement. Jay, bright and quick to laugh, recalled being carried on the shoulders of an old Wyandot chief, Ogontz, who often slept in the Cookes' barn.[4]

Eleutheros became an attorney, promoter, real-estate insider, and state legislator and was elected to the 22nd Congress (1830). When William Henry Harrison visited Sandusky, Old Tippecanoe stayed with the Cookes. Like many Sanduskians with New England backgrounds, the Cookes adamantly opposed slavery, and their house became part of the underground railroad. Jay recalled the Fugitive Slave Act with anger: a local judge, his brother Pitt's father-in-law, freed some fugitive slaves and was then successfully sued. "This . . . [law] was one which was very distasteful," he wrote, "[because] it made us all liable to do duty as slave catchers."[5]

In 1836 a New Yorker (remembered only by his last name, Seymour) became enamored of one of Jay's cousins and went to St. Louis to start a dry-goods firm. Wishing to ingratiate himself, he offered Jay a job at a whopping $600 per year, "not only for my own merits," Jay recalled, "but as a link [to my cousin]." By July young Jay, who had spent his life in tiny Methodist Sandusky, was in St. Louis. Five years earlier the *Yellow Stone* had been the first ship to steam up the Missouri to its confluence with the Yellowstone. The ship carried over a hundred tons of goods, including thousands of gallons of Monongahela whiskey, peach brandy, cherry bounce, and concentrated spirits of wine. Soon a half-dozen steamers made the annual trip, each one inexorably increasing America's dominance over British traders, who had to transport their goods across the Atlantic.[6]

With a population of some 7,500, St. Louis was the nation's western commercial hub. The town was wide open at night, with people carousing in the bars, gambling halls, and brothels along the waterfront. During the day it was a mixture of New Orleans, Canadian, and U.S. culture. Jay quickly learned French and also heard Lewis and Clark stories almost firsthand. Clark, infirm and in his sixties, lived in St. Louis, and Jay was swept along by the grand saga as steamers, bateaux, canoes, rafts, and virtually anything that could float a few thousand miles arrived from the Upper Missouri loaded with furs.

The Panic of 1837 ended Seymour's business and his relationship with Cooke's cousin. Decently, he paid Jay, who returned to Sandusky. The next year William Garroway Moorhead, Jay's 26-year-old brother-in-law, invited him to Philadelphia. Moorhead had formed a company to take passengers from Philadelphia to Pittsburgh by a combination of rail, stage, canal, and steamer. Jay sold tickets, kept books, wrote ads, paid bills, and quite likely performed janitorial duties. But Moorhead, whose skills never lay in the humdrum world of business operations, soon faced extensive competition. As bills piled up, Moorhead faded away like Alice's Cheshire cat, and by mid-autumn the company was bankrupt. Before returning home, the now self-confident Cooke,

17, wrote his parents that he would arrive with "a trunk full of presents and plenty of cash in my pockets . . . [feeling] as healthy as a rat in a granary."[7]

Jay had every reason to feel good: his herculean efforts had caught the eye of banker Enoch W. Clark. Clark's private banking house dealt in stocks, bonds, promissory notes, private and public banknotes—anything that offered a profit for a financial middleman. Tightfisted, Clark offered Jay a clerk's position at $300 a year. Clerks often worked thirteen-hour days, six days a week, and had to write legibly, do arithmetic quickly, keep books, and place a value on everything that came across their desks—to say nothing of spotting counterfeit items. By 1840 Jay balanced Clark's books, did legal work, and wrote ads and a daily financial column. Clark was no fool; Jay soon became part of his family, eating with them on holidays. On January 1, 1843, he was made a full partner, gratis, with one-eighth of the company. At Clark's death in 1856, Jay was running the company and successfully steered it through the Panic of 1857.

In Philadelphia, unlike Sandusky, Jay never found a bachelor niche for himself. In 1842, while visiting his brother Henry at Allegheny College in Meadville, Pennsylvania, he met the president's sister, Dorothea Elizabeth Allen, just 15, visiting from Baltimore. "I lost my heart the first day," he wrote 50 years later, "and the second day we were sworn friends and life long lovers." Despite the objections of her parents, Jay bombarded Elizabeth with letters and visited whenever possible. "I occasionally spent a day or two with her there—moonlight horseback rides of course and lots of other pleasant adventures," he recalled. Finally the Allens capitulated, and the two married on August 21, 1844. But the union had its strains; the Cookes were abolitionists, while the Allens owned slaves, and two of Elizabeth's brothers later fought for the Confederacy. Philadelphia's Methodists were too liberal for Elizabeth, so the couple joined the Episcopalian church. In the years to come, Elizabeth would bear eight children, four of whom survived childhood.[8]

In Philadelphia Cooke went from one success to another, investing in canal, telegraph, and railroad companies. "Rather than a gambler," Carl Sandburg wrote, "[he was] a speculator with an eye for good risks." At the opening of the Mexican War (1846), to raise $50 million, the U.S. Treasury called for bids. When the dust settled, Clark's firm (led by Cooke) was one of two companies selected. But in 1858 Cooke, bored and worth perhaps $250,000, announced his retirement. He continued putting deals together, but he did what he wanted: "free foot," he called it. A rare setback was his investment in the Vermont Central Railroad, which turned sour after a protracted legal battle. On January 2, 1861, he opened his own firm, Jay Cooke & Co. To drum up business, he gave one-third ownership to Moorhead, then president of the Philadelphia & Erie Railroad. He "knew nothing" of banking, Cooke wrote, "[but] I had the benefit of the large business which from time to time flowed into the firm through his position."[9]

Jay's tiny banking house opened just as the Civil War began. The first lengthy conflict of the industrial era, the war forced both sides to design, construct, and operate effective logistical systems as well as to raise money systematically. Besides raising taxes, another option was to print paper money and hope for battlefield success. This salutary approach (if one is not upset by inflation) worked quite well for the South but proved flawed after Gettysburg and Vicksburg. Unfortunately for the North, the Treasury had just $1.7 million in hand when Lincoln took office and was soon spending a million dollars a day. Given the lack of cash and what little tariffs and fees brought in, the federal government decided to assume a 90-day war.[10]

The North's finances were guided by treasury secretary Salmon P. Chase. Chase was in the cabinet because Lincoln, believing Chase had strong Republican Party support but not trusting him, wanted him where he could control him. But, as economic historian Theodore J. Grayson wrote, "[Lincoln's] greatest mistake of all" was picking a man who "knew very little about finance and . . . proceeded to prove his ignorance." Neither Chase nor Lincoln wanted to finance the war by printing money or adding high income taxes; so they temporized, attempting to sell bonds.

Following Fort Sumter, Cooke was determined to assist the North. He felt that slavery was a mortal sin and was embarrassed that the North had not acted earlier. "I have always felt that God designed punishing the whole nation, north and south for the evil and crime of slavery," he wrote. Cooke also appears to have been a quiet prewar activist, although to what degree is not clear. Following the Harper's Ferry raid, he harbored two of John Brown's sons, John and Owen, and later openly employed Owen as a caretaker on Gibraltar, the Lake Erie island he owned. Owen was "very strange in his ideas and ways," wrote Cooke, delicately avoiding the fact that Owen kept with him the mummified corpse of his brother Watson.[11]

Cooke's war involvement began just after Lincoln's inauguration. In Ohio Henry Cooke had close ties with Chase (he was Chase's executor), publishing a Republican paper that Jay subsidized. Henry brought Jay and Chase together; while everybody said the right things afterward, the meeting was chilly. Nevertheless, on April 20 Chase offered Cooke the position of assistant treasurer, a high post, but one that he did not want. After some hesitation, Jay declined, seemingly losing any hope to influence Northern financial policy.[12]

While most Northern states gave the federal government men, equipment, and cash, Pennsylvania, which had promised 10,000 troops, was stymied because of previous bond defaults. Cooke volunteered to sell the bonds but was rebuffed. He then watched helplessly as the state's financial officials discovered that they could not sell the bonds. Finally, they sheepishly came back to him. Upon receiving approval on May 28, Cooke charged ahead with his old friend Anthony J. Drexel, Philadelphia's dominant banker. In three weeks they sold over $3 million in bonds. Cooke himself subscribed $10,000, which became public knowledge and added to the public's faith in him: he sold only securities in which he also invested.[13]

On July 21, 1861, the North was defeated at Bull Run. Federal censors tried to block the news, but a *Philadelphia Inquirer* reporter slipped back into Philadelphia the next morning. The news quickly spread, and businessmen wandered the streets in shock. Cooke, as surprised as anyone, swung into action. Instead of trying to gloss over the battle, he made it a rallying cry, just as the Alamo had been or Pearl Harbor and the World Trade Center would be. Going from one downtown office to another, Cooke had $1.75 million in pledges by noon, twenty hours after the battle's end. He instantly became a national hero and knew he had a workable formula, whereas Chase saw a competitor grabbing headlines. Probably prodded by Lincoln, Chase took Cooke with him to New York in August as the government tried to raise $50 million. Chase did the talking and found the banking houses unenthusiastic. The bankers, Matthew Josephson wrote in *The Robber Barons*, "had neither the bubbling patriotism of Cooke nor his dazzling vision." The bonds finally sold but only at 12 percent, debasing previously sold bonds and adding to inflationary pressures. Cooke had Lincoln's support; Chase began utilizing Cooke but constantly undercut him, reduced his commissions, questioned expenses, and treated him condescendingly.[14]

Cooke became Chase's advisor for a $150-million bond program set for late 1861, but Chase limited his sales territory to only Philadelphia and nearby New Jersey, allowed nothing for advertising or operations, and left him on a commission-only basis. Nevertheless, Cooke enthusiastically went after a wide audience by mixing patriotism, small-denomination sales, and public awareness. Traditionally only the wealthy had been solicited, but his instincts said that the North's huge number of middle-class artisans, merchants, and farmers felt that the war was a noble cause and wanted to participate. Writing much of the copy himself, Cooke advertised in English and foreign-language papers. He also played hardball: publishers not carrying the patriotic stories that he submitted could forget advertising dollars. His participation, Josephson wrote, "was so brilliant . . . he sold so much more than the other bankers (about one-fourth of the total) that his demands [to run the entire program] could not long be resisted." Cooke had done nothing less than formulate bond sales in the United States and Great Britain for World Wars I and II.[15]

In early 1862, anticipating more government business, Cooke opened a branch office in Washington on 15th Street, across from the Treasury. Jay made his brother Henry the senior partner—a wise move, as Henry made friends easily, unlike Jay.

Given Henry's lack of banking experience, Jay plucked from obscurity a brilliant young banker to head the office's operations: Harris Charles Fahnestock. Fahnestock, with the Harrisburg National Bank, was likely "loaned" to Cooke for Pennsylvania's 1861 war bond sales. By year's end he was with Cooke's firm, and in 1870 held a 14 percent interest in Jay Cooke & Co., the third largest holding.[16]

Cooke also invited Drexel to invest, but he declined, citing the risk. With no actual business, Cooke hesitated; however, a letter from 74-year-old Eleutheros tipped the scales: "It is in just such times when an enterprise like this, with a skillful pilot, will be sure to be rewarded in the exact ratio of its peril." Jay knew he needed a Washington insider and brought in a three-decade congressional factotum, Lincoln appointee, and world-class busybody, Benjamin B. French, who knew everybody and kept a detailed, fascinating diary of the times.[17]

At Lincoln's urging, on March 7, 1862, Chase appointed Cooke "Subscription Agent for National Loan," giving Jay sales control of all U.S. bonds. The position was undefined, Chase was clueless, and Jay quickly expanded his role. Josephson wrote: "[He] curbed or prodded speculators as he pleased . . . [and] in his onward rush he had scrambled over the heads of the older cliques of financiers." The Cookes knew more about government plans than any other banking house and consistently invested with their inside knowledge. As more Washingtonians banked with them further information came, in turn leading to even more profits and depositors, including John Wilkes Booth. There was never a hint of impropriety concerning bond sales; as the profits from the Philadelphia and Washington offices were a fraction of Jay's wealth at the war's end, the explanation for his great wealth lies in his timely use of insider information.[18]

The Cookes soon branched out. One wartime venture that was quickly profitable was a Capitol Hill–to–Georgetown trolley-car company. But Jay did not permit African Americans, including those in uniform, on the trolleys. Chase, an early abolitionist, was furious. "Why cannot colored people ride in the cars?" he wrote Jay. "Grant writes that the colored regiments are indispensable. . . . Their exclusion is a shame and a disgrace. . . . Let all decent people ride in any car convenient when they get it." Properly humiliated and having no satisfactory answer, Cooke ducked the issue by selling the company.[19]

In the 1863 campaign Cooke sold $511 million in bonds. Drawing not a penny in advance, he fielded an organization including 2,500 salesmen. Sales reached $3 million a day; and the Treasury, which had to sign each bond, was backlogged for weeks. After all expenses were paid, Jay Cooke & Co. netted $220,000: $\frac{1}{25}$ of 1 percent. Nevertheless, the figure stirred up a storm of protest. The problem arose from Jay's making the sales look effortless: predictably, other bankers and politicians now wanted to share in the profits.[20]

Cooke never wanted to admit that, having had the opportunity, he was not on intimate terms with Lincoln. The two men had little in common, and Cooke and his family were allied with the ambitious Chase—a cost of the bond business. What most damaged their relationship was an incident following General George B. McClellan's 1862 Richmond fiasco. Cooke, meeting privately with Lincoln one evening, asked him to fire McClellan. "I told him I came direct from the people and knew their thoughts [and] I impressed these views upon Mr. Lincoln [for two hours] earnestly and almost pleadingly." After that their relationship was strictly *pro forma*.[21]

In 1864 Cooke came under congressional investigation but was fully cleared. A new bond program, without him, failed. Cooke's personal style did little to help. Testifying before the powerful Thaddeus Stevens, he was asked about legislation he supported. "I felt that in answering," he later wrote, "I was stating a great truth . . . and said, *raising myself to my full height and pointing towards Heaven*, 'in the name of God I believe every word will be fulfilled that I have promised if this bill is enacted'" (emphasis added). One can only imagine the thoughts of congressmen as the wealthy Cooke, wearing already dated clothing, gaunt, full-bearded, his eyes ablaze, invoked the name of the Almighty. Afterward the legislation died.

Mid-1864 saw another Northern crisis. Grant and William Tecumseh Sherman were stalled, casualties were horrific, Jubal Early's raid on Washington left Lincoln's reelection uncertain, and the $3 million–a-day war effort was in chaos. Chase resigned on June 29 and was replaced by Senator William Fessenden, who met with Cooke in July but—put off by him—gave him no business. In October, however, with only $5 million of a $40-million bond program sold, Fessenden gave Cooke $10 million, which he quickly sold. Cooke asked for the remaining $25 million and also sold these bonds. With Lincoln reelected and Congress now friendly, Cooke had sold another $200 million by February. On March 3, 1865, Congress approved the largest bond sale of the war, $600 million. Cooke said he could sell it all and, without opposition, was given the contract. Yet die-hard Southerners thought that they might still outlast the North. As the *Richmond Examiner* wrote:

> The Federal Government is now selling a large amount of what they call seven-thirty bonds, being hundred dollar bills bearing interest at two cents a day. Under the auspices of an eccentric financier named Jaye Cook [*sic*] . . . The efforts of the Yankees to sustain this explosive and inflated paper system, has [*sic*] so far been marked by great ingenuity, resolution and success. Whether they will succeed in conquering the South, depends in a great degree upon their continued success in upholding this paper system.[22]

Sales ended in July at $830 million. With over 500,000 people purchasing bonds, Cooke's success came not just from advertising—which failed for others—or from his sales force, but rather from his feel for the country's mood, public relations creativity, and receptiveness to new sales ideas. Cooke, liking challenges, personally sold war bonds to Quakers, saying the money would go to hospitals but knowing, deep down, that they did not want to know how the money was spent. When told that there were no sales to soldiers, Cooke's agents were soon sitting next to army paymasters; he had salesmen follow victorious Union armies and was not surprised as gold emerged from previously patriotic Confederate homes.[23]

Cooke's final war service followed Lincoln's assassination. Hearing the news on Saturday morning, April 15, Cooke caught a train to New York and, to his relief, found that Wall Street, normally open on Saturdays, had closed. Treasury officials soon authorized him "to do as you think best." On Monday federal bonds fell, but Cooke conspicuously walked down Wall Street (setting an example of confidence that J. P. Morgan would follow in 1907) and began buying bonds with his own money. By Wednesday a major financial crisis had been averted—with Cooke again making a profit.[24]

Cooke raised just over a quarter of the Union's estimated total of $6.2 billion. Grayson wrote that the "War would quite likely have come to an inglorious close for the North had it not been for [his] relentless energy, flair for publicity, and supersalesmanship." Cooke's remarkable stewardship of $1.6 billion—"the tumbling river of cash," as Sandburg called it—was handled with perfect fidelity. Cooke's contributions should not be underestimated—not just during the war, but in setting expectations for honest money management ever since. Many also knew that his commissions were low (one-fourth of what European bankers received) and that in a dispute he always accepted the government's rulings.[25]

By the war's end, Cooke was a millionaire many times over. While no one will ever know his actual worth, $7 million to $10 million would be a reasonable estimate. As the war ended, Cooke built a million-dollar home, purchased large parcels of land and an island in Lake Erie, gave $50,000 for the construction of an Episcopal church near his new home, and made scores of smaller donations.

Cooke's mansion, possibly the country's finest at the time, was just north of Philadelphia. The 200-acre site had brooks, paved roads, flower walks, woods, a deer park, an aquarium, pools and fountains, stables and riding and pony paths, a farm, a greenhouse, mock Roman "ruins," and the family mausoleum. Cooke largely designed the home himself, naming it "Ogontz" for the Wyandot chief of his boyhood. The marble-walled building (190 by 157 feet) had over 75,000 square feet, 53 rooms, and a five-story tower. It contained a conservatory, music room, library, "amusement" room with a stage, and also multiple dining, living, smoking, bed, and guest rooms, all lit by 500 gas outlets and served by private telegraph. Ogontz was decorated with stained-glass windows and over 300 paintings, statues, and tapestries.[26]

At dinner Cooke epitomized patrician grace, keeping conversation flowing with low-key questions and comments. What visitor would not be delighted to be the focus of the great man's attention? Ogontz became the visiting place of choice for the Grants as well as many church, political, and business leaders. Cooke spared no cost, paying close attention to his guests' happiness. When Spotted Tail and a dozen Upper Brulé Sioux visited in 1872, dinner included ice cream molded into animal forms and watermelon (the Brulés unfortunately dropped the rinds on the expensive carpeting). The evening featured a magician whose tricks thrilled the Indians, as Cooke had anticipated, and concluded with blankets spread on the lawn, as everyone smoked cigars while Cooke explained his Northern Pacific plans.[27]

For his primary vacation home (there were at least four others) Cooke chose a location that reflected his roots and afforded ample opportunity for fishing. Northwest of Sandusky are nine islands, the Put-in-Bay area. South Bass, the largest island, forms a half moon around the far smaller island of Gibraltar, whose eight acres are little more than a steep hill with a 40-foot limestone cliff on one side. Cooke purchased Gibraltar in 1864 and built a 15-room house (also named Gibraltar), with a four-story observation tower.[28]

Gibraltar's guest list was an Ohio Who's Who, but most visitors were clergy. Through 1873 over 250 clergymen visited: about seven at a time for an average of ten days. Most were poor, so Cooke paid *all* their expenses, his only requirement being participation in the theological discussions that he enjoyed so much and "assistance" with services and prayers. For the rest of their visit, the ministers did as they wished: fished, read, or did nothing at all. Cooke knew that, for many, coming to Gibraltar might be the only vacation in their life.

One of his unresolved dilemmas was whether railroads should operate on Sundays, a day of rest and contemplation. But on June 17, 1866, he was visited by General Sherman. Cooke normally fired a small cannon to welcome guests, but because it was Sunday, he refused. Sherman landed at an empty dock and was met on the house's front steps by Cooke's housekeeper. "Deeply regretting it was the Sabbath [but] extend[ed] our warmest hospitality to the great Warrior," Cooke untruthfully wrote that evening, already feeling remorse for his snub. (In late 1869, when Cooke was clearly about to move forward with the Northern Pacific, Sherman made it a point to say publicly that if the transcontinental road was double-tracked and had north–south feeders it would meet all demands for fifty years.)[29]

By 1870 Cooke employed over 300 in Philadelphia, Washington, and New York, netting a million dollars annually. While he delegated operational authority, he retained final decision-making. Cooke distinguished between "speculation," such as oil production—which he forbade—and "investment," such as a railroad serving an existing oil field. Negotiations for new business, the lifeblood of banking, could not begin without his approval. Cooke professed to support consensus, but he exercised the final say, in an absolute manner. Despite these flaws, his banking house was characterized by camaraderie, advancement based on merit, a sense of purpose, and the enthusiasm of young men working for a true leader. Of course, some of the feelings were hollow; a Cooke Christmas dinner invitation was not optional. For younger partners wishing to stretch their wings, Jay's growing inflexibility was the classic recipe for rebellion, although the firm's profits and his generosity initially made the issue moot.[30]

By 1865 Cooke no longer needed—or liked—his partner and former brother-in-law, Moorhead. With Jay's sister dead, the two drifted apart over Cooke's aggressive bond sales and Moorhead's constant pessimism. But if Jay could not fire him, Moorhead could not quit; he had become profligate, building and filling *his* new white-marble mansion with his profits as Cooke's partner. He was increasingly given high-level make-work but was invariably ineffective. Henry Cooke's Washington office was also troublesome. Henry was a superb lobbyist but, as Cooke biographer Henrietta M. Larson wrote, "he proved to be a spendthrift, a 'good fellow' easily influenced, lacking in business judgment." The problems increased after 1870, when he took on NP lobbying, and Grant appointed him the District of Columbia's first "governor" in 1871. Happily, New York was in the hands of Fahnestock, the company's financial star, supported by Enoch Clark's first partner, the widely respected Edward H. Dodge.[31]

After the war Cooke dominated government securities, and the private banking business also did well: what safer bank was there? Commercial banking, however, was weak. Jay clearly wanted to diversify and always had numerous opportunities, but he seemed to flounder outside of transportation or related businesses that he had learned in the 1840s and 1850s.

Jay Cooke believed, literally, that he had been given both great responsibility and empowerment by his God. "Like Moses and Washington and Lincoln and Grant I have been—I firmly believe—God's chosen instrument, especially in the financial work of saving the Union . . . and this condition of things was of God's arrangement."[32]

Money was never an end in itself. Cooke's cornerstone was that theft was a sin, and throughout his life he unshakably met his fiduciary responsibilities. Until the Panic of 1873, Cooke assisted the needy every day of his adult life. He and his partners split profits only *after* 10 percent had gone to worthy causes. Larson wrote that he "adhered with remarkable closeness to the pattern of the Christian gentleman . . . Where there was in business an obvious application of a moral rule, [he] took the ethical stand to be right to himself and with God." But Cooke had few friends. That William Milnor Roberts (see chapter 2), a Quaker, so quickly became part of his extended family speaks to his need for companionship with intelligent men of similar ethical outlook. And he *was* different, as Theodore Grayson's description of him notes:

> [I] well remember meeting Cooke . . . at the time a very old man, and on a sunny day in July he was found sitting on a pile of rocks on a little island in Lake Erie . . . fishing. [After] a quarter of a century his image is still clear and his piercing glance is well remembered. He was a small man, spare of figure, but with a fine head and unusual eyes—deep, piercing, intelligent, and even in [old] age full of fire.[33]

Cooke's life held numerous ethical ambiguities. He made huge profits on insider war information and would not let "colored" soldiers ride his trolleys. His attitude toward Native Americans was progressive for that era, but the Northern Pacific routinely encroached on or gobbled up huge swaths of reservation land. Jay wrote to Henry Cooke, "I hate this lobbying," but he never hesitated to bribe (with cash, jobs, loans, stock, real estate, or gifts) scores, likely hundreds, of government figures, including Grant. While bribery was as common then as campaign contributions, golf outings, "breakfasts with," paid speeches, and sexual favors are today, Cooke always knew it was wrong. In the final analysis, the reader must choose what emphasis to place on this less savory side of his character.

In 1865 and 1866 Cooke declined to sell Northern Pacific bonds, writing: "Our true future is to keep out of entanglements and to undertake nothing . . . that will require advances. We will always have plenty of opportunities." But he also found himself drawn to the Northwest and began making large land purchases in Minnesota. The following summer he visited Superior, Wisconsin, and Duluth, Minnesota, where he was paddled around St. Louis Bay by Indians in a canoe. Local legend has it that he wore a top hat, a long coat and a colored waistcoat, cloth shoes, and a gold watch and chain and carried a walking stick. The next summer (1868) Cooke was elated by bond sales of $4.5 million in a week for the eastern Minnesota railroad, the Lake Superior & Mississippi. "Whew! What grand sales. We could sell 40 millions just as well as 4 millions."[34]

At the time of Grant's inauguration, Cooke, 48, was at the apex of his power and in the prime of his life. He loved the Northwest and instinctively knew that his forte was railroads and transportation, not insurance or mining. Now he wanted to see if a cabinet position was in the offing. But, in any case, he again needed to be challenged by something substantial.

CHAPTER 2

"The Northern Pacific Must Be Built"

There is a saying in politics: if you can't count the votes, you don't have them. On the late winter afternoon of March 5, 1869, Cooke found himself waiting uncertainly for the single vote that would make him secretary of the treasury: that of President Ulysses S. Grant. No one knew who would be nominated, but Cooke had to feel that his qualifications were superior. Only the day before, on the inaugural afternoon of March 4, Henry Cooke, who had become part of Grant's inner circle of friends, had written Jay with advice on what to do in the event of his selection. But it was not to be. Cooke was passed over for a New Yorker, Alexander Stewart, a Scots-Irish immigrant who had built a gigantic dry-goods company. When Cooke received the news, he must have seen a divine purpose and obvious reason: he was free to do the thing toward which his life had been pointing, the construction of the Northern Pacific Railroad.[1]

Cooke, however, would not undertake fund-raising for the Northern Pacific until he was satisfied that the railroad—which was little more than equal parts dream and Washington lobbying—was feasible. He was unconcerned that the NP would have collapsed if he had said "no," and he did not care that publicizing his interest would cause all other sources of money to dry up. What he wanted to know was the truth: did the NP make sense?

Once Cooke had stated his interest, the financially strapped NP's board of directors raced to meet his conditions. Thomas Hawley Canfield was chosen to work with Cooke's representatives and inspect the difficult western part of the route. Canfield, hard-working, distinguished-looking, intelligent, and a fastidious dresser, knew more about the route than any other nonengineer. For nearly two decades he had been a tireless promoter of a northern transcontinental route and, at 47, correctly felt that this was his last chance to make big money.

Born in Arlington, Vermont, on March 29, 1822, Canfield was an 18-year-old freshman at Union College when his father died suddenly. Without money, slender, high-strung, and physically unsuited for farming, he became a hard-goods store clerk. By the 1850s Canfield's active mind was focused on the railroad business, and he joined forces with Edwin F. Johnson, a railroad engineer and early proponent of a northern transcontinental route. Canfield soon discovered the mysteries of Washington lobbying, and his intelligence and positive attitude made him effective at it.

At the war's opening Canfield earned recognition by finding a railroad route around Baltimore (controlled by Southern sympathizers) and bringing the first troops to Washington. Lincoln personally thanked him, and Canfield received permission to help form the 1st Vermont Cavalry. But in his purchase of horses, his greed came to the fore. He wrote an associate: "I am satisfied we must make all we can from this. Get just as cheap horses as you can." And a few days later: "I think you had better have the bills for the horses made out perhaps in the names of different men and not all in your own . . . destroy this letter." Canfield must have known many of the regiment's families, but concern for them was secondary to making a quick profit.[2]

Canfield's actions were soon discovered, and he played no further role in the war effort. In 1862, however, friends were resurrecting the northern transcontinental railroad; he was hired to lobby Congress (see chapter 3). After the war, with all eyes focused on the Central Pacific–Union Pacific transcontinental railroad, only Canfield's energy and focus kept the NP alive. He joined the NP's board and became the de facto chief operating officer. The board members, who had their own obligations, were happy to let him take the lead. Canfield was finally drawing a salary, and these days were among his happiest. When Cooke became interested, however, his importance and role were instantly diminished, a change that he had difficulty grasping for the rest of his life.

Cooke met with Canfield and NP board member William B. Ogden, 63, the highly respected past president of the Chicago & Northwestern Railroad, at Ogontz in late March 1869. Cooke said that he must be free to check out the facts before committing himself. Canfield was flabbergasted: "This was a stunner, and I became nettled." Ogden was so embarrassed that he asked Canfield to leave the room with him and then gave him the facts of life: "The provision is reasonable. This is the greatest financial undertaking the world has ever seen. I have been trying to raise two or three million dollars on a road already built, and this man undertakes to raise 100 million on a line not yet surveyed." Before going back into the meeting, Ogden told Canfield to keep still. Yet, when the two rejoined Cooke,

Canfield ignored this admonition. "I asked Mr. Cooke . . . if he understood it meant [losing] six months or a year [for the study]. He said he did, but that he must know what he was talking about when he undertook to sell bonds."[3]

The meeting broke up with an agreement to form a reconnaissance party to examine the tentative route and Ogden's promise to recommend Cooke's stipulation. In May NP president J. Gregory Smith, Canfield, Ogden, and Richard D. Rice, a Smith associate, went to Ogontz for further discussions. Cooke's request was logical: the route, while based on meticulous research, was after all just a paper study. From the standpoint of railroad construction, many hundreds of miles were terra incognita and required professional examination.[4]

Canfield never recognized the poor impression he had made. After financing terms were agreed to, he was removed from Northern Pacific's operations but, as a sop, given the presidency of a subsidiary, the Lake Superior and Puget Sound Land Company (LSPS). In this capacity he created policies consistently detrimental to the railroad's growth and Cooke's bond sales efforts. Before Canfield was stripped of power in 1873, he ran through some seven and a half cents of every dollar Cooke raised, was caught in the outright theft of NP land, and became one of the NP's most despised officers.

Canfield also made an enemy of the man Cooke entrusted to recommend the Northern Pacific's construction, William Milnor Roberts. He was born in Philadelphia on February 12, 1810. His family had arrived with William Penn; his maternal grandfather was a mayor of Philadelphia; but the family was best known for its engineering and architectural abilities. Milnor (he never used William) Roberts became a canal surveyor at 15 and over the next three decades built a reputation as one of the country's leading civil engineers. He was energetic, five foot nine, thin, hawk-nosed, with a full head of jet-black hair, working and writing compulsively. Yet he had a light touch, was known for fairness, had the ability to encourage and delegate, and was remembered for his "hilarious good will." An *Engineering News* editor, William Shunk, recalled working for Roberts. One evening, in an isolated part of Pennsylvania, they found themselves at a "wretched tavern [sharing] a little box of a room" with only one bed. Shunk gingerly asked Roberts which side of the bed he preferred, for "I could sleep on either. 'Well,' said [Roberts], 'I generally take the top side; you can have the other!' and broke into a big smile and laughter at his own wonderful joke."[5]

Most important, as Cooke wrote, Roberts was "an Honest man" (Cooke's emphasis). His friend Sam Wilkeson (see below) stated that "he was the soul of honor. There was not enough money in the U.S. Treasury to buy him away from his conscience, or make him surrender a deliberatively formed professional opinion . . . [His] patience and sweetness were inexhaustible, except when in his business he uncovered a thief or a liar." Wilkeson had it right, but to thieves and liars might be added alcoholics, a pervasive problem in that era, particularly among military and railroad men.[6]

In 1837 Roberts married Annie Barbara Gibson of Carlisle, the daughter of John B. Gibson, for over 20 years the chief justice of Pennsylvania's Supreme Court. Milnor and Annie had four children who survived into adulthood: Thomas, also associated with the NP; Annie, who married Captain George W. Yates of Custer's Seventh Cavalry; Richard, who became Custer's private secretary in 1875–76; and Milnor, also an engineer. Roberts's wife died in 1857, and two years later he accepted a consultancy in Brazil, where he stayed until 1864. On November 19, 1868, he married 31-year-old Adeline de Beelen, the daughter of a Pittsburgh coal magnate. This was a love match for Roberts, as his letters attest. In 1867 he joined James B. Eads, assisting in constructing the first St. Louis bridge to cross the Mississippi. The work was dangerous and required sinking massive caissons into the river's bedrock. "Caisson sickness" (the bends) was not understood. Roberts wrote: "The passing into and out of the air-chamber, several times a day, was sometimes attended, in my own case, with considerable suffering, caused by pains in my ears," which left him partially deaf.[7]

Roberts and Cooke were not strangers; their relationship went at least as far back as the 1850s, when Roberts did consulting work for Cooke. Later, Roberts recalled, "in May 1869 I was urgently called upon by [Cooke] to make an examination of the [NP's] proposed route . . . from the Pacific side eastward." His role was nothing less than to determine the feasibility of the Northern Pacific, the longest American railroad proposed by a single private company.[8]

While on the trip, Roberts became friendly with Samuel Wilkeson. Born in Buffalo on May 9, 1817, Wilkeson was bright, handsome, and idealistic; but like his wealthy father of the same name, he had an explosive temper. Wilkeson graduated Phi Beta Kappa from Union College in 1837. While studying law under Judge Daniel Cady, he fell in love with and married Cady's daughter Catherine, the sister of suffragette Elizabeth Cady Stanton, in 1841.[9]

Nevertheless the law was not Wilkeson's calling. He drifted for years before discovering publishing and journalism. In 1856 he purchased Thurlow Weed's interest in the *Albany Evening Journal*. Weed led the state's Whig-Republican Party and was a close friend of Senator William H. Seward. Wilkeson soon quarreled with Weed; in 1859 he was forced out of the paper and suffered a nervous breakdown. The following year he joined Horace Greeley's rabidly anti–Weed/Seward *New York Tribune*. With Wilkeson writing the editorials, Greeley attended the 1860 Chicago Republican convention and helped Lincoln by blocking Seward.

At the beginning of the war, Wilkeson managed Greeley's Washington office. After Fredericksburg (1862), he and another *Tribune* reporter (taking separate paths) eluded Union officers attempting to censor news of the battle. The other man, Henry Villard, got to Washington first by paying a bribe of $50. The two met at the Willard Hotel, where Wilkeson, exhausted but fortified by alcohol, lost his temper over the $50. He took a swing at Villard but was quickly floored. Years later, Villard became president of the NP, but he retained Wilkeson and treated him generously.

In the spring of 1863 Wilkeson clashed with Greeley and joined the *New York Times*. He arrived at Gettysburg during the first day's fighting, knowing that his 19-year-old son Bayard, an artillery officer, was on the field. Bayard's unit went into action; astride his horse in front of his battery, he was an obvious target. Hit in the thigh by a cannonball, he was carried to a first-aid station, which was later overrun by Confederates. That afternoon Wilkeson, who was cool under fire, and famed war correspondent Whitelaw Reid were in an animated discussion of how best to describe the sound of an artillery barrage when Wilkeson received news of his son. For two days, as the battle raged around him, he frantically searched for Bayard, only to find him just after the boy's death. Wilkeson's cry of anguish, reflecting every parent's deepest fears, appeared in the *New York Times* (July 4) and was considered by some the most powerful writing of the war:

> Who can write a history of a battle whose eyes are immovably fastened upon a central figure of transcendingly absorbing interest—the dead body of an oldest born son, crushed by a shell in a position where a battery should never have been sent, and abandoned to die . . . I leave details [of the battle] to an associate . . . My pen is too heavy. Oh you dead, who at Gettysburg have baptized with your blood the second birth of freedom in America, how you are to be envied! I rise from a grave whose wet clay I have passionately kissed and I look up to see Christ spanning the battlefield . . . sweetly beckon[ing] to those mutilated, bloody, swollen forms to ascend.[10]

One person who was undoubtedly moved was Cooke. Within a year Wilkeson was working for him, writing brochures and advertising for Cooke's war bond campaigns. Wilkeson became a close confidant, frequently receiving letters beginning "Dear Uncle Samuel." He had found the business leadership for which he had been emotionally searching. After the war he became the Northern Pacific's secretary, managing its publicity while retaining access to Cooke. An 1871 visitor described him as "engaged ten to twelve hours a day . . . arranging materials for newspapers, circulars, pamphlets and books . . . in that ready, rapid, charming way that has given him distinctive character and prominence . . . above all other [journalists] in America."[11]

The scene at "Camp Yellowstone" on August 30, 1869, would have given Izaak Walton pleasure, as a dozen men spread out along the Yellowstone, trying their luck with trout. The men were at present-day Livingston, just east of the Bozeman Pass, 4,500 feet above sea level, where the fast-flowing Yellowstone makes a sharp eastern turn. Seven of the party were cavalrymen; the others were Canfield, Roberts, Wilkeson, William S. Johnson (Edwin's son), and W. E. C. Moorhead (W. G. Moorhead's son and Cooke's nephew). These five had already traveled through a score of states and territories by railroad, stage, steamer, rope ferry, canoe, and horse and mule and now—at the end of their "reconnaissance"—were very aware of standing where William Clark had been 63 years earlier. They were there because Jay Cooke's decision regarding the financing of the Northern Pacific rested on their recommendations.[12]

Almost four months earlier, on May 10, 1869, the first transcontinental railroad had been completed. In fact, the concept of a single railroad is misleading; in actuality a series of railroads had been linked. Traveling from the East Coast to Sacramento remained a week's adventure. Just a month later, in June, Cooke's reconnaissance team set out. In addition to Moorhead and Johnson, Roberts brought his wife, and Cooke asked his close friend R. Bethell Claxton, 54, an Episcopalian minister, to join them. With Canfield and Wilkeson delayed, the larger party left first, deciding to meet them in Salt Lake City.

From Omaha, the group coincidentally traveled with William H. Seward, who went as far as Cheyenne. West of Sherman's Summit the train ran at four miles per hour, crossing the 700-foot-long and 126-foot-high wooden Dale Creek trestle in three minutes. The bridge was like "scaffolding erected for the purpose of painting a house . . . more than one passenger . . . breathes more freely and gives audible expression [of relief] once the cars have passed [over it] in safety." Just afterward came a descent of 1,000 feet in 20 miles. It would be a year before George Westinghouse's airbrake first became available, and railroads still relied on men stationed on every other car who manually slowed the train by turning a brake wheel—the "Arm-strong" system, as it was wryly called.[13]

Canfield and Wilkeson arrived in Salt Lake to face an unpleasant surprise; Roberts's wife was pregnant. Newly married and in love, he faced a difficult choice: send Adeline back or resign his consultancy, thereby wrecking Cooke's plans. Roberts temporized and, blaming Canfield, sent his wife east. In fact, Wilkeson had huffily written Cooke that "a woman could not possibly [make the trip] unless she was born and bred a squaw." They left Salt Lake on June 14; west of Reno, the train gradually climbed higher. But the downhill part, 7,000 feet in 127 miles, was the worst. One traveler wrote: "The axle-boxes smoked with friction . . . The wheels were nearly red hot. In the darkness of the night they resembled disks of flame . . . [On] reach[ing] Sacramento, not a few were specially thankful." From Sacramento they went to San Francisco, vacillated about sailing to Portland, Oregon, returned to Sacramento, and left by stage on June 29 for the 650-mile ride to Portland.[14]

The six travelers arrived on July 4 and were promptly invited to participate in the holiday speeches. The orator was the eccentric George Francis Train, who helped finance the Union Pacific by developing the Crédit Mobilier concept.

The Crédit Mobilier was designed to get around the fact that it took years after a railroad's completion for investors to make money, because of high capital (construction) costs. In contrast, construction companies made money immediately. In the most simplistic form, dummy corporations such as the Crédit Mobilier were established and owned by insiders. These companies then purchased and resold "iron" (the physical sections of track) to construction companies, for example, or sold the construction contracts that they had been awarded to another company that performed the real work. The actual Crédit Mobilier scandal in 1872 was caused by insider greed and impatience, the huge sums of federal dollars involved, and the large numbers of officials (both regulatory and elected) who were bribed to cover up construction delays and deficiencies.[15]

Train, who favored Irish independence, was an expert on the British penal system—an insight gained during a period of well-publicized incarceration for sedition. (In 1870 Train traveled around the world in 80 days, a feat that drew the attention of Jules Verne.) Later, with his usual panache, Train joined the six in their travel, graciously permitting them to pay his expenses. Continuing north toward Puget Sound, they were awe-struck. Wilkeson wrote Cooke: "Such timber—such forests—such orchards—such fish—such climate! . . . my wildest hopes are more than satisfied . . . Salmon are not caught here, *they are pitchforked out of the streams.* Jay, we have got the biggest thing on earth" (Wilkeson's emphasis). On July 8 they reached Tacoma, later chosen as the Northern Pacific's western terminus.[16]

In Seattle the party members boarded a steamer on July 9, determined to see as much of Puget Sound as they could. The possibility that Train might cause trouble never occurred to them; but at Whatcom, Washington Territory, he telegraphed the mayor of Victoria, British Columbia, that he "would be there the next day to deliver a lecture, subject 'The downfall of England! Get out your guns!'" The steamer arrived about 3 A.M. It turned out that the mayor was not amused. By dawn's early light "a few rods" from the party's ship was a British man-of-war, which, while obsolete, nevertheless had its crew on deck, its gun ports open, and its cannon out and "shotted." After a frantic search for the American consul, everyone except Train came ashore. With the local economy weak, the British were concerned about the loyalty of the colony's numerous Americans and were likely unhappy to find out about the Northern Pacific.[17]

On returning to Portland on July 14, the party, minus Train, headed east. At a crowded Walla Walla meeting, the Reverend Claxton stole the show. A newspaper wrote: "[Claxton said he] had come expecting to see icebergs and polar bears . . . [but] he declared amid laughter, he would go home . . . [to] tell Mr. Cooke, 'on the word of a clergyman which ought always to be good' what Walla Walla . . . really looked like." But behind the public camaraderie, infighting had developed. Canfield and Wilkeson did not want Claxton along; he had to be back east by September, so they encouraged his leaving. Roberts, meanwhile, complained to Cooke that the two were trying to influence his report. Canfield later admitted: "During the trip the engineers had been very reticent as to their views of the route, which created no little anxiety on [my] part."[18]

On July 21 the party, now without Claxton, left Walla Walla. The five of them and a guide, Philip Ritz (for whom Ritzville, Washington, is named), averaged 24 miles a day. Crossing the Snake River at Old Kentucky Ferry, they scooped up gravel in a bread pan and "could see the gold glistening in it." At Idaho's Lake Pend d'Oreille they sailed along the shore in a small steamer for 30 miles to the tiny, 60-year-old trading post of Hope, Idaho's first community and the gateway to western Montana, a dozen miles away.

Idaho and Montana represented the most rigorous and important part of the trip: could the gorges and passes be crossed by a railroad, and how real were the stories about hostile Indians, for whom they were no match? After Hope, the party steamed up the Clarke Fork River to Cabinet Rapids, unloaded, and then rode along the river to its junction with the Flathead. Following the Flathead some 35 miles, they went up the Jocko to Evaro, 20 miles north of Missoula. Roberts excitedly wrote Cooke that the land was similar to Argentina's famed Pampas—ideal for cattle. At Missoula, they were met warmly and given "wheel[ed] conveyance over to Deer Lodge City," which may mean that some of the horses or men, or both, were played out.[19]

On August 12 they arrived at Deer Lodge, a bustling agricultural and mining center. One paper tactlessly recorded its surprise at their "rapid trip considering that Mr. Wilkeson and Roberts have reached the meridian of life and are unaccustomed to the saddle." The next day the "evangelists of the trail" inspected Deer Lodge Pass. The approach, Roberts wrote Cooke, was "far more smooth and valley-like than any mountain divide . . . I have ever encountered"; and Wilkeson noted that the grade was "as imperceptible as that of Broadway from Canal Street to the St. Nicholas Hotel." The pass became Roberts's first choice; but later the Northern Pacific would, for business and political reasons, select the Mullan Pass near Helena.[20]

From Deer Lodge the party went up Little Blackfoot River to the Mullan Pass. Today one takes Mullan Pass Road up the gentle, alpine-looking slope on the western side of the Divide. There is really no pass per se but rather an immediate, steep decline, correctly called by Roberts "quite abrupt in its descent." (Later a high trestle and tunnel were built, with great difficulty.) The *Helena Herald* had been tracking the men for weeks, and they were welcomed with a band and speeches when they arrived on August 16. Territorial governor James M. Ashley, speaking to a large, enthusiastic audience, concluded his remarks to tremendous applause by stating:

> Following the example of the great Roman Orator who, at the close of every speech, no matter what the question, declared that however senators might differ on the subject before them, one thing was unquestioned— "Carthage must be destroyed." So I say to you . . . in Montana, at all times and on all occasions . . . however we may differ among ourselves . . . one thing is unquestioned—the Northern Pacific must be built![21]

Over the next two and a half weeks the party members found themselves dodging Indians and desperados. Wishing to inspect Cadotte's Pass, they went by stage to Fort Benton, for decades the steamboat terminus of Missouri River navigation. Then they doubled back to Fort Shaw, on the Sun River. The commandant was Philippe Régis de Trobriand—a fascinating diarist, brave general, and dismal politician. De Trobriand, who wore any hat at the jauntiest of angles, was at the army's most isolated, coldest post for good reason: his *Campaigns of the Army of the Potomac* had been singularly uncomplimentary toward Grant. That August, with some 50 Blackfeet on the warpath having killed several settlers, de Trobriand was opposed to reducing his small garrison by providing an escort. But, after extensive pressuring, he assigned six solders to the party. The pass proved unsuitable, however, and the party returned to Helena, frustrated by losing a week and calling in favors unnecessarily.

Their final stop was Fort Ellis, adjacent to the Bozeman Pass. Roberts wanted to take the Yellowstone all the way to the Missouri, following Clark's 1806 route. But the fort's commandant, Albert G. Brackett, was against it because of rumors of Indian concentrations. Wilkeson angrily wrote Cooke: "[O]ur government has abandoned [the valley] to the Sioux . . . and yet the road has got to go through— the imbecility of Washington is [unbelievable]." Fortunately the Yellowstone trip was vetoed: Sitting Bull was apparently consolidating his leadership at this time, and Sioux and Cheyennes had gathered with him. While Sitting Bull wanted to avoid confrontations, no one knows what would have happened had the party and 100 cavalrymen—no more were available—blundered into at least 1,000 warriors. The end result was a harbinger of Indian problems: the issue of safely escorting surveyors into the Yellowstone Valley did not disappear in the years to come.[22]

In July the Northern Pacific began a "reconnaissance" west from St. Paul, led by famed guide Pierre Bottineau. The group included Minnesota governor William R. Marshall, NP president Smith, and chief engineer Edwin Johnson. They were

accompanied by numerous newspapermen, including the well-known war correspondent Charles C. Coffin of the *Boston Journal*. The group also included various
railroad executives, possible investors, five ministers (some with their wives, and one
who brought his single daughter), and, intriguingly, "N. P. Langford of Montana," in
1870 the co-discoverer of the region that became Yellowstone Park. To meet the
rigors of outdoor life, the party was provided with large tents, carpeting, cots with
bedding, extensive food stuffs, hunting and fishing equipment, and even a canoe—all
carried in eighteen wagons. Teamsters, servants, cooks, and Indian scouts accompanied them, all paid from the railroad's dwindling funds. Upon reaching Georgetown,
Minnesota, on the Red River on July 22, the group split—a decision apparently
caused by Marshall and Smith's mutual dislike.[23]

Smith's group traveled east and reached Duluth about August 14, while the
Marshall party rode west, guarded by 19 mounted infantry and Indian scouts.
Many thought the Sioux were no longer a problem east of the Missouri. However,
after Marshall reached Fort Stevenson (on the Missouri) on July 30 and turned
back, they were tracked for two days by Sioux, who tried to steal their horses but
gave up after a brief exchange of rifle fire. At Fort Totten an inaccurate rumor had
Sitting Bull and 150 Sioux east of the Missouri. Racing across the prairie and
bypassing the regular route, the party was back in Minneapolis on August 10. The
biggest surprise was seeing only one buffalo. While accomplishing nothing, the
reconnaissance generated wide publicity as well as Coffin's popular book about the
railroad's potential, *The Seat of Empire*.[24]

The Canfield-Roberts reconnaissance party returned to Fort Ellis, Montana, on
August 31 and arranged to be driven 75 miles to Virginia City. On September 3, at
6:30 P.M., they began the uncomfortable, dangerous 400-mile ride to Corrine. In fact,
bandits robbed the Corrine stage on August 31 and September 6, taking $30,000 in
gold. Roberts noted that it took "four days and nights hard riding through alkaline
dust [before] we arrived." Upon reaching Omaha, Roberts left for St. Louis. Canfield
and Wilkeson went to St. Paul, telling the local press that when they reached New
York they would have traveled some 10,070 miles: 6,440 by rail, 1,936 by stagecoach,
1,070 by steamer, 509 on horseback, 70 by mule, and 45 by canoe.[25]

Cooke promptly asked Roberts to come to Ogontz, an invitation that was, of
course, not optional. Once there, fed by their mutual enthusiasm Roberts completed
an exceptionally positive, optimistic report on September 25. In it, potential investors
saw exceptional opportunities for business, industry, and agriculture and found no
hostile Indians or insurmountable engineering problems. Roberts estimated the
road's cost at $85,277,000, adding, "I have purposely made no allowance for the
reduced cost . . . of Chinese labor." Roberts clearly threw caution to the wind
when he wrote that the Northern Pacific "can certainly be built and opened

between Lake Superior and Puget Sound in 1873." His dislike of Canfield colored a key conclusion, however: unlike Canfield, he did not believe the rumors of an easy-to-cross "lost" Marias Pass that might save hundreds of miles. In fact, the pass—south of present-day Glacier National Park and long known to Indians and trappers—had been seen by a surveyor in the 1850s but was not "discovered" until 1889.[26]

Roberts's reconnaissance achieved its goal—Cooke's commitment. However, 25 years later Cooke ruefully admitted that Roberts's "preliminary examinations occupied several months and future events proved that I was entirely too careful and conservative in expending so much time and money in examination, but I felt that I could not conscientiously undertake the [NP's] financial agency unless fully satisfied in my own mind." Ironically, Canfield's May worries proved correct: precious time and ideal market conditions were forever lost.[27]

CHAPTER 3

"Free from Fatigue"

Robert Fulton's 1807 demonstration of a steam-powered ship could hardly have come at a better time for the United States, whose borders then stretched to the Rocky Mountains. Reflecting its limited capital and scarcity of engineers or large population centers, the country had fewer than 50 miles of canals, perhaps 150 miles of macadamized road (akin to today's "improved gravel"), and a handful of bridges over major rivers. Although sailing ships had undergone constant improvement since the Middle Ages, the transport of people and goods by land in the United States—split by dozens of rivers—was slower than in Roman times. Yet 25 years after Fulton's *Clermont,* the land from the Louisiana Purchase was under firm U.S. control, and no foreign power disturbed America's cross-continental vision. Its natural resources seemed unlimited, an economic and educational infrastructure was emerging, and American culture rewarded inventors of time-saving machinery. American mechanics and inventors were also looking at steam power as a means for movement over land.

The use of wheeled vehicles on "tracks" traces back to 1676, when a New-castle miner sent a load of coal in an open container mounted on wheels downhill on a wooden track. After reaching the track's end, the empty container was then hauled back by rope. Experiments began 125 years later with steam-powered engines that could move on similar tracks. George Stephenson and his son built such an engine in Great Britain; on or about September 27, 1825, the *Locomotion* carried 600 people 12 miles. For his first run, Stephenson placed modified stage-coaches to ride on wooden rails, spaced to meet the coaches' wheels. The train had no brakes, nor was it able to go up an incline or even make wide curves. A friend wrote: "Nothing can do more harm to the adoption of railroads, than the promulgation of such nonsense that we shall see locomotive engines traveling at a rate of 12, 16, 18, and 20 miles per hour." Four years later Stephenson's *Rocket* carried passengers at 30 miles an hour.[1]

In America John Stevens put a steam engine on a platform in 1825, carrying a half-dozen people on a small circular track. In 1830 the Baltimore & Ohio railed road began horse-drawn service from Baltimore to Ellicott's Mills. On September 18 Peter Cooper, with 36 people aboard his *Tom Thumb*, made the run in an hour. On the return trip, Cooper raced a man in a carriage and was well ahead until a crack developed in his engine. That December, 140 guests rode four miles on *The Best Friend of Charleston*, just outside Charleston, South Carolina. The first regularly scheduled train, the Mohawk & Hudson's *DeWitt Clinton*, ran 17 miles from Albany to Schenectady on August 9, 1831. The same trip via the Erie Canal and the Hudson River was 41 miles long; boats passed through more than two dozen locks for the 240-foot drop between the two cities. In addition to the time difference, canals froze in winter. Entrepreneurs and investors quickly threw their support behind railroads, while those who had invested in or were employed by canals fought back with repressive legislation, sabotage, and occasional murder.

Nevertheless, American artisans were soon designing, constructing, and operating railroads, discovering as they went novel concepts such as centrifugal force. They thought, fiddled, and filed patents so that trains ran and stopped with a modest degree of regularity. Safety requirements brought dramatic change. Wood track, for example, gave way to wood with an iron overlay, "strap iron." But it often broke; "When that happened it became a 'snake,' in railroad lingo, knifing its way through car floors and impaling hapless passengers." Track quickly became all-iron, gradually increasing in weight per yard because of heavier trains. Virtually every piece of railroad construction, equipment, signaling, and operations had to be invented or modified from stagecoaches and steam ship engines.[2]

About 1829 Edwin Johnson, the future Northern Pacific chief engineer, correctly predicted that "when their merits become more fully appreciated, by far the greater portion of the inland trade will be conducted by [railroads]." Well into the 1830s, railed-roads were powered by steam engines, horses, or both. New York businessman Philip Hone wrote in his diary in 1832 (following a trip by steamer to Albany): "We set off to the railroad and embarked in one of a train of carriages; arrived in Schenectady, breakfasted, walked a short distance to the commencement of the Saratoga road . . . This is a very pleasant mode of traveling; not very rapid but free from fatigue or inconvenience of any sort. The Mohawk and Hudson is traveled by the power of a steam locomotive engine; the Saratoga by a horse-power [*sic*]."[3]

The key was "fatigue"; compared with bumpy or mud-slowed stagecoach, railed travel was more comfortable, more reliable, and faster. Travel from Lancaster to Philadelphia via horse car rail in 1833 took 12 hours; but steam engines proved faster and more efficient and by 1836 were replacing horses for longer trips. In 1838, despite ice, snow, and having to take two ferries, Hone traveled from Philadelphia to Baltimore in seven hours, commenting on "what a contrast this is to the old winter traveling between the two cities on a detestable road and a dangerous ferry, and two days and a night consumed."[4]

The concept of railed travel spread rapidly. In 1839 daily service between Boston and Springfield was inaugurated. A one-way 90-mile trip in the wooden, double-decked passenger train took 12 hours; but just 32 years later express trains traveled twice the distance (Boston to Albany) in half the time. In the 1830s regional promoters like Hone, Eleutheros Cooke, and hundreds of others developed routes, raised money, and built roads. Despite swindles and failures, the successes allowed dramatic growth to continue.

Complementing and greatly contributing to the leap in railroad construction in the 1850s was the perfection of the telegraph, first demonstrated in 1844. The telegraph ushered in a new era. Most American railroad construction was single track, so trains had to wait at sidings to meet or be passed by other trains. With telegraph operators sending signals from stations, trains could increase their average speed, and more trains could use the same track.

By the time of Jay Cooke's birth in 1821 there had been modest growth in macadamized toll roads (no figures are available, but the total was possibly in the 500-mile range). While only a handful of completed canals existed, the Erie was under construction. A boom was underway: 2,500 miles of canals built and $75 million invested in the 25 years after the War of 1812. The canals fully complemented steamboat routes by connecting rivers and lakes. One incentive for canal builders was public land grants. Although these were irregularly given and exceeded a million acres only in 1827, the precedent of offering public land to encourage commerce was well established when the first railroad land grant was made (1847). Growing numbers of surveyors and engineers received their training by building canals, including Edwin Johnson and Milnor Roberts. By 1840 there were 3,326 miles of canals—almost entirely dug by hand. Ultimately, as in so many technological booms, canals were built with little more than the hope that traffic would develop once they were completed. Predictably, given the high labor cost to build and maintain them, many canals became virtually idle in the 1840s. Still, by 1848 a network of over 9,000 miles of railroads and canals was operating east of the Mississippi; an unanticipated side effect was that macadamized toll roads were all but driven out of business. Even more spectacular than canal building were the results of steam-powered shipping. By 1840 over 16,000 miles of water routes were being served. St. Louis became the nation's central hub, as freight and passengers plied the Mississippi, Missouri, Ohio, Tennessee, and other rivers. Deeper-hulled,

Table 1
Gorwth of Railroad Mileage in the United States, 1830–1873
(All figures rounded to nearest whole number)

Year	Mileage	(Avg.) Annual Gain	Investment (millions $)[a]
1830	23	NA	NA
1835	1,098	220	NA
1840	2,818	344	NA
1845	4,633	363	NA
1850	9,021	878	318
1855	18,374	1,871	763
1860	30,626	2,450	1,149
1865	35,085	892	1,172
1869	46,844	2,940	2,041
1870	52,922	6,078	2,476
1871	60,301	7,379	2,664
1872	66,171	5,870	3,159
1873	70,628	4,457	3,784

Source: U.S. Department of Commerce, U.S. Bureau of the Census, *Historical Statistics of the United States: Colonial Times to 1970,* p. 731.
[a] U.S. Department of Commerce, U.S. Bureau of the Census, *Historical Statistics*, p. 734. The actual category is "Stock, mortgage bonds, equipment, obligations, etc." Investment figures are not available prior to 1850.

large-capacity sailing ships continued on the Great Lakes and along the Eastern Seaboard but soon gave way to steam power for time-sensitive traffic.[5]

Philip Hone's 1847 travel from New York to St. Louis, northern Michigan, and back illustrated the era's mix of trains, stages, canals, and steamers. After reaching Philadelphia by train (June 10), he took another train to Harrisburg, 106 miles in eight hours. From there to Pittsburgh, Hone could choose between stage and canal but took the canal, due to the heat. One canal was breached and blocked by a large coal boat, the *Commet*—"what better could be expected from a fellow who spells Comet with two m's?" Hone grumbled. On June 14, at Holidaysburg, he took the Allegheny Portage railroad, a Rube Goldberg mechanism with 10 percent grades controlled by ropes and pulleys, partially built and designed by Milnor Roberts. At Johnstown, Hone returned to a canal barge, arriving in Pittsburgh five and a half days after leaving Philadelphia.[6]

Hone's next stop was Cincinnati, via an Ohio River steamer, which was "exceedingly pleasant . . . a fine boat, excellent fare, comfortable staterooms." The 496 miles to Cincinnati took two days. Hone then took a stage to Lexington, Kentucky, breakfasted with Henry Clay, and went on to Louisville by stage. There Hone took another Ohio steamer to St. Louis, which "astonish[ed]" him: "Fifty large steamboats, at least, lie head on, taking in and discharging their cargoes, constantly arriving . . . The whole of the levee is covered, as far as the eye can see, with merchandise landed or to be shipped."

Table 2
Regional Railroad Mileage in the United States, 1841–1872

	1841[a]	1851	1861	1871	1872
New England	589	2,800	3,697	4,898	5,053
Mid-Atlantic[b]	1,237	3,795	6,963	12,380	13,499
Mid-West[c]	196	1,846	11,320	27,187	30,499
West Central[d]	0	0	0	1,201	1,804
Southern	913	2,541	9,283	13,446	14,112
Western[e]	0	0	23	1,790	2,137
Totals	2,935	10,982	31,286	60,902	67,104

Source: Railroad Gazette, July 19, 1873. The Gazette, unlike U.S. Department of Commerce, U.S. Bureau of the Census, Historical Statistics, shows construction by region. While the numbers themselves are slightly different, they clearly have the same order of magnitude. Also note that some numbers were not entirely legible.

[a] 1841 is the first year shown by the Railroad Gazette.

[b] Includes Delaware, Maryland, the District of Columbia, and West Virginia.

[c] Includes Missouri, Nebraska, and Kansas.

[d] Includes Wyoming, Utah, North Dakota, South Dakota, Colorado, and Oklahoma.

[e] Includes California, Nebraska, Oregon, and Washington. No track in Arizona, Idaho, Montana, or New Mexico.

After touring St. Louis with Senator Thomas Hart Benton, Hone left for Chicago via steamer up the Illinois River to Peoria or Peru, where he switched to stage and rail. He reached Chicago on July 4 then went to Milwaukee, Sheboygan, and Fond du Lac. The last leg was by wagon over a rough dirt road; he was bothered by mosquitoes and watched settlers clearing the land—literally the frontier, with "the trees still burning; a log-cabin with swarms of children . . . Every mile we meet a family of German emigrants." A week later, near Sault St. Marie, Hone noted that he was "now on Lake Huron, steaming down to Detroit, almost home—only about 1,200 miles to go." He reached Detroit two days later and then Buffalo, whose "basin and harbor are so obstructed with steamboats and lake craft that hours are consumed in ingress and egress."

Hone was back in New York June 30, having traveled 3,967 miles. Despite gaps in his diary, it is clear that railroad travel was only one of many options. Yet his trip illustrated the advantages that railroads had over stage and canal travel. Even as Hone completed his trip, events were underway that would further spur railroad growth. The end of the Mexican War and its huge land annexation coincided with the discovery of gold in California. Almost immediately, Americans began seriously thinking about a transcontinental railroad.

In 1845 Asa Whitney, considered by many the driving force for such a road, drafted a proposal to Congress calling for a railroad beginning at Lake Michigan, crossing Illinois and Iowa, and paralleling the Platte River and Oregon Trail. At South Pass (the continental divide in Wyoming) the road would split: one part would go toward San Francisco (Mexican Territory), and the other would follow the Oregon Trail to the Columbia River. Given sectional hostility, the route was immediately opposed; but in the political infighting of the early 1850s a compromise emerged from Washington. In addition to the Gadsden Purchase, which permitted a southern route, surveys (actually reconnaissances) to study five east–west routes were begun in 1853.

Many hoped that the plan would be studied to death, including Secretary of War Jefferson Davis. Davis, who opposed any central or northern route, made sure that the only result would be some beautifully bound reports. In reality, the technical and financial requirements for a transcontinental road, combined with sectional politics, guaranteed that nothing would happen in the 1850s. The need for a railroad became apparent because of California's explosive population growth (380,000 by 1860) and the discovery of silver at the immense Comstock Lode in Nevada (1859).

Before the Civil War, water transport still carried more freight and possibly more passengers than railroads, although railroads had over 30,000 miles of track. However, once the war was underway, commerce was shut down along numerous rivers and canals. Additionally, hundreds of paddle-wheelers were requisitioned by both sides, destroyed, cannibalized, or left to rot. Simultaneously, railroads underwent dramatic growth. In the North, track mileage increased by some 20 percent, available locomotives and rolling stock rose by 50 percent, and overall traffic jumped by over 250 percent. The leap in productivity was due to cooperation between the railroad and military, improved operating techniques, coordinated schedules, the adoption of common track gauges, and increased nighttime and Sunday operations. Advances in track and bridge building were dramatic: in 1864 Nathan Bedford Forrest's men are said to have complained that, as fast as they tore track up, they heard the whistle of repair trains following them.[7]

Northern war requirements spurred technological development. Increased train weight required longer-lasting track with more iron per yard. Thousands of engines were converted from wood to more efficient, cheaper coal. As a result of the burst in productivity and invention (for example, better headlights were needed for round-the-clock operations), hundreds of patents were filed each year. With each new product came the need for additional capital to manufacture or purchase the equipment. Railroad operators worked with longer-lasting, higher-quality raw materials (including steel) and added products that ranged from signaling equipment to larger, more efficient engines. When the golden spike was driven at Promontory Point (1869), the railroad business was seemingly new compared to what it had been in 1861. And with thousands of miles of new track being built annually, the last thing on most people's minds was a second transcontinental railroad.[8]

All but forgotten during the late 1850s and early 1860s was the idea of a northern transcontinental road. Only the efforts of Isaac Ingalls Stevens and Edwin Johnson kept the idea alive. Stevens (West Point, '39) joined the Corps of Engineers, served gallantly in the Mexican War, was named governor of Washington Territory in 1853, and en route there led Jefferson Davis's northern transcontinental railroad study. Elected territorial delegate to Congress in 1856 and 1858, he was "the only major active proponent of the northern route." Defeated for reelection in 1860, Stevens rejoined the army and was later killed at the battle of Chantilly (1862).[9]

After Stevens died, Johnson was the man who kept a northern Pacific concept afloat. Born in 1803, he was teaching mathematics and civil engineering by the mid-1820s. According to the *Dictionary of American Biography:* "His record from 1833 to 1861 is practically a review of the transportation facilities that were constructed." An activist, Johnson held elective office, invented canal and railroad equipment, and energetically advised the government during the Civil War. As early as 1840, he published articles about a northern transcontinental route; and in 1854, with Canfield's support, he wrote *Railroad to the Pacific: Northern Route, Its General Character, Relative Merits, etc.,* which suggested the route that the NP did in fact follow. Northern Pacific historian Eugene V. Smalley wrote that Johnson "placed it upon a practical basis . . . and show[ed] the actual advantages of the route for railway construction."[10]

While Stevens and Johnson kept the concept alive, they could not answer two critical questions: Why should investors be interested in a transcontinental route with such a small population base and was the road really necessary? In 1860 only 237,000 Americans lived in the states and territories along the route, all but 13,000 in Minnesota and Oregon. At the same time, 1,169,000 lived along the central route. In 1870 the northern tier's population was 593,000; but not until 1881–82 did it equal the central route's *1860* population. Political indifference was another hurdle. Prior to the war, Southern hostility alone gave it some legitimacy in the North. Ironically, when the war broke out, opposition to the route vanished, as did most of its support. While legislation for the central route was approved on July 1, 1862, interest in a northern route was nonexistent. However, shortly after the vote was taken, gold was discovered in Montana.

The northern route needed a financial savior, and in 1863 the quixotic Josiah Perham suddenly stepped forward. Born in 1803 and bankrupted twice in the 1840s, Perham became rich in 1849 with the "Seven Mile Mirror," a panoramic illustration of the Great Lakes that was cranked forward to give the feeling of motion. Perham rented a theater in Boston and began cutting deals with railroads to offer combined train and panorama tickets. More than 200,000 visitors came via rail to see the panorama, some from as far away as Canada.[11]

Perham began promoting discounted railroad tickets; in 1861 he was working to sell tickets to soldiers on leave in Washington when he became interested in a transcontinental railroad. Pushed aside from the central route, he began working with Johnson and added a twist to the financing to entice Congress: a "People's Pacific Railway" with tens of thousands of small investors, an idea remarkably similar to Cooke's bond sales. Perham soon had a key ally, Vermont-born Speaker of the House Thaddeus Stevens. Two years later, propelled by the necessity of safe-guarding Montana's gold, legislation shepherded by Stevens created the Northern Pacific Railroad. The act, loaded with legislative pork and signed by Lincoln on July 2, 1864, contained no dollar subsidies but did include some 50 million acres of land.

The act stipulated that construction had to begin within two years and be completed by July 4, 1876. Moving quickly, Perham held his first board of directors meeting in Boston (September 1, 1864), raised some cash, and received pledges for $200,000. Most of the cash went to pay off debt; with the remainder, Perham set up operations in New York. But the idea that had sounded so good to Congress failed to interest the public. Debt-ridden and ill, Perham resigned and sold out on December 12, 1865, dying "in extreme poverty" in 1868.[12]

While the Northern Pacific had no cash, its charter included huge grants of land. The men who bought the NP from Perham were New England businessmen who, if not wealthy, had the wherewithal to legitimize the new company. Their leader was a former Vermont governor, J. Gregory Smith, who for a decade had been interested in a northern route. Smith was, on one hand, far-sighted, energetic, and persuasive; on the other hand, he was considered "ruthless, and arrogant." Smith's photographs depict a solemn, austere appearance, with his hair prematurely white. But correspondent Charles Coffin saw another side, dedicating *Seat of Empire* to Smith, "whom I first saw tenderly caring for the sick and wounded in the Hospitals of Fredericksburg [winter of 1862–63]."[13]

Smith's father, John, was a businessman, attorney, state legislator, and congress-man. A brother, Worthington, led the Vermont Senate (1855–65) before serving three terms in Congress (1867–73); and one of his first cousins was the well-known engineer and general William F. "Baldy" Smith. Gregory Smith was born July 22, 1818, in St. Albans, 15 miles south of Canada, just east of Lake Champlain. He attended Yale Law School and joined his father's railroad business in the 1840s. In 1863 and 1864 the Vermont legislature elected him governor (then a one-year term). In 1858, following his father's death, Smith became president of the Vermont Central. His railroad skills and sense of purpose seemed considerable: the railroad was the nation's eighth largest by 1871.

Smith's Northern Pacific presidency is critical to any understanding of its sub-sequent problems. In 1843 his father and some friends incorporated the Vermont & Canada (V&C), and two years later John Smith became its president. The railroad, like so many others springing to life around the country, was undercapitalized, served a limited market, lacked economies of scale, and was invariably in financial difficulty. Just south of the V&C was the Vermont Central (VC). Begun the same year, but far more robust, the VC raised over a million dollars, including an unknown amount from two Philadelphia bankers, Jay Cooke and Anthony Drexel. In its first full year of operation the company had 70 miles of track, 200 pieces of rolling stock, 15 locomotives, 47,000 passengers, and $100,000 in revenue. The VC was on its way to being a major force in the Vermont railroad industry, while the V&C struggled, serving a far smaller market.[14]

In 1850 the Vermont Central signed an agreement with the Vermont & Canada to lease its track, the first step in a de facto takeover of the smaller, less competitive line. With John Smith on the VC's board, the agreement was friendly. However, a provision gave the V & C operational control of the VC if it failed to make the semiannual lease payment of $54,000, until such time as payment could be made.

There seemed little to suggest that John Smith would ever be more than a successful investor, with his small Vermont & Canada fated to be an acquisition for the Vermont Central. But then, out of nowhere in late 1851, came astonishing news. Among other things, the VC's treasurer, Josiah Quincy, had personally sold 1,240 of the company's shares to investors and then sold another 3,462 shares of nonexistent (unauthorized) stock. By the time the facts were sorted out, the VC was all but out of cash and its credit ruined. "Quincy's financial misdeeds," Vermont Central historian Robert C. Jones wrote, "had probably cost the railroad at least a half million dollars." But the story soon got worse; the VC's president, Charles Paine, had sold and rented personal land to the railroad and also submitted numerous "incidental claims," all highly inflated.[15]

When the economy slid in the mid-1850s, the badly weakened Vermont Central was unable to make its first 1855 payment to the Vermont & Canada. John Smith demanded control; after the legal dust settled, he and Gregory controlled the larger railroad. The VC soon made money again, and its investors asked the Smiths to make the payments and return the VC to them. It never happened; the investors were no match for John and Gregory Smith, who operated the company during the day and cooked the books at night, always being "unable" to pay back the V&C. The final lawsuit, supported by Cooke, failed in 1861. At this point, Gregory Smith was running a railroad three times larger than his V&C, which he had acquired for little more than attorney's fees. (In 1928 Gregory's son retired as president, ending 73 years of "temporary" Smith management.)[16]

During the war, Smith managed a 250-mile railroad with 40 locomotives, hundreds of pieces of rolling stock, and a booming business. Gradually he took over smaller, less profitable lines. Smith dropped the Vermont & Canada name but made St. Albans the Vermont Central's base; by 1871 the railroad had 1,700 employees headquartered in a new red brick station and office building. He was also increasingly powerful, as Vermont's governor and the owner of two St. Albans banks, its largest hotel, and a newspaper. His new home had three towers and a mansard roof, and he generously gave to his Congregational church. Little was to mar his fiefdom until October 19, 1864. In a famous incident that became a movie 90 years later, 20 Confederates slipped across the border, stayed in his hotel, and robbed his two banks and a third bank of $200,000. Although $80,000 was recovered, it is not known how much was returned to Smith.[17]

Smith continued to expand the Vermont Central in the late 1860s, as the railroad industry began to experience the brutality of industrial Darwinism: eat or be eaten. In Vermont it was only a question of time before one or two railroads would control the area between Lakes George and Champlain and the Connecticut River. Smith was well aware of Vermont's geographic and size limitations, and his goal was to consolidate regional operations; but he was unprepared for the declining traffic after the war or the presence of a strong rival: the Rutland & Burlington. The Rutland's president was another former Vermont governor, John B. Page.

Smith met this threat as he had others, through rental-purchase. Knowing Smith, Page agreed, but under firm conditions. On December 30, 1870, the VC took over the Rutland, renting it annually for $376,000, a figure partially based on wartime traffic. Considering the circumstances of under which he and his father took over the VC, it seems amazing that Smith signed. Yet he was working with Cooke; the economy was strong; and with the Rutland no longer a threat, its payments looked safe. Railroad historian David B. Sargent, Jr., noted that the "plausible excuse for the lease . . . was the fear that the [Rutland's] continued expansion . . . would seriously impair the [VC's] western and Canadian business."[18]

In addition to the large payments, the "merger" saddled Smith with more equipment, employees, and track than needed. It appears likely, however, that under the contract's terms Smith could not significantly cut the Rutland's overall operations. By mid-1871 he faced the payments plus declining freight and passenger business in Vermont. The ink was barely dry when he tried to break the contract but lost in court. Thus just as the Northern Pacific was beginning to build a transcontinental railroad, Smith, over 50 and with a small staff, found his Vermont operations in deep financial trouble.

No one seems to have had qualms in 1870 about Smith's being president of two railroads. While his correspondence reflects energy, intelligence, and common sense, his actions reflect an inability to delegate; and he managed the Northern Pacific from St. Albans. Sam Wilkeson read his incoming mail in New York, summarized its contents on a cover sheet, and forwarded it. Even urgent messages were telegraphed to New York and retelegraphed from there. Smith's decisions were made by mail or by telegraph, usually routed via New York. The process was slow; but if one approaches Smith's business style on the assumption that he was acting illicitly to keep the VC afloat, the last thing he needed was decision-making by a real management team.

Even if Smith had been thoroughly honest, he had no experience directing large-scale construction. In contrast with the Northern Pacific's needs, the Vermont Central's growth had been snail-paced. Acting on a small stage, suffering few defeats from which to learn, blissfully unaware of his limitations, never facing well-financed, motivated competition, Smith had gone from one success to another. Now he had to manage the design, construction, purchasing, and operations of a transcontinental railroad simultaneously with the VC. He had to attract settlers, develop traffic, and build an effective staff. He also faced the likely collapse of the VC unless he found $376,000 a year for his Rutland obligations. The cash could not be borrowed or come from VC operations, which left only one source: the money Cooke was raising.

In addition to his inherent management deficiencies, Smith appears to have been guilty of misusing the Vermont Central's resources, further contributing to the line's financial collapse in 1872–73. In 1873, when a slow-moving, Smith-friendly Vermont legislative committee reluctantly called him to the stand, Smith refused to testify. One impartial mid-twentieth-century source, which treats him gently and never addresses Smith's personal ethics, nevertheless summed up the problems of his management style by noting that "he was doubtless over-optimistic and extravagant [concerning Northern Pacific Railroad construction], and has been charged with neglect and the entrusting of important matters to incompetent and dishonest persons."[19]

Why, it may be asked, did Smith want to work with Cooke and vice versa? The answer seems to be that it was a marriage of convenience. Each held something that the other desperately wanted: Cooke gave Smith the key to a financial kingdom, while the NP gave Cooke's ego a project of singular proportions. Neither could know, of course, that within a few years the other would begin to flounder desperately: Smith, flailing like a drowning man; and Cooke, the pied piper, glancing over his shoulder only to discover that his financial tune had not attracted enough followers. Yet at the time many thought it was an outstanding marriage of proven complementary skills.

In the winter of 1865–66 Smith found himself sitting on an exceptional opportunity but also with a requirement to begin construction of the Northern Pacific before July 4, 1866. He sent Canfield to Washington to get a delay for the construction and to see if Congress would grant financial aid. Fortunately for the NP, the Union Pacific had not met its charter obligations and, to modify its charter, bribed numerous congressmen with Crédit Mobilier funds. Canfield, who had a nose for such things, followed close behind, arguing in essence: "You can't give them a break and not give us one." What made things work was Canfield's relationship with House Speaker Stevens, who, as Fawn Brodie wrote, "feverishly promoted" the NP. While Congress granted the NP the delay, Canfield could not get construction subsidies;

for, as Eugene Smalley noted, "the temper of Congress and the country was adverse to further favors."[20]

Smith knew the Northern Pacific needed more than just New England directors to be taken seriously, and he approached businessmen of national stature. Ogden and William G. Fargo agreed, as well as officers of the Erie, New York Central, and Pennsylvania railroads. Smith sold 12 shares at $8,500, paid off some debt, and hired Sam Wilkeson to publicize the NP. (Smith also began cooking the books: by the time the bill was presented to Cooke, it included $924,276 in expenses, a figure four times too high.) The new board began on May 23, 1867, selecting New York as its headquarters. Construction preliminaries were also begun, with survey crews from Duluth and also between Puget Sound and the Columbia River. To manage the company Smith appointed Canfield general agent. When funds proved inadequate for the surveys, he raised $25,000 by dunning the new board members.

Chief engineer Edwin Johnson saw the Northern Pacific going from Duluth on Lake Superior to Portland and Puget Sound: in all over 1,775 miles, costing $140 million. For a variety of construction reasons, since the 1850s Johnson had preferred paralleling the Yellowstone River versus following the Missouri River. Without a compelling alternative, and with mid-central Montana's growing population and gold, this route remained the NP's first choice. (Because of its limited finances the railroad could, of course, build nothing.) While the general route was known, the "middle" route contained a 750- to 800-mile gap running west from present-day Fargo, crossing the Missouri and west to the Yellowstone and following the river to the Bozeman Pass. It was assumed that, technically, this route's only difficult section would be the long ascent and descent of the Bozeman Pass. Crossing the pass would not be easy, but it was within the era's construction norms; and its challenges were modest compared with the Central Pacific's crossing of the Sierra Nevada.

While some might disagree, civil engineering is clearly among the world's oldest professions (perhaps even the second). From the moment when an unknown tribe chopped down a tree, angled it to fall across a stream, and trimmed its branches to reduce roll, civil engineering began. Construction of bridges, roads, military fortifications, canals, harbors, tunnels, and civil and religious edifices started at least 12,000 years ago, and recorded engineering knowledge dates back 5,000 years. The successful execution of these works lies in the ability to plan and measure accurately. Peoples in the Nile and Tigris-Euphrates valleys, facing annual floods that washed away property markers, learned to determine whose land had been where and also positioned buildings based on celestial observation. Gradually, military needs, expanding population, trade, societal ambitions, and religious practices galvanized technical and mathematical thought.

Most of the Romans' engineering skills were, in fact, not lost in the early Middle Ages. The stabilization of European societies and the combination of eastern mathematical skills with preexisting technology led to a period of technical advancement and invention in the first part of the second millennium. The greatest surge of civil engineering innovation, however, came from gunpowder and the breaching of Constantinople's walls in 1453. Military engineers not only had to sight cannon accurately and construct precisely designed fortifications; but to transport the heavy iron cannon, they also needed better roads, bridges, and canals. (Canal locks, for example, were invented in the 1400s.)

Politics also changed measurement. In England, Andro Linklater wrote, "a surveyor still filled his original, feudal role as the executive officer of a landed nobleman. His duty was primarily to oversee (the word *surveyor* is derived from the French *sur* [over] and *voir* [see]) the estate. He was to walk over the land and make a note of the boundaries . . . of the tenants' holdings, and then to assist in drawing up the official record or court roll of what duties they owed." Land was owned by the crown or church; the king's land was held in trust (leased) by nobles and followed a pecking order down to the villein who farmed a fraction of an acre. When Henry VIII seized and sold the land of hundreds of monasteries, buyers, not surprisingly, wanted to know precisely what they were purchasing. The difficulty in uniformly answering this question (many surveyors measured with knotted ropes) led to Edmund Gunter's early-1600s invention of a 100-piece iron chain that, though heavy, could be folded and did not change in length. Despite its defects, Gunter's 66-foot chain was the most efficient tool available and became the British measurement standard.[21]

Peculiar as Gunter's chain might appear, it *was* replicable. Because of America's immense area and the poor training (or dishonesty) of many surveyors, squares were chosen to measure land just after the Revolution, versus the European style of using streams or hilltops. The distance of the side of each American square was 480 Gunter lengths (six miles), an easily divisible number. Although use of a Gunter chain made no intrinsic sense as the basis for the Northern Pacific's surveys, NP surveyors used the same standard measurement as the rest of the United States, which was reason enough.

Surveying further evolved with the invention of the theodolite (circa 1550); its rotating telescope for measuring horizontal and vertical angles permitted accurate topographic surveying. In the early 1600s the slide rule was invented, permitting high-speed mathematical computations. Other tools used by American surveying teams included "plane tables" going back to the Greeks and the (water) level, of Roman origin. The addition of "spider lines" (crosshairs) to telescopes, circa 1670, further facilitated measurement. Sextants became available 60 years later and were a favorite surveyors' tool. While the steel tape measure was invented in America in 1841, it was not trusted for decades; hence Northern Pacific surveyors used Gunter chains. Similar leaps took place in technical education; surveying texts and field manuals were published in the late 1500s and continued to improve for centuries. Thus, when NP surveying began, the tools were well in place and were not to change significantly until the electronic era.[22]

With land considered wealth in America, surveying attracted many of the country's best and brightest men. In 1802 the Corps of Engineers helped establish West Point; and by 1845 railroad engineering was being taught at nontechnical colleges. Engineers had surveying skills but generally were better trained than surveyors, especially in mathematical computation. Gradually a gap developed between surveyors and engineers; but at the time of the Yellowstone surveys and for fieldwork a mature, intelligent surveyor was no less skilled than a college-trained engineer.

Steam-powered locomotives brought new engineering issues into play. For example, engines needed to add water after some 15 miles in the 1830s, but requirements varied by locomotive size, weight to be pulled, terrain crossed, and desired speed. Larger tenders holding more fuel and water became necessary as engines became larger and pulled more weight; ultimately Northern Pacific water towers were 15 and 20 miles apart. Engineers were challenged by rivers, wetlands, hills, mountain passes, buffalo, and even grasshoppers (which got into braking systems and disabled them). Trial-and-error design soon discovered ideal curves and angles for climbing and descending. The role of centrifugal force and the pressure it placed on a locomotive, its parts, and the cars it pulled also had to be learned. As the Baltimore & Ohio's chief engineer, Benjamin H. Latrobe, laconically expressed it, "[A]n abrupt bend upon a railway [will] bring down the speed of an engine or, if the speed is kept up, some part of the train must be cast off."[23]

An early example of Latrobe's insight had occurred on November 11, 1833, when a Camden & Amboy train, "speeding" around a curve at some 25 miles an hour, broke an axle and rolled off the tracks, causing the first railroad fatality. One gentleman suffered two broken ribs and vowed never again to have anything to do with railroads: Cornelius Vanderbilt. Also on board was John Quincy Adams, who escaped injury. Ironically, improvements in track design, brakes, telegraphy, and signaling equipment resulted in more trains with greater loads running at higher speeds. The admittedly minimal figures in the *Railroad Gazette* show close to six deaths a week in 1872–73. The era's illustrated magazines feasted on train wrecks, while newspapers happily described decapitations, squashings, and manglings suffered by railroad workers, passengers, inebriates, and other luckless souls. Despite all these problems, railroad investment and traffic continued to grow explosively throughout the nineteenth century.[24]

When the Northern Pacific began construction, America had 50,000 miles of track in operation, seemingly providing adequate experience to eliminate construction surprises. But before construction could begin, each section of the route had to be surveyed and designed. Once the NP decided to follow the Yellowstone versus the Missouri, the next step was to determine the location of a general route by a "reconnaissance survey." Despite major Army Corps of Engineer exploration in the 1850s between the Bozeman Pass and the Missouri, this work did not come close to meeting the needs of a railroad's reconnaissance, and large areas west of Bismarck had never been formally explored.

Preconstruction engineering involved three basic stages: a reconnaissance and a first and second (or final) survey. Northern Pacific surveyors, however, often performed all the three stages in parallel. The equipment for a reconnaissance included a compass, a pedometer (showing the number of steps taken), a hand level, an aneroid barometer, and sometimes a sextant and chronometer. All could be hand held, with the data recorded by a single individual, as Milnor Roberts did in 1869 and 1871. His skills illustrated how an experienced engineer simply "eyeballed" a perspective route to determine its feasibility. In unexplored areas between the Missouri and Yellowstone, the survey leader often made horseback reconnaissances, sometimes beginning a preliminary survey the next day. Three stages were not usually needed in the Yellowstone Valley, because the route was generally dictated by the river's path and adjacent hills and cliffs.[25]

After he became the Northern Pacific's chief engineer, Milnor Roberts also emphasized the importance of flexibility to his field leaders. His goal was always to find the most cost-efficient route in terms of construction and later operations. To assist the surveys, the Roberts teams always had copies of earlier NP and pertinent government reports and maps, reconnaissance equipment, Gunter chains, and transits and levels on tripods. A "level" party calculated topographic details with a "stadia"; the distances were recorded by noting the intervals between the telescope's crosshairs on a marked rod. The resulting map showed line direction, profile and landscape contours, and features. Based on this information, individual roadbed sections and track cross-sectional plans were drawn, thus permitting the determination of the amount of "cut" and "fill" required as well as the road's gradient. There were also management variables. Wanting to emphasize the Yellowstone Valley's economic benefits in 1872, Roberts wrote the Helena office manager, "If you can find some one who is good at *sketching*, try to get him into the party to take striking views: especially of all appearances of coal—including the region traveled last year" (Roberts's emphasis).[26]

Other refinements were added. Infantry captain Augustus W. Corliss wrote of the surveyors: "[Their] wagons were most admirably fitted for their use and were wonders of labor-saving and space-economizing expedients, most of them the result of Gen. Thomas L. Rosser's experience during the war." Tents were large, specially made, and equipped with folding tables, drawing stands, and chairs, allowing crews to produce finished maps. Corliss noted that "a thorough system prevailed in every part of the whole organization. Duplicate notes of the surveys were made and kept in the tent of the commander . . . so that in case of accident . . . all would not be lost." Corliss also wistfully recalled that the surveyors' food was "much superior" to the officers' mess; they looked forward to escort duty because they "were always invited to luncheon with Gen. Rosser."[27]

Survey teams varied in size. When the college-trained engineer Edward C. Jordan was hired (1870), his crew consisted of 8 men and a cook. The Yellowstone surveys were both reconnaissance and preliminary surveys, each fielding at least 15 men. Rosser employed 25 men in 1871 and in 1872 managed two crews, with over 30 members, including cooks and teamsters. While each survey team varied, the composition, work ratios, and pay of NP surveyors were similar to those in a *New York Times* story: chief of party ($175 a month), first assistant ($150), assistants ($125), topographer ($125), transitman and leveler (not available), rodmen ($75); picket-flagmen, chainmen, axemen, and cook ($60 each), and assistant cook ($40). Teamsters were paid $40 a month or $3.50 a day if they had their own team of mules.[28]

Roberts could not control daily operations, but he carefully outlined key surveying tasks in an 1871 letter, "General Arrangement of the [Surveying] Parties." The chief of party led the survey, scouted ahead for the most feasible route, and checked daily to see that technical readings and topographical features were properly recorded and logged. Roberts wrote: "He will make up a brief synopsis of the work accomplished during the week showing distances, heights etc. *the main features*" (Roberts's emphasis). He wrote that "early rising and starting of the surveys must be a regular feature . . . the encampments should be arranged . . . [for] the least walking to and from camp," something neither western survey ever did. "Success," Roberts said, "can only be secured by a strict adherence to regular discipline." "It is [in] the interest of every member . . . to be always courteous, one to another, without exception."[29]

The "leader of the field work" (first assistant) was responsible for compass and transit readings, a book with data on streams to be bridged, levels, "abrupt elevations or depressions," and ground composition (rock, grass, swamp, or hard dirt). Rodmen were responsible for individual segments and height changes and for giving the data to the leveler or his assistant "to guard against error of hearing or sight." The final work product had a "profile" and "alignment" of the route. The profile section was a center line showing the "ups and downs" in ground level at each measured point. The alignment was the drawing showing distance as well as the deviations of the route from a straight line, particularly important at curves. Most surveys did not have topographers. The team leader, through his observations and field notes, was to give a "good general idea of the character of the ground traversed . . . rather than minute accuracy."

Roberts did not mention the menial positions of picketmen (holding markers and driving stakes), chainmen (measuring distances), or axmen (clearing trees and underbrush). Yet their work could not be taken for granted. An 1872 diary noted: "One of the axemen sick and progress slow." Roberts was concerned about keeping a night watch to prevent "stealing of animals" and fully understood that surveyors needed protection. In 1872 he telegraphed an assistant: "Get arms and ammunition if you can . . . Use your best judgment. See [the fort's commandant]." His last instruction noted one of the era's major problems: "It is to be understood that intoxication will be regarded as sufficient cause for dismissal." In fact, heavy drinking by both surveyors and army officers was to plague all five Yellowstone surveys.[30]

Most Northern Pacific reconnaissances and surveys in Montana and Dakota had military escorts. (In one 1870 case, an army officer, Lt. Edwin Turnock, was court-martialed for leaving a small group of surveyors east of the Missouri; while he was acquitted, he was later forced out of the service.) Although as few as six men accompanied NP personnel, the mere presence of soldiers told both Indians and outlaws that the surveyors were under the full protection of the United States. And indeed, from 1869, when a small band of Indians attempted to steal Governor Marshall's horses in Dakota, this protection would remain unchallenged until 1872.[31]

As Cooke and Smith negotiated their contract in 1869, they had every reason to believe that the Northern Pacific could be built in a timely manner. Railroads had evolved with amazing rapidity in the four decades since the *Tom Thumb* and *DeWitt Clinton*, the first transcontinental railroad was operational, and Cooke was confident that he could raise the money for a second. While there probably was concern over the *costs* of crossing the Bozeman Pass and the Continental Divide, no one, including Roberts and Johnson, appeared concerned about Minnesota's wetlands (the subject of chapters 5 and 6). Additionally, other than viewing them as nuisances, little notice was paid to Sioux, Cheyennes, and Arapahos who lived in and adjacent to the Yellowstone Basin. Nevertheless, that summer "militants" were coalescing around the leadership of the Hunkpapa Sioux Sitting Bull: they wanted little more than to be left alone to follow their traditional way of life. These limited goals and the Northern Pacific's route would soon meet head-on.

CHAPTER 4

"The Buffalo Will Dwindle Away"

The real defeat of North America's Native peoples, beginning with the landing of Christopher Columbus and ending at Wounded Knee, was not the result of Western metallurgy, engineering, use of horses, gunpowder, and military discipline or Indian losses in battle. Neither was it caused by alcohol or treaty violations or governmental corruption: all these paled in comparison to microbes that neither Indians nor whites knew existed. William H. McNeill's classic *Plagues and Peoples* indicates that 50 years after Hernán Cortés landed in Mexico the death rate was 90 percent; he survived in part because Aztec leadership was decimated by smallpox. In describing sixteenth-century losses from disease, Roger G. Kennedy notes that "it is likely that as many as five million people in the Mississippi Valley were reduced in the Great Dying to a few hundred thousand."[1]

Similarly, as the Pilgrims stepped onto New England's stern and rockbound shores, the woods were fortuitously empty. Squanto, who guided them through their first winter, returned home to find his *entire* tribe destroyed by disease. William Cronon writes of European arrival: "Mortality rates in initial onslaughts were rarely less than 80 or 90 percent, and it was not unheard of for an entire village to be wiped out." Disease and epidemics continued for centuries and included smallpox, influenza, typhus, measles, tuberculosis, dysentery, and syphilis. Mental health also suffered. With faces disfigured by smallpox and their religions and medicines powerless, suicide was not uncommon among Indians, alcoholism took root, and for many the will to fight vanished. Other Native Americans, however, united under charismatic leaders such as King Philip, Pontiac, Tecumseh, and, ultimately, Sitting Bull.[2]

Scarcely 200 years elapsed from the destruction of the Pequots in Connecticut (1636) to the birth of the last Sioux war chiefs. From 1640, when 24,000 English-speaking peoples hugged the Atlantic Coast, to 1840 the Euro-American population soared to 17 million. Just 30 years later, a few thousand warriors faced a nation of 39 million Euro-Americans. By this time the issue facing the United States was how to apply Christian principles to its Native peoples—while removing them from land of economic value. The pragmatic question was often decided by the slow nature of the democratic process. When valuable land (for example, with gold) was discovered, members of the heavily armed frontier society—later augmented by those trained to kill in 1861–65—took matters into their own hands. Only where the land was of lesser value did the frontier expansion temporarily slow.

The election of Grant came at a time of adequate farmland and no new mineral discoveries. Grant was sympathetic to the plight of the Indians; but he could only nudge the system, not change it. In general, "peaceful" Indians lived on land reserved for their use, administered by the Department of Interior's Bureau of Indian Affairs. The BIA was responsible for providing food, shelter, clothing, and basic education. Nineteenth-century politics and business practices, however, combined with a lack of public interest, were a sure recipe for services that, if delivered, were at best second rate.

BIA's Indian agents were often indistinguishable from frontier ruffians or parts of the spoils system. Of course, working on the reservations was not for the faint of heart; a handful of agents were responsible for thousands of armed, often sullen, and sometimes volatile individuals. Grant did what he could to improve the situation by his radical selection of a full-blooded Seneca (Iroquois) as the BIA commissioner, his friend Ely S. Parker (he was the best man at Parker's wedding). Sadly, Parker was in over his head: his well-meaning attempts at reform were usually thwarted, he was a weak administrator who made numerous errors, and he was all but forced to resign in 1871. By the end of his first term, and with the death of his wife's first cousin at Indian hands (chapter 11), Grant appears to have given up trying to reform the BIA.[3]

In 1869 one of the few and by far the best and largest areas under Native American domination was the high northern plains and the adjacent Yellowstone-Missouri basin. The majority of these Indians were Sioux (Ojibwa for "snakes"), or Dakotas ("allies" or "friends," as they called themselves). Historian Kingsley M. Bray estimates that 28,000 Sioux controlled 60,000 square miles in 1665, mostly in woodland Minnesota, western Wisconsin, and Iowa. By the nineteenth century the Sioux had been pushed west—divided into Eastern (Santee or Dakota), Middle (Yankton or Nakota), and Western (Teton or Lakota) Sioux. The Tetons included the Brulés (Sicangus), Hunkpapas, Miniconjous, Oglalas, Oohenonpas (Two Kettles),

Itazipacolas (Sans Arcs), and Sihasapas (Blackfeet). Most of these lived on reservations, but the BIA estimated that there were 8,000 "roving Sioux," mostly followers of Sitting Bull. This figure, in addition to being a third too high, also included Santees, Yanktons, Cheyennes, and Arapahos. The northernmost, poorest, and most militant of the Lakota subtribes were the Hunkpapas, one of whom was Sitting Bull.[4]

From 1750 to 1870, approximately every 15 years, disease swept the plains. In 1780–82 smallpox decimated the Missouri's Arikaras, Hidatsas (Gros Ventres), and Mandans. When Lewis and Clark arrived near Bismarck (1804), there were 1,500 Mandans, just 15 percent of the population 23 years earlier. In 1837 smallpox killed 90 percent of the Mandans and also caused high death rates among the Arikaras, Hidatsas, Blackfeet, and Assiniboines. The Indian Affairs office estimated that "at least 17,200" were dead. If their enemies were devastated, the Tetons' more nomadic life spared them the worst; and their population slowly grew from 8,500 in 1805 to 14,370 by 1870. Of these, approximately a fifth consisted of warriors who participated in offensive operations (war parties), which usually did not include men older than 38.[5]

Following the 1837–38 epidemics, the Lakotas found themselves commanding a huge area bordered on the south by the Platte, on the west by central Wyoming and southeast Montana, on the north by current Interstate 94, and on the east by central North and South Dakota. As Francis Parkman recognized in *The Oregon Trail* (1847), however: "Great changes are at hand. With the stream of immigration to Oregon and California the buffalo will dwindle away, and the large wandering communities that depend on them for support must be broken and scattered. The Indians will soon be abashed by liquor and overawed by military posts."[6]

In the mid-1850s Sioux hunting territory encompassed over 150,000 square miles but was controlled by only a few thousand warriors. Even when the Northern Pacific began its surveys, there was less than one warrior per five hundred square miles. But as Parkman predicted, the Oregon Trail's toll was high. In 1851 the Brulés, other Lakotas, and another half-dozen tribes signed a treaty giving safe passage to Oregon Trail emigrants. Just before the Great Sioux War began, Edwin T. Denig described the plight of the Brulés: "They being nearest to the trail cholera, smallpox, measles, etc. have year after year thinned their ranks so that [only] a remnant [remains] . . . badly clothed, without game, and with but a few horses to enable them to hunt."[7]

The first formal clash in the Great Sioux War began in 1854, when a Mormon immigrant complained to the military at Fort Laramie that a Miniconjou Sioux had stolen his cow. The incident escalated into the "massacre" of the foolish Lt. John Gratten and thirty troops, which, in turn, led to Col. William S. Harney's brutal murder of some 85 Brulés the next year. Despite mutual animosity, a peace then

Table 3
Kingsley Bray's Estimated Teton Sioux (Lakota) Population History, 1805–1881

Tribal Division	1805	1825	1839[a]	1855	1870[b]	1881
Brulé	2,400	3,000	3,450	3,120	4,050	5,700
Oglala	1,000	1,500	2,250	2,950	3,600	4,800
Miniconjou	2,000	2,200	2,080	1,715	1,620	1,290
Two Kettles[c]				650	990	740
Sans Arc	800	900	880	1,090	1,170	870
Sihasapa	700	900	890	1,055	1,050	1,090
Hunkpapa	1,600	1,500	1,770	2,330	1,890	1,620
Totals	**8,500**	**10,000**	**11,320**	**12,910**	**14,370**	**16,110**
"Warriors"[d]	1,700	2,000	2,264	2,582	2,000[e]	NA[f]

Source: Kingsley M. Bray, "Teton Sioux Population History, 1655–1881," *Nebraska History* (Summer 1994), table 3, "Reconstructed Teton Sioux Population," pp. 174–75. Original charts also include estimates for 1849 and 1869 as well as breakdowns by men, women, children, lodges, and percentages of total population for each of the tribal divisions.

[a] Follows the smallpox epidemic of 1837–38.

[b] The 1869 *Annual Report of the Commissioner of Indian Affairs* lists 17,980 but also includes the Upper and Lower Yanktonais [*sic*] Sioux.

[c] Two Kettles figures for 1805, 1825, and 1839 are included in Miniconjou numbers in the original chart.

[d] Bray estimates (p. 169) that "[t]he 'warriors' would comprise the majority of adult males [who made up 27 percent of the population], excluding the aged, and account for approximately one-fifth of the total population."

[e] Significant numbers of Teton Sioux were living all or some of the year on reservations, so the available number of warriors, even in summer, had to be smaller and most likely was in the range of 1,750 to 2,250.

[f] Not applicable, as virtually all Teton Sioux were living on reservations or in military confinement (followers of Sitting Bull and Gall).

descended over the northern plains, not to be broken until 1862. The Bureau of Indian Affairs had trouble living up to its various obligations even before the Civil War began, but by mid-1862 the Dakotas living on a constrained reservation in west-central Minnesota were starving. Desperate, they rebelled; after killing over 800 settlers and soldiers, they ran out of momentum and were crushed at the battle of Wood Lake on September 23. The Dakotas had been assisted by the Yanktons; but, buttressed by rumors of Confederate and British support, Lincoln and the northwestern war governors decided to push the Sioux out of eastern Dakota in 1863.[8]

Under Gen. John Pope, a double pincer movement was planned, the first column coming directly from Minnesota and the second coming up the Missouri from Iowa. The first column under Henry H. Sibley caught up with Yankton and Teton Sioux who were hunting buffalo, and some 80 Sioux warriors were killed at the battle of Big Mound (July 24, 1863). Two other battles quickly followed; the Sioux were defeated both times, although with lighter losses. Meanwhile, the second column under Alfred Sully had been delayed and missed its rendezvous with Sibley. However, on September 3, 1863, at Whitestone Hill, the column stumbled into a large encampment of Sioux hunting buffalo. The battle resulted in horrendous Sioux losses: over 150 warriors were killed, some 400 lodges were destroyed, and their entire winter food supply was lost.

From a tactical standpoint, 1863 saw the combined Sioux tribes suffer terrible casualties, as well as the loss of their hunting grounds east of the Mississippi; but they had not been destroyed and were understandably enraged. Pope knew that they had to be subdued; but the necessity for safe passage of gold (which had been discovered in quantity in Montana in 1862) meant that the 1864 campaign would have to be west of the Missouri. Pope's plan was to build a string of forts in Dakota and at the confluence of the Powder and Yellowstone Rivers then bring the Sioux to one final battle. As planned, forts were built at Devil's Lake, on the James River, and on the Missouri (Fort Rice). Then the Sioux chose to fight 2,200 troops under Sully at the base of Kildeer Mountain (July 28). Facing both a dozen cannon and cavalry, the Sioux were overwhelmed; over 150 warriors were killed, 1,600 lodges burnt, and the camp's 3,000 dogs killed. Marching to the Yellowstone, Sully and many of his troops later contracted dysentery; they did not reach the Powder River or build the Yellowstone fort. In the years to come, the implications of not having a Yellowstone post were to loom large for the Northern Pacific and, of course, for 263 members of the 7th Cavalry.

The Sioux suffered grievously at Killdeer Mountain, and the establishment of Fort Rice meant the effective loss of their hunting grounds adjacent to and east of the Missouri River until its western turn north of Bismarck. This loss was magnified by the disappearance of the buffalo for at least 150 miles west of the Missouri. Although disease clearly played a role, a comment by Capt. William Raynolds during his 1859–60 Yellowstone expedition is noteworthy: "[T]he wholesale destruction of the buffalo . . . is due first and mainly to the fact that the skin of the female is alone valuable for robes . . . The result is that females are always singled out by the hunter, and consequently [today] the males in a herd always exceed the females . . . [by] ten to one."[9]

In 1865 Pope again tried to subdue the Sioux; but a complex pincer movement with troops being sent from Wyoming, Iowa, and Minnesota failed in its strategic purpose. However, the 1862–65 fighting had all but destroyed the Dakotas and Nakotas, and at least 15 percent of the Teton Sioux warriors were probably killed or badly wounded. Because of the destruction of their camps, the army posts on the Missouri, and the disappearance of the buffalo, the various Sioux tribes were forced to live west of the Missouri. During 1867–68 the Sioux under Red Cloud's leadership forcefully attempted to block traffic moving along the Bozeman Trail between Fort

Laramie and Bozeman. Despite the tactical success that came when Capt. William H. Fetterman and 79 other soldiers and civilians were killed to a man (December 21, 1866), by 1868 the Sioux were a badly weakened, increasingly desperate people.

On the Euro-American side, the motivations for the 1868 Fort Laramie Treaty (signed at Fort Rice) ranged from the highest Christian tenets—the Indians were starving—to pragmatic territorial goals. On the Indian side, motives ranged from near-starvation to the cynical acceptance of otherwise unobtainable gifts. How accurately the treaty's details were translated and to what degree Indian signatories realized what they had signed are unknown. It was obvious that Sitting Bull was against the treaty, and lesser chiefs under Gall were sent. Gall not only did not know the treaty's details but actually spoke against the treaty on the same day he signed it. Western historian Robert M. Utley notes: "The treaty that Gall so innocently signed addressed no fundamental grievances of the Hunkpapa." Similarly, the government did not consider the Northern Pacific's needs; the railroad, if thought of at all, was considered a pipe dream.[10]

Following the treaty, Sitting Bull and his followers continued living in their traditional way. Later that summer he led a raid on Fort Buford, killing three soldiers and stealing 250 head of cattle. Some 5,000 generally younger Lakotas and perhaps 1,000 others (Arapahos, Cheyennes, and Dakota and Yankton Sioux) were followers of Sitting Bull; but given their nomadic hunting patterns, they camped with him only a few times a year. Each spring he was joined by young warriors from reservations, possibly 1,000 more. But in 1870, in another raid at Buford, one civilian killed five Indians before going down. After this, Utley notes, Sitting Bull shifted "the direction of his leadership, from the offensive to the defensive."[11]

In fact, Sitting Bull had few options: his followers found themselves virtually in a state of siege. Most trapper-hunters, "wolfers," and Hidatsas, Arikaras, and Flatheads killed any Sioux on sight. Crow warfare seemed never-ending; one 1869 clash left 30 Crows and 14 Hunkpapas dead. Miners were interested in the rumored gold of the "yellow-stone" river, and only the fact that there was none prevented the valley's being overrun. Sitting Bull also faced pressure from Métis (Chippewa and French-Canadian mixed-bloods) who lived along the Red River. The Métis, better armed and organized, were also affected by the buffalo's disappearance and now hunted in western Dakota and Montana. And Sitting Bull's followers had a final problem. The only way to get repeating rifles, powder, and whiskey was to kill and barter more pelts and hides—from a contracting habitat. Making matters worse, 6,000 Dakotas and Nakotas were moved to Montana's Milk River agency in 1871, putting further pressure on the land. To minimize his losses, Sitting Bull kept as far away as possible from the army, now spending most of the year in eastern Montana. Not until 1872, and seemingly without options, did he reluctantly determine that he had to block the Northern Pacific's surveyors.[12]

The postwar U.S. Army averaged just over 30,000 men between 1869 and 1873. It was administered by the secretary of war, followed by the general-in-chief and then divided into functional and geographic lines of responsibility. Sherman succeeded Grant as general-in-chief; and his former position, commander of the Division of the Missouri, was filled by the combative Philip H. Sheridan. Sheridan's command ran from Canada to Texas, divided into the Departments of the Gulf, Texas, the Platte, the Missouri, and Dakota. The Department of Dakota, headquartered in St. Paul, contained about 1,700 men (the number shifted slightly year by year) and 370,063 square miles, including Montana, Dakota, and Minnesota—some two-thirds of the Northern Pacific's route.[13]

On May 17, 1869, Winfield Scott Hancock, the hero of Gettysburg, angrily assumed command of the Department of the Dakota, feeling it was beneath him. An 1868 Democratic presidential nominee, he ran second as late as the twenty-second ballot, which fed his not unsubstantial ego but further frayed his relations with Grant (a West Point classmate) and Sheridan. On leave and walking near the White House in 1870, he passed Grant, who tipped his hat. Hancock boorishly pretended not to see him. Shortly after Gen. George H. Thomas's death, Hancock sought a promotion. When he stated his choice to Sherman, he soon received a reply: "The president authorizes me to say to you that it belongs to his office to select the commanding generals of divisions and departments, and that the relations you chose to assume toward him officially and privately absolve him from regarding your personal preferences." Hancock remained in St. Paul.[14]

In 1869–70 Hancock was lukewarm about the Northern Pacific; but later, when his twin brother, John, sought employment in St. Paul, the NP became a "great national enterprise." With his eye on the presidency, Hancock wrote of his department's 100,000 Indians and 4,000 hostile Sioux in Montana, noting that Fort Buford was "constantly in a state of siege" and that "traveling in [the] vicinity [of Fort Rice] is never safe." But despite Hancock's suggestion of danger, Sheridan reported limited fighting in the Department of Dakota during 1869–71. In 1869 Sheridan's division took part in two Indian campaigns and saw 65 incidents; but only 4 were in Hancock's department, and, at most, Sitting Bull's followers were involved once.[15]

In 1869 six Montana civilians were killed by a band of Piegans—the "crisis" that had an impact on the Roberts-Canfield party. In response, Sheridan bypassed Hancock and placed the able but alcoholic Maj. Eugene M. Baker in command of a 200-man strike force. On January 23, 1870, Baker found a Piegan camp (the

Table 4

Military Posts and Indian Agencies, Department of Dakota, 1869–1873 (Officers and Men)

Districts[a]	1869	1870	1871	1872	1873
Montana					
Fort Shaw	NA	278	186	394	NA
Fort Ellis	NA	271	291	271	NA
Fort Benton	NA	65	48	63	NA
Camp Baker	NA	72	51	62	NA
subtotal	879	686	576	790	NA
Fort Buford	NA	285	167	428	NA
Middle (Dakota)					
Fort Sully	NA	234	253	268	NA
Fort Rice	NA	250	268	254	NA
Fort Randall	NA	205	223	245	NA
Fort Stevenson	NA	98	132	122	NA
Fort McKeen[b]	—	—	—	111	NA
Lower Brulé Agency	NA	111	51	56	NA
Cheyenne Agency	NA	191	114	91	NA
Grand River Agency	NA	182	115	124	NA
Old Ponca Agency	NA	118★	—	—	—
Whetstone Agency	NA	118★	57	—	—
In Camp [temporary]	—	—	—	54	—
Crow Creek Agency	NA	120★	—	—	—
subtotal	1,243	1,912	1,380	1,753	NA
Minnesota					
Fort Ridgely	NA	1	1★	—	—
Fort Snelling[c]	NA	104	93	78	NA
Fort Ripley	NA	79	56	53	NA
Fort Abercrombie★★	NA	110	56	57	NA
Fort Wadsworth★★	NA	98	123	57	NA
Fort Ranson★★	NA	88	68	—	NA
Fort Totten★★	NA	182	110	104	NA
Fort Pembina★★	NA	144	86	92	NA
Fort Cross	—	—	—	103	NA
subtotal	246	806	593	544	NA
Temporarily Attached	NA	—	—	399	NA
Recruits en route	NA	317	429	504	NA
Grand Totals	**2,368**	**3,721**	**2,978**	**3,990**	**4,148**

Source: Annual Report of the Secretary of War on the Operations of the Department for the Fiscal Year Ended June 30, 18 (varies by year).

Note: The Department of Dakota was under the command of Winfield Scott Hancock from the spring of 1869 through the end of 1872. Alfred H. Terry commanded the department both before and after Hancock. Both officers reported to Philip H. Sheridan.

★ Last year troops were stationed at agency or fort.

★★ Actually located in Dakota Territory.

[a] "District" lines did not necessarily correspond with state or territorial boundaries.

[b] Fort established in 1872 and renamed Fort Abraham Lincoln in 1873.

[c] Figure likely includes one company plus Department of Dakota staff and the staffs of some regiments, such as the 7th Cavalry in the fall of 1873.

wrong one) at Marias Creek in Montana and killed 173 people (17 of whom were men) without a single U.S. casualty. Of 160 prisoners taken, the males were later killed and the rest turned loose without food. The details leaked out, caused a national outcry, and worsened relations between Sheridan and Hancock, who pointedly called it "the Baker massacre." Baker was to accompany Milnor Roberts down the Yellowstone Valley in 1871 and to lead the surveyors' escort in 1872.[16]

Despite the Baker slaughter, there was no other fighting in Hancock's command in 1870. During Hancock's inspection of Fort Ellis in 1869, he had crossed the Bozeman Pass to the Yellowstone and had concluded (referring to both technical and Indian issues): "We found no obstacles in the way to the passage of a railroad."[17]

CHAPTER 5

"Knee Deep in Mud"

The year 1870 began with Cooke and Smith formally completing their agreement on New Year's day and the Northern Pacific facing the daunting task of living up to its expectations and promises. During the year NP surveyors spread out across large parts of four territories (Washington, Idaho, Montana, and Dakota) and worked frantically in Minnesota to perfect a final route. Cooke's construction and bond sales also began in earnest, but management problems soon appeared, one result being Milnor Roberts's replacement of the aging Edwin Johnson as chief engineer.

Congress had stipulated that the NP build at both ends of the system. While 25 miles were completed in Washington in 1870–71, the NP's primary effort was in Minnesota, between Duluth and present-day Moorhead on the Red River.

The Minnesota route was mostly level or had gentle hills, except for a climb just southwest of Duluth, where track was being built by the Lake Superior & Mississippi (LS&M) Railroad. Yet no lengthy stretch of railroad except for the Central Pacific's crossing of the Sierra Nevada raised more construction problems. Minnesota contains 11,842 lakes larger than ten acres and unnumbered thousands of smaller ones. The glaciers that created these lakes also scraped central Minnesota flat, and the gradient per mile is often measured in inches, not feet. West of Carlton, water flowed east to Lake Superior, south to the St. Croix River, and west to the Mississippi; and NP track crisscrossed the watersheds five times. For over a hundred miles the area consisted of porous glacial moraine with lakes, swamps, peat bogs, sloughs, pine barrens, sinkholes, quicksand, and sometimes floating "islands" of solid ground. Besides visible creeks and rivers, underground streams flowed just below what appeared to be firm land. The deceptive covering was a forest of pine, spruce, tamarack, birch, and some elm protected by seemingly impenetrable undergrowth. As the daughter of a surveyor wrote, the wetlands were

> sometimes mere potholes into which a man would step and find himself wallowing waist deep, sometimes stretches three or five miles wide, but all . . . filled with black muck which was not water, for no one could swim in it, nor land. For no one could walk upon its surface . . . [When a] wind blew over it, [one] could see great heaving ripples, sinister and unbelievable, go across its surface. [It was] a dark expanse . . . with stunted evergreens, bright insects hovering in the damp air, and the twisted knees of roots running back and forth everywhere.[1]

The unchanging water level made the land ideal mosquito habitat. The few Indians who lived there learned to cover themselves with bear fat. Sometimes mosquitoes balled themselves up and were carried by a breeze, panicking horses that smelled them downwind. Humans caught by a mosquito cloud became unrecognizable, and horses, livestock, and dogs often died. Fortunately, the insects carried no life-threatening illnesses. Additionally, Minnesota's winters were exceptionally long and cold, which shortened construction seasons; each fall the land froze and expanded, while in the spring it thawed and contracted.

The man chosen to head the NP's Minnesota effort was Ira Spaulding. Spaulding led the 50th New York Engineers in the Civil War, building fortifications, bridges, canals, roads, tunnels, railroads, and pontoon bridges, and was promoted to brigadier general. After being wounded while bridging a river, he developed a chronic cough and suffered frequent pleurisy attacks. Six feet tall and blue eyed, he was a natural leader; one surveyor remembered "a kindly man, genial and much respected." Gregory Smith's decision to hire him (ca. 1868) seemed sensible; but while he ably led the surveyors, he proved a weak construction manager.[2]

Railroad construction contracts were riddled with graft; but, in general, if the theft was not excessive and the project was satisfactorily completed, the public was satisfied. Graft was so rampant that an obscure Tammany Hall politician, George Washington Plunkitt (who became a millionaire operating a shoe-shine parlor), is remembered for distinguishing between honest and dishonest graft. In Plunkitt's example, if an almshouse was sturdily built, it was not unethical to give your brother the contract and let him turn a nice profit. "Dishonest graft" meant shoddy materials or an unsafe building. Dishonest graft permeated the Northern Pacific; but after 135 years the only "proof" lies in strange contracts, purchasing that defied common sense, shoddy construction, and so forth. To what degree, if any, Spaulding was involved will never be known, although ex-Minnesota governor William Marshall believed he was in on the take.[3]

One of the first men Spaulding hired in 1870 was a down-on-his-luck 33-year-old veteran who had not held a steady job since the war. Rumor said he applied for an axman's job, cutting trees and clearing brush at $40 a month. With war memories still sharp and Spaulding in frequent pain, this man's hiring was even less likely because he had been a Southern officer. But Spaulding, a good judge of character, was impressed by Confederate major general Thomas Lafayette Rosser. Rosser, of French Huguenot descent, was born in Virginia's Piedmont area. After the Mexican War his father, a slaveholder, went to Texas, acquired land, and sent for his family. Tom, at 12, drove the animals and wagons over a thousand miles. Likable and intelligent, he was encouraged by his teachers and friends to attend West Point, which he did in 1856. It was then a five-year program. For a number of years the room next door was occupied by a close friend, George Armstrong Custer.[4]

Just before his 1861 graduation, Rosser resigned to enlist in the Confederate forces. There he rose quickly; he was self-confident and tall (six feet two inches, weighing some 220 pounds), with excellent coordination, a prerequisite for cavalry longevity. Decades later, he estimated that he was in more than a hundred battles and skirmishes, noting that he had been wounded nine times. Rosser caught J. E. B. (Jeb) Stuart's eye, commanded a regiment in 1862, and the next year became a brigadier general. He fought Custer in central Virginia and the Shenandoah Valley throughout 1864 and late in the year was promoted to major general. Rosser believed in slavery and the South. When Lee was surrounded at Appomattox, Rosser broke through Union lines, the last troops to escape, which was one of his proudest moments. He met the fleeing Jeff Davis and, like Davis, wanted to keep fighting. Rosser stayed out of Union reach; but in early May, rather than surrender, he let himself be captured—to him an important distinction.[5]

Rosser's bravery, leadership by example, and character were unquestioned, but his management skills were modest. Civil War historian Robert K. Krick wrote that "subordinates invariably attested to [his] bravery, but with almost as much unanimity they complained of his incompetence, particularly when he assumed division command in 1864." Two surveyors had similar thoughts. Montgomery Meigs complained that Rosser "muddle[s] things up so awfully. He has not the slightest method in him, and rushes engineers off their own work into somebody else's and makes confusion all the time." Edward C. Jordan, picking his words carefully, stated: "[B]y his force and directions and his ability to enlist the best labors of others he soon showed [his superiority] . . . over those who possessed perhaps more technical engineering capacity."[6]

In late 1862 Rosser stopped at a house near Ashland, Virginia, and asked a boy for water. After peeking through a window, the boy's stunning 19-year-old sister, Betty ("Lizzy") Winston brought the water. It was love at first sight; and on May 28, 1863, they married at the Winston's ancestral home, Courtland. The large, well-publicized wedding included cavalry luminaries such as Stuart and Fitzhugh Lee. Years later in Minneapolis, a man approached Lizzy and asked if she was Mrs. Rosser. When she said yes, he said that he had been a Union spy who had crashed the wedding, hoping to pick up Rebel secrets.[7]

As in so many wartime romances, the two barely knew each other. After the war Rosser, with a growing family, found himself unemployed. He attended law school, began businesses in New Orleans, Mobile, and Baltimore, and tried lecturing. Nothing worked. Christmas Eve, 1869, found him alone in a St. Paul hotel, his family in Virginia. Subject to frequent depression, he despondently wrote Lizzy: "I failed utterly with my lecture [yesterday], the night was bitter cold, the thermometer stood 23˚ below zero, and no one came out [to hear 'Adam's Transgression and Life beyond the Grave']. I now have only three cents to my name." Some men would have shot themselves. However, Rosser pulled himself together and continued: "But [I] am not in the least dismayed." Rosser's optimism was justified: for a change he was in the right place at the right time and was soon hired by Spaulding.[8]

Spaulding also hired three others who were to play key supporting roles in the years ahead: Albert O. ("Eck") Eckelson, Edward C. Jordan, and Montgomery Meigs. Eckelson, for whom a North Dakota town and a lake are named, enlisted at 16 in the 36th Illinois and was wounded at Stone's River (Murfreesboro). He contracted chronic bronchitis while hospitalized afterward; he was employed by a railroad, where he learned surveying, and in 1870 joined the Northern Pacific.[9]

Another Rosser assistant was Montgomery "Monty" Meigs. His father (Montgomery Cunningham Meigs) was a notable civil engineer, architect, and the Union army's quartermaster general during the Civil War. Meigs's maternal grandfather, John Rogers, commanded the 44-gun frigate *President* in the War of 1812. Meigs graduated from Harvard's Lawrence Scientific School and the Royal Polytechnic Institute in Stuttgart, Germany. When he returned to the United States, the Northern Pacific was only too happy to hire him. Fortunately, some of his letters and drawings survive.[10]

The Meigs-Rosser relationship was complex. Meigs's older brother, John, first in his West Point class (1863), was on Sheridan's Shenandoah Valley staff when he was shot behind Union lines by a Confederate cavalryman in civilian dress in 1864. A never-settled controversy erupted over whether he had an opportunity to draw his pistol. Ironically, John Meigs's killers were nominally under Rosser's command, of which Monty had to be aware. His letters show that, while he resisted Rosser, he fell under his spell. Monty's daughter, Cornelia L. Meigs, wrote a novel about the surveyors, *Railroad West*. A key figure is an ex-Confederate, "General Arnold," drawing a clear parallel to Benedict Arnold. Yet, reflecting her father's ambivalence, she wrote of the thinly disguised Rosser: "Besides the charm and courtesy of a Virginia birthright he had something rarer and deeper, a warmth of magnetism that drew men to him and held their admiring loyalty. [My father heard], many times, the observation, 'Oh, I do not know if [he] is really a great engineer, but how I do like to work for him!'"[11]

In 1870 Spaulding also hired Edward C. ("Ned") Jordan. Ned's roots went back to Robert Jordan, a penniless minister who left England in 1639. His pro-royalist position during the English Civil War forced him north to the "uninhabited" Portland, Maine, area, and later his stand against witchcraft in Maine earned him many enemies. During King Philip's War he and his six sons barely escaped the Indians, fleeing to Newcastle Island, New Hampshire, where he died and is buried in a long-lost grave. For three decades, the Jordan family took part in the sporadic warfare with the French and their Indian allies, pushing back into Maine, only to be driven out again. One of Jordan's sons, Dominicus, nicknamed "Indian Killer," was renowned for his accuracy with a six-foot musket. On August 10, 1703, with peace presumably reigning, Dominicus let three Indians into his Maine trading post. When he turned his back, an Indian split his skull open with a hatchet. As Dominicus lay dying, 23 other Jordans were killed or captured, and his wife and 6 children were taken as captives to Canada, later returning to Maine.[12]

Ned's father was a successful businessman and railroad investor, securing a job for Ned with the Portland & Ogdensburg Railroad until 1866. Given his interests, Ned went to Union College, one of the few schools with civil and railroad-engineering courses. The town also housed the Schenectady Locomotive Works, handcrafting three to four locomotives a month, which gave the engineering department a more practical bent. Ned entered the class of 1868 as a junior; George Westinghouse, the inventor of the air brake, was in the same class but had flunked out earlier. Besides French, German, and mathematics, the curriculum included drafting, engineering statistics, leveling (for construction), mechanics, mensuration (measuring), roads and railroads, stability of structures, stereotomy (cutting through solids, such as rocks), and surveying.[13]

Following Union College, Jordan went to work for the Central Pacific and was at Promontory Point when the final spike ceremonies took place. Probably through his father's intervention—no one was hired at his level without good connections—he began work in May 1870 and kept a diary (which survives) through mid-1871. Of average height, thin, balding, and well liked, the determined and energetic Jordan was likely the best-trained *railroad* engineer of all the surveyors. His first assignment was to manage a small surveying crew, and he kept Spaulding's first instructions:

> To be of value your work must be done as rapidly as possible consistent with sufficient accuracy for our purposes. The object of the Survey is to obtain the information necessary for us to locate the line of the Rail Road [southeast of Moorhead]. . . . All time and labor expended in detailed surveys,

beyond what is necessary to obtain the information mentioned above, would be a waste of money and should be avoided.[14]

After Milnor Roberts's report of his reconnaissance was completed, it was clear that Cooke would undertake the Northern Pacific's financing. The agreement was dated January 1, 1870, and signed shortly thereafter. Under it Jay Cooke & Co. received broad power, controlling capital expenditures and establishing an independent land company, a likely source of quick speculative profits. NP historians state that Cooke got the "better" of the deal and/or that its terms were "harsh." Yet, had the railroad been successful (that is, if the bondholders had been paid), Smith's group would have retained some 40 percent—quite fair, considering that in 1869 the NP had no cash or hard assets. Cooke, who had ample investment options, understood the vast difference between established concerns and "start-ups," the riskiest of all ventures. There was also bad blood from eight years earlier, Cooke had more to lose than Smith (and did), and Cooke was fully aware that lenders of last resort do not survive by being eleemosynary institutions.[15]

On January 24, 1870, Cooke wired Smith that he had raised $5.5 million, more cash than Smith and his "Vermont clique" ever thought possible. While many of the nation's wealthiest people had invested, it was ominous that bankers and railroad men approached by Cooke had uniformly declined. Although Smith had told Cooke that he wanted to establish a million-dollar pool with some friends, Cooke moved so fast that Smith's group was excluded. Later Cooke let Smith buy in, but at a premium. Cooke's insult and short-sightedness seem inexplicable, unless they were related to an inflated $975,000 bill for previous NP expenses that Smith presented. If the seeds of mistrust had not already been sown in the late 1850s, they were by the time the contract was two months old.[16]

The February 15, 1870, ground-breaking was merely for Cooke and public relations purposes—the cold precluded real construction. Nevertheless, 300 to 400 attended: reporters, dignitaries, Northern Pacific personnel, and residents on sleighs from Superior and Duluth. Those on the St. Paul train trudged through two miles of snow. People crowded around a bonfire and downed spirits as the ceremonies began. After a prayer, J. B. Culver of Duluth shoveled some dirt into a wheelbarrow. Next came the main oration, followed by a dozen others. Northern Pacific employee Hiram Hayes, a tough war veteran who laughingly recalled that he had wheeled the first load of dirt to a dump, noted: "Gen. Rosser, a Confederate cavalry officer of much renown, was [there]." George W. Cooley, an 1869 surveyor, also noted Rosser's presence and that evening turned his notes over to him.[17]

The *St. Paul Weekly Press* stated: "The direct line, as surveyed, is in reality a pretty crooked one, for, through the first 150 miles . . . it winds among the sloughs, and lakes, and bogs, and wooded and sandy ridges of a curiously broken and barren country." The reason behind the decision to cross Minnesota via Brainerd (named after Smith's wife's family) to Moorhead, almost exactly 250 track miles—versus a northern and straighter route saving over 25 miles—is not known. Indeed, Cooke biographer Ellis P. Oberholtzer strongly suggests that the purpose of this route was to put more cash into the hands of Gregory Smith and his group: "It was a cause for remark that the road had not been allowed to take a more direct course."[18]

However, getting meaningful construction underway proved to be more than Smith's team could manage and two 1870 actions ignited firestorms of protests. Spaulding's decision to move his office from St. Paul to Minneapolis infuriated investors and politicians in the then-larger city. Oberholtzer states that Spaulding seldom left Minneapolis, where he stayed in an "elegant mansion . . . free of cost." Of more damage was the selection of tiny Duluth over the established port of Superior, probably because it offered greater opportunity for speculative profits. Had the decision been made tactfully, the end result—an implacable Wisconsin congressional delegation—might have been avoided.[19]

Amazingly, Smith wasted over six months after Cooke's intentions were known and did not issue bids for grading, bridging, masonry, ballasting, rails and ties, and other items until early May. With a June 1 deadline, bidders rushed to submit proposals. By mid-June contracts were let, but the process was too rapid to be honest and hurt Cooke's fund-raising and lobbying. Highlighting everybody's paranoia, the major contract went to two unqualified French immigrants, Charles and Ferdinand Canda. More humorously, many thought it was a *Canadian* company, sparking further protests. Oberholtzer wrote that the Candas' company was "said [to be] composed of officers and employees of the railroad," and the process left Cooke looking naive and out of touch.

Cooke, in the back of his mind, expected Congress to give the Northern Pacific both land grants *and,* if not cash upon track certification, at least bond guarantees. It was no more than what had been done for the Central and Union Pacific roads, and he anticipated "that Congress would give the NP a direct money subsidy [west of] the Red River or would guarantee its bonds as it had the central line." But the mood of Congress had changed; a northern route served no vital national interest, most of the land was devoid of settlement, many neutral observers felt that a transcontinental railroad would not be needed for decades, and there was strong opposition from Wisconsin, Illinois, Indiana, Ohio, Pennsylvania, and New York. Grant was also against cash payments or bond guaranties but told Cooke that he would be neutral.[20]

Ultimately, Cooke asked Congress only to amend the Northern Pacific's charter to let him sell bonds, secured by property mortgages and the 47-million-acre land grant. Even this was difficult; but when it came to distributing cash, stock, jobs, consultancies, waivers of debt, and other gratuities, Cooke never hesitated. His financial wand touched senators, congressmen, governors, and the vice president—men who voted or controlled votes and "friends" who simply wanted to be paid off. Was Cooke wrong? Had he not jumped into the cesspool, the NP would have died in 1870. Larson noted that Cooke "saw in the hungry politician a force which would work against him if he did not pay, and being a man of action he chose to pay the price." When the dust cleared (on May 26) the NP had survived but had no additional financial support.[21]

Spaulding sent four 16-man surveying teams into the field in late January. Three went to Superior-Duluth, and a fourth to St. Cloud. We do not know *why* they went there: the Northern Pacific company had let it be known that it had been working at least a year, but now it was apparently starting over. For whatever reason, the NP's 1867–69 surveying, if performed, was largely useless. Later in 1870 other teams went into central and western Minnesota. If surveying in winter was difficult, the same work once the snow melted was even harder. Years later the surveyor Richard Relf described some of his crew's difficulties:

> [We were at] the watershed of between the St. Croix . . . and the Mississippi. . . . Plenty of open swamps or floating bogs were encountered. . . . This wet season had filled the swamps compelling us often to wade out sometimes almost waist-deep before getting onto the floating mass—which was anything but reliable, and several comical rescues were witnessed. Our intrepid head chainman had to take the lead and keep to the line while the rest of us could steer around whatever open water was in the swamp so he was the one most often in need of brush and poles to help him out.[22]

Most teams encountered similar difficulties. Jordan's first crew included an assistant, two chainmen, a picketman, an axman, a man with an undefined position, a cook, and a teamster (the last two driving wagons). In early 1871 Jordan wrote a friend about some of his experiences in Minnesota's Ottertail–Detroit Lakes area. In Ottertail ("two stores, three dwelling houses, and a sawmill"), Jordan noted that his team spent a few days with 300 Chippewas, joined in "a feast composed of fat dogs, baked beans, and fish," and then returned to work:

> [N]othing was left but to push through a dense growth of timber some 40 miles wide—full of lakes, swamps, marshes, and mosquitoes. I packed three horses with 20 days rations, one blanket per man and a cooking kit . . . and started in to cut our way through at the rate of one mile per day.
>
> All this was very interesting, time passing quickly in our contest with mosquitos and Tamarac swamps. Most of the so called Tamarac swamps are floating forests of trees, and beneath the network of roots and moss there is

generally a mud lake from ten to 20 feet deep; one has to only step on the interlacing roots to walk along quite safely. My Indian pony was adept at this; he carried a pack of 200 lbs. and jumped from root to root occasionally floundering but always recovering.

But with the horses it was different. A misstep would send them through the sod discouraged [*sic*] only to be got out by slipping poles beneath and lifting them by [our] strength. This, together with an occasional disappearance of everything but the head of some unlucky chap, to be extricated in the same beastly manner, gave a variety that was not to be harkened after, but which serves its purpose in giving spice to our life. For 15 days this life continued, the men growing cross and surly from the prolonged hardship of wet clothes, disturbed sleep and the incessant warfare with mosquitos.[23]

Jordan's companions included Edwin Johnson (with Roberts the year before), Meigs, and the artist Seth Eastman's son. The others were two bankers' sons, a Yale graduate, and Smith and Morse (first names unknown), protégés of NP board member and Smith confidant Richard Rice. "These young men," Jordan wrote, "laughed and sneered at by some of the rough, common members of the party, were more willing and suffered the many little disagreeable duties with less complaint than the very men that [we] hired for *tough* [work]" (Jordan's emphasis). Smith was unable to swim, and Jordan recounted with delight the various mishaps of Smith and Morse:

Smith land[ed] safely and after several [lengths of the 66-foot] chains got on with varying [degrees of] floundering success when suddenly Morse disappears again and on rising swears that some one pulled his shoe off while he was down. "26 feet and no bottom," called the sounder, [and Morse said,] "I guess I will let the shoe remain." Smith was trolled across this and other places.

Plodding through the bogs and swamps, Jordan said, "was like walking on a feather bed; at each step I took it billowed up before me, threatening to engulf me constantly, but the secret of success was in rapid motion . . . [and Meigs was like] a drowned, slimy rate rat." But the survey failed as Spaulding had them "back up and swing to the north, this crossing is impracticable!" When Spaulding asked him at a meeting if he "was used to getting out of difficulties," Jordan said he replied that "he should have seen me in a slough, with the horse and wagon hitched on a hundred feet of rope with fifteen men in knee-deep mud, pulling and shouting like fire-jakeys or else he should have seen me ferrying swollen rivers swimming the horses and rafting the outfit." (What should not be missed here is that Spaulding debriefed his surveyors and therefore must have known about the wetland problems well before 1870.) Later Spaulding sent Jordan's team on a reconnaissance to look for possible alternative routes:

Having reached the Red River of the North, Meigs and myself took . . . an old Chippewa scout, and started across the country with a canoe and hunting [gear]. We followed the chain of the Buffalo Path Lakes, carrying the canoe on our head across the connecting portages; and through the lakes and rivers we traveled for a hundred miles or more . . . several times we snagged and had narrow escapes from dangerous swims.

Jordan's letter does not indicate that anything came of this last trip in the fall, although he proudly noted he was acting "Resident Engineer." He mentioned the "bitter experiences . . . [from] the wading of brooks, marshes and river[s] during the latter part of the cold fall months." Jordan also noted the winter's "astonishing cold," which made it a "terror," a particularly interesting comment considering that he was raised in Maine.

Construction difficulties in wetlands were well known. In 1870 Benjamin H. Latrobe wrote that "construction of a permanent road bed over *boggy* ground is often an interesting problem for the engineer" (Latrobe's emphasis). In Britain earth for embankments "sunk out of sight almost as fast as it was thrown in"; and in the United States "railways crossing our western prairies [in] deep swampy spots have been successfully crossed by various expedients." While the Northern Pacific had a major problem, Spaulding knew about the issue and should have known about the successful precedents. But the NP was soon stalled. The Union Pacific had purchased four of the newly invented Otis steam shovels (called "scoops") at $12,000 each, but they were useless in the swamps. It is even more baffling that the NP purchased only a single pile driver.[24]

Wetland construction specified that pilings must be sunk; but even when this was done, the requirement was often evaded and the ground was packed with anything to meet the specifications calling for a 12-foot-wide roadbed. Smalley noted that workers found it almost impossible to find solid ground to sink piles: "The filling of one day would disappear during the night." Every day "pathfinders" moved forward with shovels, axes, two-man saws, and pickaxes, clearing brush, felling trees, and filling. Rock and gravel came in by rail. Contractors were paid by the completed mile, so they took shortcuts in both piling and fill, using inadequate piling and filling with wood and brush. Only the best roadbeds did not crack, slide, or compact after heavy use; and improperly built sections could buckle the first time an engine passed over them. While the wetlands *were* exceptionally difficult, the problems were a greater reflection of the Northern Pacific's mismanagement.[25]

Even worse, the Northern Pacific quickly became a "good news" company. Problems were swept under the rug by a bureaucracy that stretched from the wetlands to St. Albans and back. Management was characterized by incompetence, buck-passing, and dishonesty; it chose to believe everything and inspect nothing. Cooke was soon flooded with reports of problems "as well as some actual dishonesty in the awards of contracts and the execution of them on the line." General Alvred B. Nettleton, a trusted Cooke associate who had served under Custer, "inspected a portion of the line and reported that much of it would have to be done over within a short time." Of course, Cooke should have visited Minnesota. The shoddy work received wide press coverage, hurting bond sales. An oft-told story was that when one section was finished, a locomotive came up with supplies. As the train moved forward, the roadbed began shuddering. The engineer attempted to move forward, the track dipped, the engine rolled backward, and, as the crew escaped, the locomotive and supply cars sank into the muck.[26]

In 1870 George A. Brackett, from Maine, became the Northern Pacific's general agent, which included outfitting all surveying parties.[27] An entrepreneur, he and some friends decided to float ice in barges down the Mississippi to Memphis in 1859, losing $15,000 in a particularly warm spring. Undaunted, Brackett began selling supplies to the army, which soon became a growth industry. He took part in the 1862 Sioux war—cheerfully pointing out later that he ran and hid more than he fought—and then became a flour mill owner, conservationist, real-estate dabbler, fire chief, Minneapolis mayor, and Yukon road builder. The *Minneapolis Tribune* called him a "steam engine in breeches." Brackett personified "honest graft." He and Rosser quickly became friends and partners, happily joining in endeavors that would raise unending conflict-of-interest issues today. Yet, in an era when "shaving" was normal, Civil War and NP veterans held him in high regard; and without his zeal in setting up the 1906 surveyors' reunion, there would be huge gaps in the story of the Yellowstone surveys.[28]

On September 5, 1870, the *New York Times* reported (in a story dated August 29 from Toronto) that the Canadian government, with full British support, had decided to give its highest priority to building a railroad to the Pacific. Cooke's European leverage was further weakened by protectionist congressional language in his 1870 land grant: "in the construction of the Northern Pacific Railroad, American iron or steel only shall be used, the same to be manufactured from American ores." Cooke had anticipated selling NP bonds in Europe and made a major effort in France and Germany, but the relationship between the two countries began disintegrating. France declared war on July 19. Cooke could only shake his head: it would be impossible to sell bonds in Europe for the immediate future.[29]

The actual construction of the Northern Pacific did not begin until the Lake Superior & Mississippi finished building between Duluth and Carlton in mid-August. The completion of the line technically meant that Minnesota grain could be shipped east from Duluth. But the *Railroad Gazette* noted that a finished harbor, grain elevator, and storage and warehousing facilities were still needed, and until then "the trade of the town may be light at first and then develop slowly." Duluth would soon have the necessary infrastructure, but most of the funds came from Cooke's bond sales.[30]

Why some Lake Superior & Mississippi and Northern Pacific work could not have been done in parallel is not known, but by the end of August all 1,600 LS&M workers had been shifted to the NP. The *St. Paul Weekly Press* wrote: "[I]t requires no small executive ability to manage such a force as this in a new country, far away from all settlements and still farther away from every base of supply." On October 22 the *Duluth Minnesotian* reported that less than two miles of track had been completed, but "iron [had been] laid" on 17 of 30 graded miles. A month later there were 25 miles of track, and grading and iron laying were rapidly progressing, with the work force jumping to 3,000. With construction far behind schedule, Smith decided to work through the winter despite the weather, the only way to reach the Red River by the date that he had contractually established, July 1, 1871.[31]

Worker dissatisfaction was soon high, and food quality was scandalous. Workers made $14 a week, $5 of which was subtracted for "board," a practice leading to contractor shortchanging. The LS&M futilely attempted to bar liquor from being sent (a sure sign of heavy drinking), while the workmen blamed the "Philadelphia Executive Committee" (that is, Cooke). Although published construction figures vary, Renz's *History of the Northern Pacific Railroad* indicates that by February completed track was 28 miles east of Brainerd, while grading was 20 to 30 miles west of it. A Mississippi bridge was also under construction and was completed on March 15. (Typifying the shoddy workmanship, the bridge collapsed in 1875.) By mid-winter the NP was operating or had ordered 9 locomotives, 26 boxcars, and 130 flat cars. Operational facilities, including engine houses, coal sheds, and water tanks, were also coming on line.[32]

During the summer of 1870, Northern Pacific surveys were at work at Dakota, Montana, Idaho, and Washington. In Idaho 51-year-old engineer Walter W. DeLacy ventured down part of the Salmon ("the river of no return") but found the route "impracticable." DeLacy's report made it clear that a northwestern route, from central Montana to the "neck" of Idaho toward Spokane and from there southwest toward Walla Walla, would have to be taken. Cooke and his supporters in the East, increasingly dissatisfied with the NP's progress, focused their discontent on chief engineer Edwin Johnson, 68, who was deaf and unable to travel or to process the data pouring in. Smith, although angry, made no effort to block Cooke. Only Milnor Roberts had the prestige, knowledge, and Cooke's support; without bothering to ask Roberts, the board decided to hire him (on October 1). Meeting Smith in New

York for what he thought was consulting work, Roberts wrote, "I was surprised to learn that I had already been appointed Chief Engineer." It was an offer that no engineer could refuse: building a transcontinental railroad. Johnson's hurt was cushioned by retaining his desk, full salary, and a consulting title. Roberts, beginning on November 1, faced mountainous paperwork and only 16 miles of operational track.[33]

The *Duluth Minnesotian,* which had peppered the summer and fall with articles detailing Northern Pacific problems, headlined: "Light Dawning—The Beginning of the End of a Swindle, We Hope!" The editorial stated: "It was about time that [Cooke] came to the rescue of their Bondholders . . . from a most corrupt, villainous, scampish combination of forty thieves . . . [with] affiliations . . . amongst the highest officials of the company itself." Roberts was soon inspecting Minnesota operations. Smith, angry at Spaulding, left him in charge of construction; but he brought a Vermont friend, Daniel C. Linsley, an able engineer, to manage Minnesota-Dakota engineering while "reporting" to Roberts. Smith sent his ally Richard Rice to the West Coast. Rice promptly awarded a contract to the Canda Brothers and purchased unneeded rail and rolling stock on an emergency, whatever-it-cost basis, leaving in his wake more anger and a nasty exchange with Cooke, forcing Roberts to clean up the mess.[34]

As 1870 ended, Cooke also completed a series of business maneuvers that gave him control of the strategically placed St. Paul & Pacific Railroad (over 175 miles). For what little it was worth, Smith admitted to him "grave mistakes made in the location of the road . . . but there has been no deliberate fraud intended." Smith was not contrite, however: "Even if it were true, it would seem as if the wisest way for the friends of the project would be to say as little as possible. . . . I hope you will put your hands on these Duluth people and stop their clamor, or they will ruin us." If the letter smacked of extortion, the worst was still in store: Smith was about to get himself into deeper financial trouble in Vermont than anyone could have imagined.[35]

CHAPTER 6

"No System Observed"

Concern on the part of Jay Cooke, his associates, and their allies about the efficacy and honesty of Gregory Smith and his management team, often referred to as the "Vermont clique," had been growing throughout 1870. In 1871, however, concern changed to anger and hostility. The two camps were bound by little more than the thin veneer of nineteenth-century civility and occasionally issues that required them to assume a public image of solidarity.

The previous year, 1870, had ended with Edwin Johnson's forced resignation, highlighting the split. Board members, investors, and employees had conflicting loyalties and were at first neutral, although some, such as Frederick Billings and Sam Wilkeson, wound up in Cooke's camp.

Smith favored Daniel C. Linsley as Johnson's replacement, but he voiced no objections to Cooke's choice of Milnor Roberts. Nonetheless, Smith wanted to be sure there was no confusion as to how he felt: in June he summoned Roberts to St. Albans. After an hour, Smith walked out, stating that he had to go to another city. He also gave Roberts one assignment after another outside of Minnesota, keeping him away from the focus of the company's efforts. Thus Linsley, a Vermonter whose family was close to Smith, took over the Minnesota engineering and for all intents and purposes worked for Smith. While Linsley formally reported to Roberts, and the two had a courteous professional relationship, Roberts had been effectively shunted aside.[1]

The NP's New York headquarters became an unresolved issue. The location was chosen at Smith's behest; but, as Oberholtzer noted, "if Smith were almost never in Minnesota, so was he also seldom in New York." Smith's first priority was his troubled Vermont Central, and NP employees frequently had to travel to St. Albans to see him. The New York offices included a private dining room serving lunches but were regularly used only by Wilkeson, Johnson, treasurer Ashbel Barney, and clerks. These costs were minuscule, however, compared to Minnesota, where stories of construction irregularities were not easy to sweep aside, leaving Smith on the defensive and hurting bond sales.[2]

Cooke's concerns are seen in a letter from Moorhead: "One . . . large subscriber [is] very emphatic in his . . . condemnation of the manner in which the road has been built . . . If there is to be a ring to manage our contracts please count us out of any further participation." Smith's team, Cooke thought, was unable to see the big picture, slow to make major decisions, unnecessarily quick to spend cash, and inattentive to operational details. Although he did not state it in absolute terms, sometime in 1871 Cooke's opinion of Smith's team undoubtedly evolved from being perplexed to the ultimate negative conclusion: he had dishonest partners.[3]

Throughout 1871 Cooke was flooded with letters from friends, associates, investors, and NP personnel, complaining about management. The president of the Pennsylvania Railroad, a good friend of Cooke and Milnor Roberts, wrote Cooke in March 1871: "I do not think that any amount of bonds you sell can complete the line. . . . At present, according to Roberts, there is no system observed in the management of the work whatever." Five months later Cooke was told: "One perplexing thing about the road east of Brainerd is this: portions of the track over or near lakes continue to sink."

Other than Washington lobbying, there was little cooperation between the two camps. Efforts to patch up the differences were doomed; as the Vermont Central floundered, Smith's focus was on its survival and quick Northern Pacific profits. Cooke's goal was different: to build a second transcontinental railroad, populated along the route with communities reflecting his Christian values. Oberholtzer's comments about Smith are scathing: "That the Smith party was not competent to manage such an enterprise is very clear. It had no time to devote to the business of the road . . . [Smith] and his associates were connected with the enterprise for gain and they [ruined it] . . . by their intermittent and tactless administration of affairs." By year's end little more than proper manners between gentlemen remained. Smith's letters to Cooke were usually moderate, frequently logical; his comments attempted to reflect the imperfect world of railroad operations but never, of course, the root causes of so many of the NP's problems.

In addition to construction, one of the Northern Pacific's real-estate arms, the Lake Superior and Puget Sound Land Company (LSPS), became another embarrassment. The company would purchase land where the NP would build, plan communities, and sell the land to new businesses, residents, and speculators. The LSPS was responsible for buying rights-of-way and land *before* railroad construction and then engaged in the speculative activity of selling private but not federal land. The federal land, awarded after certification, was to be sold by the Northern Pacific Land Company. It was expected that both companies' land sales would have a multiplier effect by attracting easterners and European immigrants, creating railroad traffic, and in turn strengthening bond sales.

The Lake Superior and Puget Sound Company not only knew just where the railroad would go but, with Smith's consent, at times actually selected the route, forcing engineering to follow Smith's wishes and giving him enormous speculative opportunities. Of Cooke's initial $5.5 million 1870 investment, LSPS received $2.4 million.[4]

To manage the company, Smith chose his old friend Thomas Canfield. Smith, who was wearing himself out keeping his Vermont Central afloat, was certainly aware of Canfield's flaws; but with the Northern Pacific under construction, he undoubtedly felt that it was impossible for the land company not to make rapid and large profits.

Under Canfield, the strategy to assist the NP while making large insider profits quickly collapsed. Canfield's greed resulted in improperly located, unattractively designed communities; their lots were too small, not only hemmed in by narrow alleys and streets but also outrageously expensive. What had seemed like a sure thing soon stalled. Canfield was supposed to attract new businesses and homeowners; instead, prospective buyers balked, often writing bitter letters that received wide circulation. Touring Minnesota and Dakota in 1873, Charles Loring Brace noted Canfield's operations: "For a time there was . . . what seemed like a kind of Crédit Mobilier affair of a small kind before it was quashed." Historian John L. Harnsberger wrote: "[T]he methods [Canfield] used handicapped the actual construction of the railroad and interfered with the sales of Northern Pacific securities which [Cooke was] trying to popularize."[5]

Sales of federal lands had a dollar potential second only to bond sales, but various tasks were required before the land could be sold. The most important step was "certification": the transfer of federal land upon meeting the congressionally mandated construction standards. Only *after* certification, in segments of no fewer than 25 miles, did the land belong to the NP. Even then sales would be challenging, considering that adjacent, virtually free federal land was available, an issue apparently not factored into NP calculations.[6]

The Northern Pacific Land Company, responsible for the sale of federally certified land and for attracting immigrants, was managed by Frederick Billings. He had become wealthy in California; but in 1864, in ill health, he retired and returned to his Vermont home. Through Smith, he developed an interest in the NP, was an early investor, and became a board member in 1870. Billings approached land sales logically and honestly, putting the railroad's interest ahead of personal investment.

For sales, he hired John S. Loomis in March 1871. Cooke actively followed Billings's operations, and the two were soon working closely, more often than not in agreement on policy issues and increasingly unhappy with Smith's leadership.[7]

Like so many other Northern Pacific assumptions, colonization proved more expensive, time-consuming, and competitive than anticipated. The goal was to attract Civil War veterans and Europeans of Anglo-Saxon and Nordic stock. The logic was that Minnesota-Dakota winters were similar to those of northern Europe, whose "hardy" peoples felicitously reflected the day's pseudo-scientific racial prejudices. Priority was given to farmers who were being replaced by labor-saving machinery, who, it was hoped, wished to purchase their own farmland. What the short-sighted Canfield never seemed to realize—but Billings and Cooke did—was that the money made from land sales was not as important as the economic impact of a farming family that sold and received goods and produce shipped by rail. The colonization costs were shared with Northern Pacific bond programs, and in 1871 a public relations effort was launched in Denmark, Germany, Great Britain, Norway, and Sweden.[8]

Billings's land company had a solid story to tell. Iowa's best land was already taken, but the Red River Valley (formerly a huge glacial lake) offered tens of thousands of square miles of rich, black bottomland, often two feet deep. The soil was ideal for grain, potatoes, sugar beets, and dairy farming, and a program to publicize the area became operational in early 1871. The publicity was so overdone, however, that "one enthusiastic writer went so far as to state that the only illness which even remotely touched residents were the pangs of overeating." The ink was barely dry on the first circular when a Scotsman, Lord Gordon Gordon, arrived in St. Paul, deposited $20,000 in a local bank, and said he wanted to purchase 100,000 acres. Besides wining and dining him, under Loomis's direction the NP outfitted a dozen men (a scout, a French cook, two white-gloved servants, and so forth) and six wagons and gave him a two-month tour of NP land. In all, Loomis spent well over $15,000 (perhaps as much as $45,000) before the delightful but totally fraudulent Gordon Gordon quietly vanished one frosty evening, a step ahead of numerous creditors.[9]

Billings's approach to colonization was logical; but even if everything had gone well, the turnaround time for European immigrants had to be measured in years. Nevertheless, in 1871 brick reception houses were built in Duluth, Brainerd, and Glyndon (just east of Moorhead). Each could sleep more than a hundred in bedrooms (not communal living), and all had furnished living rooms and kitchens. Staff was hired but, of course, had little to do. In part, the lack of initial success was due to the desire of European countries after the Franco-Prussian War not to let their able-bodied young men immigrate. A related NP initiative established hospitals and clinics for immigrants and construction workers. The health care system was controversial, however, as workers were charged two and a half cents a day. By mid-1871, with the NP footing the bill, a number of operational clinics existed, including a mobile one operating from a boxcar.[10]

There are no known figures showing immigration effort expenditures. Totaling the work by both Cooke and Billings's land company, 1871 expenditures were perhaps $500,000, all taken from bond sales revenue. Results were minimal. Settlers from eastern states using the facilities were in the low hundreds per month and European immigrants far fewer. From January 1870 through September 1873, total expenditures were likely over $1 million.

While the Northern Pacific had not certified its land, its public relations campaign was contributing to rapid settlement from the East, which compounded these problems. One man wrote: "Without an exception this is the best stock raising country in the West." Another stated that "the roads leading [to the Red River] are literally covered with . . . two hundred wagons per day." The land was not surveyed, so the settlers took what they wanted. When the land company finally claimed its federal land, it had to remove hundreds of them. In July 1871, however, settlement came to a screeching halt; huge swarms of grasshoppers appeared, devouring everything in their path and wrecking the year's harvesting prospects for new settlers.[11]

Without federal funds or guarantees, land sales from the Northern Pacific's millions of federal acres in Minnesota were desperately needed. In one of 1871's nastiest surprises, not a single mile of track was certified. Billings and Smith had known each other for decades but had never worked together. Billings soon became angered by Smith's slow decision-making and offended by having to veto Smith's candidates. Like Cooke, Billings wanted certification after each 25 miles. Smith, however, chose to wait until all Minnesota was finished, arguing that there was little sales value in heavily forested, swampy land that, if settled, would only lead to complaints. Billings felt that the land had value because of its timber sales and would generate much-needed rail traffic, but Smith never filed a foot of track for certification. Most likely, Smith knew that the track was too shoddily built to be certified. Indeed, when the NP's directors went over the track east of Brainerd, "the cars were separated by means of long links to permit of safety to them, and the passengers were asked to walk around [a] sink hole."[12]

How much land might have been sold had certification been requested is speculative. Adding to the problem, Loomis fell behind in the surveying, platting, and requisite filings. In December he told the *Railroad Gazette* that he had a dozen teams of "examiners in the field" and had completed work on 1,529,000 acres, half the Minnesota land. However, the teams did not begin until August, too late for 1871; even when the fieldwork was completed, months were needed to get the data processed, filed, and ready for final recording.[13]

Meanwhile, Jay Cooke asked his brother Henry to "watch over" commission appointments. It was a delicate game, but Henry had Grant's consent to *show* him

names chosen from a Smith-approved list. In May, answering Jay about certification, Henry wrote: "I have written [Smith] several times about this subject but for
some inexplicable reason my suggestions have received no attention . . . I had
become disgusted and let things drop . . . [as he] seems to be extremely indifferent."
In short, Grant had been willing to ignore his ethical obligations and do the
Cookes a major favor, but they were unable to follow through. In the years to
come, Grant was to be far less compliant when critical favors were needed.[14]

On paper there was considerable progress in 1871. On the West Coast, 25 miles of
track were built between the Columbia River and Puget Sound. The Northern
Pacific/Cooke influence was enormous in Minnesota. Besides 229 miles of NP
track, the NP and Cooke controlled the St. Paul & Pacific (292 miles) and Lake
Superior & Mississippi (209), a total of 730 miles. Only one critical gap remained;
some 60 miles from Brainerd south to Sauk Rapids. Until this was completed,
passengers and freight from the Red River Valley had to travel 200 extra miles, via
Carlton, to reach the Twin Cities. Construction costs also *appeared* reasonable if
slightly on the high side: for the 229 miles in Minnesota, the cost was put at
$5,397,843 or $23,571 per mile. Millions of dollars were missing, however, and were
never accounted for. The real figure was probably far closer to $50,000 per mile.[15]

The Northern Pacific also faced stiff competition. The St. Paul & Sioux City
Railroad planned to connect Minneapolis/St. Paul with Sioux City, Iowa. Nevertheless, picking up traffic from the west and sending it to Duluth would still benefit
the NP, as it was less expensive than sending Iowa and Minnesota grain to the
Northeast and Europe via Chicago. As 1871 began, some 150 miles of the 276-mile
St. Paul & Sioux City road needed completion; it was adequately financed and would
be finished on schedule in 1872.

In 1870 and into 1871 the Northern Pacific's construction workers were living in
squalid tent cities. In January 1871 over 200 of them rioted, possibly because of late
pay, causing extensive damage near Brainerd. By July living conditions had become
intolerable for some 3,500 workers. The long list of problems also included the
summer's heat, mosquitoes, armed theft by small gangs, and occasional drunken
Indians. One of them, a Chippewa known only as "Horace," passed out on the tracks
and was decapitated when the midnight train came down the line. Lawlessness
became so bad that NP officials brought in U.S. marshal Alfred B. Brackett. The tough
but evenhanded marshal, who had led "Brackett's Battalion" in a sabers-drawn cavalry
charge at Killdeer Mountain, became the NP's all-purpose enforcer. In July, with a
dozen heavily armed men, he entered the NP's forward tent city. Troublemakers were
"invited" to leave; a dozen were placed in chains and sent to St. Paul. Brackett "served
notice upon all parties along the entire line of the road, to discontinue the sale of
liquors . . . within the five mile limit." The unruly elements were only temporarily

cowed, and in October the NP sent Brackett back. The *Minneapolis Tribune* candidly commented: "All of the gamblers, pimps, bullies, and harlots that have been following up the [NP] road have been driven out of Moorhead, and are now located in Fargo, the new town on the Dakota side of the Red River."[16]

As 1871 began, some 1,600 men were working near Brainerd. The *Railroad Gazette* said that the most difficult part of the road was built, but the ground was frozen to two and a half feet; ominously, it noted that "grading is very difficult—good grading quite impossible." On March 13, with 94 miles completed, the Mississippi bridge was finished, and "the first passenger train containing Northern Pacific officers passed over the structure." The road's infrastructure was more successful, as water tanks, railroad yards, and related facilities were completed. In March, with the ground still frozen, the NP announced that the Red River would be reached by late summer or early fall.[17]

Legal barriers were quick to fall. A letter from Otter Tail noted: "The chief from Red Lake arrived here and is very indignant at the railroad's running through the reservation without first negotiating with him." When Indians' land "blocked" the road, Cooke secured legislation extinguishing their title.[18]

By April employment reached 3,000, with a mile of track laid daily. As the ground warmed, however, the stupidity of winter construction became apparent. Track driven into icy surfaces began buckling, and soon many sections were sinking. The *Duluth Minnesotian* (April 15) stated: "The frost leaving the ground . . . the track in many places sink[s] further into it; and there would be guaranty neither for the [passengers'] lives . . . nor the [freight's] safety. . . . All had better possess their souls with patience until the line is ballasted and surfaced . . . it will take two or three weeks yet to put the line in working order."[19]

The *Minnesotian*'s prediction of a few weeks was wildly optimistic; the roadbed was in worse shape than anyone realized, and the NP's management was caught totally unprepared. Soon locomotives, rolling stock, and equipment became stranded. Each day saw more problems, with holes under and adjacent to track, track buckling, and entire sections slipping under water. Repair crews had to collect their equipment and ride by mule or walk to each site. Frequently log piling had to be sunk first for bracing before refilling could begin. By June, with 3,500 men working, estimates for completing the *repairs* were pushed back to August. Rosser telegraphed Linsley on June 23: "It will be at least 30 days before a loaded train can run up safely over the road between [Brainerd] and the Junction." West of Brainerd 800 men abruptly halted work: the route was discovered to be impractical, and a new route had to be located and surveyed.[20]

Smith's management highlighted the dangers posed by absentee managers' retaining tight control even when they are honest: decisions are slow, are not necessarily correct, and waste valuable time for those in the field. Further hurting the Northern Pacific, as the Rutland's pressure on the Vermont Central grew, Smith probably used Northern Pacific economies of scale to benefit the Vermont Central by reducing NP "discounts" to get lower prices for the VC. He undoubtely received kickbacks or other benefits, directly or through third parties (with variations of the Crédit Mobilier concept), from equipment contracts, from companies that were grading, laying track, or building bridges, from construction of the numerous facilities directly involved in railroad operations (water towers, roundhouses, repair and maintenance sheds, and so forth), and from buildings such as NP hotels and reception facilities for immigrants. Railroad historian Kevin Graffagnino writes: "[Smith] came under attack for the same sort of tactics he had perfected in Vermont, as a growing number of observers charged him with extravagance and misuse of [NP] funds to enrich himself and his associates."[21]

Bad as Smith was, however, he never envisioned paying dividends with other people's money, looting the NP's treasury, stock manipulations, or similar activities that are commonplace today. His actions might be described as parasitic: leeching himself to a viable host body. It never seemed to occur to Smith, who genuinely believed in the Northern Pacific, that his actions or example could badly hurt the company. But graft permeated the NP down to the surveyors. In its most innocent form, Meigs's 1872 letters are filled with accounts of small-scale quick profits from land speculation. Rosser, always in financial trouble, went a step further, helping his brothers-in-law form a construction company that built small bridges as an NP subcontractor. It was no accident that Rosser was noted for designing exceptionally long straightaways, thus forcing the NP to build bridges over bends in streams that in most cases could have been paralleled.

Besides building to the Red River, the Northern Pacific also planned to complete the St. Paul & Pacific line from Sauk Rapids to Brainerd. However, in June, the *St. Paul Weekly Press* learned that this had been "given up for the present"; the NP's entire effort focused on rebuilding and completing track to the Red River. Not until August 7 was new track laying resumed. The NP still thought it could reach the Red River by mid-October, a disappointing but acceptable 45-day loss. Just a month later the *St. Paul Pioneer* said track would reach the Red River on November 20. In early October the *St. Paul Pioneer* was told that the crews were laying track at the rate of 2.5 miles a day but were still 48 miles from Moorhead. Meanwhile the NP's board announced contracts to build from Fargo to the Missouri by July 1, 1872, and to the Canadian border (Pembina) by the end of 1872. Then, reversing field again, it decided to complete the Sauk Rapids to Brainerd track.[22]

In keeping with the Northern Pacific's luck, the first snow fell in mid-October. On November 23, with track 11 miles from the Red River, 16 inches of snow fell. One paper stated: "King Winter [is] master of the situation . . . there now seems little

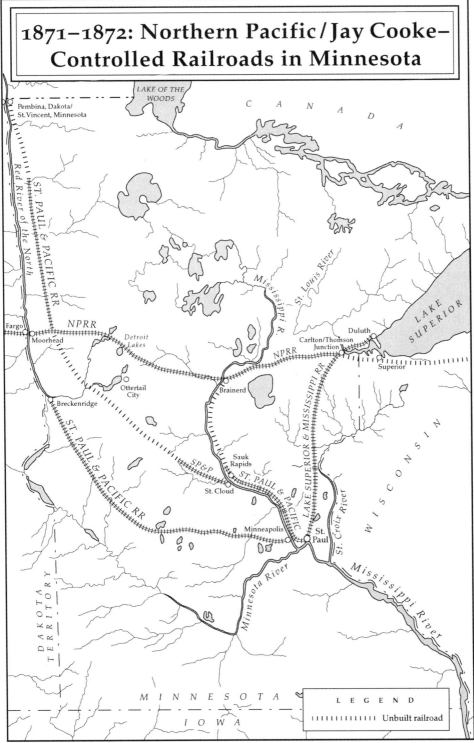

1871–1872: Northern Pacific/Jay Cooke-Controlled Railroads in Minnesota

LAKE OF THE WOODS

C A N A D A

Pembina, Dakota/
St. Vincent, Minnesota

Red River of the North

ST. PAUL & PACIFIC RR

Mississippi R.

St. Louis River

LAKE SUPERIOR

Fargo
NPRR
Moorhead

Detroit Lakes

Duluth
Carlton/Thomson Junction
NPRR
Superior

Ottertail City
Brainerd

Breckenridge

ST. PAUL & PACIFIC RR

SP&P
Sauk Rapids
ST. PAUL & PACIFIC

St. Cloud

LAKE SUPERIOR & MISSISSIPPI RR

St. Croix River

W I S C O N S I N

Minneapolis
St. Paul

D A K O T A   T E R R I T O R Y

Minnesota River

Mississippi River

M I N N E S O T A

I O W A

L E G E N D

|||||||||||| Unbuilt railroad

Map by Vicki Trego Hill adapted from map in 1873 *Duluth* pamphlet by H. T. Johns,
courtesy St. Louis County (Minnesota) Historical Society

prospect of striking another blow until spring." But construction continued, despite the weather. One accident, reflecting the slipshod operations, happened 20 miles from Moorhead. Two engines were pushing 39 boxcars "quite rapidly" when they hit half-spiked tracks; 16 cars slid down an embankment, many flipping over. On the train were George Brackett and Thomas Canfield's son, who respectively suffered a compound leg fracture and "severe injuries on the head and face." In Moorhead (population 220) speculators sat in a hotel waiting for the sound of a train whistle. Although Cooke received a December 31 telegram stating that the first train had arrived the day before at 4:45 P.M., a *Railroad Gazette* article states that track was a mile and half from the river while the temperature averaged minus 36 degrees.[23]

During 1871 the St. Paul & Pacific, with Moorhead as chairman of its executive committee, paid the price of Cooke's make-work for him. Valuable resources were squandered as track was completed from St. Paul to Breckenridge, located on an unnavigable part of the Red River; and as soon as the Northern Pacific reached Moorhead, Breckenridge lost its strategic value. It remains difficult to fathom the decision to finish the Breckenridge line while not completing the Saux Rapids–Brainerd run, a far more cost-effective section of track.[24]

Cooke also was blindsided by an informal alliance of economic interests along the Omaha–Chicago–New York economic axis, which did everything possible to block Duluth traffic—an unexpected, fiscally draining battle. With little support or apparent interest from Smith, Cooke found himself devoting time to developing traffic for the NP and Duluth. Cooke had hoped to sell NP bonds via European and American consortiums and in 1870 strengthened his European presence by establishing a London branch under Hugh McCulloch, Andrew Johnson's treasury secretary. While London proved a commercial success, the British government discreetly blocked NP bond sales. Hiring McCulloch also infuriated Grant (who hated him) and frightened the Morgan family, then based in London. The opening of Cooke's new office ushered in the drumbeat of negative articles about the NP in the *London Times*, apparently instigated by J. P. Morgan with British government cooperation.[25]

By 1871 Cooke's European hopes were reduced to a consortium led by the Union Bank of Vienna, which sent five "commissioners" to the United States. The five, traveling coast to coast, chewed up $25,000 of Cooke's cash. Cooke, who did not like them but kept his fingers crossed, was a perfect host. "A little German wine and a few cigars won't demoralize them," he wrote Wilkeson. But it was to no avail; the group, led by Regierungsrath Haas, submitted a negative report. Haas's painstakingly logical findings were based only on what *existed;* unlike Alexis de Tocqueville or Cooke, he thoroughly misunderstood America's dynamic growth.[26]

With European markets foreclosed, little interest and less cash from American banking houses, and NP dollar demands worsened by Smith's mismanagement,

Cooke had no choice but to sell NP bonds to the public. The campaign began in January 1871. Cooke played an active role, but its day-by-day direction was overseen by Abe Nettleton. Cooke's Northern Pacific bond sales approach was the same as in the war; the "7-30s" were to run 30 years and bear 7³⁄₁₀ percent interest in gold. Agents were placed around the country with sales materials and ads. The effort was unprecedented for a private enterprise. Cooke's advertisements were placed in 1,371 publications, although the 1872 number was to be far smaller, averaging some 140 publications per month. Nettleton, with Wilkeson's assistance, opened the floodgates with maps, pamphlets, lectures, articles, books, rallies, and exhibits at fairs and expositions supporting the effort. By mid-1872 Nettleton had printed 2.5 million large circulars and 30,000 maps, with advertising and printing costs topping $350,000.[27]

Newspapermen were wined and dined, junketed, assisted on the lecture circuit, or paid for favorable stories. On June 12, 1871, Cooke rented Philadelphia's Academy of Music, where 4,000 guests listened to the governor, other notables, and a two-hour oration by congressman William "Pig Iron" Kelly, a supporter of railroads and the gifts that they bestowed, especially on him. Kelly's speech was reprinted by the thousand and sent around the country. But Cooke was fishing at Gibraltar and did not attend, wasting an exceptional sales opportunity. Later in the year a dozen well-known writers and editors toured Minnesota and Dakota. Charles A. Dana (*Two Years before the Mast*) slyly wrote that Duluth's air was "cheerful and embracing [and] wonderful to breathe . . . [P]eople who can not live elsewhere find health and vigor in it. The sick become well here, and the weak strong."[28]

An unstated quid quo pro was that publications carrying Northern Pacific advertising also print articles submitted by Wilkeson, as well as endorsements from governors, Senate and House members, generals, and various organizations. Cooke also had Vice President Schuyler Colfax write and speak on behalf of "the great enterprise." Cooke even urged Colfax to *resign* and work for the NP, an offer the open-palmed Colfax respectfully declined. Nevertheless, the effort became overbearing. One unknown Kentucky congressman, J. Proctor Knott, delivered a tongue-in-cheek speech "praising" Duluth, the "Zenith City of the Unsalted Seas." Cooke's enemies had the speech reprinted nationally, and Knott became a household name. His remarks negated a year of Wilkeson's public relations work, making the NP and Duluth a national joke and damaging future promotional campaigns.[29]

In the fall of 1870 the country had been dumbfounded to hear of a newly discovered area in northwest Wyoming filled with great waterfalls, geysers, sulphur and hot springs, and a mud volcano "with explosions resembling distant discharges of a cannon." Cooke understood the tourist implications for rail traffic before anyone. As early as mid-1869, he was associated with Helena resident and ex–vigilante leader Nathaniel P. Langford, who, with Cooke's financial support, became one of the key figures on the 1870 exploration.[30]

Aubrey L. Haines (in *The Yellowstone Story*) indicates that Langford met with Cooke at Ogontz on June 4 or 5, 1870, and that the meeting "probably had much to do with getting the Yellowstone exploration off dead center." On returning east that winter, Langford was booked at prestigious locations, delivering at least twenty well-publicized lectures on the wonders of Yellowstone. The lectures were so well received that Cooke extended them into the spring, including one at Ogontz in May 1871 for Cooke and some influential friends.[31]

Cooke and Langford agreed on the necessity of a formal, government-sponsored study and enlisted the respected geologist Dr. Ferdinand V. Hayden, who had been on the William F. Raynolds/Jim Bridger explorations in 1859–60. With the Cooke brothers greasing the Washington skids, Hayden secured $40,000 for his 1871 Yellowstone exploration, which included the famed wartime photographer William H. Jackson. Cooke felt that an artist was also needed, and Nettleton recommended the then unknown Thomas Moran, who had illustrated Langford's articles in the May and June 1871 *Scribner's*. Hayden's funds were committed, so Cooke loaned Moran the money and sent him west to join Hayden. Cooke got the better of the financial deal, as Moran repaid him with some of his 1871 artwork, but Moran walked away with an enduring national reputation.

Cooke next set about having the federal government create and maintain a national park. When Hayden and Moran returned, Jay and his brother Henry began lobbying to create a park. Cooke's efforts were supported by "Wonders of the Yellowstone" stories that began to appear ever-so-spontaneously in newspapers and national illustrated magazines. The Cookes arranged to exhibit Moran's breathtaking *The Grand Canyon of the Yellowstone* at the Capitol in Washington, D.C. As 1871 ended, the legislation to create a national park, and thus indirectly a major tourist destination for the Northern Pacific, was just months from congressional passage.

With his financing options narrowing, Cooke began selling directly to the public. In addition to overhead (advertising, commissions, and so forth), he frequently repurchased bonds to keep prices high. For example, of $700,000 sold in July 1871, $600,000 was repurchased. The results were so disappointing that Smith wrote Cooke: "[I] am sorry to see you so much discouraged." In January bond sales averaged just $2,500 per day, with most sold at $100 per buyer. While the numbers began improving, the paperwork involved became immense, because most purchases were in small denominations. Before the 1873 collapse, over 80,000 people purchased bonds. Sales fluctuated wildly. May's gross was only $150,000, but June's was $600,000. Ultimately, while a handful of months broke a million in sales, most were closer to a half million.[32]

Just after the Chicago fire, Cooke, the country's leading banker, granted an interview to the *New York Herald*. His refusal to sugarcoat bad news and his prescience strike today's reader. When asked about insurance companies, Cooke replied: "Well, you see, some . . . will undoubtedly have to go under. . . . Then some of the banks and bears will hold tight and make money as tight as possible; of course you know the [negative] effect of that." On bank stability: "The banks will certainly feel panicky for a few days, perhaps; but it will be nothing—nothing." Concerning Chicago's being rebuilt: "The chance is a certainty, sir. Her situation is most advantageous . . . the rebuilding, I feel certain, will in point of rapidity and completeness surpass anything that ever this country has witnessed." Asked if Duluth would benefit, he answered: "Yes, perhaps so; but I don't think anybody, even in Duluth, will rejoice over the immediate cause of its good fortune."[33]

Despite the fire, or perhaps because of Cooke's reputation, November sales exceeded a million dollars. Sales through July 1 were about $2.5 million, and sales for calender 1871 were probably about $7 million. Subtracting fees, commissions, and expenses, the Northern Pacific's net was $5.5 to $6 million. Sales for 1872–73 were about the same, and ultimately cumulative bond sales were around $13.5 million. While it is not possible to quantify the impact, bonds sales were also hurt by increasing railroad competition for investment dollars, the success of the Sacramento-Omaha route, and the 1871 announcement of the Southern Pacific, which said it would use inexpensive Chinese labor. Investors and existing bondholders had to wonder if traffic could be found for a second transcontinental railroad, let alone four lines including the Canadian Pacific.[34]

Throughout this period Cooke's standing remained high. One paper noted: "[His] great achievement in 'placing' our government [war] bonds has given him a peculiar hold on the popular confidence. . . . Whatever he may say as to the prospects of the . . . [Northern Pacific] will be believed by millions of those who have found from experience that he is to be trusted." As the NP's problems grew, Cooke took on more responsibilities, including those of salesman. In February 1871 he was invited to speak at the home of a leading Brooklyn resident to a "few hundred prominent gentlemen," representing "every department of trade and finance to the extent of [a half billion] of capital," one paper wrote with awe. After a warm introduction and the host's apology for "bringing business affairs into a social gathering," a map was hung in the parlor, and Cooke began:

> His remarks were more in the nature of [a] free and offhand talk than of a systematically arranged speech, and were probably more impressive from this very fact. By no means an orator or given to rhetorical flourishes, Mr. Cooke talked on his favorite theme like a man who is so full of interesting

facts that his constant difficulty is that of selection—"an embarrassment of riches." He does not possess his subject, but it possesses him; absorbs him and makes him eloquent in spite of himself, and eloquent in just the way to inspire cautious financiers with confidence in an enterprise which has so evidently captivated so practical a man . . . [after a history of the railroad and a review of its prospects, he said that he] regarded the bonds as the safest and soundest securities in the market.[35]

Yet Cooke would not give a completion date, saying only that if "asked for his personal opinion, however, he would say that within four years the trade of the Indies would be carried over this route." Cooke's remarks confirm Larson's observation that his lack of specificity hurt sales. Perhaps reflecting his ambivalence, investors had no feel for when the road might be finished or become a going concern; and, unlike most salespeople today, Cooke felt constrained in directly asking his audience to invest. Also, in a highly competitive market, the bonds were neither fish nor fowl; they returned too little for a speculative venture and too much for a "safe" one.[36]

As pressures mounted, a great personal loss further drained Cooke. Three of his children were married or engaged, and a fourth was away at school. In 1871 his wife, Elizabeth, became ill with an undiagnosed heart disease. Cooke went to Gibraltar on June 5, while she stayed at Ogontz. A week later he wrote: "Wife much better & hopes to get to Gibraltar"; and then: "News from wife—she is better—God be praised." Elizabeth soon arrived, but Cooke's June 29 notation was ominous: "Our visit . . . has been saddened by the [sic] dear wife's sickness who has been unable to do more than sit on the porch or in the hall for a few moments at a time." Back at Ogontz, Elizabeth weakened, and Cooke stayed at her side. "I cannot leave the house," he wrote Wilkeson on July 17, "my wife is so sick." On the evening of July 21, Elizabeth Cooke, 43, died. One can only speculate on the depth of Cooke's pain and emptiness as he wandered, likely in a daze, now truly alone, down Ogontz's great marble hallways. He never again married or openly courted another woman.[37]

Despite Elizabeth's death, there was no respite from his pressures. Because of Cooke's increased Northern Pacific commitment, his relations with his partners began eroding. By 1871 many were becoming apprehensive and beginning to question his growing commitment to the NP; ironically, this was the same issue he brought up with Smith: the ability to manage two businesses simultaneously. For his firm to succeed, Cooke's *active* presence was needed, as others, especially Morgan and Drexel, were competing for the same business. Sometime in 1871 Cooke began devoting more of his time to the NP than to Jay Cooke & Co.

Additionally, Cooke was running out of cash and had to reduce his charitable contributions. With his wife gone, he began quarreling with the Episcopal archdiocese "over its exclusiveness and high-church tendencies." His daily life became constrained, painful, and without emotional reward. Larson writes that Cooke "was no longer the buoyant, masterful man that he had been . . . He was, instead, tired and irritable, and he lacked the decisiveness that had earlier characterized his work." In September the exhausted Cooke candidly wrote Wilkeson:

> If I know my own heart, it is that I have engaged in this great work and have been sustained in it thus far, in the midst of great trials and troubles, from the consciousness that I was in the faith of Christian duty. . . . I would rather be out of the Northern Pacific than see it go to pot and be instrumental in building up cities and towns without the blessed influences of the school, the college, the seminary and the church going with it and filling in a godly and moral population.[38]

The year 1871 came to a symbolic end with Cooke not being told the truth by Northern Pacific management. A December 31 telegram stating that a train had reached Fargo stretched the facts: the train was actually 1.5 miles from the Red River.

However, and certainly far more importantly, both Yellowstone surveys had been successful despite constant rumors of their likely destruction by hostile Sioux. Most others would have been thoroughly crushed by 1871's business and personal losses, but Cooke was not about to quit. He felt that there was a higher reason for what was happening and, equating himself with Washington and Lincoln, also resolved to prevail through this most trying time. Cooke literally felt that he was being watched and judged by history and his God. Fortunately he did not know what the future held.

CHAPTER 7

"Stop Firing at Me"

By August 1871 the Northern Pacific had yet to send a man into the Yellowstone Valley. While the NP had finished surveying from Duluth to Bismarck and from Bozeman to Tacoma, fear of Sioux retaliation had resulted in a 600-mile information and engineering gap in western Dakota and eastern Montana—no way to build investor confidence or a railroad. The NP assumed that Sitting Bull and his followers would fight its surveyors, fully realizing that the road would destroy their traditional way of life. Gregory Smith wrote Milnor Roberts in June: "It will probably be unsafe to carry on the work between the Missouri River and Bozeman Pass without a proper military escort. Negotiations are now underway to supply this, and it is hoped that a sufficient military force will be detailed and placed at your disposal."[1]

Later that summer, despite army infighting and red tape, infantry and cavalry units were assigned to protect the surveyors, permitting the Northern Pacific to enter the Yellowstone Valley from the east (Fort Rice) and the west (Bozeman–Fort Ellis). The upper Yellowstone was under the control of friendly Crow Indians and the Sioux generally hunted east of Billings, so a far smaller military escort was required than the one necessary to protect Rosser's survey leaving from the Missouri River (chapter 8).

Roberts had remained on the West Coast until late April 1871, making sure that the Northern Pacific did not default on its charter for lack of West Coast construction. The Roberts family suffered the tragedy of the death of their firstborn, a girl only a year and a half old, a heartbreaking blow for both of them. Roberts had been absent from home for most of his first marriage and had missed seeing his children grow up. He wrote Tom Rosser's wife: "One of the great drawbacks in an engineer's life is the very limited time he can command for home enjoyments.

I have always said to young ladies, 'Don't marry an engineer, it is worse than the army.'" Now he probably second-guessed himself about bringing his wife and child with him.[2]

By May Roberts was back at New York headquarters presenting plans for both Yellowstone surveys. But if he thought that he would get back to Minnesota he was mistaken; he was next sent to Helena, Montana, to direct six surveys in Montana and Idaho as well as follow through on a key part of his instructions. "The passes through the Rocky Mountains being of special importance," wrote Smith, "you will as far as practicable make a personal examination of these . . . [and] render a full and complete report on the subject." The instructions were a result of rumors of an "undiscovered" gap heard by Thomas Canfield in 1869: "The Marias Pass to the north has never been fully examined," Canfield had accurately written. Aside from Minnesota, few things were more important than finding the shortest, most cost-effective route across the Rockies.[3]

In June Roberts stopped in Sandusky, at Cooke's invitation, to attend the wedding of one of Jay's nephews. Continuing west, on July 10 he met with his survey leaders in Corrine, Utah, admitting: "A majority of the Engineers had previously been unknown to me." Most were from Pennsylvania and New York, likely with limited western experience. Roberts, his pregnant wife, his son Thomas (who led a survey team), and Thomas's wife and their child met and traveled to Helena, arriving July 20. The next evening, several hundred residents and a brass band gathered in front of the hotel to cheer and serenade him. Roberts responded "at some length, in a plain and practical manner," describing the Northern Pacific's efforts and plans.[4]

Roberts was soon finishing his plans for the various surveys. Three Montana surveys included routes to Missoula from west of the passes, and a fourth was from Three Forks (the head of the Missouri River) through Deer Lodge to the Little Blackfoot River. The final Montana effort was the "western" Yellowstone surveying expedition, the subject of this chapter. The survey would begin at Three Forks and go to Fort Ellis, three miles east of Bozeman. Here the survey team would receive a cavalry escort, cross the Bozeman Pass, and follow the Yellowstone downstream as far as weather and the Sioux permitted. Because the Crow (Mountain Crow or Absaroka) reservation was by treaty on the south bank of the river, the team would survey the opposite side.[5]

After visiting eight passes between Deer Lodge and Cadotte's Pass, no easy task for a 61-year-old, to his dismay Roberts was ordered back to Utah to meet a party of European bankers and show them the Pacific Coast area he had visited in 1869. Unable to take his wife, who went to live with a sister in Kansas, Roberts left Montana, not to return until late October. This unexpected development caused him to lose three months' time, effective operational control of the surveys, and the opportunity to search Montana's passes fully.[6]

The Yellowstone survey team consisted of 17 men, including a "chief of party," an assistant chief, one topographical engineer, one transit man, a leveler, and a rodman. There were also two flagmen, two chainmen, three axemen, a cook, an all-purpose "assistant," and one teamster as well as a pair of two-horse wagons and a pack train of mules. The survey's leader was the alcoholic, ineffectual Edward D. Muhlenberg, a Pennsylvanian wartime artillery officer and a descendant of Muhlenberg College's founder. His key qualification was the support of Senator Simon Cameron, a Lincoln cabinet member who retained enormous political clout. Later Roberts received a less than subtle letter from Cameron, on Senate stationery, stating: "I have a deep interest in E. D. Muhlenberg . . . and am anxious that he should find a friend in you." Cameron admitted that Muhlenberg "was once 'wild,' but has now put that fully behind him."[7]

In 1871 Roberts had heard rumors of Muhlenberg's drinking but was misled about it, writing the Northern Pacific Board that "Mr. Muhlenberg has worked most industrially and faithfully since leaving the fort." In March 1872, after discovering that he had been lied to, Roberts was livid. He adamantly refused to rehire Muhlenberg, "nor any man or boy who is in the habit of drinking . . . I will not [be used as] a school for the care of inebriates; they *can't go*" (Roberts's emphasis). By that time, of course, the 1871 survey had long since ended.[8]

Muhlenberg left Three Forks in late July; it took him almost three weeks to get to Fort Ellis, just over 30 miles away, traveling over open, relatively flat land. As for the Indians, Roberts telegraphed New York: "[I] do not apprehend danger to any of our [surveyors]." Further delays followed, although they were not Muhlenberg's doing. Unwilling to wait for an army escort, he surveyed over the Bozeman Pass. He stopped at the Crow Indian Agency, some four miles east of where the narrow Shields River entered the Yellowstone, until an escort arrived. Ellis, established in 1867, was an active post in the lush Gallatin Valley at the northern end of the Bozeman Trail, with some 300 officers and men from four 2nd Cavalry companies (F, G, H, L) and Company A, 7th Infantry. That summer, one cavalry company escorted Ferdinand Hayden's expedition into Yellowstone Park, two other companies futilely chased Indians who had killed two settlers near Bozeman, and the final two stayed at Ellis in reserve. [9]

To Muhlenberg's frustration, General Hancock's written orders had not been received at Fort Ellis, and telegraphic orders to Ellis authorizing the survey's escort were not sent until August 5. Only after the cavalry in the field had returned could an escort (consisting of 91 men and 5 officers from H and L Companies) be assembled, but it did not leave until September 16. Food, clothing, ammunition, tents, and reserve grain for the horses and mules were packed in ten six-mule wagons, two four-horse wagons, and one two-horse spring wagon. With ample grass in the western Yellowstone valley, the cavalrymen, supplied with scythes, cut hay daily.

The escort was commanded by Capt. Edward Ball, a career soldier who had seen extensive combat in both the Mexican War and Civil War. Ball, made a captain in July 1865, was well respected, able, and honest—too much so for his own good, as it turned out a few years later when he apparently would not take a bribe from Montana pioneer Nelson Story. Without money or influence, and perhaps not getting along with the commanding officer at Fort Ellis, he seems to have drawn many long and difficult assignments. The 1871 survey proved to be both.[10]

Ball could not speed up Muhlenberg, of course. From the time the survey left Ellis until it turned back in November, it averaged only 2.5 miles a day. Ball and the surveyors met no later than midday on September 17, but work did not resume until September 22. Part of the problem was Muhlenberg's drinking, which was likely the cause of his quarreling with at least one intelligent subordinate. The problem was compounded by his inflexibility and the specificity of his orders to survey the Yellowstone's north bank downstream.[11]

From the Livingston area, the Yellowstone flows through a valley ranging from a half mile to four or five miles wide. The south bank of the river is generally wider and much less rugged as far as present-day Columbus. After Shields River, the north bank is bordered by Sheep Mountain and then by frequent hills and bluffs, intersected by numerous deep-cutting creeks. Ball wrote that "a greater portion of the time the camps had unnecessarily to be pitched on the [south] side of the river to which the parties were at work, which made it necessary for the guards to cross twice a day and many of the crossings [were] quite deep and rocky, and the water colder every day." This meant that every day the surveyors and their escort had to find a safe crossing, do their work, and recross the Yellowstone. One officer wrote of the area: "These fords are all difficult, the current of the river being very swift and the bottom covered with large boulders. At this season the depth was about three feet at the fords."[12]

Until they reached Columbus, if there was no ford near the day's work, the surveyors and their guard either had to walk extra miles to find a ford or had to take greater risks by crossing directly. Either way, they all had to know that their work would not be used: while it was technically possible to build on the north side, it was obviously too expensive; even today there are no roads paralleling the river or communities between Livingston and Columbus. Clearly the railroad had to rework the 1868 Crow treaty so that the south side of the Yellowstone could be used. Had Roberts been in Montana and not with the European bankers, he could have resolved the problem rapidly; but Muhlenberg floundered for months, effectively cut off from Roberts and numbly following orders.

Adding to the survey's problems, 47 miles from the Crow Agency a fire swept through the camp on October 10. Ball wrote that "it broke out in one of the tents of the officer's line . . . and although a number of men were within a few feet of the tent in which the fire originated their efforts to extinguish it availed [them] nothing, the wind blowing such a terrific gale not more than one minute could have elapsed from the time the fire was first discovered until it swept down to the river." The fire destroyed Company H's tents, blankets, clothing, rations, and stacked carbines. A number of men were napping in the tents; the fire spread so quickly that, despite the shouting, many suffered from burnt clothing, hair, or hands. Attempts to put out the fire abruptly ended when "about eight hundred rounds of carbine and pistol cartridges exploded in the burning debris . . . sending their missiles in all directions." No one was seriously hurt. Ball sent one wagon back to Ellis to restock some supplies, but Company H remained short of tents and blankets, later a matter of serious consequence.[13]

In late October Roberts returned to Montana and became fully aware of Muhlenberg's problems. He quickly made the decision to join Muhlenberg and undertake a parallel "reconnaissance" of his own. Roberts was the guest of honor at a banquet in Helena on October 29 and left for Fort Ellis the next morning, arriving 36 hours later. Joining him were G. D. Chenoweth, an engineer, to "assist" Muhlenberg with his maps; C. A. Broadwater, active in Montana freighting; and "Major" Fellows D. Pease, the respected and recently appointed Crow Indian agent, who had lived in Montana since 1856 as a trapper, scout, prospector, and trader.[14]

The commandant at Fort Ellis was Eugene M. Baker, born near Lake George, New York, and an 1859 West Point graduate. A classmate described his "very strong and vigorous mind, as well as a marvelously powerful and perfect physique." Dark-haired and of average height, Baker did well his plebe year, but later something "caused him to neglect study and depend on his natural ability to keep him up in his class," in which he was 12th of 22. Baker had a solid war record, catching Sheridan's eye at Winchester (1864), where he was cited for "gallant and meritorious service." Baker was promoted to major in April 1869 and received command of Fort Ellis on December 1, 1869.[15]

As noted in chapter 4, Sheridan ordered Baker to attack a band of militant Piegans and "strike them hard." With some 200 Piegans dead, and his force without casualties, a national outcry followed. Baker became a symbol for all that was wrong with the army's treatment of Indians. An enlisted man, William H. White, stated: "Baker was known as a hard-hearted man . . . [and] a heavy drinker." His West Point obituary noted that, "believing that nothing could injure his constitution, [he] neglected such precautions as he might have taken and broke down sooner than he had the slightest idea he could." White called him popular: "[C]arr[ying] his strong body in [an] erect, soldierly manner . . . his familiar mingling with all subordinates did much toward bringing them into forgetfulness [about] some of . . . [his] reprehensible traits." Baker, likely angered by Hancock's order to accompany Roberts, found himself with a Quaker who disliked alcohol and killing of any kind. Roberts was no prude and had a number of in-laws in the military (including Confederate lieutenant-general Richard Anderson), but he would have been discomforted by being with a man he abhorred by reputation. Now circumstances had put the two together; as Roberts was to reveal, it was indeed a bad mix.[16]

At 9:00 A.M. on November 2 Roberts, Baker, Chenoweth, Broadwater, Pease, another officer, 25 cavalrymen, a half-dozen wagons, and a light wagon left Ellis. Despite six inches of snow, the weather was warm. Roberts wrote: "As soon as we passed the divide, lo! The scene changed—there was no snow left, and the road was dry, looking almost as it did [in 1869]." Upon reaching the Yellowstone, Roberts, ever inquisitive, measured its flow, estimating it to be "more than double the low water flow of the Ohio at Pittsburgh." At sunset, after crossing to the south side of the river, they arrived at the Crow Agency.[17]

The Crow Agency consisted of a small stockade with room for horses and wagons, several storehouses, quarters for four men, and a one-room school. Outside its walls were over 300 Crow lodges, where some 800 or 900 warriors lived. They were frequently gone, however, hunting in the Yellowstone and Musselshell valleys. The next day Roberts visited their farm, noting the "good crop of potatoes, very good turnips and cabbages, and . . . two acres of sweet corn." At Pease's suggestion two Métis guides were hired, Pierre Shane and Mitch Boyer (or Bouyer), who later died with Custer. Three Crows were also hired: Blackfoot (or Sits-in-the-Middle-of-the-Land); Wolfbow, "a big-nosed, six footer Chief [and] middle aged"; and Pretty Lodge, "a young but large Indian, nearly six feet high." Blackfoot was a war chief, one of whose wives was a Sioux captive; and Wolfbow later became a tribal leader.[18]

On November 4 the party recrossed the Yellowstone, inspecting Muhlenberg's survey by following the brightly marked stakes. Roberts immediately realized that track could not be constructed on the Yellowstone's north shore; "The reservation side is obviously the better." Bridges would be necessary, but he saw few problems: "The Yellowstone, although it has a strong current, does not rise high, [so inexpensive] piers and short spans will answer." For the next two days camp was on the Boulder River because, Roberts noted, "Col. Baker, not feeling well, concluded not to start till we should see what kind of weather we are to have." He knew that Baker was surreptitiously drinking, his symptoms being an inability to be wakened, late sleeping, and "the shakes" upon awakening. However, the weather was raw, with the temperature in the low forties, and a heavy snow began falling in midafternoon.[19]

As Roberts rode down the Yellowstone Valley, he was impressed by the large stands of cottonwoods, fascinated by the large prairie dog cities, and delighted at the likely prospect: "Thus far down the Yellowstone . . . it will be a cheap line to construct." The scouts and Crows provided game. Roberts, with a mattress and ample blankets, slept deeply in a tent he shared with Chenoweth. Baker, Broadwater, Pease, and the handsome Lt. Charles B. Schofield (West Point, '70) occupied another tent. The scouts and Crows shared an "improvised wigwam," and the enlisted men likely had pup tents. As rich bottomlands and meadows appeared, Roberts saw large herds of antelope, deer, elk, and other wildlife. He was stunned by the lush grass, the "clear as crystal" Yellowstone, and the box elder, cottonwood, and pine along its banks and on the hills. "This is a beautiful place," he wrote. Roberts also noted that during the breaks the teamsters sprinted to the streams feeding the Yellowstone, enthusiastically, if unsuccessfully, panning for gold.[20]

Roberts's sketch of the evening of November 7–8, which survives, gives a good feeling of a typical encampment. The next morning, up at five, he observed Venus and wrote that "the white light in the east contrasts charmingly with the clear blue almost black of the west, and the atmosphere is as pure as a virgin." The previous evening the temperature fell over 40 degrees, standing at 23 degrees at 5:30 A.M., and the hardened ground allowed the wagons to make better time. By 11 A.M. Roberts had recrossed the Yellowstone and reached the Ball-Muhlenberg camp. After a half day's rest, and with good weather and no sign of Sioux, Roberts and Baker decided to "borrow" most of Ball's command and ride to the Big Horn River, an estimated 115 miles away.

Accompanying Roberts and Baker were three officers, 90 men, Boyer, Shane, Blackfoot, and Wolfbow. They took no tents or wagons, only pack horses with five days of rations. The group assumed, incorrectly as it turned out, that there would be ample grass for the horses. One officer was the charming, hard-partying, politically well-placed New Yorker Lovell H. Jerome (West Point, '70, 56th of 57), the ne'er-do-well son of playboy Lawrence Jerome. Lovell's uncle was Leonard Jerome, who became Winston Churchill's grandfather in 1874. The column left Ball near present-day Park City. Despite a temperature of 37 degrees and light rain and snow, Roberts enthusiastically wrote: "[W]e have all been charmed with the beauty of the valley and its surroundings. . . . For sheep, cattle and horses, this region . . . surpasses any that I have ever seen in North or South America." Game was becoming abundant, including buffalo and antelope. Riding east, Roberts noted: "We have passed through the finest valley by far that I have seen in Montana . . . 175 sq. miles of very superior land." Supper was buffalo and a wild goose. Roberts spotted the first veins of soft, brown coal (lignite), which stretched east 300 miles.[21]

Around 10 A.M. on November 11 Roberts wrote that he was atop a "100-foot high flat [plateau], Pryor's Creek opposite, but does not come in till 2 or 3 miles." They crossed back to the right bank and found a ford, likely close to today's Huntley bridge. As a horse slipped in the swift current, Roberts simultaneously wrote: "Man overboard [!]" The horse rolled over a trooper named Shavers, pinning him underwater "long enough to make me feel very uneasy about him. Captain [George L.] Tyler and several soldiers got to him after awhile with a rope and got him back to [a] gravel bar. . . . He was chilled, frightened nearly to death." The next day Roberts discovered that Shavers had served under Muhlenberg during the war; not realizing that he had been lied to, he wrote to his wife that "Capt. Ball and the other officers here say that Mr. M. has worked faithfully and well since they left Ellis, and that he has been entirely abstinent. He is all right now, and they all like him."

About noon on November 11 Roberts rode to a bluff overlooking the river, "about 170 miles from Fort Ellis, whence we had a good view of the valley for 20 miles farther, to Pompey's Pillar." He was likely close to present-day Interstate 94, seven to eight miles east of its I-90 junction. They were all cautious, aware that they were nearing Lakota hunting grounds. Roberts and Pease were in front— where Baker should have been—watching small buffalo herds. Roberts, who had exceptional eyesight, thought he spotted something peculiar: "I was the first to suggest that they did not move like buffalo and after awhile Major Pease took out his [binoculars] . . . as I had said one of them was a man and a horse." Pease reached a similar conclusion, and the two wasted little time in turning back. It was as far down the Yellowstone as Roberts ever went.

In fact, Roberts had spotted Crows. The Crows also saw them and were even more disconcerted, assuming they had been encircled by Sioux who were chasing them, for they had stolen a number of horses from a large Sioux camp near the Big Horn River. Some had taken horses across "to the Musselshell where there is a large Crow camp"; these Crows, likely decoys, "had ridden all night they said. They were young, good looking, and had on their war paint! Without any invitation they . . . followed us into camp." The Crows, of course, were delighted by the survey's food and protection. Roberts wrote his wife: "[W]e saw immense quantities of game . . . this being near the upper boundary of their range this season." The officers were enthusiastic, enjoying freshly killed buffalo, cool evenings, and plenty of sleep. Roberts wrote: "The Doctor has a sinecure. Nobody gets sick; rather, they are fattening. Lt. Jerome thinks he has gained 30 pounds. He looks as if he weighed 200. Such days! Such nights! Such game! Such appetites!" Roberts also loved a horse that Ball had loaned him: "[T]he best horse I have ridden for years so that five minutes after dismounting, after riding 30 miles, with scarcely a pause, I felt no fatigue, and my appetite was, as you may believe, good."[22]

Roberts was unaware that Sitting Bull's scouts had seen them and were concerned by their being so far into the valley. Fortunately, Sitting Bull and over 1,000 warriors were hundreds of miles away at the Milk River Indian Agency. Assured that the column would soon turn back, he made no effort to intercept them. Yet with Sioux near and the grass apparently eaten by buffalo, on November 12 the reconnaissance party turned back. By late afternoon they were with Ball and Muhlenberg, who had camped near the "Place of Skulls." His work completed, Roberts focused on returning; but the next morning he wrote: "Col. Baker had last night a chill fever." This and the earlier notation are Roberts's only public comments about Baker; in their time together there is not a single mention of their talking, riding, or eating with each other.[23]

Before returning to Fort Ellis with his escort, Roberts had breakfast with Ball, with whom he had formed a quick friendship, noting: "Ball thinks this part of the Yellowstone Valley, say for 25 to 30 miles, is worth as much as all of the [lush] Gallatin Valley for farming." But cold weather was setting in: "It snowed a little last night . . . [I]ce is running in the river today and stands along the edges, and [is] ¼ inch thick in our tent."[24] With growing concern about the weather, it was agreed that Ball would determine the survey's return date. And the weather was turning colder: by late afternoon on November 13 the temperature was 37 degrees.

The next morning the party made a 6:45 A.M. start. Thoroughly enjoying himself, Roberts had awakened, hearing "Breakfast is ready, Col!" as an enlisted man came over to his tent. The title was, of course, in deference to his age and status; everyone addressed him that way. Roberts kept taking notes on the return trip: "thousands of Pine, cross-ties can be had in this vicinity on both sides of the river." About three, near a ford, the party camped. Shortly after an event occurred that was so bizarre that Roberts told it only to his wife and apparently never mentioned it to another person or even in his field notes.

> Directly opposite the camp, on the same side of the river, is a pretty Mount . . . And soon after we stopped I took my pistol, barometer and thermometer and started across the beautiful natural meadow to its foot, and ascended to the top, which I figured to be 400 feet above the plain. It took me 8 minutes rapid walk to reach the foot and 25 minutes, slower gait, to ascend to the top; where I had a fine view of the valley for many miles up and like distance down—the windings of the river and its islands opened out like a map before me. As soon as I reached [the top] I fired my pistol, while standing on the highest peak of rock. Soon after I heard a ball whiz and strike the rock about 20 feet below me, and a little while after another ball whizzed and struck the rocks not far below me. I called out to the party to stop firing at me. It was, as I learned when I returned, [because they thought] their rifles *would not* carry that far; while it is very clear to me that they did [know]. Col. Baker had fired the first shot, but none of them had believed that the balls had struck so high up. (Roberts's emphasis)[25]

Why did Baker fire at Roberts? No one can know the reasons for his animosity, but perhaps it reflected Roberts's compulsiveness and Baker's resentment at having to accompany him and being forced to drink furtively. It is also likely that, no matter how hard he tried, Roberts was unable to conceal the fact that he found Baker abhorrent. In any event, shooting directly at the Northern Pacific's chief engineer, even as a "joke," speaks to Baker's state of mind. Having described the incident to his wife, Roberts clearly wanted to put it behind him and immediately changed the subject: "We had an elegant supper this evening; oyster stew, buffalo meat, antelope and breakfast bacon, with excellent potatoes, grown at the [Crow] Agency."

On November 15 the men started before 7:00 A.M., making good time. Just after nine, Roberts noted that a place they passed was where "Rev. Thomas and his son were killed by the Indians." The tale was a part of Bozeman Trail lore. In 1866 Thomas, a man of great faith traveling almost alone and against everybody's advice, decided to place his safety in the hands of the Almighty. Roberts did not say that Thomas was from Chambersburg, Pennsylvania; having lived there himself, he may have known the family. Just west of the Boulder River, as the temperature dropped, they made camp "on a small island in the Yellowstone."[26]

Awaking on November 16, Roberts recorded four inches of snow and a temperature of 16 degrees; but by making good time they reached the Crow Agency that afternoon. The next day they slept late, were at the Bozeman Pass by 3:30 P.M., and, notwithstanding darkness and a foot of snow on the western slope, arrived at Fort Ellis that evening. Roberts was back in Helena on November 20, scribbling notes even as he arrived at the International Hotel at 5:45 P.M. During the next two weeks he caught up on his mail, wrote reports, sent thank-you notes to Baker and the public (via the *Helena Herald*), and met with other survey team leaders. Finally, on December 5, he began the rugged 450-mile stage ride to Corrine, where he boarded the Union Pacific for the trip back to his wife and home.[27]

Even after Roberts left, the "summer's work" was not over for Muhlenberg's surveyors and Ball's escort. Work continued a few days until Ball, concerned about the weather, decided on November 15 to break camp and return to Ellis the next day. He had waited too long, however. That evening a snowstorm began that lasted until Friday morning, when Ball was able to break camp. For nine days, until reaching the Crow Agency, the party traveled 110 miles upriver, through seven days of intermittent snow, usually with a biting wind from the west and, it is safe to guess, a wind-chill factor seldom above freezing. Six to ten inches of snow gradually built up, making it difficult for the animals to forage for grass and impossible for the men to cut hay.

As the horses gave out, the cavalrymen had to walk, further delaying the column. While there was ample food, not all of the blankets and tents had been replaced after the October fire, and the delay and cold weather added to the men's hardships. By November 20, increasingly nervous about the condition of the horses,

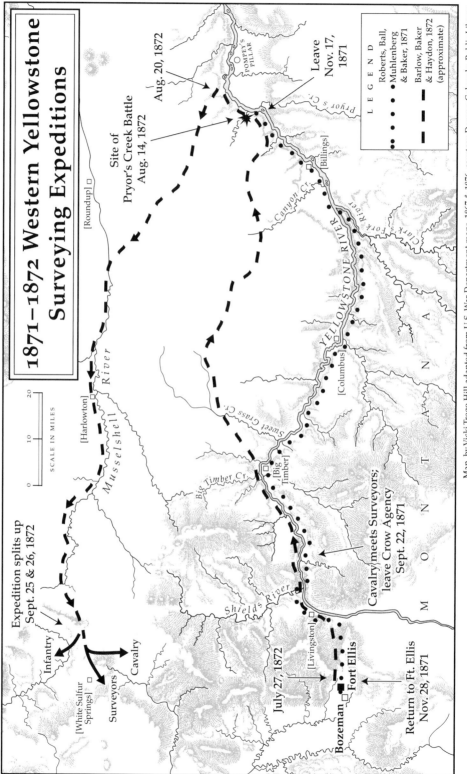

1871–1872 Western Yellowstone Surveying Expeditions

Map by Vicki Trego Hill adapted from U.S. War Department maps, 1867 & 1876, courtesy Denver, Colorado, Public Library

Ball felt that large numbers would be lost unless they had grain. Turning the command over to Capt. George L. Tyler, an able war veteran, he set out with seven troopers for Fort Ellis.[28]

That evening Ball's small party marched through the night, finally reaching the Crow Agency by 8 P.M. the next day. The following morning, with little sleep, facing another storm and snow two to four feet deep in the Bozeman Pass, Ball left for Ellis, arriving at 3 P.M. on November 23. A rescue party of 30 mounted men, including Lt. Edward J. McClernand (see appendix A), "26 pack horses (the snow being too deep for mules)," grain, and blankets was quickly assembled. The plan was to leave on Friday morning, but with a huge storm moving in from the west they were forced to wait until it blew over.[29]

That same afternoon (November 24) Tyler and Muhlenberg were marching alongside the now frozen Yellowstone when they were engulfed by the storm as it blasted its way through the Bozeman Pass. The *Bozeman Avant Courier* reported: "The severe snow storm of [last] Friday came upon them in all of its fury, the blinding snow coming in [like] a hurricane, drifting to the depth of many feet in the line of march." With gusts perhaps as high as 70 miles per hour, visibility fell to a few feet as officers took turns leading, often on foot. The temperature dropped; and, as the light faded, men began moaning to be allowed to go to sleep.[30]

Pack animals began stumbling under the accumulating extra weight of snow and ice. Officers and sergeants gave up on the animals but kicked and pushed the men forward. Others screamed that their feet, hands, or faces were freezing. The *Avant Courier* noted: "They would tumble off of their horses perfectly benumbed, and it required the greatest exertion of those not so badly affected to arouse them from the stupor that was fast coming on." Some five hours after the storm hit, the first men reached a clump of willows and cottonwood that offered fuel and some shelter. A trumpeter, Sgt. Edward Page, sounded the "Rally" again and again, leading the men to the woods, but his lips probably were sticking to his brass trumpet. One surveyor became lost but survived the night by himself, although his feet were frostbitten.[31]

On Saturday Fort Ellis's able-bodied soldiers began digging a path through the snow. Although nine miles were cleared, they were unable to crest the pass. Rather than spend the night in the open, almost a thousand feet above Fort Ellis, they returned to the post. Earlier that day Tyler and Muhlenberg's men had staggered into the Crow Agency, where they were met by Pease, who was expecting them, and helped to the extent possible. On Sunday they rested at the agency while Ball's rescue party made their way over and down the eastern side of the pass.

By November 27 Pease's grain was almost gone. Tyler, leaving the wagons, mules, equipment, and some horses with Pease, despite being dangerously low on blankets, marched west as best he could. At dusk he spotted Ball's rescuers near the Shields River and camped with him. While the steeper, eastern side of the Bozeman

Pass had to be climbed, by 3 P.M. on November 28 they were back at Fort Ellis. Ball reported that 57 soldiers—he made no mention of the surveyors—"had their faces, hands, feet, ears, and noses painfully frozen." Although they required no amputations, 100 miles to the north the same storm had caught 65 men from the 7th Infantry in the open, resulting in 22 amputations. "All of the party highly commend the action of the commanding officer, Capt. Ball," the *Avant Courier* reported, "for his humanity, courage, and foresight, under circumstances of the most trying nature."[32]

Considering the lateness of the season and the severity of the storm, Ball's leadership was remarkable. Once back at Ellis, Muhlenberg refused to take any responsibility for the loss of more than a dozen carbines and revolvers that had been loaned to the surveyors and discarded during the march back, leaving the officers stuck with the cost of replacing them.[33]

Despite its modest expectations, the survey was successful. Disappointments such as not reaching the Big Horn River or Muhlenberg's performance were inconsequential. Roberts came away with a good feeling about construction in the Yellowstone Valley and also learned that he had to build track on the river's south bank: "It so happens that the largest portion of the most favorable ground is on the Reservation side . . . [so] it will probably be advisable to put [track there and make] . . . an arrangement with the Crow." Roberts was also pleased with the land's "rich, black alluvial soil" and the large stands of timber. Because the river fell 11 feet per mile, Roberts felt that it was unsuitable for navigation but would make for easy irrigation. Regarding the Sioux, he was optimistic but wary: "I am convinced that a fort, well equipped with cavalry, has a most soothing influence on Indian warriors . . . [and then] judicious, peaceful arrangements can be made and maintained with the Indians without serious fighting."[34]

The survey and Roberts's reconnaissance might best be remembered not for what was accomplished in 1871 but for some tantalizing "what ifs." Roberts never had time to look for the Marias Pass, which was not "discovered" until December 1889. The pass led to a shorter, easier route from the Great Lakes to Puget Sound, but the beneficiary was the Great Northern Railroad not the Northern Pacific. What the NP would have done with the information had Roberts discovered the pass in 1871 is, of course, speculative. Roberts also never told Cooke that Baker had shot at him, although they likely discussed his drinking. Cooke, who had the wherewithal to remove Baker, never asked this favor of Grant, but would surely have done so had he known of the incident. Roberts's reticence was to haunt Cooke and the NP (chapter 10), and his escorting of the European bankers proved useless. When the railroad reached the area in 1881, the Crows received $25,000 for the land paralleling the Yellowstone.[35]

CHAPTER 8

"The Army of the Glendive"

As the Northern Pacific and the U.S. Army prepared for their first large-scale surveying expedition, stories concerning hostile Indians began to circulate. An August 3, 1871, *New York Times* report cited the death of the Santee Sioux chief Standing Buffalo at the hands of militant Sioux, suggesting that this faction, with 1,000 lodges, now controlled northeastern Montana. Other stories indicated a convergence of hundreds of lodges to prevent the surveyors from entering the Yellowstone Valley. The *Sioux City Journal* predicted that, as the soldiers had been sent up the river to protect the surveyors in the valley, "a general Indian war will follow this move."[1]

In fact, by early September soldiers, surveyors, and their supplies were beginning to converge on Fort Rice, the jumping-off post, 20 miles south of present-day Bismarck. The purpose of the survey (or expedition as the military called it) was to find a practical railroad route, running as directly west as possible from Fargo-Moorhead to the Yellowstone. Previous surveys had pinpointed a crossing at Bismarck, but west of the Missouri the maps were poor. Most of the area was unknown from a railroad engineering viewpoint. The work was anticipated to take two months, and it was hoped there would be no Indian problems.

The surveyors were led by Thomas L. Rosser, the obvious leader for the potentially dangerous assignment. Also on the survey were the now experienced younger surveyors such as Jordan, Meigs, Eckelson, Eastman, and Charles "Shorty" Graham. Rosser had been promoted to chief engineer, Dakota Division, just before the survey began, reflecting his leadership and an offer of $5,000 a year from the St. Louis & Cairo Railroad. His wife was "quite disturbed about my going to the Yellowstone"; but family considerations aside, the ex-cavalryman was invigorated by the prospect of again being in the saddle and commanding men. Despite perfunctory references to "my sweet little family," Rosser's actions reflected a man happy to be away from the constraints of family, business, and civilization. But, at 35, he was not without qualms, writing in his diary on August 23: "Took leave of my precious wife and dear little children and left on the train. God preserve me." Before leaving he met with Gregory Smith, engineering personnel, and General Hancock to finalize "escort matters."[2]

On August 28 Rosser and most of the surveyors left St. Paul and by the next afternoon were some 40 miles from Fort Abercrombie, at the end of the track, where the Northern Pacific had a supply depot. The agent running the depot wrote that he had furnished Rosser with six four-horse teams for wagons, four saddle horses, and "a complete outfit of camp fixings . . . I think to his entire satisfaction." In a letter to Rosser's superior, D. C. Linsley, the agent meekly complained that the swarthy, forceful, hard-drinking, six-foot-two Rosser had cleaned out most of the depot's cigars and liquor, for "I knew not how to refuse him." Rosser was in his element and likely showing off for his young surveyors, gleefully playing the role of Rebel swashbuckler and taking what he wanted for his 24-man surveying team.[3]

Three days later, the surveyors left Fort Abercrombie and by the next evening were just east of present-day Lisbon, where the Sheyenne River makes a U-turn to the north. The next day they crossed the virtually imperceptible Hudson Bay/Gulf of Mexico continental divide. On September 3 they found a James River crossing, and from there they made good time, skirting some of the hundreds of tiny lakes that dot that part of Dakota. But what astonished them most was the eerie quiet of the country: plains that had teemed with buffalo as late as 1863 were now empty.

The party was without guides, as Rosser's war experience had left him contemptuous of them. He wrote: "Regarding that class of creatures called guides . . . [y]ou can rarely get one who has been over the exact ground that you wish to explore, and although they will tell you in almost every instance that they are perfectly familiar with it, but after a few day's march they begin to become confused and soon become a perfect nuisance." Based on his compass readings, Rosser made 20 to 25 miles a day without guides and by the morning of September 7 had them at the Missouri, directly opposite Fort Rice. That night Rosser noted in his diary that "the wind [was] blowing a fearful gale and [we] could not cross with wagons."[4]

Despite the wind, Rosser crossed in a rowboat, probably not realizing how dangerous the river was. A few days before his arrival, a large rowboat had been ferrying a company of men from the 17th Infantry across the river. For years the army had refused to buy a new boat, and the rowboat was considered a "miserable old tub, worn out and unsafe." After most of the men had crossed to Fort Rice, rather than make two trips, the boat squeezed in 20 men for one final run. Halfway across the quarter-mile-wide Missouri, the overcrowded boat apparently hit a tree stump, began to swamp, and finally tipped over. As horrified onlookers at the fort watched, unable to help, the river's cold water and swift undercurrents quickly drowned every man, despite the fact that many were believed to be strong swimmers.[5]

At Fort Rice, Rosser met Colonel David S. Stanley of the 22nd Infantry, who was in charge of field preparations and also commanded the Middle District of Hancock's Department of Dakota from Fort Sully (present-day Pierre, South Dakota). On September 1 Stanley, angry that the steamer *Silver Lakes* had not arrived to carry his soldiers to Fort Rice, had chartered the *Far West* from his old friend the legendary Missouri River steamboat captain Grant Marsh and loaded four companies and their supplies, reaching Fort Rice on September 5. The next day more troops and 55 "civilian" wagons arrived on the *Peninah,* and the surveyors were spotted marching over a distant hill, east of the river. All the survey's elements had come together.[6]

On the morning of September 8 Rosser, disgusted at paying the *Peninah*'s captain an outrageous charge of $139, nevertheless had him take his surveyors across the river to Fort Rice. Later he met with Stanley, who gave him bad news: reports had arrived of Indians who were burning the grass west of Fort Rice. Stanley made the army's grain supplies available and sold him two wagons, but Rosser still had to leave behind clothing and equipment. In the evening Stanley, Rosser, and Rice's commandant, Col. Thomas Leonadis Crittenden, had a private dinner. One member of the escort was conspicuously absent: its commanding officer, Maj. Joseph Nelson Garland Whistler.[7]

With Indian fighting expected, the composition and the preparedness of the army's escort were critical for the surveyors' safety, but its leadership was not imposing. Whistler, 49, the first cousin of artist James McNeill Whistler, was in West Point's class of 1846 with Thomas "Stonewall" Jackson, George McClellan, and A. P. Hill but graduated 47th of 59. In Mexico he served with distinction, but his career soon faltered. In Texas when the Civil War began, he was captured then exchanged and held administrative positions; when he finally saw combat in 1864, he was wounded at Petersburg, Virginia. Although breveted a brigadier general, he had few connections and was sent to Dakota in 1866. Philippe Régis de Trobriand wrote in his diary that Whistler was a decisive, "fine man"; but with the cost of educating children in the East, "[his] family is in poverty, a poverty in which not even appearances can be kept up." He correctly predicted that, while Whistler wanted an eastern assignment, "he probably will not get . . . [it, for] the old soldier has spent his life on the plains, far from the political world and sources of favor, and can not exert enough influence." By 1871 Whistler was drinking heavily and had apparently burnt out; his leadership in the weeks ahead was questionable on all but one occasion.[8]

A key officer in the escort was the quartermaster, Capt. Henry Inman, 34. He was the son of a gifted but penniless artist of the same name, but his mother was a

New York Dutch Ryker, from the family that owned Rikers Island. Inman enlisted as a private and rose rapidly during the war, afterward joining the quartermasters—the wrong place for an irresponsible person. In 1870 he was court-martialed for selling two army horses and pocketing the money; the charges appeared true, but the popular Inman was acquitted. In early 1871, however, an angry Gen. John Pope took the unusual step of reversing the court's findings. Inman appealed and was as popular as ever—"a great favorite with the civilians," one paper commented—but he served with a cloud over his head.[9]

No diary from any survey is more detailed than that of Capt. Javan Bradley Irvine. Irvine, 40, from New York, moved to St. Paul in 1855 and became a building contractor. When the war began, he joined the red-shirted 1st Minnesota Volunteers and, when passed over as an officer, simply stayed with them. At Bull Run, in the battle's smoke and confusion, Col. Bartley Barry Boone's similarly red-shirted 2nd Mississippi and the Minnesotians became entangled. Boone walked over to Irvine, who had only a bayonet, and was starting to give orders when Irvine asked if he was a "secessionist." Confused, Boone answered "yes," and Irvine took him prisoner, the highest-ranking Confederate captured that day. For his Gilbert and Sullivan–like heroism, Irvine was made a lieutenant in the regular army and spent the war as a quartermaster. After the war, Irvine remained in the army. Stationed at Fort Sully under Stanley, he and his wife, a woman of deep faith, became close to Stanley and his equally devout wife.[10]

Another diarist was Lt. Lafayette E. Campbell, 27, the personable, good-looking (despite having been shot in the mouth during the war) officer responsible for the escort's two Gatling guns. While most of Campbell's early entries reflect his pining for a "Miss Mary," once the expedition began, his diary offers a substantive account of daily activities.[11]

One of the army's scouts was Isaiah Dorman, a tall African American man about 40, who later died with Custer. Irvine called Dorman "the best [scout] in the country, honest and reliable . . . [He] was with Gen. Sully through this country during his campaign in 1864 and [186]5 against the Sioux." Dorman was likely an escaped Texas slave who had made his way to Dakota. He made friends easily, both white and Sioux. In 1865 he married a Hunkpapa, briefly lived with the tribe, and perhaps became friendly with Sitting Bull. Five years later, badly wounded, Dorman would be captured and mercilessly put to death by Hunkpapa women who knew him, but in 1871 he owned a "wood yard" where he sold cut wood to passing steamers.[12]

The lead scout was Basil Clement, 47, of French, Spanish, and Indian blood. Raised in St. Louis, he joined the American Fur Company at 16, worked for Jim Bridger, and was associated with army operations throughout the 1850s and 1860s. Like Dorman, he owned a wood yard and did government work when possible.

Stanley wrote Hancock: "I think that the half breed, Clement, understands the country at the head of the Heart River." Clement knew the area that the survey would follow but was of limited assistance to Rosser, never really understanding railroad requirements. He was not about to get the survey lost, but he was also unable to find an optimal route from the Missouri to the Yellowstone (which Rosser succeeding in doing in 1873).[13]

Seven infantry companies escorted the surveyors. While Whistler's report never states the exact numbers, the total likely stood at some 375 officers and men and about 550 including all others. Stanley's 22nd Regiment supplied Companies A, C, H, and I and two Gatling guns. The group also included companies D and H from the 17th Infantry, Company B of the 20th Infantry, and 26 Indian scouts, 2 surgeons, and the army scouts as well as beef-herders (including Whistler's nephew), Rosser's surveyors, and a few others. Supplies were carried in 114 wagons. The army issued each teamster a breech-loading rifle and 100 rounds, adding to the firepower. For fresh meat, a herd of a few hundred beef followed the formation.[14]

The logistical requirements for the planned 60 days included food and water kegs, tents, blankets, clothing (including cold-weather buffalo coats), ammunition, extra shoes, tools (axes, picks, scythes, spades, and so forth), officers' belongings (including large tents, cots, and portable writing desks and chairs), portable blacksmith materials, and grain for some 650 horses and mules. Inman assumed seven pounds per day per animal and thus needed at least 275,000 pounds of oats and barley for two months in the field. In all, over a ton of grain per wagon had to be packed, every ounce sent up the Missouri by steamer.[15]

Waiting for the surveyors, the soldiers went through final drills, tested weapons and equipment, wrote letters, and readied themselves for inevitable inspections. Most anticipated combat. Campbell wrote: "Close to the post, I am out with my mules and horses and in the afternoon try my [Gatling] guns. Find they work very fine, and I am confident that I can work them very effectively against any living thing." Fortunately he never had the opportunity; in 1872 a Gatling proved incapable of traversing fast enough to hit Indians galloping full speed over broken ground. But Irvine was pessimistic: "Our greatest difficulty will be to protect our [wagon] train and animals. I am of the opinion we will meet with disaster in this regard. We certainly have not troops enough to guard our train and supplies."[16]

September 9, 1871, was surprisingly chilly, but by 9 A.M. everybody was ready to depart. As Fort Rice's band jauntily played the ubiquitous "The Girl I Left Behind Me" and (almost unknown today) "Sister to the Walking Bird," wives and remaining soldiers waved as the column departed. Half the Indian scouts led the column, followed by four infantry companies with a Gatling gun. Next came the wagons in four columns, each side flanked by an infantry company in skirmish formation. At the column's rear was a final company, the second Gatling gun, and the remaining scouts. The daily formation was similar, but the companies rotated; and when surveying began, one company always accompanied Rosser's men. "The precautions taken by the prudent commander of the escort to guard against surprise gave every assurance of perfect safety," Rosser graciously wrote in November, but the truth was the opposite.

Whistler apparently suffered from a hangover as the column left Fort Rice, perhaps explaining his absence from the Stanley-Rosser-Crittenden dinner the previous evening. Sutlers (men who ran the army's commissaries) had bribed him with liquor to let them come on the survey, but Stanley squelched the idea. Irvine wrote: "For two days after our arrival [Whistler] devoted himself exclusively to testing the five gallon demijohn of brandy sent him on the *Peninah* and got very much fatigued. Aside from him we have not a soaker in the command."

Three miles from the fort, the column ran into its first problem: a series of steep, rugged hills that made it necessary to double-team the wagons. Irvine wrote: "We were led out of our way by [Whistler,] who thought he was a better guide than the one we employ at $100 per month." The problem was symptomatic of Whistler's leadership: before their mid-October return he misdirected the column at least nine times, causing a minimum of 55 extra miles marched and three lost days. Whether his problems were caused by alcohol, stubbornness, inability to use a compass, bad maps, or a combination of these factors, the end result was badly frayed nerves, especially for those on foot. Also slowing the column was an almost daily breakdown of one or two wagons. With the column moving only as fast as the slowest wagon, daily progress was sluggish even without natural obstacles. If a drawback of the September start was increasingly shorter and cooler days, however, the daily march was nevertheless aided by drier ground and lower streams.

On September 10, with Rosser scouting ahead, Whistler failed to meet them at their planned location. Rosser bitterly noted: "We lay out [for the night] on the prairie without food, forage, or blankets." Irvine wrote that Whistler, who was responsible for the surveyors' safety, was apprehensive that Rosser was not in camp but did nothing to find them. With no signs of Sioux, all personnel began relaxing as they passed through plains with good water, lush grass (the buffalo that formerly had eaten the grass had all but vanished), and numerous antelope. Irvine noted: "[Whistler] not with column while marching, but off hunting and cavorting over the country . . . [He] gives no attention to the order of march but lets everybody look out for himself." That night he wrote his wife: "No one has any confidence in . . . [Whistler] and he has failed to exhibit any good sense or judgment so far in his conduct of affairs."

Whistler was not the only one confused; problems were developing for Dorman, who incorrectly thought that they had reached the 180-mile-long Heart River.

When it was discovered that Rosser had begun surveying the wrong river, he and Whistler were embarrassed and angered. Whistler's report evasively states that they "encamped on a river emptying into the Missouri"; and Rosser's diary notes: "[The army's] having mistaken a small creek for the Heart River, I was dreadfully annoyed." Apparently Dorman stopped the column on what is now called the Little Heart River. In hindsight, Dorman was too eager to prove his worth, the shrewd Clement held back, and the army's incorrect maps added to the confusion.[17]

All larger army expeditions, to say nothing of formal explorations, carried area maps produced by the Corps of Engineers. The post–Civil War northwestern maps traced back at least to Lewis and Clark, and the army had undertaken extensive studies of the Yellowstone basin in the two decades following the Mexican War. The Missouri basin was better known and had been thoroughly mapped earlier, but the area between the two rivers was either poorly mapped or—on the maps at least—*terra incognita*.

At least one army topographical engineer accompanied each Yellowstone Surveying Expedition (with the possible exception of the 1871 western survey). One of his tasks was to update the existing maps. None of the maps, however, showed the suitability of the land for railroad construction. (There have been numerous books on this subject, but the classic remains William H. Goetzmann's *Army Exploration in the American West, 1803–1863* [1959]).

The real Heart River was reached on September 11. Irvine wrote that the surveyors' "little red flags are flying among the trees [and] foliage along the river bottom." Rosser called the shallow, 50- to 100-foot-wide Heart a "tortuous stream," full of twists, turns, and bends in a valley half to three-quarters of a mile wide, with cottonwood and maple as well as scrub oak, ash, and elm. The water was clear but slightly alkaline, and the land was "susceptible of cultivation." In his diary Rosser noted that the soldiers were already complaining about the marching and wanted a day's rest. "I will oppose it all I can," he wrote in disgust.[18]

Although there were no indications of hostile Indians, everybody remained apprehensive. Late that night, as the sentinels were being relieved, someone thought he saw something. The sentinels and their relief began firing at each other, which, Irvine noted, "created some excitement in camp." A surveyor later recalled that Rosser had told them that as civilians they were not to get involved in Indian fighting. But at the first shots, Rosser sprinted out of his tent "half dressed and rushed round so that if there was any fighting to get in, he would be in it." Dawn's early light revealed no signs of Indians and fortunately no injuries.[19]

September 12 was hot; and the climb out of the steep Heart Valley was difficult, even with every wagon double-teamed. Rosser followed the Heart upstream, temporarily taking him south. The wagons paralleled the surveyors, staying on the plateau's top, overlooking the river, but they still had to cross numerous small streams and often stalled. As was standard practice, Whistler established a "pioneer corps" of enlisted men who built roads and corduroyed soft ground with brush, tree limbs, and grass. "We go on and find some almost impassable [buffalo trails]," wrote Campbell, "[and] we cut down the banks and then get along the best that it is possible." The pioneers worked with picks, shovels, and axes while fighting off gnats and mosquitoes under a strong sun. On September 12 scouts killed some game; Campbell wrote with the satisfaction of an officer on a full stomach: "We had part of the elk for dinner . . . [and I] find it to be very fine."[20]

The next day the column marched seven miles in the wrong direction. Whistler blamed Dorman: "We found our guides had misled us, and we had to make a turn almost back on our track." Campbell calmly noted: "So we change directions and march down [and] back in the very way we came"; but Rosser was angry, writing that they "walk[ed] eight miles back to camp . . . [Whistler] is worthless." Irvine noted that Rosser had "repeatedly designated [Whistler] an 'old fool' and spirited him to warmer regions." There was also the disturbing news that two Sioux had spotted them, causing Irvine to worry about the surveyors: "I fear [they] proceed *too far in advance* [for us] to support them in case of attack" (Irvine's emphasis). Meanwhile Dorman, disgusted, quit and disappeared. Was Whistler's attitude racially motivated? Certainly both Stanley and Custer liked, respected, and later employed Dorman. Irvine was furious:

> The officers in charge gave but little attention to [Dorman's] counsel, made no provisions for his comfort and cast a great deal of opprobrium on him for calling Fawn Creek Heart River. They first disregarded him as a guide . . . and rendered him no assistance . . . keeping him near the train when he should have been permitted to ride ahead . . . he was made to shift for himself. All this disgusted him and he left.[21]

Rosser, who was likely out of shape from not being in the field for six years, nevertheless pushed himself hard; his exhaustion and hands-on leadership are seen in his September 15 diary: "Everything begins to drag and it requires almost super human efforts on my part to keep things going. I carried [stakes] all day afoot and am very tired." Nevertheless, he had enough energy to kill a deer brutally; "[T]he Indian scouts had wounded . . . [the deer] and I ran it down on horseback and shot it several times with my pistol then jumped off my horse and killed it with a stone." On September 16 Irvine wrote: "[W]e proceeded some distance without difficulty and approached the river. . . . Suddenly the train was halted and . . . [Whistler] commenced prancing around frantically declaring that the guide did not know the country and that he was going to be his own guide. He then turned the train . . . [and] led us at least six or seven miles out of our way."

The next day, as they saw prairie fires to the west, they came to 2,509-foot-high Heart Butte (13 miles south of present-day Glen Ullin), the area's dominant landmark. Campbell climbed it and found "the top to be of stone and full of wolves." Whistler's report makes the fascinating comment: "Timber was very scarce and . . . [beavers] had used stone instead." The column would now stay on the Heart until it ended in numerous, almost dry stream beds over 80 miles to the west. Reacting to the rumors that the Indians had started the fires, Rosser wrote: "If that is true they intend to give up the country themselves and will not be there to fight us."

Rosser wrote in his journal on September 18: "I have just made a proposition to . . . [Whistler] asking for his [Indian scouts] that I may establish his line of march for him so as to suit the work of my party of engineers." Rosser's request is indicative of a weak relationship. In 1872, while he and Stanley had little in common, their relationship was courteous, and Stanley invariably acquiesced to Rosser's engineering needs. But Rosser's comments paralleled Irvine's: "Officers are indignant at [Whistler's] want of judgment and lack of administration . . . [including] his weak and churlish direction." Intriguingly, Irvine had been avoiding Rosser, possibly reflecting an ambivalence that many officers felt toward the ex-Confederate. That night Irvine wrote: "[I] introduced myself to Chief Engineer Rosser." In the weeks to come, Irvine's diary reveals that he and Rosser were spending more time together. If Irvine was half as sarcastic and irreverent in person as he was in his diary, Rosser would have found his company delightful.

The column marched 18 miles on September 18 and camped 8 miles south of present-day Richardton. The Heart was now so narrow that Irvine called it a creek. The next day Whistler gave the men a much-needed break; Irvine noted that "the vapor from our breath [is] distinguishable . . . [in] the cold morning air." Marching on a windswept prairie, versus in the Heart's valley, made each morning's chill more pronounced. Some enlisted men, not bothering to put out the fire with which they had boiled water to wash their clothes on their day off, started a grass fire that would have signaled their position to any Indians within 30 miles.

Despite seven pounds of grain per day, good grass, and firm ground, some of the horses and mules began to weaken and die. As the Heart narrowed, more lignite coal was seen, and the fields continued to increase in size. On September 21 Rosser and Inman, in front, apprehensively watched large fires in the west, which everyone assumed the Sioux had set. The next day the column followed a picturesque sheltered valley and crossed the Green River, which enters the Heart from the north (present-day Gladstone). For years, maps designated the area as "Whistler's Crossing"; and later Stanley and Custer camped there.

Prairie fires were moving east, but fortunately on the Heart's south side. Whistler's report for September 21 stated that after sunset the clouds of smoke were eerily lit by the burning grass, while the southwest "was one vast ocean of flame rolling on like some troubled sea." Given the country's dryness and the disappearance of buffalo, the grass was quite high, thus making a prairie fire far more frightening and dangerous than it had been a decade earlier.

September 22 proved horrific. The day began as the wagons moved west, north of the Heart, while the fires were to the south of the river, moving east. In midmorning the wind suddenly shifted, blowing from the southwest. The fire jumped the Heart and headed directly at the column, driving crazed wildlife before it. Whistler now acted, instantly becoming the leader that few thought possible. "The commanding officer," wrote Irvine, "with a party of mounted escorts and officers rode in advance to reconnoiter . . . [and] shortly they were seen riding rapidly toward the train." Whistler, calculating the fire's path, raced back, barking out instructions for some men to start a backfire on a nearby hill. "We soon had a vast conflagration of our own burning the grass off . . . ," Irvine continued, "so that the [wagon] teams [could] move on to it as a harbor and [be] safe . . . [as the prairie became] one vast ocean of flame rolling on like some troubled sea [as] the flames would shoot toward the heavens in angry columns."

The train was following a path through a low ravine with thick, dry grass—no place to be in a fire. It instantly became a scene from a John Ford film: more than a hundred wagons bouncing forward as fast as possible through the backfire's smoldering grass and toward the comparative safety of the hill that Whistler had selected. Teamsters cursed, whipping frightened horses and mules, and the herders did their best to keep the cattle under control. Officers and noncommissioned officers screamed orders and encouragement to infantrymen, who double-timed as best they could while carrying 15-pound rifles, ammunition, canteens, and personal items.

Looking over their shoulders, soldiers surged forward, watching the fire that threatened to swallow them up. Men, wagons, horses, and cattle barely reached the hilltop sanctuary. For half an hour, Whistler's report states, "the wind [was] blowing fearfully carrying ashes, cinder, and smoke into our eyes, ears, and nostrils, but there was no help for it as the prairie was one black mass." Just one accident occurred. Rosser described what happened to one of his wagons as it came up a steep hill and then sharply turned: "[D]espite all our efforts . . . it passed over a bluff of 75 feet; wagon, horses, cargo, etc.—carrying off stumps, brush, saplings and making several revolutions landed at the bottom, without injuring the horses or load, but broke the pole."

Once the fire passed, Whistler realigned the column, zigzagging forward through previously burnt areas. That evening some cooks lost control of their fire, which destroyed an entire company's blankets and clothing and came close to stampeding the animals. Later, with everyone relaxing as best they could, they watched the fire slowly move east. Whistler's report stated that the fires made "a panorama for which many would pay to see. The fires would run up the valleys resembling long streets lit up with gas."

In Dakota the Whistler-Rosser column was unaware of newspaper stories concerning their progress and hostile Indians. The *Sioux City Daily Journal,* whose city would be hurt by the Northern Pacific's reaching the Missouri, gave the latest "news" on September 21:

> [A]ll the Indians at the several posts and reservations along the Upper Missouri have disappeared . . . everybody is satisfied that their object . . . [is to] drive back the surveyors. Many of the people in the upper river country who are familiar with the facts . . . are fearful for the safety of the expedition. The Indians, we are informed, will outnumber the expedition ten to one, and they are said to be very hostile.[22]

At the same time, Montana's Governor Benjamin Franklin Potts wrote Secretary of the Interior Delano a letter that received national attention: "I understand that he [Sitting Bull] has declared open hostility against the [Northern Pacific] engineers . . . I hope that there will be no collision between our troops and Sitting Bull's band, as that would irritate the whole Sioux nation." The situation was explosive; some papers even reported that the survey had already turned back. Reacting to "the reported retreat of a surveying party," an anonymous retired cavalry officer wrote the *New York Herald,* arguing for a preventive war. "I have no hesitation in saying that the only way to deal with Sitting Bull . . . ," the officer harrumphed from 2,000 miles away, "is to send a sufficient number of cavalrymen, under good officers . . . and let them deal with Mr. Sitting Bull as they deem fit."[23]

With no news from Whistler, the drumbeat of ominous stories increased around the country, as one paper passed on another's rumors. The *Minneapolis Tribune* said that the Sioux had set huge prairie fires, two thousand lodges had banded together to combat the surveyors, Sitting Bull was personally leading 500 Hunkpapas from Montana, the Indian scouts and their "half-breed interpreter" had fled in terror, and another several hundred Santee Sioux had headed west from Fort Totten, "ostensibly for a hunt but more probably for the war path."[24]

On September 23, Whistler, apparently exhausted by his demonstration of leadership, made camp at 2 P.M. and the next day camped near present-day Belfield. Rosser, impatient, wanted to see the badlands: "I now begin to feel we will not find that fearfully rough country I have been told of." He need not have worried.

As they marched west, the soil became sandy and then gave way to a red and at times white, bricklike clay. Coal became more frequent; describing a vein that had been ignited, Whistler said that it gave off "smoke like the bituminous coal of Indiana and Illinois." Signs of Sioux were numerous and fresh but indicated only 30 warriors. Like Rosser, the scouts were not worried; with the grass burned, large war parties could not feed their ponies and thus were no immediate threat. But Whistler's sense of direction worsened, possibly because of his drinking. Irvine noted with relish that a few hours after Whistler rode up and "affirmed that we were marching in the wrong direction," the surveyors came up from behind a hill and headed in the direction the column was initially going. Irvine wrote that when Whistler "came up to me, he endeavored to lie out of his blunder."[25]

On September 25 the column reached the badlands. "A grand spectacle of broken bluffs taking on the most fantastic forms imaginable," Irvine wrote. Whistler's report stated that "the sight was magnificent beyond anything we had yet seen or had hoped to see"; and Rosser wrote: "A grand sight!" As one drives west today on Interstate 94, the prairie appears to rise slightly then suddenly drops some 250 feet to reveal the beauty of the badlands' multicolored formations. The column was just a mile away, at Sully Springs, which offers another dramatic view, but with a more gradual descent toward the Little Missouri.

The following morning the column headed west and then south, coming to a stream that Rosser named Davis Creek, possibly for surveyor Henry Chandler Davis. Whistler noted the valley "so resembled a street that the men were calling the different points after large hotels . . . some vast dome-shaped hills rose out of the valley resembling Mosques, others looked like gasometers." On the valley floor the view was more "beautiful to look upon than when we were standing above it." Rosser wrote: "Upon rising to the top of this well defined ridge the . . . [badlands] come so suddenly into view as to shock the vision of the beholder by their strange and wild grandeur. The prairie is cut short off your feet, and dropped 200 feet below the plain on which you stand." He noted that taking Davis Creek to the Little Missouri was a "very easy descent" for constructing track; "The work of changing its channel is so light as to be of small consequence."[26]

With bluffs on all sides, a river in front, and new reports of Sioux, Irvine apprehensively wrote: "[I]f we pass through these dangerous locations unharmed it will be through . . . [luck], and not through any . . . preparations by [Whistler, who] . . . has given no thought to the subject but has directed his whole mind to antelope hunting." Any Sioux could easily have found them; they were like little boys, delighting themselves with bugle calls that "re-echoed from one [hill] to another until you could hear [them] half a dozen times, the effect of which was truly grand." The valley was filled with game; a hunter who was lost for two days told the story of killing two deer and then being besieged by wolves, who would not leave until he gave up his deer.[27]

At the base of Davis Creek is the 560-mile Little Missouri River, which drains parts of North and South Dakota, Wyoming, and Montana. Like the Bighorn, Powder, and Tongue, the Little Missouri has its headwaters in Wyoming and runs north; but instead of flowing into the Yellowstone, some 75 miles north of present-day Medora, it suddenly cuts east to the Missouri. The river's narrow drainage basin and the arid country through which it passes usually result in low water, but the region's frequent summer cloudbursts can cause violent flooding.

While the scout Basil Clement had chosen Davis Creek, the question was: would it lead to an exit on the western side of the Little Missouri suitable for rail-road construction? The Little Missouri's valley floor at this point was seldom a half mile wide, a series of loops, half-moon lakes, and steep banks. While the bottomland looked solid, it was little more than gravel that became quicksand when wet. The badlands were a maze, the river a trap, and getting in and out of the valley with the shortest mileage was a necessity. Clement had taken them to the best crossing he knew, but it was not a good *railroad* route. For Rosser to succeed, they needed to find a western exit; and no one knew if such a route out of the valley existed.

Then Rosser became lucky. What might have taken weeks to find was quickly discovered. Sully's trail crossed south of Medora; but just to its north, diagonally opposite, was a gap in the hills, Andrews Creek. The creek, with gentle curves, ran west out of the badlands. Better yet, it could easily be connected to Davis Creek with a four- or five-mile run. By finding Andrews Creek, where trains still run, Rosser's survey instantly became an enormous success. Everyone could breathe a huge sigh of relief; now the Northern Pacific had a functional route from Duluth to the Yellow-stone River. Although Rosser would spend several days finding the optimal branch of Andrews Creek, he had found a practical route through the badlands.

Meanwhile the weather was getting colder, freezing small pools of water on the morning of September 26. The next day an 80-man pioneer corps began cutting brush to build a corduroy bridge across the Little Missouri. The work was completed by mid-morning, with the wagons following Sully's 1864 trail and crossing what later became known as "Custer's Flats." (The site is now a golf course.)

After long weeks of marching, however, tempers were raw. On September 28 Irvine wrote that Whistler, feeling that the teamsters were too slow, stormed into their camp, screaming: "You drunk, lazy sons of bitches, why haven't you got these teams harnessed?" A teamster who was watching accidentally stepped into a smoldering campfire and yelped in pain. Another teamster, named Arbuckle, laughingly cursed him in a stage whisper. Whistler, thinking the comment was directed at him, yelled:

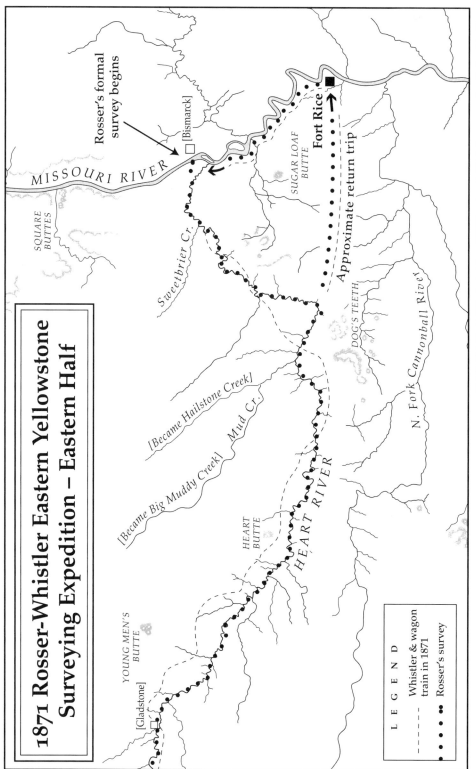

1871 Rosser-Whistler Eastern Yellowstone Surveying Expedition – Eastern Half

[Gladstone]

YOUNG MEN'S BUTTE

HEART BUTTE

HEART RIVER

[Became Big Muddy Creek]

[Became Hailstone Creek]

Mud Cr.

SQUARE BUTTES

MISSOURI RIVER

Sweetbrier Cr.

Rosser's formal survey begins

[Bismarck]

SUGAR LOAF BUTTE

Fort Rice

Approximate return trip

DOG'S TEETH

N. Fork Cannonball River

L E G E N D

Whistler & wagon train in 1871

Rosser's survey

Map by Vicki Trego Hill adapted from 1875 Department of Dakota map, courtesy National Archives

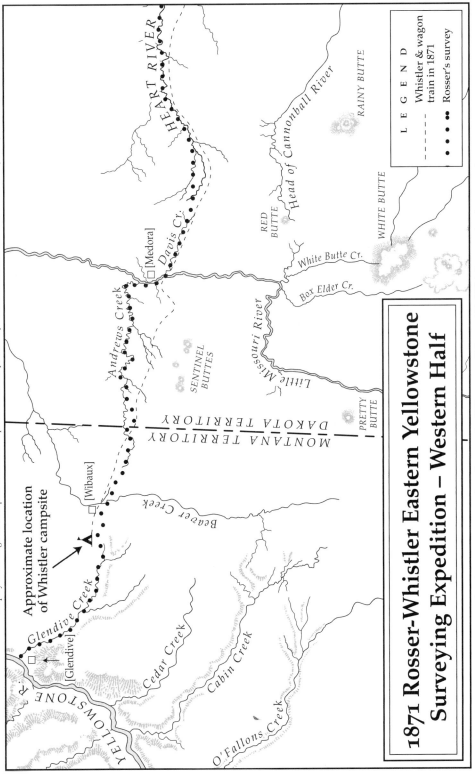

Map by Vicki Trego Hill adapted from 1875 Dept. of Dakota map, courtesy National Archives, and 1876 U.S. War Dept. map, courtesy Denver Public Library.

YELLOWSTONE R.

[Glendive]

Glendive Creek

Approximate location
of Whistler campsite

[Wibaux]

Beaver Creek

Cedar Creek

Cabin Creek

O'Fallons Creek

MONTANA TERRITORY

DAKOTA TERRITORY

PRETTY
BUTTE

Andrews Creek

SENTINEL
BUTTES

Little Missouri River

Box Elder Cr.

White Butte Cr.

RED
BUTTE

Head of Cannonball River

WHITE BUTTE

RAINY BUTTE

[Medora]

Davis Cr.

HEART RIVER

L E G E N D

Whistler & wagon
train in 1871

Rosser's survey

1871 Rosser-Whistler Eastern Yellowstone
Surveying Expedition – Western Half

From Whistler's campsite Rosser and 200-man escort continued on to the Yellowstone River while Whistler remained at campsite.

"You shout at me, will you!"; grabbing Arbuckle, he said, "You come with me!" But Arbuckle pushed Whistler away, saying: "No, I won't come with you, and you can't take me!" Whistler said that he had someone who would, called a guard, and arrested Arbuckle. There is no further mention of the incident, so Arbuckle's arrest must have been brief.[28]

The day was made worse by a consistently dusty wind. Whistler again got the column lost, refusing Rosser's suggestion to change direction. Still angry after his altercation with the teamster, Whistler turned down Inman's afternoon request to stop when they passed a pond with woods but later chose a barren campsite with sulphur-laced water. By now Rosser was suffering so severely from piles (hemorrhoids) and a fever that he had to ride in a spring wagon that doubled as an ambulance. The month ended with the column in Montana, about ten miles west and slightly south of present-day Wibaux. They crossed the fertile but narrow Beaver Creek valley and, after a slight rise, entered the Yellowstone basin. Irvine noted that, the day before, "the C.O. managed to lead us eight miles north out of the direct line, and we were compelled to turn and come back again. . . . Yet at the same time, he had his compass before him and was endeavoring to make a [reading]."[29]

West of Beaver Creek the country became barren, and the only water found was invariably laced with soda and sulphur. Irvine wrote that "the animals are almost famished"; five of Rosser's horses became useless, and one had to be shot. Irvine thought that the lack of good water was causing discipline to crumble; Whistler no longer sent out Indian scouts, and the wagon train became "strung out and scattered." Morale slightly improved when two buffalo were shot; Campbell wrote in his diary that he killed one with his revolver.

With Rosser sick, the men and animals exhausted, the water and grass poor, Whistler stayed in camp on October 1 but sent the Indian scouts ahead to pick a route to the Yellowstone. They returned that evening and reported no signs of Sioux. Whistler assembled a column of some 235 men: three companies (including Irvine's), a Gatling gun, scouts, surveyors, 17 lightly loaded wagons, and the ambulance for Rosser. The infantry was led by the able Capt. John C. Bates, the son of Lincoln's attorney general. Why Whistler declined to continue is not known. The river was the column's goal, and Whistler was responsible for reaching it, but one suspects that he had stashed liquor away and was craving to drink. Irvine sarcastically wrote that "[his] brave heart failed him"; significantly, Whistler's report has no details concerning the final leg to the Yellowstone.[30]

The Bates-Rosser column marched west, soon reaching Glendive Creek or a slightly northern tributary, Hodges Creek. Rosser was too ill even to sit up: "[I] have been very sick of a violent inflammation and ulceration of the rectum." With Whistler absent, Irvine was in a fine mood and enthusiastically recorded the day's events, noting that "the valley we surveyed today is beautiful." Although the country was barren, the creek, fed by numerous springs, offered fresh water and frequent growths of cottonwood and box elder. Progress was only 13 miles, but Irvine was pleased, no doubt helped by the fact that they were marching gradually downhill.

On October 3, just before the Yellowstone, the column reached present-day Makoshika State Park. Campbell noted: "The bad lands are far more grand here than on the Little Missouri. One hill on our right looks like the ruins of an Abbey, while on our left the hills rise in majestic grandeur almost kissing the skies." For Irvine, it was a red-letter day: "REACH THE YELLOWSTONE, the battle is fought, the victory won" (Irvine's emphasis). On arriving at the river, which he thought beautiful, Irvine wrote: "[W]e found the largest prairie dog town I have yet to see, it is more than a mile long and of nearly equal width." He estimated the Yellowstone "about ¼ of a mile wide and about three feet deep, clear and cold, with an abundance of fish."

Upriver from Glendive, past the place where the Bighorn enters the Yellowstone, the river's beauty is not of the same intensity that one associates with Yellowstone Park. The Yellowstone winds its way for 200 miles through a valley 5 to 10 miles wide, surrounded on both sides by a landscape of parched buttes. Here it is closer to an Asian watercolor. Its beauty comes from subtle splashes of soft, white-green cottonwoods, other small trees, and shrubbery that parallel the river's sparkling dark blues, with occasional ripples of white. It was this unspoiled vista that so impressed the 1871 and later Yellowstone Surveying Expeditions.

As Rosser reached the Yellowstone and noted the time (12:15 P.M.), his surveyors showered him with congratulations. By mid-afternoon their work was completed; but Rosser, wanting some sketches, sent Meigs, Eastman, and two Indian scouts wading across the river for a better perspective. Sadly, neither the sketches of the two talented artists nor Meigs's letters have survived. Rosser calculated that from the Missouri to the Yellowstone was 226.96 miles, a figure that he significantly lowered by finding a shortcut in 1873. No one mentioned Indian burial scaffolds, but decades later Edward Jordan recalled "an enormous Sioux burying grounds . . . containing the corpses of dead braves wrapped in blankets and wampum." A number of soldiers and surveyors tore the scaffolds apart, looking for items that might be sold and personal souvenirs or simply for the hell of it. The extent of the damage is unknown, but large numbers of scaffolds still remained in 1873.

Whistler's first dispatch of September 14 arrived in St. Paul on October 4. The brief message was bland, stretched the truth ("The men are all well and in good spirits and growing fat [on game]"), and contained no bad news. The October 7 *Sioux City Daily Journal* reported that many Sioux were returning to their reservations, which "indicate[s] that they do not intend to co-operate with the hostile Indians in seeking to prevent the survey." The next day the *Journal* published a telegram stating that Whistler was returning. Despite difficulties, there was no really alarming news to report, and the story was buried next to a shoe-store advertisement. Soon the lack of problems coupled with Chicago's great fire (October 9) pushed the survey out of everyone's minds.[31]

With their goals met, Irvine wrote: "Such sights as we have seen one would hardly believe and today we rejoin the Army of the Glendive. . . . Took a last, long, lingering look at the beautiful Yellowstone and turned . . . homeward." Whistler's sarcastic "Army" comment referred to the wartime practice of naming Union armies after important rivers. It was 28 miles to Whistler's camp, and everyone arrived exhausted: the surveyors at 2 P.M., the last wagons three hours later. With Rosser feeling better, the next day the column marched to a Beaver Creek campsite and prepared for its return to Fort Rice. Irvine noted that he and Rosser discussed NP construction costs but, frustratingly for today's reader, gave no other details. His comments concerning Whistler were scathing:

> Here we rest today to enable the troop to wash their clothes and . . . reload or equalize the loads in the . . . [wagons]—nothing of the kind being done [when] we were absent at the Yellowstone. [He was] . . . too fully occupied hunting and playing poker to give attention for something so unimportant . . . as preparing the train and command for the return.[32]

Once the march began, the column made good progress: 59 total miles on October 6, 7, and 8. Rosser, now better, was again in the saddle. With an Indian attack unlikely, Irvine focused on the minutiae of the march: a wagon that broke down, the discovery of fossils, and his surprise and disappointment at not seeing buffalo or *some* Indians. Late that evening, however, ten hours of driving rain and sleet set in. The original plans had been to break camp at 8 A.M.; but as Irvine wrote on the night of October 9:

> [Whistler] got engaged in a game of poker and around 11 P.M. orders were given not to move until tomorrow morning; it cleared off around 11 A.M. and the wind soon died sufficient[ly] to enable the command to march had they been directed to do so . . . we could have made ten miles this afternoon and we would have been so much nearer home and the end of our trials under such an imbecile commander.

On October 10, with the ground covered by frost and the column again moving, Rosser and some Indian scouts discovered a grizzly bear. After chasing it two miles, they brought it to bay and "had a desperate fight [and] killed it at last." As Rosser chased his grizzly, Whistler was misdirecting the column again by refusing to take a shortcut that the guides told him Sully had taken in 1864. This time the column marched an extra ten miles. Some of the edge was taken off on October 11: Irvine wrote that everyone had a good laugh as a jackrabbit, chased by hunting dogs, fled under a long line of wagons, scaring one set of mules after another.

The weather became so cold that the soldiers unpacked their buffalo-hide over-coats. Campbell, riding ahead with Rosser, wrote, "I find him to be a very agreeable companion, a fine engineer and the stamp of the southern gentleman," but said nothing else. The day began with a snowstorm, then sleet, and finally rain, ending at noon. Whistler considerately let the men ride in the wagons but nevertheless selected a camp half a mile from the Heart River. "Chief Rosser," wrote Irvine (as always refusing to acknowledge Rosser's Confederate title "General"), "Capt. Inman, and [others] who were at the . . . [Heart] waiting for the train to come up were quite indignant at the C.O.'s capricious action."[33]

Bad weather or not, the column marched 70 miles in three days. When Heart Butte was sighted, everyone knew they were in the backstretch; but the mornings stayed cold. Irvine blamed Whistler for the death of two good horses "from over-work and irregularity of rations." With tempers short, and Fort Rice near, Rosser took his revenge on October 14. "The train went the wrong way and I turned it back, which threw the Command[er] into quite a rage." Rosser had done nothing less than countermand Whistler's military orders by force of personality. Whistler, returning from hunting, was humiliated; his officers had obeyed a civilian's orders! Worse yet, he could do nothing, as Rosser was not under his authority. Barely on speaking terms, the two decided to separate: the main column to Rice, Rosser and an escort to survey a bit more. Despite Rosser's correction, Whistler had added ten miles of marching, leaving Irvine livid: "[His] mismanagement or rather want of management . . . condemns him as a man and officer of no capacity, judgment, or common sense whatever."[34]

On the last evening together, October 14, they camped near the Heart River's "great bend." The next day Campbell wrote in his diary the only known statement about Irvine: "All are anxious to get into . . . [Fort Rice] and of course they march right along. Even Capt. Irvine pulls out at a fine gait." Campbell's comment indicates that caution needs be taken with Irvine's comments; he too had his enemies and might not have been such an exemplary officer as he pictured himself. Rosser, reflecting in his diary that night, commented, "Today is my 35th birthday and the eighth year of my marriage. Heaven help the future as the past."

On October 16, after 48 miles of hard marching and more argument over the correct route, Whistler reached Fort Rice; but he had neglected to send a messenger. He had not been expected for weeks, so Rice's garrison was stunned to see his column march in. Meanwhile Rosser cut northeast to the Missouri, just below Bismarck. On October 17, at 10:15 A.M., he told the surveyors that their work was over. At Fort Rice they were met by the fort's band. Rosser was too anxious to go home to bother with anything but the most perfunctory thanks. Irvine wrote: "The Engineers crossed the Missouri and went into camp on the other side: thus ended the far famed Yellowstone Expedition."[35]

News of the survey's safe return reached the country on October 25. But the facts were devoid of excitement: a dozen buffalo seen, no hostile Indians, and no casualties. Large lignite deposits were not the stuff of higher newspaper sales, and public interest evaporated. A story in the *Sioux City Journal* blamed many of the delays on faulty maps, reflecting an interview with either Whistler or an officer friendly to him. Rosser, however, still angry, told the *St. Paul Press* about Whistler's drinking. The paper wrote: "General Whistler himself is said to have exhibited some considerable scarcity of piety, especially when he had no water for drinking purposes, considering that his wants in this respect were limited." The story soon appeared, verbatim, in other papers. As a good NP employee, Rosser wrote a formal glowing letter thanking Whistler and adding the era's usual profuse embellishments. Likely more damaging to Whistler was Irvine's letter to his wife, expressing feelings that he must have known would be passed on to Stanley:

> [Whistler's] administration of military affairs [was] a decided humbug and farce. It is conceded by everyone that . . . if God had not been on our side and [if] there had been any Indians, we never would have survived. [His] whole mind was given to antelope hunting and poker . . . and when he did attempt to give directions and orders, it only created confusion and more marching. . . . Everybody is completely disgusted with his imbecility, incompetency, and mismanagement . . . [Rosser] gave him a letter thanking him for his *ability, energy*, and *courtesy* with which he had conducted the escort. Such is the manner in which West Point whitewashes its imbecile graduates. (Irvine's emphasis)[36]

While Whistler's ineptitude caused no long-term harm, after the survey Stanley gave him no meaningful assignments. Inman was cashiered from the army in 1872. While the Indians were blamed for the prairie fires, 1871 saw not just the great Chicago fire but also huge conflagrations across the northern plains and western Great Lakes that burned millions of acres, destroyed scores of communities, and killed over 2,000. Sitting Bull was fully aware of the Rosser-Whistler survey but chose not to confront it. In 1906 some surveyors expressed modest disappointment that they had not "smelled powder," but one gets the impression that they were pleased that they "saw no more of Indians than as if we had been on Broadway."[37]

For the Northern Pacific and Jay Cooke, Rosser's survey was an unqualified success. As in the case of its western counterpart, the nay-sayers had been completely wrong concerning hostile Sioux, and the NP had met its goals without a casualty. Much of the 1871 eastern survey's route was never built, but only because Rosser found a better route in 1873. Most importantly, a practical, cost-effective way through the badlands was discovered. Based on Rosser's success, Cooke and NP officers had every reason to look forward to 1872. What none of them realized was that Sitting Bull, uncertain regarding the purpose of the two surveys, had given them the benefit of the doubt. He would not make this mistake again.

CHAPTER 9

"The Fear of Red Skins"

On July 26, 1872, over 600 men and 100 wagons lined up on the plains outside of Fort Rice. An observer recalled a "line of loyal blue wind[ing] out among the hills," marching west. Women and children waved handkerchiefs, remaining soldiers cheered (many thankful for avoiding the work), bugles called, horses pranced, barking dogs raced alongside the column, flags snapped in the wind, and Rice's band played "The Girl I Left Behind Me." Each enlisted man had been issued three pairs of new shoes, a message not lost on anyone. As in 1871, the army's mission was to escort Northern Pacific surveyors into the Yellowstone Valley. This year a second survey, coming from Fort Ellis, would be met at the Powder River (see chapter 10).[1]

That same day the surveyors were ferried across the Missouri at Bismarck and marched west, escorted by an infantry company and Indian scouts. The two groups would complete the Yellowstone work begun in 1871, giving the railroad a continuous "line of survey" from Duluth to Puget Sound. If the surveyors looked forward to completing the work, many officers were apprehensive: they were about to cut across land that Sitting Bull had said not to cross.

Three months before, the *St. Paul Weekly Pioneer* ran a story reporting that Spotted Eagle, a Sans Arc Sioux and Sitting Bull emissary, had met with Col. David Stanley in early April, refused to accept government rations, and objected to the "building of the . . . [Northern Pacific] through his territory and said he would tear up the railroad and kill its builders." The *Pioneer* said that Spotted Eagle knew "the driving away of the buffalo was death, and he would fight knowing he was beaten. . . . Stanley believes . . . that it [will] be necessary to employ a large force of troops to guard the working force west of the Missouri." Stanley then wrote Rosser:

I want to come up and see you.... I had a long talk with Spotted Eagle ... [He said] he would destroy the road and attack any party that tried to build it.... I tried to make him understand the fatal consequences. He said he did not care, "it was life or death and he would fight it out." [T]here will be constant danger west of the ... [Missouri], and it should be impressed on all persons that eternal vigilance is the price for keeping their scalps.[2]

In June the *Army and Navy Journal* reported: "[T]here are now collected about 2,000 hostile Indians ... who have declared their intention to oppose [the NP] ... They have torn up the stakes planted by the [1871] surveying party ... [and] are well armed and equipped." Then the *New York Tribune* carried a War Department story that 700 lodges were camped on the Little Missouri near where the surveyors might cross. More accurate reports had Sitting Bull's followers gathering in the Yellowstone Valley to block either Stanley or the Fort Ellis survey.[3]

The military escort for the eastern survey was commanded by Stanley. Today Stanley is reduced to sound-bite proportions that emphasize his drinking and presume a lack of military skill, intelligence, and sensitivity. But, although he was born June 1, 1828, in a log cabin near Wooster, Ohio, he would have been more at home in the twentieth century. Stanley's early years were typical of the life of any frontier boy whose family cut down the forest and eked out a living from farming. When he was 12, his mother died; the father remarried. Introspective and moody, Stanley was apprenticed to a nearby Dr. Firestone. He clearly was not wanted by the new bride, his father, or both. Once with the doctor, however, he appears to have found a home and soon devoured all the doctor's books. Stanley was always torn between medicine and the military and eventually married the daughter of the well-known army physician Joseph Wright. Of medicine he later wrote: "The practice was very different then from now. The thermometer, the antiseptic and anaesthetic, the cocain [*sic*]—all have come into use since that time."[4]

In 1848 blind luck changed Stanley's life; the West Point appointee from his district was found "deficient," and a replacement had to be found. Firestone pushed for Stanley's appointment, but Stanley vacillated. He had begun to notice girls (although not vice versa), however, and felt that he would look good in a uniform. "I fear vanity had a share in my decision," he wrote. En route to West Point he met "a little, dapper, and rather dandified young man," Phil Sheridan, with whom he formed a special bond. Stanley graduated 9th of 43 in 1852 and was in the top 5 in chemistry, engineering, mineralogy, and geology; only mathematics (in which he was 16th) held him down. He was 8th in the field artillery course of George H. Thomas, whom he served under and whose innovative tactics he copied later. He loved West Point and gave its 1885 graduating address but a few years afterward wrote: "I regret today that I did not tie myself to scientific pursuits."[5]

Little tells more about Stanley than an 1858 incident in western Kansas, when Stanley and a friend chased a Comanche to a spring. The Indian, hiding in the water 20 feet from them, suddenly jumped up and fired three arrows at Stanley before he and his friend shot back. Stanley wrote: "I do not know whose [shot] killed the Indian. . . . When it is seen how close I was to . . . [him] it is strange that he could miss me. Of course the poor fellow was dreadfully excited and as one arrow followed another he took no aim . . . one arrow passing between my legs." Given the racial attitudes of the day, Stanley's sympathy for the "poor fellow" may be surprising. Nevertheless, Stanley reflected the anti-Semitism then prevalent and also owned slaves. While traveling up the Arkansas River just after the attack on Fort Sumter, Stanley met a Southern congressman he knew, who enthusiastically but casually told him to go to Little Rock, where he would be given a Confederate regiment. Why the congressman believed Stanley would support the South is not known (perhaps because Stanley owned slaves).[6]

Stanley was a brigadier general in the Union army by late 1861 and, after acquitting himself well at Iuka and Corinth, Mississippi (in the fall of 1862), was promoted to major general. By the late summer of 1863, however, he was emotionally exhausted and sick, suffering from acute dysentery. On September 15 he relinquished his command, five days before Chickamauga.[7]

Stanley's bravery was exhibited at Resaca, Georgia, on May 14, 1864, when his division (on the federal left) was pushed back in a massive attack by Confederate John B. Hood. The only things stopping Hood from rolling up the Union's left were six cannon. Stanley galloped over to assist. Facing 5,000 attackers, he knew he had no chance of survival if Hood's men reached his position. But his accurate fire broke up a first attack, and a second was thwarted when reinforcements arrived just before his position was overrun. Stanley's coolness and heroism resulted in his being given command of a corps in July.[8]

When Sherman began a sweep around Atlanta on September 1, Stanley was seemingly positioned to trap the Rebel army. But Stanley, who was tearing up rail lines, never arrived, and the encirclement failed. Was Stanley's delay caused by too literally following Sherman's orders to destroy the Confederate rail lines? While historian Albert Castel guardedly supports Stanley in *Decision in the West,* it is nevertheless clear that Sherman was not inaccurate in saying that Stanley lacked "dash." Stanley was clearly a superb defensive tactician, but he was cautious on the offensive. More importantly for Stanley's career, he and Sherman had an angry confrontation on the morning of September 2, and Sherman never forgave him for failing to trap Hood. The immediate upshot was that Stanley was excluded from the March to the Sea and pointedly placed under John M. Schofield, with whom he had been feuding.[9]

The fall of 1864 saw Schofield and Stanley transferred to south-central Tennessee. In mid-November Hood marched north with 40,000 men. Schofield's smaller army was scattered and included many regiments recently formed or taken from garrison duty. Schofield did not see the danger, and on November 29, at Spring Hill, the two sides unexpectedly met. Outnumbered, Stanley beat back Hood's best units with artillery and regiments with repeating rifles while clinging to the only escape route. Hood, exhausted, camped atop a low hill overlooking a dirt road (that separated the Union army from Nashville), which Hood thought he held. When the evening turned black, Stanley stealthily directed the escape of some 15,000 men, a thousand wagons, and the artillery safely past Hood's camp a few hundred yards away. The Union army retreated north and hurriedly built defensive positions around Franklin. Hood, furious about the escape, followed and attacked that afternoon (November 30) in a series of violent assaults that resulted in six Confederate generals and thousands of men dead. At the battle's height, the Rebels broke the federal center. In *Ordeal by Fire* (1935) Fletcher Pratt describes the counterattack:

> [Stanley] flung himself into the struggle around the road; the reserves followed him in. . . . There was a savage melee for a moment; Stanley's horse, shot dead, pitched him to the ground; he rose and led the line on foot; a bullet hit him [in the nape of the neck] . . . ; he slashed down the rebel who fired it with a stroke that split the man from head to navel, and then, as though by magic, the Confederates were out of the trench-line.[10]

If Stanley, who had almost bled to death, felt afterward that he was being conspired against, it was not without reason. His wound prevented him from writing a report, and official reports reduced his role as well as Schofield's blunders. Today some accounts of Spring Hill-Franklin make no mention of Stanley, why Schofield's army was almost trapped, or the implications of a Hood victory. Ironically, Stanley also saved Sherman's reputation—which Sherman fully understood. There had been considerable second-guessing when Sherman marched east that he had left the Ohio Valley exposed. In essence, Stanley's effort had prevented Hood from advancing north. Decades later Stanley gleefully quoted a comment that "Nashville, Louisville, Cincinnati and Chicago were defended at Spring Hill [and Franklin]."[11]

After the war, the United States turned its attention to Mexico's French-installed emperor. In the diplomatic maneuvering, 25,000 troops were sent to Texas under Sheridan. Intriguingly, he had his pick of officers (essentially an "all-star" team) and gave both Stanley and Custer divisional commands. The two were both stationed in Texas but probably did not meet. In the army downsizing that followed the war, Sherman gave Stanley a poor posting, sending him to Fort Sully, Dakota, in May 1867. Stanley remained there seven years, a painful assignment for a man intellectually dissatisfied with routine army life.[12]

Stanley began drinking and—putting further strain on his marriage—appears to have been a disinterested churchgoer, while his wife was devout. Stephen R. Riggs, describing his missionary work, noted, "We found also, good and true Christian friends in Captain Irvine and his wife, and in the noble Mrs. General Stanley," but pointedly omitted Stanley. In 1870 Edward Duffy stabbed Patrick Pender to death in a drunken brawl between the two enlisted men. Stanley brought Duffy to the funeral. Still seething, he grabbed Duffy and marched him to the open coffin: "Come here sir; put your hand on the dead man's heart and look into the face of the man you have murdered."[13]

Stanley was clueless about helping himself, noting with pride that war correspondents never stayed in his camp. He felt it was beneath him to flatter superiors, disliking those who did so. His reports were invariably labored, possibly reflecting an inner anger, for when writing about his Ohio youth and early career he had a graceful touch. Stanley had not a gregarious bone in his body, was devoid of humor, and was quick to take offense. He had few army friends, the exceptions also being army "outsiders." Yet Stanley could relax with civilians like the Jesuit Father Pierre-Jean de Smet and riverboat captains Joseph LaBarge and Grant Marsh, who named the *Josephine* after Stanley's oldest daughter. While Stanley and Sheridan were not close, Stanley's career was first saved and then advanced by Sheridan; nevertheless, Stanley was gratuitously nasty about Sheridan in his memoirs.

When all was said and done, however, Sheridan made a good call in 1872: the veteran Stanley was skilled, conservative, handled troops well under pressure, understood the Sioux, and was loyal to Sheridan—traits difficult to put together. Anybody who thinks that Stanley's assignment was easy should simply picture Custer commanding the same *infantry* in 1872.

The survey's escort consisted of 33 officers and 553 enlisted men, including a company with a twelve-pound Napoleon gun and a one-inch and two half-inch Gatling guns. Stanley's request for two cavalry companies was turned down. Almost half the men were from the 8th Infantry, the rest from the 17th and 22nd Regiments. J. P. Wright, Stanley's brother-in-law, was the chief medical officer. There were 5 Métis guides led by Basil Clement (again the chief scout) and Louis Agard and 13 Indian scouts, including Bloody Knife, who died with Custer. Rosser had been unhappy with Clement in 1871; through his friend George Brackett, he coaxed the legendary Pierre Bottineau out of retirement to be the Northern Pacific's guide, describing him as "an intelligent fellow [who] had lived a long time on the plains." How much friction, if any, Rosser created is unknown; but he would not have hired Bottineau if he had trusted Clement (and, to a lesser degree, Agard) to under-stand railroad requirements.[14]

Stanley hired "Lonesome" Charley Reynolds, who would die with Custer, as the expedition's hunter. The expedition also included over 100 teamsters, support personnel, the surveyors, staff, beef-herders, Sheridan's observer (Capt. Sanford C. Kellogg), two "English noblemen," servants for some officers (including Stanley)—altogether about 725 men. The exact number of wagons taken is not known, but it was over 100. Stanley indicated that the wagons pulled by the six-mule teams had an average weight of some 3,600 pounds. Two-horse teams pulled lighter wagons and ambulances, and most of these carried over a ton.[15]

Second in command was the survey's oldest officer, at 53, the corpulent, inef-fectual Lt. Col. Henry D. Wallen (West Point, '40). During the war, Wallen was kept as far away from fighting as possible, not because he was from Georgia but rather because of his lack of ability. Western historian Dan L. Thrapp writes of one postwar assignment that Wallen "was not very effective, and not greatly interested in the position or anything else." Except for presiding at the funeral of a teamster who died of disease, Wallen's efforts in 1872 were equally minimal.[16]

One might ask why Wallen, who was about to retire, was chosen. The reason probably went back to the fall of 1848, when Wallen was temporary quartermaster at Detroit's Fort Wayne. When the new quartermaster arrived with his wife, Wallen pulled some strings and got them sent, instead of himself, to Sackets Harbor on the St. Lawrence River. Thanks to Wallen, the couple circled the icy shores of Lakes Erie and Ontario to spend a long winter in cold stone barracks. In fact, the young officer Wallen had literally sent packing back in 1848 would later do quite well for himself in military and civic endeavors. Among the now middle-aged civilian's other qualities was a long memory. Thus, as 1872 began, from his residence at 1600 Pennsylvania Avenue in Washington, D.C., President Ulysses S. Grant took his sly revenge.[17]

Third in the command chain was a capable, short-tempered, popular Irish-born major, Robert E. A. Crofton. When the Civil War broke out, he was appointed from Delaware as a captain in the 16th U.S. Infantry and served with distinction in the Army of the Cumberland, where he probably met Stanley. But the real reason for his 1872 inclusion might be a bit more prosaic: although he had married into the DuPont family after the war, Crofton was, as his *New York Times* obituary indicates, an active ladies' man. In assembling the 1872 escort, Stanley all but emptied a number of posts. Many married men would have been nervous leaving their wives for months in close proximity to the handsome, rakish Crofton.[18]

Leading the Indian scouts, a difficult, thankless assignment, was the ferocious-looking Lt. Daniel Harmon Brush (West Point, '71), who had begun his army career by enlisting at 16 in 1864. He took after his father of the same name, a legendary figure who enlisted at 48 and ended the war a breveted brigadier-general. The energy and glare in his eyes can be seen in photographs today. Stanley's choice was wise, for Brush exemplified the energetic leadership characteristics that Stanley knew the scouts would respect.[19]

In 1871 the Northern Pacific surveyors had essentially headed due west to reach the Yellowstone River. A glance at a map showed that, instead of going via Glendive Creek, 40 to 50 miles might be saved by building west and south after Heart Butte and then to the Yellowstone and Powder Rivers. The route had not been explored, and thus the survey's secondary purpose (meeting the Fort Ellis survey came first) was to see if the extra track might be eliminated. Rosser was again chosen as the survey's chief and had most of the same enthusiastic team from 1871. However, he was saddled with Daniel C. Linsley, the chief engineer for Minnesota and Dakota. Why Linsley, 45, with a wife and two children in Vermont, was on the grueling survey and whether his participation was mandated or voluntary are unknown.[20]

Regardless of the reasons, the surveyors did not like Linsley. Meigs wrote: "Mr. L is a peculiar man. He is as kind as a razor. . . . Every word of a statement to him must be expressed in language which leaves no room for a possible double meaning . . . Woe unto the young man so unfortunate as to make a loose statement. . . . At times he is quite genial and a moment after as cold and hard as a glittering icicle." By July the surveyors were fed up, their anger fueled by numerous quarrels. Meigs wrote: "Mr. Linsley, [is] a talented man but a perfect specimen of the hard, cold, calculating Yankee . . . [but] we are hoping he will soon be shipped [out]." However, it did not happen quickly, and problems with Linsley continued until he left a month later.[21]

As the survey began, Rosser divided his personnel into two 15-man crews, directed by "Eck" Eckelson and W. E. Welch. Rosser had two assistants (Ned Jordan was one) and at least six support wagons. They reached Edwinton (a temporary tribute to former chief engineer Edwin Johnson, who had died on April 12, 1872), at Apple Creek's junction with the Missouri, on July 21. The community was rife with land speculators, including Rosser and Meigs, who had actively invested, albeit on a small scale, earlier in the year. The town had other temporary names until early 1873, when the Northern Pacific, in an effort to secure money and immigrants, chose the name "Bismarck." In turn, Otto von Bismarck wrote an effusive letter of thanks on heavy paper, stamped with colored ribbons and symbols but signifying nothing.[22]

Rosser's surveyors had arrived at the Missouri from eastern Dakota and Minnesota in the early spring, joined by some bachelor surveyors who wintered in walled tents at present-day Valley City, North Dakota. The time was used to complete the engineering for track and bridges to the Missouri and for their Yellowstone survey. On July 4 Gregory Smith, Milnor Roberts, Linsley, and numerous Northern

Pacific directors arrived in Fargo-Moorhead for the opening of the Red River bridge and the next day rode to the track's end at the Sheyenne River. Cooke should have been in attendance but was not; his presence clearly would have been welcomed.

Leaving Fargo, Rosser, Roberts, and Linsley rode in a light wagon to Eckelson's camp on the Missouri, reaching it on July 8 and staying there briefly before returning to Fargo. By July 22 Rosser was back at Fort Rice (taking the steamer that Smith had purchased for the NP). He was loaned 24 carbines for the survey's duration and had dinner with Rice's commandant, Col. Thomas L. Crittenden. Rosser then returned to Eckelson's camp at Bismarck, picking up his men, Linsley, and the supplies. Rather than have the surveyors go to Fort Rice, a company of soldiers had come upriver with Rosser and became their temporary escort. On July 26 everyone was ferried across the Missouri and marched west and slightly south, meeting Stanley the following day.

Stanley had taken Spotted Eagle's threats seriously. Once on the march he assigned an infantry company daily to be with the surveyors. The rest of the men were "pickets" or marched in formation around the wagons and beef herd. The half-inch Gatling guns were front and rear, the 12-pound Napoleon and the one-inch Gatling gun in the center. Each afternoon, after selecting a camp, Stanley put the wagons in a square, not a circle as is usually assumed. Cattle, horses, and mules grazed nearby until dusk then were driven inside, with the soldiers sleeping just outside the wagons as one company kept guard each evening. Given the summer's heat, reveille was sounded before sunrise. Decades later Jordan recalled: "Our commander, although we did not see an Indian for . . . [a month,] never relaxed his vigilance."[23]

The pressure on Stanley was unremitting: he alone was responsible for the safety of the column and the surveyors, who usually worked miles away. He knew that they might be surrounded by overwhelming numbers at any time, like Fetterman, as even his Indian scouts could not spot an ambush. Stanley likely anticipated the same Sioux ferocity as on the Bozeman Trail, where Crazy Horse, Gall, and Hump "invented tricks to taunt, infuriate, and then lure soldiers . . . into well laid traps." But Stanley had only infantry, and his few score horses quickly wore out. "Hostiles" frequently rode close by, taunting and challenging soldiers and surveyors, knowing that no reprisals were possible. Most officers knew of Xenophon's *Anabasis* and probably felt like the 10,000 Greeks who had to march through the Persian Empire toward the Black Sea, surrounded by native tribes who hated their presence. Major Crofton later wrote that "the fear of red skins [was] before your eyes all the time."[24]

The first two weeks were uneventful: the weather was generally fair and the ground dry—critical for a good day's march. But Linsley immediately proved to be a problem; Rosser's July 26 diary noted: "D.C.L. very troublesome about selecting roads and looking after latter details greatly to the annoyance of us all." Adding to Rosser's frustrations, as the surveyors waited for Stanley the next day, Rosser went out hunting alone and killed an antelope; but his horse ran away, and he had to walk back to camp. Rosser and many officers frequently hunted for pleasure, while Reynolds "went ahead with the Ree scouts, killed the game and marked the meat for each company, and left it where we could pick it up as we came along." The hunting was critical: as Stanley wrote, "The complaint of hunger was constant." The enlisted men's rations were low in quantity and quality, and their meat was mostly salted pork. In the hot, dry country the only available water was often highly alkaline: drinking too much to wash away the salt taste often resulted in dysentery or similar problems.[25]

The column reached Heart Butte on July 31 and followed the Heart River until Antelope Creek. In the first two weeks they marched some 180 miles. Two Indians, likely Hunkpapas, were seen on August 4 near present-day New England, North Dakota. The next day Rosser, some surveyors, and Indian scouts rode to the Little Missouri to select a route while Stanley encamped. Rosser was back on August 6; despite heavy rain, the column reached the Little Missouri about 20 miles above present-day Marmath on August 9. Many teamsters had hired on so that they could safely pan for gold. A surveyor noted: "[W]e had with our party many gold prospectors and hunters who took the trip with us to seek for gold. At nearly every creek we came to we would see them out with their pans washing the gravel for color."[26]

To everyone's fascination, "petrifications" began to be found. The Surveyors' Journal recorded: "The finest specimen is an immense fern tree, said by the [amateur] geologists of the party to be a species extinct before the creation of man." The rain-swollen Little Missouri kept everyone in camp on August 10, and they spotted three old bull buffalo, a remnant of the huge herds of a decade earlier. The following day Rosser began taking the surveyors' wagon across the river; but Linsley, nervous, insisted on ropes. Rosser, who had crossed a few rivers in his Confederate days, stormed off in disgust as Linsley began supervising. On August 13 a surveyor noted without comment: "Mr. Linsley had all the engineer corps out picking and shoveling." That same day Stanley's scouts reported seeing a score of hostile Indians.[27]

The column marched west on August 14 and crossed into the headwaters of Beaver Creek, a dozen miles north of present-day Baker, Montana. Here it entered a dramatically different, stark, sun-baked climate. Imagine a cloudless sky, 100-degree temperature, and marching across a treeless, rolling landscape. Soldiers in woolen pants, carrying at least 35 pounds of gear, walked gingerly to avoid the little cactus plants whose spines easily penetrated their shoes. Both the O'Fallon and Yellowstone Valleys were wildernesses by August, with feeder streams dry and the main streams having only a trickle of water. Over a month would be spent there.[28]

With Indian scare stories appearing in newspapers as in 1871, the Northern Pacific answered with a carefully orchestrated rebuttal. The *Red River Star* noted on July 27 that Rosser "informed us before starting that the fresh reports of anticipated trouble in the Yellowstone Valley with the Indians is [*sic*] a malicious invention without the least fabric of truth." Rosser was so convincing that the *Star* went on to say that "the trip is one of great interest and we doubt not [it] will be highly enjoyed by the participants." In early August a letter by Milnor Roberts appeared in leading papers, brushing off the possibility of Indian problems. "The newspaper stories about Indians and dangers from them to the railroad across Dakota, have no solid foundation in fact," Roberts said. Rather, the blame lay in "[f]rontier speculators . . . [who] will doubtless furnish the newspapers with prophesies of imminent 'Indian Wars.'"[29]

The first attack on Stanley came on August 16, led by Hunkpapa war chief Gall. Stanley recorded: "[B]efore reveille and just before daybreak, a party of probably 20 Indians rushed out of one of the clumps of wood, yelled, fired a volley into camp, three or four riding very close to our sentinels, and ran away just as fast as their ponies could go." Rosser wrote in "The Death of Adair": "[T]he wild 'hi-I, hi-I' of savage men in war paint and hideous disguises breaking in upon your slumber in the dead stillness of night, for a moment paralyses you, then braces every nerve in your body for defense." The raid came close to the surveyors, who grabbed their carbines and fired into the darkness. After daylight it was discovered that the surveyors had killed one mule and wounded five. Stanley was not amused. Each evening thereafter—Sioux or not—he confiscated their rifles, although, one can be certain, not Rosser's. The raid also ended straggling, as the scouts reported that no sooner had Stanley vacated the camp than the Hunkpapas rifled through it.[30]

Despite the attack, August 16 ended with a 14-mile march down O'Fallon Creek, totaling 45 miles in three days. They were just 10 miles from the Yellowstone and making good time, but Indian signal fires reminded them that they were being closely watched. The next day the surveyors were at the Yellowstone by ten, although the wagons did not reach the campsite until four. At one point, Stanley was told that a large Sioux force was advancing, and he corralled the wagons and sent out skirmish lines. Whatever the Indian intent, if any, the show of force and the sight of the unlimbered artillery were enough to drive them away.

(That same day, and of course unbeknown to Rosser, a personal tragedy was unfolding. Some 400 miles to the east, in the Northern Pacific's "city" of 15 tents in Fargo, close to the mosquito-infested Red River, a nightmare was beginning for Lizzy Rosser. In her August 17 diary entry she penned a brief line concerning their year-old son, John Pelham Rosser: "Poor little Pelham is not very well.")[31]

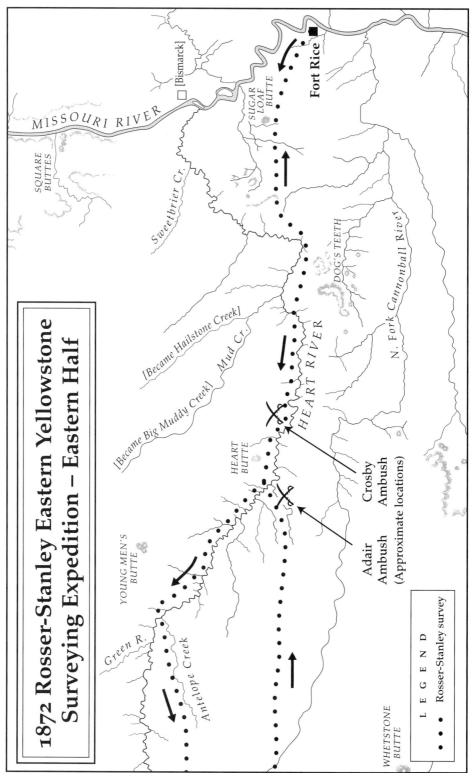

1872 Rosser-Stanley Eastern Yellowstone Surveying Expedition – Eastern Half

MISSOURI RIVER

[Bismarck]

SQUARE BUTTES

Sweetbrier Cr.

SUGAR LOAF BUTTE

Fort Rice

DOG'S TEETH

N. Fork Cannonball River

[Became Hailstone Creek]

Mud Cr.

HEART RIVER

[Became Big Muddy Creek]

HEART BUTTE

Crosby Ambush

Adair Ambush
(Approximate locations)

YOUNG MEN'S BUTTE

Green R.

Antelope Creek

WHETSTONE BUTTE

L E G E N D

••••• Rosser-Stanley survey

Map by Vicki Trego Hill adapted from 1875 Department of Dakota map, courtesy National Archives

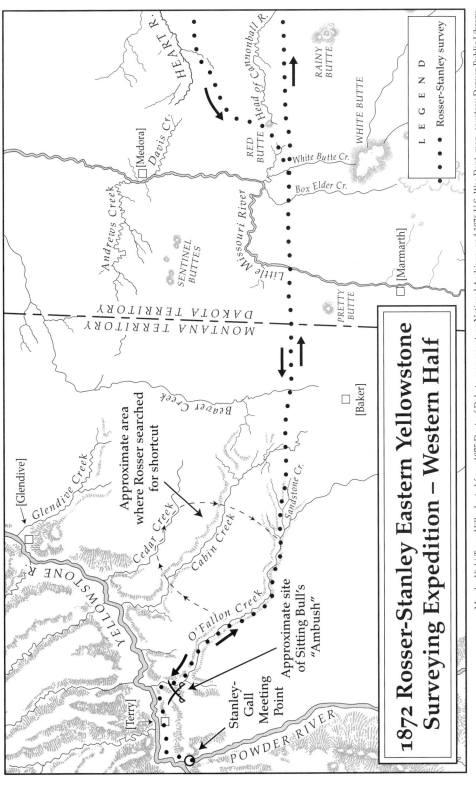

1872 Rosser-Stanley Eastern Yellowstone Surveying Expedition – Western Half

LEGEND
● ● ● ● Rosser-Stanley survey

HEART R.

Head of Cannonball R.

RED BUTTE

RAINY BUTTE

WHITE BUTTE

White Butte Cr.

Box Elder Cr.

[Medora]

Davis Cr.

Andrews Creek

SENTINEL BUTTES

Little Missouri River

MONTANA TERRITORY

DAKOTA TERRITORY

PRETTY BUTTE

[Marmarth]

[Baker]

Beaver Creek

Approximate area where Rosser searched for shortcut

[Glendive]

Glendive Creek

Cedar Creek

Cabin Creek

Sandstone Cr.

O'Fallon Creek

Approximate site of Sitting Bull's "Ambush"

Stanley-Gall Meeting Point

YELLOWSTONE R.

[Terry]

POWDER RIVER

Map by Vicki Trego Hill adapted from 1875 Dept. of Dakota map, courtesy National Archives, and 1876 U.S. War Dept. map, courtesy Denver Public Library.

By mid–morning on August 18 the surveyors and some 200 infantry, supported by their Napoleon gun, were finishing an easy march. After crossing a low ridge that separated O'Fallon Creek from the notoriously shallow Powder River, they emerged on the floodplain that formed the Powder's mouth. Stanley was about to meet the most charismatic of the younger generation of Hunkpapa war leaders, Pizi, who was born about 1840 and was known by the English translation of his name: Gall.[32]

If Pizi had been given a choice, he would be remembered as Man-Who-Goes-in-the-Middle, as in wading into the center of a fight. Gall was just under six feet tall, heavy boned, and with the ramrod-straight posture that epitomized Indian dignity. He was sensually handsome, a man with numerous wives and children. Even Elizabeth Custer's heart appears to have skipped a beat, for she wrote: "Painful as it is for me to look upon the pictured face of an Indian, I never in my life dreamed there could be in all the tribes so fine a specimen of a warrior as Gall." Like so many other Indian leaders, he was a good listener and outstanding orator.[33]

Gall's father died in his infancy. Little is known about his mother's death, but he appears to have been adopted by Sitting Bull's father. As a youth Gall had been stronger than others, once winning a wrestling match with the famed Roman Nose. Gall counted two coups at Rainy Buttes (southwest North Dakota) in 1859, a battle between Crows and Hunkpapas in which Sitting Bull's father was killed. Also growing up in his village was a boy with a Sioux father and an Arikara (Ree) mother, Bloody Knife, who developed a hatred for Gall. The feeling was apparently mutual, for in 1862 he killed, scalped, and then quartered two of Bloody Knife's Ree brothers or half-brothers.[34]

By the early 1860s Gall had a reputation for personal valor and leadership. He was probably at Big Mound and likely wounded at Killdeer Mountain. Other Hunkpapa warriors gradually joined his war parties and bold raids. In the winter of 1865–66 he and his followers brazenly pitched their tents in front of Fort Berthold. Coincidentally, Bloody Knife was there and that evening led an officer and three or four soldiers to Gall's tent. Gall, seeing them, dove to the ground, rolled on his back, grabbed the tent, and tried to propel himself out, but he was tackled, yanked back into the tent, and bayoneted while still on his back. When one trooper's bayonet became stuck in his body, the man put his foot on Gall's chest and yanked the bayonet out. Fearing that any noise would rouse Gall's friends, instead of shooting him they ran back to the fort, believing he was dead or dying.[35]

Somehow Gall recovered, becoming more of a hero, and later was active in Bozeman Trail fighting, including the Fetterman "massacre." His status rose higher when Sitting Bull selected him to sign the 1868 Fort Laramie Treaty. Gall signed, but his speech was hard-line: "Suppose the people living beyond the great sea should come and tell you that you must stop farming and kill your cattle, and take your houses and land, what would you do? Would you not fight?" He concluded: "We are blamed for many things. I have [even] been stabbed" and dramatically threw open his robe to reveal his scarred body. In 1872, acting in concert with Sitting Bull, Gall attempted to block Stanley as best he could.[36]

"In the angle between the Yellowstone and Powder," Rosser recalled, "we determined to mark the beginning of the survey back to the Missouri. A large cottonwood post was cut and planted well in the ground, and in pencil we wrote on its clear white peeled surface a note to our delayed friends whom we had expected to meet." The post was the survey's benchmark for their 1872 engineering. The Indians, Rosser wrote, "swam across the Powder River, danced around our cottonwood post, shot at our stakes, and yelled defiantly at us." Another source noted: "After the roadbed had been located and surveyed and stakes had been driven, the Indians would come at night and shoot arrows at the stakes." Why? One possibility is that the Indians' perception of how railroads worked was different from the view of a person raised in an industrial society. To them, each surveyor's stake (with its colored ribbon) was magic. They did not perceive stakes as markers but rather as an intrinsically evil force that attracted trains. The stakes were spirit-enemies, to be killed by their own weapons and incantations. Brave as they were, the Indians would not touch a stake (or the large cottonwood post) but instead shot them with arrows, leaving them where they fell.[37]

The measurements taken at the rivers' junction completed the engineering line from Duluth: Rosser's surveyors had accomplished their mission. Unlike 1871, steps had been taken to celebrate properly. The surveyors' diary noted that "some of the officers opened some wine, etc. and we were just beginning to enjoy ourselves . . ." Rosser wrote: "[W]e went down to the bank of the river, with Gen. Stanley and his staff to clear our throats of alkaline dust with a glass of champagne." After the bottles had been emptied, they were refilled with dispatches for St. Louis newspapers, recorked, and thrown in the Yellowstone. (Given the heat, strong sun, and ample champagne, it was probably just as well that the bottles never reached civilization.) Stanley noted: "[W]e fired our 12 lb. gun several times, hoping to apprize [sic] Col. Baker's command . . . of our whereabouts." There was no response, but decades later Jordan recalled that "the shell hovered above the mountain and then exploded. Before the echo died away the hilltops were alive with hostile Indians when we did not suppose [one] to be within 50 miles."[38]

Stanley wrote: "[T]he engineers were . . . [placing their post when] an alarm of Indians was given and 25 or 30 Indians were seen coming down the hills full speed after a foolish young . . . [surveyor] named Davis . . . who had strayed off to hunt agates." The surveyor was the popular Henry Chandler Davis, 23, described by Rosser as a "jolly and witty rodman"—the man who helped drive the first and last

Northern Pacific spike. For Davis, it was to be an eventful day. As he wrote in his diary that night:

> Wishing to . . . collect specimens I started out ahead of [the] escort with the intention of following the Yellowstone till I joined them. After . . . taking a good bath I heard the Napoleon gun firing some distance away. Seeing that I had missed my calculations . . . I made good time to the top of a butte nearby to ascertain the exact location of the firing and the cause. No sooner had I reached the top of the butte than I saw to my left—about 3 miles distant . . . something like 150 horsemen . . . and from every movement showing themselves to be Indians . . . Now it was that I had a lively conversation with myself regarding what direction it was best for me to take—whether toward camp . . . [with] a good chance of running into these redskins . . . [but] I concluded to make for the point where I heard the firing and took the precaution to get down under the river bank and follow it as far as possible. Up to that time I don't think that the Indians saw me but after I had walked about an hour I came upon . . . rapids where the cut bank of the river came close to the water's edge. At this point I was obliged to go onto the bluffs and take my chances of being seen . . . Trusting to luck . . . [and] wishing I was anywhere on earth but where [I] was I struck out over hills and through coulees—after making about half a mile I reached the trail made but a short distance before by the escort. I followed it a short distance when my worst fears seemed in fair way to be realized.
>
> My situation was this[:] I could see no trace of the . . . [surveyors] save the trail I was on and I was so near the place where the gun was fired that [I] concluded they had moved after firing the last shot. I didn't know but what they might have gone back and I [had] missed [them] . . . In the midst of my confusion I was startled by hearing the sound of running horses—the jingle of bells on their saddle and the well known war whoop . . .
>
> There I was, how far from help I knew not with a band of blood-thirsty Sioux coming down on me like the wind. The imperfect expression of language forbids me telling all I felt, I remember that [I] told myself my time had come and that to run was useless for I could see no place to run—I felt real deep-seated home sickness—a terrible longing to be anywhere else . . . I had with me an army rifle and 40 rounds of ammunition and coolly—lemme see—and coolly concluded to walk along at my regular gait and trust to luck as soon as they showed themselves. . . .
>
> All of this ran through my head in a tenth of the time I take to tell it . . . I now passed down through a deep canyon and as I rose on the further side my attention was attracted to the Scouts coming at a flying rate of speed to my rescue. . . . The scouts were coming at a fearful pace . . . [and] I knew I was safe when I saw the Redskins to the top of a hill 500 feet behind me and seeing the scouts turn and run without firing.[39]

The Surveyors' Journal noted that "we were just beginning to enjoy ourselves when the alarm of Indians was sounded . . . [W]e saw a footman [Davis] about a mile out on the plain and about a dozen Indians on the full run after him and our scouts also going on a full run to the rescue." Following his none-too-soon rescue, Davis became the subject of heavy-handed humor, but everybody's attention was quickly drawn to the beginning of skirmishing between the Ree scouts and Hunkpapas. Rosser described the clash with professional detachment:

> I had never seen an Indian battle and looked on with a most animated interest. The hostiles were numerous but [our] scouts were better armed and as they approached each other, in the most apparent headlong manner, I fully expected to see the hair and scalps fly, but they did not close. As soon as they got within range they scattered to the right and left, rode in circles and fired without effect. Finally the scouts formed a line as skirmishers and advanced on the hostiles in the order of cavalry and drove them back into the bluffs. But when the scouts attempted to follow . . . the hostiles dismounted and repulsed them. Then the hostiles would remount and ride in pursuit of the scouts, but when turned upon they would scamper back . . . A great deal of noise was made and many shots fired, but no scalps were lost or taken and no one was hurt.[40]

Davis picks up the story again:

> A medium sized fellow seemed to be riding down toward us—he dismounted when a thousand yards distant and taking off his blanket approached us on the opposite side of the river giving signs of peace. He called loudly for our interpreter Louis Agard who coming forward announced the infamous character of the Sioux renegade. [It was] *The Gaul* [sic] who wished to have a talk with Gen. Stanley. The general came forward and [had] a few minutes talk with the red rascal . . . [and it] developed that he wanted us to leave what he called his country. He did not ask for but discussed rations and at the same time declared that he'd give the white man no more peace . . . [Then] it became evident that an attempt was going to be made to assassinate the General. [Davis's emphasis][41]

Rosser's memory two decades later was remarkably similar to Davis's diary:

> We had moved but a short distance from the bank of Powder River when a tall Indian riding a sneaking, cowardly looking wolf of a pony appeared on the bank of the opposite bank of the river and asked for a conference. He was in full war regalia, wearing nothing but paint, breach cloth and an old, weather beaten stove pipe silk hat, which gave him a most grotesque appearance. This August prince of the plains was at once recognized as The Gaul, a minor chief of the Hunkpapa band of Sioux, distinguished for his cunning, cruelty, and

courage. After the usual complaint, that we had invaded his country . . . he majestically ordered us to be gone.[42]

Accounts vary as to whether Stanley met Gall in the middle of the river. Stanley wrote that after he and Gall laid down their arms, he invited Gall to meet him in the middle of the shallow, hundred-yard-wide Powder. Gall refused. In Rosser's account, with the guides "translating as quickly as the Indians spoke . . . [Gall] declaimed on the courage and heroism of his people whom the 'white dogs' had made poor [and] beating his breast said that his braves, their wives, and their children were starving [and] that their ribs were as bare as their '*travois poles.*'"[43]

According to Jordan, Gall said: "I shall never make peace while the land measurers stay; go home and make no marks upon the ground" and promised a battle. Stanley replied that he wanted peace and was willing to buy the land and give the Indians presents, but Gall cut him off, saying: "You lie." Meanwhile Gall's warriors were creeping forward. "As [Gall] could or would not stop them," Stanley wrote generously (considering that he was about to be shot at), "I thought it time to leave, and had hardly retired a few paces when the Indians fired on our party." Light skirmishing followed for half an hour from each side of the Powder. "We drove them out of the bushes," wrote Davis, who, like so many others, claimed to have hit an Indian. Lt. Philip H. Ray of the 8th Infantry, a good marksman who would play a major role in 1873, stated: "[I] plugged one of them who ventured rather a little too near." Davis, who had badly cut his feet on the rocks and cactus, concluded his diary: "[We] then turned homeward [to O'Fallon Creek]. I was obliged to ride in the ambulance. . . . Thus ends one of the most full days of my life."[44]

CHAPTER 10

The "Battle of Poker Flat"

The mission of the 1872 Western Yellowstone Surveying Expedition could not have been clearer: cross the river to the south side and survey downstream to the Powder River. There it would meet the Stanley-Rosser survey, thus completing the Northern Pacific's line of survey from Lake Superior to a Puget Sound. After meeting Stanley, the survey would cross the Yellowstone to the Musselshell River and follow it to its headwaters due north of Fort Ellis and east of Helena. The officer leading the escort was Maj. Eugene M. Baker. Sheridan considered Baker a good leader of men despite his known drinking, a man who knew the upper Yellowstone and appeared to be militarily competent.

Replacing Muhlenberg as the lead surveyor was John A. Haydon, often confused with Dr. Ferdinand V. Hayden of Yellowstone Park fame. Little is known about Haydon's Northern Pacific career because only one item written by him survives; how he came to the attention of Milnor Roberts and where he went afterward remain question marks. Like Rosser, Haydon had been a Confederate officer. Born near Morgantown, (West) Virginia, in about 1827, Haydon was trained as a civil engineer and in 1860 was living in Nashville. Commissioned in the engineers when the war began, Haydon was captured at Fort Henry (February 6, 1862). Prisoner-of-war records show he was five feet eight inches tall, with hazel eyes and "iron gray" hair. After a year at Johnson's Island prison in Sandusky Bay, a dozen miles from Cooke's Gibraltar, he was paroled, became a captain (May 1863), and spent the rest of the war in Tennessee, Georgia, and the Carolinas. The few references to him indicate a trusted officer who performed difficult assignments under intense pressure.[1]

One can assume that, like most Confederate engineers, Haydon had to make do with limited supplies and equipment; nevertheless, he built (or blew up) bridges, railroads, artillery positions, tunnels, and canals, sometimes under fire. Haydon was no quitter; he surrendered with Joe Johnson's army on April 26, 1865. Haydon's record testified to his technical competence (the quality of an engineer's work, after all, being subject to objective measurement), resourcefulness, and tenacity—all critical qualities for a Northern Pacific surveyor.

Haydon's wife stayed with Joseph W. Flenniken, the Helena paymaster and office manager, and his wife that summer. No other personal information is known. Whether Roberts even met Haydon is unknown but unlikely. At 45, however, unless he was a vigorous outdoorsman, Haydon was too old for his grueling, life-threatening assignment. Making matters worse, like Roberts the year before, Haydon likely had little in common with Baker. To some degree, his Confederate service probably was a detriment in working with Baker.[2]

Partially offsetting the paucity of Northern Pacific materials is the report of Sheridan's official observer, the engineer Maj. John W. Barlow, whose journal was printed by the Senate as *The Report of J. W. Barlow, Who Accompanied a Surveying Party of the Northern Pacific Railroad, in Relation to Indian Interference with That Road* in 1873. Barlow (West Point, '61) was intelligent, reliable, and no stranger to combat. In 1870 he was appointed Sheridan's chief engineer and in 1871 explored Yellowstone Park with Dr. Hayden. His report, rushed into print despite the loss of his backup data in the Chicago fire, was so brilliant in its descriptive powers that it played an important supportive role in the establishment of the national park.[3]

By late May Roberts had three surveys at work in Montana and Idaho, but the *Railroad Gazette* reported: "The Yellowstone parties have not been formed as yet." Even today, the size and the composition of Haydon's survey team are not known. Some Roberts to Flenniken letters survive, as well as letters from Flenniken to Cooke, who, interestingly, addresses him as "Jay." Roberts told Flenniken to procure supplies for three and a half months: "the proper number of wagons with good teams & good teamsters . . . [and] good horses and equipment" for Haydon and three others. Roberts, noting that it was Flenniken's second year and expecting higher-quality work, stated: "I must insist on having our topography in better shape than last year. . . . If you can, find some one [*sic*] who is good at sketching, try to get him into the party to take striking views: especially of all appearances of coal— including the region traversed last year."[4] This last sentence was another indication that the survey was expected to cross the river near Livingston.

Roberts told Flenniken that "General Sheridan has promised a good escort— perhaps five hundred" and thought that everyone should be at Ellis by July 20; if they arrived earlier they could double-check the measurements west of the Bozeman Pass. Roberts sent maps and profiles from 1871 and noted tongue in cheek: "Doubtless you will find Col. Baker disposed to aid us in so far as he may be authorized in the most friendly way as before." His June 5 letter said that he still had not hired a survey chief, because "I have not yet any definite authority to act in connection with escort matters." Whatever the cause (most likely Gregory Smith's infighting with Cooke), Roberts had to wait until mid-June, when many of the best candidates were probably gone. Even after Haydon was hired, Roberts was not entirely satisfied; he told Flenniken to "go over yourself to Fort Ellis and be there when they start and keep things in as good shape as possible."[5]

Haydon's escort included all of Fort Ellis's 2nd Cavalry (companies F, G, H, and L), 187 officers and men, and companies C, E, G, and I of the 7th Infantry, with 189 officers and men. Besides the military, surveyors, and teamsters, about 20 heavily armed prospectors and wolfers attached themselves to the column (including two running from the law). The survey had 65 military wagons and ambulances, three NP four-mule wagons, and a small herd of beef. Including headquarter personnel (such as Barlow), scouts, and beef-herders, the column was made up of just under 500 men and about 700 horses and mules. Not everyone was pleased: worried about Indian raids, the *Bozeman Avant Courier* pointed out that Fort Ellis now held fewer than 30 soldiers, many too sick to be considered able-bodied.[6]

On July 27 the wagon train, infantry, and surveyors crossed the Bozeman Pass. This unexplained late start gave Baker and Haydon only a limited margin of error to meet the Stanley-Rosser survey. Because of a late snow melt, unseasonable rain, and snow in Bozeman on July 1, the Yellowstone was high. As the main body camped just below Livingston on the north bank of the river, the group's leaders crossed at Mission Ferry to the Crow Agency. The water was flowing at eight miles an hour, and the crossing was made "with great difficulty." The plan had been to cross to the south bank here, but with the river so high they decided to wait until they were opposite present-day Big Timber. Had they known that the river would remain high, Baker, Barlow, and Haydon might have devised a ferry system; but instead this became the first example of a collective lack of imagination and energy.[7]

Despite all the preparations, Baker had not hired scouts. At the Crow Agency no Crows were interested, likely because of rumors of a Sioux-Cheyenne attack. Two mixed-blood scouts were hired, however: Joe Hozay and, as in 1871, Mitch Boyer. Boyer's mother was Santee, and his father French-Canadian. Boyer, a protégé of Jim Bridger, spoke English, Sioux, and Crow, knew the area well, and was one of the few scouts who understood the concept of measuring in miles.[8]

At first the survey members marched in hot weather through soft bottomland, then they skirted the rugged base of Sheep Mountain and camped near Hunter Hot Springs. As the weather grew warmer, progress slowed. On August 2 they made only seven miles: "roads" had to be built by pioneers working with picks and shovels in the 90-degree heat. About mid-afternoon of August 3, after four days of difficult marching, the column reached Big Timber Creek, which was "alive with trout, yielding a supply for the entire command."[9]

Opposite Big Timber, Barlow wrote with dismay that the Yellowstone "is 300 feet in width, some 12 or 15 feet deep, and booms along in great waves at the rate of seven or eight miles an hour." The column wanted to cross the Yellowstone, but it was impossible. Reluctantly, with steep hills and bluffs on their side of the river, they were "therefore compelled to work back among the hills." Much of the day's marching was in a zigzag pattern. August 4's camp was on Sweet Grass Creek, eight miles east of the previous evening's camp. "This stream derives its name," Barlow wrote, "from an aromatic grass which grows along its banks and which has an exceedingly agreeable and lasting perfume."

Crossing the creek typified the column's difficulties. The stream cut so steeply into the hill that the men had to lower each wagon by rope down the west side of the creek, push and pull the wagons across the 40-yard-wide rocky stream, and then pull each one up by rope on the far side. Under Boyer's direction, the column followed the Sweet Grass generally north and east, making eight miles a day, crossing and recrossing the creek and its tributaries until at midday on August 7 they reached the divide between the Yellowstone and Musselshell.

That afternoon violent thunderstorms followed by a long, soaking rain turned the ground to mud and held the column to just four miles on August 8. The next day the column reached dry "prairie country" and made 18 miles. On August 10 they continued east but suddenly stopped "after a march of only six miles," perhaps because of Baker's drinking, some 15 miles north of Young's Point on the Yellowstone. Game became frequent, including buffalo, and there were no signs of Indians. Marching southeast on August 11, they came "upon the brow of a high bluff" that led to the Yellowstone. After partially descending, they became stymied and had to U-turn and march 18 miles, likely camping on a tributary of Canyon Creek. Finally, on August 12, tired and frustrated, they reached Billing's Rimrock area after 10 miles. From here they went east, camping near Dover's Island on the Yellowstone.

At this point, from Fort Ellis to their camp on the Yellowstone via the river was some 155 miles. Had they been on the correct side of the river, and assuming a conservative 15 to 20 miles a day, they would have been between Rosebud Creek and the Tongue River, approximately 60 miles from the Powder River. Instead, 16 days after leaving Ellis, they were between 100 and 125 miles upriver from where they should have been, had not surveyed an inch, and were on the wrong side of the river. Despite this inauspicious start, things were soon to get worse.

The surveyors quickly found the last stake that Muhlenberg had placed nine months earlier, as they all enjoyed their new camp. "Where we struck the river one of these rich meadows was found," Barlow wrote, "fringed with cottonwood trees, willows, and rose bushes, whose rich green color was a gratifying contrast to the brown and withered vegetation . . . we had just left." There were no signs of Indians, but disquieting incidents indicated their presence. A Sioux horse wandered up to some hunters, three Indian dogs were spotted, some prospectors told of articles being stolen, and an army dog was mysteriously killed. Yet, if each incident caused concern, no one believed that a large force of Indians could be close. Lt. James H. Bradley of the 7th Infantry, although not on the survey, wrote a few years later that "the general feeling was of confidence and security [and] no especial precautions [were] taken" the evening of August 13.[10]

Sitting Bull was aware that both surveying expeditions were underway but knew little else. If historian Robert Utley's time frame is correct, by mid-July as many as 2,000 lodges of Lakotas (Hunkpapas, Blackfeet, Brulés, Minneconjous, Oglalas, and Sans Arcs), Cheyennes, Arapahos, and Kiowas gathered on the Powder River near the Montana-Wyoming border, a location equidistant from the two surveys. Sioux historian Doane Robinson has suggested that Red Cloud was sympathetic to Sitting Bull's call to block the Northern Pacific and lent tacit encouragement. As most sources indicate, a war party to attack the Crows was formed after a sun dance ceremony, with perhaps 1,000 warriors, including Crazy Horse. As they neared Crow land, scouts brought word that soldiers were on the north side of the Yellowstone, but this likely came as no surprise to Sitting Bull. While he did not know Baker's location—the column had been masked by its turn toward the Musselshell—Sitting Bull likely had a good feel for its size and composition. Similarly, he had Gall's information concerning Stanley's location as well as the composition of his troops: no cavalry but infantry supported by artillery.[11]

Nevertheless, Sitting Bull's decision to attack the Crow Agency, over 200 miles to the west, is militarily perplexing: it would have left his large camp weakened and exposed to two large army columns. It is even more surprising that on or about August 10, rather than riding west and slightly north in a relatively straight line toward the Crow Agency, Sitting Bull rode *northwest,* directly toward the Billings area. By taking this route, Sitting Bull's scouts soon found the Baker-Haydon campsite sometime on August 12.

Late on August 13 a war council began to discuss attacking the soldiers, stealing their horses, or swinging upriver against the Crows. Sitting Bull had been at nominal peace since the Fort Laramie Treaty, but he now found himself just miles from hundreds of horses and the surveyors. As the story has been told since 1872, Sitting Bull and the older Indian leaders were against attacking, but the younger warriors wanted to steal the horses. During the debate Sitting Bull, realizing that his younger followers had become agitated, actually established a picket line to keep them in check. Just after sunset, some Brulés slipped away. The trickle soon became a flood of young warriors. Most swam the Yellowstone with their horses, while others crossed

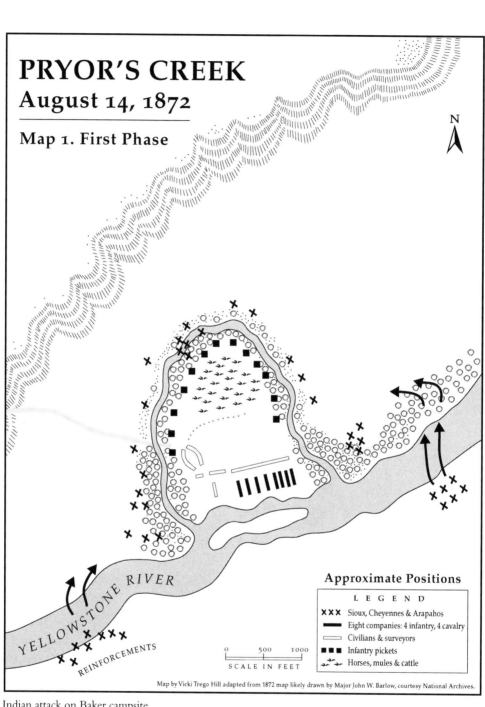

PRYOR'S CREEK
August 14, 1872

Map 1. First Phase

N

Approximate Positions

LEGEND

✕✕✕ Sioux, Cheyennes & Arapahos

▬▬ Eight companies: 4 infantry, 4 cavalry

▭ Civilians & surveyors

◼◼◼ Infantry pickets

🐾 Horses, mules & cattle

YELLOWSTONE RIVER

REINFORCEMENTS

0   500   1000
SCALE IN FEET

Map by Vicki Trego Hill adapted from 1872 map likely drawn by Major John W. Barlow, courtesy National Archives.

Indian attack on Baker campsite

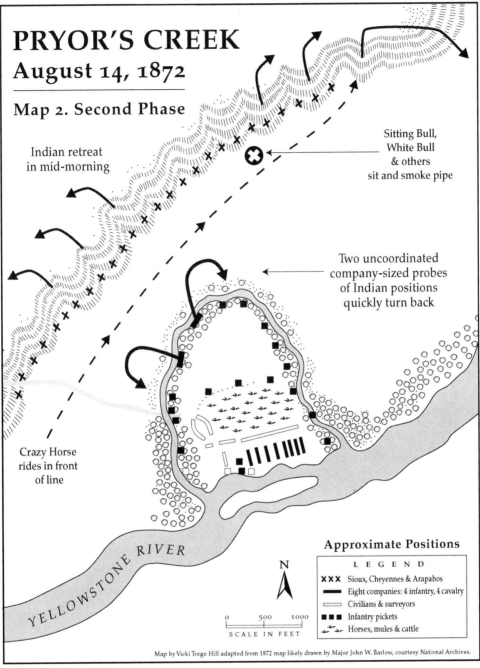

PRYOR'S CREEK
August 14, 1872

Map 2. Second Phase

Indian retreat
in mid-morning

Sitting Bull,
White Bull
& others
sit and smoke pipe

Two uncoordinated
company-sized probes
of Indian positions
quickly turn back

Crazy Horse
rides in front
of line

YELLOWSTONE RIVER

N

Approximate Positions

0   500   1000
SCALE IN FEET

L E G E N D

✕✕✕ Sioux, Cheyennes & Arapahos
▬▬▬ Eight companies: 4 infantry, 4 cavalry
▭▭▭ Civilians & surveyors
■ ■ ■ Infantry pickets
⟶ ⟶ Horses, mules & cattle

Map by Vicki Trego Hill adapted from 1872 map likely drawn by Major John W. Barlow, courtesy National Archives.

Both sides in defensive position

in "bullboats" (buffalo hides over a round wood frame that could be paddled short distances). Sitting Bull, about 38, found himself having to choose to lead, follow, or get out of the way. He chose to lead and crossed the Yellowstone by dawn.[12]

By 3 A.M. perhaps 300 warriors had crossed the Yellowstone. They were thoroughly disorganized and did not constitute a cohesive force as they inched forward in small groups toward the Baker-Haydon campsite. The Indians apparently had no plans other than to steal as many horses as possible, or anything else for that matter— or so they said later.

Most of the camp was asleep, including Baker, who, according to Bradley, "permitted himself to become unfitted for the proper performance of his duties by an overindulgence in strong drink." One large tent was lit, with a number of partially dressed officers playing poker, "from which circumstance," Bradley continued, "the fight is sometimes called the 'Battle of Poker Flat.'" On guard duty were 26 men commanded by Lt. William Logan, an inadequate force considering that men, horses, and wagons were scattered over "two or three score acres." The prospectors and wolfers had camped in the thick grass under some willows, a few hundred feet upriver, west of the camp. One of them, an outlaw, Jack Gorman, had his rifle propped against a tree but slept with his revolver on. Half awake in his blankets, stirred by some slight noise, he slowly opened his eyes and saw an Indian crawling up to steal his rifle. Gorman, barely moving, carefully found his revolver, brought it up slowly, and pulled the trigger.[13]

Within seconds thunderous gunfire broke out along the camp's perimeter. At first it was thought that the shots were fired by nervous sentries, and officers tried to calm sleepy troops who poured out of their tents. But when the shots were answered by war whoops, everyone realized that they were under attack. One can imagine the initial chaos and noise as soldiers and Indians, equally surprised, suddenly understood that a battle was underway. Fortunately for the military, the officers playing poker took charge. Capt. Charles C. Rawn, a 34-year-old veteran who commanded the four infantry companies, rushed into Baker's tent for orders but "found [Baker] in bed, stupefied with drink, skeptical as to the presence of an enemy, and inclined to treat the whole alarm as a groundless fright upon the guard. It was difficult to get any order from him." Without hesitating, Rawn acted on his own.[14]

In the course of exchanging shots in the dark, Logan and most of the guard gradually began herding the horses, mules, and cattle toward their camp. The teamsters and beef-herders dashed forward to assist, rounding up the animals, firing as they went. Rawn, "disgusted and angry" with Baker, "upon his own responsibility" drew up two infantry companies where the milling animals were pastured and advanced through and past them. Firing a number of volleys, he temporarily drove the Indians back. Except for 15 head of cattle and a few horses and mules, the animals were herded into the main camp, protected by a loose corral formed by some wagons. With the animals secured, Rawn's infantry slowly retreated toward the main camp.

On the left, where the shooting had begun, firing was heavy. The well-armed prospectors and wolfers gradually fell back, firing and buying time for the soldiers, hitting a few Indians and mortally wounding one. When some soldiers joined them, they surged forward, pushing the Indians back. The wounded Hunkpapa Plenty Lice, now lying within the army's line, was shot dead by some soldiers and his body dragged back into the main camp. Boyer was in this section of the field, along with Thomas Laforge and a man named Peeples. "As the conflict warmed up," Laforge recalled (admitting he hit nothing with his repeating rifle), "Peeples left us and ran for shelter behind a tree. On the way a Sioux bullet laid him out dead."[15]

The preliminary exchanges ended about 4 A.M., as both sides regrouped. Amazingly, some Indians were still hidden directly in front of the camp's center and had not given themselves away. As the sky lightened, a number of infantry cautiously extended their line forward. Moving through underbrush and trees, they made slow progress until they suddenly noticed a slight movement in front. Firing three volleys rapidly, they caught the Indians unprepared. The Indians quickly broke and, in running, were also subjected to gunfire from the right. Here they suffered their heaviest casualties of the day, likely a dozen killed or wounded.

With the day's first light, Baker's soldiers were inside or on the camp's perimeter. While Baker was awake, his orders were apparently incoherent. As more Indians crossed the Yellowstone, their number equaled Baker's. Many were within 200 yards of the camp, on top of a long 40- to 50-foot-high bluff, looking directly into the camp but angling away from it. From there they began a heavy fire that pinned down Baker's men but produced few casualties because of the large trees that blocked the Indians' line of fire. Twice infantry and cavalry companies advanced to force the Indians back; but, as Barlow pointedly wrote in low-key but militarily damning words, they were "not acting in concert" and failed.[16]

Sitting Bull arrived sometime after the fighting began and took a position on the bluff on the north side of the camp. There was little he could do: the "attack" had failed, and both sides were stalemated. The soldiers were safe but lacked the will and leadership to drive the Indians off the bluff. While they might have taken the bluff in a determined attack, they would have had to climb its steep, soft, and gravelly face on foot (horses could not have been ridden to the top but would have had to be led) in front of over 500 warriors, hundreds of whom had repeating rifles. Even if they had reached the top, they could not have trapped their more agile foe. But Sitting Bull had equally limited options: he was facing 500 well-armed men, positioned behind trees and wagons.

With daylight, as bullets whizzed back and forth, the Indians began taunting the soldiers and, knowing that Mitch Boyer was in the group, called on him to show himself. But their braggadocio turned to horror when four men threw Plenty Lice's body into a campfire and left it to smolder. Gradually the firing slackened as adrenalin wore off and the lack of sleep took its toll. Sitting Bull now hoped to boost his warriors' morale with a show of personal bravery. Taking a nephew (White Bull), another Sioux (Gets-the-Best-of-Them), and two Cheyennes, he slowly walked down from the bluff and sat down in plain sight with his companions a few hundred yards from most of the soldiers and his warriors. Taking out his pipe and tobacco, Sitting Bull started to smoke, passing the pipe around. The soldiers were at first amazed but then began firing. Bullets kicked up the dirt as each warrior took a few puffs. One bullet grazed the shoulder of a Cheyenne.

Another Sioux, Two Crow, to show his daring, galloped in front of the soldiers until his horse was hit. Two Crow's momentum caused him virtually to slide into the five seated Indians, who pretended to pay no attention. Long after, White Bull (who lived until 1947) recalled that except for Sitting Bull they were terrified: "Our hearts beat rapidly and we smoked as fast as we could." With the pipe smoked, and as bullets continued to whine past them, Sitting Bull methodically cleaned the pipe and then walked back to the top of the bluff.[17]

After Sitting Bull's return, Crazy Horse (to show *his* bravery) and White Bull mounted ponies and raced in front of the soldiers. When Crazy Horse's pony was shot, White Bull scooped him up and carried him to safety. Soon, however, the warriors began to disappear. About 8 A.M. Captain Ball was sent to scout their position and reported that the Indians were fleeing across the Yellowstone. Bradley noted that "Major Baker at one time ordered Captain Rawn to get two of his companies in readiness to move, announcing his determination to take them and two companies of his companies of 'busters'—as he was pleased to call the cavalry—and pursue; but he soon forgot all about it or changed his mind."[18]

Sitting Bull had been defeated. The battle of Pryor's Creek (a misnomer, as the creek is on the other side of the Yellowstone and five miles downstream) was over. By mid-morning the Indians were gone, taking their dead and wounded across the Yellowstone. Baker's losses were comparatively light. An infantry sergeant was killed when shot through the head, and three cavalrymen seriously wounded: one was shot through the eye, another through the bowels, and a third suffered a serious leg wound. Numerous soldiers sustained lesser wounds. Most sources indicate that a civilian was killed, likely Peeples. In the afternoon Haydon's men surveyed three miles, and the column marched four miles before camping.[19]

As evening fell, Baker, various officers, and Haydon were busy writing dispatches. A small party left that night, reaching Fort Ellis late on August 18 or the next morning (the route they took is unknown, although they likely followed the Yellowstone and would have had to cross it twice). Col. John Gibbon at Fort Ellis, who commanded Montana's posts and reported to Hancock, then telegraphed St. Paul on August 19. Gibbon relayed the news of the fight but also noted: "The information from reliable officers of both cavalry & infantry is of such a character regarding Maj. Baker's condition at the commencement of the attack (2:30 A.M.) and during its continuance for several hours that . . . [if could I communicate with them] I should place . . . [Rawn] in command & arrest Maj. Baker." He also noted that "once the troops commenced to act they repulsed the Indians with but little difficulty." Nowhere did Gibbon express concern about the survey's continuing its mission; in fact, he stated: "The warning it has had will be of advantage to it."[20]

Hancock in turn notified Sheridan, who telegraphed the War Office later that afternoon. While there was some confusion about the exact number of casualties, the order of magnitude was correct. Yet while casualties were low, the telegrams indicate a high level of apprehension felt by Baker's officers. Haydon was equally fearful, and his dispatch to Flenniken survives, albeit only in references to it and quotations from it by others. Haydon called the Indians "strong, persistent and brave" and also noted that the "infantry and cavalry fought well . . . [but the] military mistake [was] in not putting forth full energy at the right time . . . there appears [to be a] lack of command." Haydon felt more troops were needed and considered the "escort inadequate for [surveyor] duty." Interestingly, Haydon stated that "Baker has issued orders to send for 200 Crows to assist in defense, harass the enemy, and steal horses." Hancock, seeing Haydon's comments, was angered and commented in a telegram to Gregory Smith: "I think that the dispatches Haydon signed must be unreliable." Smith, who (whatever his flaws) understood the corridors of power, wired Hancock: "It is more than probable that Haydon telegraphed under some excitement. I have confidence in your superior judgment, and shall consider the party safe so long as you regard them so."[21]

When news of the fighting reached Helena on August 19, the *Daily Herald* carried a brief story. However, the next day two detailed stories appeared, with remarkably accurate accounts of the fighting but, surprisingly, with no mention of Sioux, identifying only Arapahos and Cheyennes. The August 22 *Bozeman Avant Courier,* still nervous about undermanned Fort Ellis, played up Indian strength ("the force engaged is but a small portion that can be brought . . . against the expedition") and predicted disaster ("they can certainly annihilate them by a concentration of forces"). The article also noted that "Capt. Ball says the fight was one of the most determined he ever witnessed with the Indians, who fought with dogged determination."[22]

For Baker and Haydon, there was soon more bad news: four "large" Indian trails and several large camping places were discovered, indicating far more "hostiles" than had been estimated. The officers were also disconcerted by the Indians' determination: for the first time in memory, they had not run away after the initial volleys. Morale was made worse, of course, by Baker's drinking. On August 17 they saw

Pompeys Pillar, but they felt that the river was still impossible to cross. The accuracy of this judgment cannot be assessed after 130 years. All that can be stated with certainty is that Yellowstone's fall per mile was just half that at Livingston, which reduced the current's speed; but after the Big Horn River entered it, the Yellowstone's volume increased by almost 50 percent. In short, they were at a good place to cross.[23]

It was obvious to everyone that, besides being on the wrong side of the Yellowstone, they were outnumbered, faced difficult terrain, and had suspect leadership. On August 15 the surveyors (guarded by a company of cavalry) moved ahead five miles, while Baker, finding a strong defensive position, moved his column half the distance. On all other surveys, the main column routinely moved parallel with the surveyors. Yet after August 15, except for a quarter-mile march to cross a creek, Baker refused to break camp. No reason was offered for his passive-aggressiveness, which must have frightened the surveyors and their escort. Each day they had to walk to where their surveying had ended the day before, moving farther and farther away from camp. Surveying progress became minimal, and everyone increasingly jittery. During the night of August 17–18 a guard fired at a log, mistaking it for an Indian; and another sentry, who had gone out in front of the pickets to relieve himself, was shot at when he returned.

On the morning of August 18 Haydon apprehensively questioned Baker about the escort's size. Baker replied that he and his officers unanimously felt that the surveyors were safe and could reach the Powder River. The next day, "intensely hot with a fierce wind blowing," the surveyors walked 6 miles to where they had stopped the day before, surveyed 2½ miles, and returned, a total of 17 miles. To add to the surveyors' and the escort's feeling of vulnerability, day after day they took the route marked by the stakes and had to go well beyond the sight and sound of the camp: in short, they could be ambushed at any time. On returning to camp, the exhausted 45-year-old Haydon gave up. He told Baker that he did not consider the escort sufficient for their safety and wished to return to Fort Ellis. Baker said he would grant his request but made him put it in writing. At that instant, Sitting Bull's defeat was reversed: because the column turned back, the battle suddenly became a strategic victory for him. For Jay Cooke and the Northern Pacific it was a stinging, unmitigated defeat, more damaging than any other event to date.[24]

Haydon had to know that his Northern Pacific employment and possibly his entire career was over, but he believed that his life and his surveyors' lives were in imminent danger. While Haydon attempted to avoid the blame, when it came to maneuvering, Baker easily countered his attempt to pin it on him. Barlow said: "The difficulties under which Colonel Haydon labors, the impossibility of continuing work without dividing his force, determined him last night to notify Baker that he could not operate any farther. . . . This is probably a just and wise determination, in consideration of all the circumstances in this case." Flenniken wrote to Roberts:

> From the day I left them until the day I received news of the attack, I lived in a semi-fever—a dread that they would be caught "napping"—and the commanding officer sleeping so sound[ly] that he would be hard to wake. I am afraid my forebodings were too true. . . . I feared that Baker would continue drinking—and he has. I felt so strongly that while at Ellis, I remarked to one of his friends with the hope it would be repeated to Baker, that if he, Baker, made a mistake—this time it would be fatal to him—cost him his commission. . . . Had I thought that speaking to Baker . . . would have done any good I would have done it, but I feared it might work in the opposite direction.[25]

In his last paragraph Flenniken mentioned Haydon's wife: "I have a pretty tough time in keeping Mrs. Haydon's spirits up to zero, but Tom [Roberts's son] and I manage between us to convince her that the Col. is safe."

Fifty years later McClernand agreed, as did Barlow: "[T]he survey was resumed but under conditions that did not inspire confidence . . . [T]he strength of our escort was not sufficient to guard the . . . [wagons], and at the same time give proper protection to the surveyors, who frequently were strung out two or three miles." Bradley, conversely, laid the blame on Haydon, who, "though wholly responsible for the failure to prosecute the survey to Powder River . . . afterwards endeavored to shirk it on the military . . . [as] the great majority of the officers were eager to go on, to save the command from any suspicion of having been frightened from its purpose by Indian hostility." The *Bozeman Avant Courier*, however, wrote:

> We are informed that after the fight at Pryor's Creek, the camp moved down the valley about four miles, when a council was held, and to Col. Hayden's [sic] inquiry as to whether the military had sufficient men to protect the surveyors at their work as well as the supply train, Col. Baker replied that he did not; therefore Col. Hayden concluded that it would not be practical to carry on operations . . . and turned back.[26]

After Haydon's capitulation, Baker prepared to break camp and march to the midpoint of the Musselshell River. On August 20 the column left the Yellowstone and headed northwest, gradually climbing uphill across barren land. Two days later, under a strong August sun with temperatures close to 100 degrees, they crested the plateau separating the Yellowstone and Musselshell. Finally, on August 23, they reached the Musselshell and its heavily wooded valley. Barlow described the river as 40 feet wide and just over a foot deep, with a strong current and clear, sweet water. The column, physically and emotionally exhausted, camped along the river 10 to 15 miles east of present-day Roundup, doing nothing for three days.

Work resumed on August 26 as the surveyors marched downstream to the place where the Musselshell turns north and from there began surveying back upstream. Interestingly, the farther west they went, the deeper the river became; the land closest to the bend was sandy, draining the river. Numerous fossils were found, some of which gave the river its name. Barlow, aware that Congress would publish his report, went out of his way to say something nice about Haydon ("Much skill is evidenced by [him] in the selection of the line"), who clearly was in deep trouble.[27]

On September 5 a rider who had left Bozeman on August 24 with mail and a second horse stumbled into camp. Near Pompey's Pillar, he said, he was attacked and chased dozens of miles, escaped by switching horses (but lost a horse and most of the mail), found the column's trail, and reached the Musselshell after four days without food. Barlow noted that the rider "observed . . . that the country across from the Yellowstone was literally covered with Indians." One of the few letters the rider had salvaged was a warrant for the arrest of two men, including Gorman, who had spotted the Indians first. Coincidentally, Gorman soon "escaped," making it safely, it was thought, to Fort Benton.[28]

The *New York Times* published a letter on September 30 titled "A Brush with Indians." The author was identified only as a "gentleman in the surveying party." The letter, dated September 1, was written near present-day Rygate. The surveyor wrote: "Since reaching Pryor's Fork, where 2,600 [Indians] jumped our camp, they have showed us every attention, sometimes serenading us two or three times a night." The writer then told an unlikely story of being chased and escaping from eight Sioux. But the letter's most damaging part was in its final paragraph: "You will hear before this reaches you that the Yellowstone expedition and Northern Pacific Railroad survey is a failure . . . [The Indians] demonstrated the fact that our force was totally inadequate to pass down the Yellowstone Valley."[29]

For the rest of September the column plodded west. Haydon's men listlessly surveyed the Musselshell, which, with its low gradient and obvious route, presented no difficulties. With the stress of failure taking its toll, many surveyors fell ill. McClernand, who had been taught surveying at West Point, noted that "a man who used a surveyor's compass fell ill and . . . the Chief Engineer asked me to replace him." Haydon also became ill, and McClernand claims to have replaced him: "with considerable misgivings as to my qualifications I . . . selected the line for the surveyors to follow for the next two or three days."[30]

Messengers from Helena now had no trouble reaching the column, and one brought the September 11 *Helena Daily Herald*. Seeing the paper, Haydon discovered to his horror that Baker had stabbed him in the back. An article quoted Sheridan as stating that Baker's return was caused by "the engineers deciding to go no further for fear of Indians." Haydon questioned Baker about the story on September 17, but Baker untruthfully denied writing the statement and refused to write a clarifying letter, an easy enough task. Instead, Haydon wrote the weakest of letters to the *Herald,* stating that Baker "assures me" that the September 11 statement was "utterly untrue." The letter was printed on September 25 but received little notice.[31]

On September 15 the column reached the south fork of the Musselshell, 20 miles west of present-day Harlowton and 4,700 feet above sea level. The weather had become colder, and they were moving at a snail's pace, taking two weeks to go under 100 miles. On September 22, a month after sighting the Musselshell in 100 degree heat, Barlow wrote: "Deep snow on the ground . . . The weather is bitterly cold." Despite more snow and freezing cold, on September 24 they marched six miles west, crossing the divide separating the Musselshell from the south-flowing Shields and from Sixteen Mile Creek, which runs to the Missouri. The next day the infantry marched north to Fort Shaw, the cavalry southwest to Fort Ellis. On September 26 Haydon left Baker, heading west to Helena with his surveyors and a small escort, thus ending the survey.[32]

The decision to abandon the Powder River rendezvous was instantly understood to mean that, at best, railroad construction would be delayed. The *Helena Daily Herald* editorialized on September 9 that "the return of Col. Baker's command without [meeting] . . . the eastern surveyors, with the certain hostility and trouble from Indians, show [*sic*] that greater obstacles are in the way than were anticipated." In another example of the bad luck that continued to plague Cooke and the Northern Pacific, Sheridan's staff in Chicago (he was traveling) failed to check a *Sioux City Daily Journal* story on Saturday, September 7, entitled "Indian Attack on Northern Pacific Surveying Party." On Monday the staff, clearly lethargic, released a statement based on the *Journal*'s erroneous facts, probably without checking with Sheridan, clearly without reviewing their own records, and definitely without getting Washington War Department approval. The staff's announcement, which was telegraphed across the country, stated that Baker's losses were "over 40 dead and wounded" and that his column was "so badly crippled that he is obliged to return to Fort Ellis." The action of Sheridan's office is thoroughly baffling, because three weeks earlier he had telegraphed the War Department with accurate numbers.[33]

The next day the War Department, furious over the story's implications during what was thought to be a close presidential election, released a "clarification": "Colonel Baker . . . was obliged to come back on account of the surveying engineers' . . . fear of Indians, and therefore the expedition is a failure." It made no attempt to correct the erroneous casualty figures but simply shifted the blame. Intriguingly, the independent *Army and Navy Journal* noted: "[The Indians] report that Baker is so badly crippled that he is obliged to return to Fort Ellis without having accomplished the object of his expedition." In short, the Indians knew that Baker and Stanley were supposed to meet and that they had prevented it. There was no way, of course, for Cooke to respond.[34]

The *Army and Navy Journal's* article can be read to support the belief that Sitting Bull was not primarily interested in stealing horses but rather attacked Baker to prevent him from completing his mission. Certainly Indians were not above telling white people what they wanted to hear and would cause them the least trouble. Sitting Bull had to continue buying rifles and ammunition as well as to receive rations. By saying that they found themselves near Baker on their way to attack the Crows and spontaneously decided to steal his horses, they might dispel some bureaucratic anger and confirm the white concept that "savages" were unable to plan ahead or control their base emotions—ideas, of course, that closely fit army and Washington racial stereotyping.

Later the *Helena Daily Herald* reported: "Indians who were in the attacking party said they were never so badly scared in their lives"—a surprising reaction to what was supposed to have been an impulsive raid. Is it possible to believe that, faced with a railroad through the heart of their last hunting ground, Sitting Bull and his followers did not *attempt* to formulate a plan to block it? In fact, Sitting Bull positioned himself equidistant from Baker and Stanley, where he could rapidly strike at either or both. Was the presence of Arapahos and Cheyennes from Nebraska and Colorado coincidental? Does not the knowledge, early in the battle, of scout Mitch Boyer's presence speak of excellent *previous* intelligence by Sitting Bull's forces? Is there any reason to believe that Sitting Bull and the other Indians leaders could not weigh Stanley and Baker's respective abilities, factoring in the strength of the deliberate Stanley—with his feared artillery—versus the brutal, alcoholic Baker, whom they hated?[35]

Numerous comments concerning the Indians' exceptional determination do not square with horse stealing. The fact that the attack was botched, like so many other Indian attacks over hundreds of years of white-Indian conflict, did not make it any less deliberate. Although this factor is never mentioned, the Baker-Haydon column was fortunate for the all wrong reasons, in its inability to cross the Yellowstone. What if the crossing had been made? The answer is that Sitting Bull could have had far more time to coordinate an attack with more warriors. In such an action, the defensively sloppy Baker would likely have received far higher losses than at Pryor's Creek.

After Baker returned, he offered a second explanation for the column's turning back: the land parallel to the Yellowstone was impassable, and the survey would have been forced to turn back anyway. This issue was answered in 1873 when Stanley and Custer covered the same ground in just over two weeks. In fact, the

Baker-Haydon column surmounted far greater obstacles in the two weeks before they reached their Billings campsite.

Haydon clearly did not have Rosser's will or leadership, but he was hired as an engineer. Ultimately, the decision not to continue to the Powder River reflects on Baker. On the issue of whether Baker gave Haydon adequate support to continue surveying, the answer is no. At a critical juncture Baker did what Ball, Whistler, and Stanley never did: he refused to move his camp. With everyone uneasy if not frightened, and considering the debilitating weather, Baker's action of furnishing just one company (just over half the men Fetterman had) for escort duty shifted the pressure to Haydon, who quite understandably cracked.

Shortly after Baker's return (October 15), an angry Hancock placed him "in arrest." He remained in that status until January 11, 1873. By then Hancock had left Minnesota, having been promoted after Gen. George G. Meade's death. No charges were brought against Baker; but Alfred Terry, Hancock's successor, did not reinstate him. In January the *Helena Daily Herald* reported that Baker had been ordered to Omaha, noting: "[His] name is associated with the best memories and most effective achievements of our border defense." In Omaha Baker was detailed to purchase horses. Barlow's report was printed by the Senate Committee on Pacific Railroads on January 6, 1873. His description of the fighting praised both Rawn and Ball but did not mention Baker. By then, however, Haydon had disappeared, the Northern Pacific was out of cash, and Jay Cooke was unable to sell bonds.[36]

CHAPTER 11

"Falstaff's Ragamuffins"

As John Haydon's surveyors struggled to continue on August 18, 1872, 150 miles to the east Gall's warriors broke off their skirmish with Stanley at the Powder River. While Stanley had acquitted himself well, under the accumulated pressure, he now began drinking. Rosser noted the next day that "[Stanley] shows signs of going on a spree." For whatever reasons, both Rosser and Stanley's leadership seemed to falter after August 18. Having reached the Yellowstone, Rosser had as his next goal to find a cost-effective railroad shortcut in the arid, mazelike, low-lying badlands of eastern Montana. (Rosser, of course, was unaware that at Fargo his infant son Pelham had taken a turn for the worse. Lizzy Rosser's anguished August 19 diary entry read: "Mrs. J—'s child, Max[, also] taken sick. Oh God, spare my darling boy.")[1]

What triggered Stanley's drinking is unknown, but he probably was badly upset by not finding Baker. Stanley knew no later than midday on August 20 that Baker had turned back. How? There is no question that something that was called the "Indian grapevine" existed, analogous to the "jungle telegraph" of World War II. For example, as is well known, in 1876 friendly Indians at Fort Abraham Lincoln near Bismarck knew of Custer's defeat (but not the specifics) well before the *Far West* reached them with the news. Similarly, there was constant communication—if nothing else "trash talk" in today's idiom—between Stanley's Arikara scouts and Gall's Hunkpapas.[2]

Stanley had to feel that he was caught in a lose-lose situation, where he could be endlessly second-guessed. He could wait and hope that Baker would arrive; go back to Fort Rice and later find out that Baker had made it; or, without cavalry, risk his remaining horses and punch his way upstream to Baker, an almost suicidal option. Stanley and Rosser likely discussed the situation as the surveyors continued working between O'Fallon Creek and the Powder River. Sometime on August 20 the decision was made not to wait for Baker but to return to Fort Rice. The next day the column left the Yellowstone, camping a few miles up O'Fallon Creek. It was also clear that the Hunkpapas were being reinforced; they became more aggressive, nearly captured an Indian scout, killed a horse, and chased Eckelson.

Certainly Stanley was never questioned for his decision. Whether or not Stanley knew that the Baker Haydon column was on the north side of the Yellowstone and that it had turned back is unknown. However, it is very likely that Stanley was aware of at least one and perhaps both pieces of information before he gave up trying to meet Baker. In fact, given the Indians' consistent boasting, it appears his Métis guides knew that Sitting Bull was coming to support Gall. Stanley's actions the next few days were consistent with a man who feels lucky to be alive but is not entirely sure how long the statement will remain true. The problem he faced was that, given the mercurial nature of the Indian force and Baker's defeat, it was possible that he would soon be facing a force far larger than his own. Given that he could not mount more than a few dozen soldiers, his only option was to form a walking defensive pocket.

For Stanley, the O'Fallon Creek Valley—which he had to march through—was a potential death trap. On the half-mile-wide valley's sides was an eroded plateau that left a series of steep hills 100 to 150 feet above the meandering creek. The valley began at the Yellowstone's floodplain and ran southeast ten miles until widening just before present-day Mildred. Once they entered the valley, there was no way out. Stanley, likely thinking what he would have done had he been attacking, had to be apprehensive. It was a ten-mile gauntlet of infantry against mounted Indians, without the possibility of reinforcement. Baker could have survived a siege, because Governor Potts of Montana (a Civil War combat general) could have reached him in a week with a large, heavily armed force. But Stanley had stripped Dakota of troops, and Dakota's territorial population was mostly along the Iowa and Nebraska borders. In fact, Potts was closer.

(On August 20 Lizzy Rosser's world collapsed. She numbly wrote: "Today . . . tonight at 8 o'clock he passed away." The next day she wrote: "Anguish to bear it and say, 'Thy will be done.'" Strangely, the infant was buried in a garden in back of a hotel. Lizzy Rosser emerged from her ordeal shaken, with the bond between her and Tom Rosser weakened.)[3]

The Northern Pacific Journal's August 22 entry noted: "[Charley] Reynolds . . . drove [off] a dozen of them single handed. About 9 o'clock the Indians reappeared in force and the line party had to withdraw to the train while the skirmish line was thrown out to drive them back. . . . They numbered about 100 and have evidently been heavily reinforced." The reinforcements, led by Sitting Bull, included Hunkpapas, Minneconjous, and Santees, who had ridden over 150 miles. Stanley was now in the narrow part of the valley, where, as he correctly expected, he was soon attacked. Sitting Bull's force numbered no more than 200, however, most of whom had little ammunition. As the piecemeal attack unfolded, Stanley quickly adjusted his troops. Capt. Clarence E. Bennett of the 17th Infantry wrote:

> During the firing an Indian with a new black hat hollered to Louis [Agard and] . . . said he was Sitting Bull and would attend to us after awhile. He had not all his men there but would attend to this Command and give them all their bellies full before they got to [Fort] Rice. He said the Hunkpapas, Minneconjous, Oglalas, Brule, Blackfeet, Sans Arc, and other Sioux, Kiowas, Cheyennes, and Arapahoes were all going to join and fight the whites, and they would give us plenty of fight [for] when that railroad went through there would be no more Indian.[4]

Rosser's account includes one of the few times that a Gatling gun was used in the field during the Indian Wars:

> [T]he valley was narrow with a deep canyon ahead of us and Gen. Stanley determined to keep along with us, with his entire command until we reached the open prairie. It was well that he took this precaution, for just as the head of the column was entering the canyon, the Gaul, reinforced by Sitting Bull, opened a brisk fire on us. Fortunately, they were unable to restrain their warriors and they fired too soon, for their purposes. The wagon train was on open ground, and was at once parked, which was done by closing the intervals between wagons, till the wheels almost or quite touched, and all faced the center of a large circle making the wagons afford a protection to the animals . . . [A] line of skirmishers was deployed and pushed up into the hills for the purpose of clearing the canyon . . . all were engaged except a company of infantry and a Gatling gun, composing a rear guard, about 100 mounted Indians moved up the valley in our rear. The engineers were ordered to keep themselves inside the corral [as] the Indians came on at a gallup, and in the order of veterans. The Gatling gun was opened on them, and as soon as they came within the range of musketry, the infantry rear guard began firing. But on they came in perfect order.
>
> I felt sure that they would charge on the infantry and make an effort to reach and destroy our train. The Indians maintained order and came boldly and rapidly on. There was no hope to secure and reinforce in time to meet this charge. . . . I jumped off my horse, took a stand near the Gatling gun, and began using my rifle vigorously. Their painted features and fiendish yells were indeed appalling . . . [O]ur ranks began to waver and the officers had to threaten the men, to keep them in line and make them do their duty. The Indians came up within a hundred yards of us and a collision seemed inevitable, when suddenly, as one man, they broke by the flank and dashed

up a ravine, and out of sight into the hills! Oh, my! What relief! I believe if they had come on 25 feet further, that our infantry would have broken and run [back to] ... the wagons. I then realized the difference of an army fighting for patriotism and one fighting for a business rather than work for a living. A company of volunteers in the armies of '61 and '65 would have killed every Indian in that platoon under similar circumstances, and these escaped without leaving a single one of their miserable carcasses behind.[5]

About half of Sitting Bull's warriors ranged along the hilltops, but they hit nothing and retreated when Stanley sent skirmishers up the hills. Stanley sustained no casualties, while one Hunkpapa appears to have been killed and a few wounded. The attack was Sitting Bull's last effort. Archaeological evidence indicates that his warriors were low on ammunition, likely used up against Baker. The limited ammunition probably explains their small numbers and why Stanley had so little problem storming the strong site. Nevertheless, Sitting Bull felt he was victorious, because by late August both Baker and Stanley had left the Yellowstone. For another week Stanley's column would briefly see the warriors, but then they entirely disappeared.[6]

The September 12 fighting was described by Nibsey Swipes (the pseudonym of a noncommissioned officer) in the *Sioux City Daily Journal,* who stated that the Indians "made one or two feints, but not taking the troops unaware as was expected, they withdrew, neither side losing any men." Swipes continued that "these bands have dispersed and formed hunting parties, giving up all further intentions of opposing the survey." Describing the fighting, he wrote:

> [The attacks] they have made are not sufficient against the barking Gatlin [sic] guns and breech-loading rifles. . . . If Mr. Big Gaul ever again attacks any party crossing the plains, he will, in my opinion, first look sharply to see if they have got any Gatlins with them. . . . I'm certain that if Uncle Sam saw Big Gaul and company retreating to the cover of the bluffs from the shower of grape which these Gatlins sent whistling around his red skins, he would send all Indian agents home to await orders. . . . I rather think they have given it up and gone to hunt up their winter supply of beef.[7]

With Sitting Bull and Gall gone, soldiers and surveyors soon fell back into their normal routines. Rosser later wrote: "For days and weeks after we marched and worked and saw nothing more of the Indians, and the men naturally dropped back into their careless habits." He was delighted when his boss, Linsley, announced his intention to return to Fort Rice. But whatever his flaws, Linsley was an outstanding engineer, which Rosser was not. At one of their last meetings Linsley must have badly frightened Rosser, whose actions and diaries after Lindsay left indicate a man who has been told to find a short cut *or else.* One cannot help feeling a real sense of sadness for Rosser—the man who never surrendered and the quintessential nineteenth-century man of action—in his relationship with Linsley. Linsley was an intelligent but cold-hearted number-crunching bureaucrat who brought the war hero—who feared unemployment more than anything—to his knees with the threat of discharging him.[8]

On August 24 Stanley, again confident, sent 37 empty wagons back to Fort Rice with two infantry companies, Linsley, Davis (whose feet had not healed), and Sheridan's observer, Sanford Kellogg. The wagons left after dark, reaching the Missouri on September 3. On September 25 an Indian scout, Goose, arrived after a difficult four-day ride from Rice, carrying formal news of Baker's defeat. The NP Journal stated: "He brought word that Baker had had a fight with the Indians at Price's [sic] Creek on the 14th and had been badly whipped although he had succeeded in repulsing the Indians." Just getting word to Stanley was difficult; the message went from Baker to Fort Ellis to St. Paul to Chicago (Sheridan) and then back to St. Paul to Fort Rice and on to Stanley. Sheridan's message stated that Baker had been attacked "at the mouth of Price's River [sic] by a war party of four or five hundred Arapahos and Cheyennes. Indians were repulsed. Their losses not known. Our loss is considerable."[9]

Neither Rosser's diary nor Bill McKenzie, who kept the NP Journal, expressed surprise at Goose's news, another indication of the "Indian grapevine." McKenzie happily wrote that with Linsley gone he and Eckelson could move into Rosser's tent, with its superior sleeping facilities. Intriguingly, Rosser's August 26 diary noted: "No Indians seen today. We think they have gone off after Baker." By August 29 Rosser was between Sandstone (northwest of Baker) and Cabin Creeks looking for a shortcut. Two days later he was stymied: "I failed to find an escape and returned and requested [Stanley] to go down [Cabin Creek] to the Yellowstone. Yes, [but] with much difficulty." Stanley, highlighting the difference between Baker, Whistler, and himself, wrote: "I decided that the Expedition must not fail for want of trial, on account of the military."

Rosser was to remain in the area almost three weeks, fully disrupting Stanley's goal of being back at Fort Rice in late September. During this period the column was plagued by soaking rains and thunderstorms, a "violent hail storm," and temperatures ranging from severe heat to frosty mornings. Without much wood, the party used buffalo chips. Stanley noted: "The country . . . from the head waters of the Heart River to the Yellowstone retains traces of immense herds of buffalo, which seem . . .[to have] nearly all disappeared 8 or 12 years ago. Only a few buffalo were seen on the trip. . . . Why the buffalo should have all left, or why they should have ever ranged here, the country being so poor, I cannot conjecture."[10]

At Fort Sully, on September 10, Stanley's wife delivered a boy, who was to be named David Sloane Stanley. A week later Sheridan, who was inspecting his Dakota posts and checking on the Northern Pacific's progress, visited Fort Sully. Sheridan stopped by Stanley's home to pay his respects and see the baby. With Mrs. Stanley still in bed, the oldest daughter, 12-year-old Josephine, carried the infant out on a pillow to show him. Sheridan asked the infant's name. Josephine, likely nervous in the presence of such a famous person, blurted out: David *Sheridan* Stanley. The vain Sheridan had to be gratified by the family's wisdom and continued friendship, and thus little David was christened Sheridan, not Sloane. Considering Stanley's lack of political acumen, his daughter's jitters likely did as much for his career as he himself could have accomplished in a decade.[11]

Rosser became frantic and depressed trying to find a shortcut in eastern Montana: "party very tired but no one more than myself as my horse is broken down and to ride him is a great labor" (September 12). "If I fail there will be trouble somewhere" (September 17). The NP Journal did not hide the lack of progress: "line will probably have to be abandoned" (August 30), "got to abandon the line we have been running" (September 2), "poor luck with the line" (September 9), "it seems as if we were never to get out of this cursed creek" (September 13), "[Rosser] rode at least 60 miles but did not find any route" (September 15), "impossible to get a grade line over the summit unless the [expensive] tunnel plan is adopted" (September 16), and "started a new line" (September 18). The Cabin Creek to Cedar Creek line required a tunnel, and that same day (September 18) Rosser correctly predicted: "Don't think the company will ever build it, but will go back to the [1871] Glendive Creek route. Very, very tired."

Evenings soon became cold (there were snow squalls on September 19), adding another unpleasant element. Stanley wrote that the army tents were "very flimsy . . . The companies of the 17th Infantry and scouts had begun with worn tents, and by the march's end were almost without shelter." Nibsey Swipes complained about limited rations and marching on empty stomachs. But Stanley remained vigilant; Swipes wrote that they were up at 3 A.M. "so as to be ready to receive the Indians in case they attack us at daybreak." Swipes undoubtedly knew about Stanley's binges, but he remained complimentary:

> I will here state . . . that a better commander than General Stanley for an expedition like this, it is difficult to find. He is cool and collected when any danger threatens and is particularly attentive to the comfort of his men. . . . He is a good soldier and never puts his men to any unnecessary trouble . . . [and] knows and is up to all the tricks of the Indians. He can outflank them at any one of their dodges.[12]

As Swipes wrote (September 21), some 50 wagons with supplies (and whiskey), mail, and the recovered surveyor Henry Davis arrived from Fort Rice. Here Rosser heard the news of his son's death but was stoical, almost cold: "It is hard to give him up, but these griefs are inevitable, and we must be prepared to meet them." The next evening, suffering from a headache and sleeplessness, he wrote: "How I . . . [miss] my dear wife and crave so much to be with her. She misses our dear little Pelham more than I do." The exhausted column had met the supply train where it had crossed the Little Missouri River in August. Swipes wrote:

> I hope that General Stanley and Rosseau [sic] will be through in time for us to have Christmas dinner in winter quarters somewhere. . . . We are dirty and ragged; our old war hats . . . without rim or crown. We are almost shoeless, and, in fact, as bad as Falstaff's ragamuffins, who had but a shirt and a half in their whole battalion . . . Then again, . . . [the surveyors] make mistakes which they have to go back, sometimes twenty miles or more to rectify . . . accordingly we have to follow the[ir] leader, "Old Ross." General Stanley follows as meek as a lamb with his poor, ragged, worn out troops.[13]

McKenzie had noted on September 22: "It was pretty lively around camp in the evening." The next day he reported: "Good many men were full today— Dohna got so wild and abusive that Eckelson had to send him to the guard house. Gen. S [sic] got full and Eck and myself gave up our bed to him." (The story of the two men giving up the bed they shared for Stanley is likely the one that Rosser told Custer the following year, who passed it on to his wife, albeit in garbled form.) Two days later the camp had not moved as Stanley, waiting for Rosser, remained drunk. Rosser, who wanted to be home, became increasingly frustrated: "I don't like this line at all and don't expect to see it built." The drinking continued, and the NP Journal (September 27) noted that the veteran surveyor Frank Eastman "got hold of some whisky today and got full."

The next day McKenzie noted: "Camped on the creek where Linsley and I had the row coming out," although there is no hint as to what the altercation was about. The NP Journal recorded on September 29: "Line party worked today as Gen. Rosser is anxious to get out of the Bad Lands." But Eastman, who had done good work for two years, was drinking uncontrollably; Rosser wrote the next night with disappointment: "Eastman has been drunk for several days. Tonight I offered him a pledge, he declines and I discharge him." Once past the Little Missouri the column made decent time, and morale improved as the surveyors averaged nine miles a day from September 29 to October 3.

Progress was so good that Stanley agreed to Rosser's suggestion to release some men. On October 2, as the column crossed the divide between the Cannonball and Heart Rivers, Stanley sent Major Crofton and the 17th Infantry's 125 men back to Fort Rice. What no one knew, of course, was that Gall and up to 100 Hunkpapas were shadowing them. The previous day they had chased five Santee Indian scouts, who were carrying Stanley's dispatches, virtually to the gates of Fort

Rice. Crofton camped 15 miles east of Stanley, close to the Heart River crossing, five miles southwest of Heart Butte (the location now covered by North Dakota's Lake Tschida).[14]

One of Crofton's officers was the popular and effective Lt. Eban Crosby. Crosby, with the 6th Maine at Gettysburg, had a finger shot off his left hand. The wound was improperly treated, gangrene set in, and his forearm was amputated. Undaunted, Crosby stayed in the army. On the afternoon of October 3, after a campsite was selected, he went out hunting alone on foot. He wounded an antelope then followed it, drawing farther and farther away from his camp. Suddenly he found himself surrounded by Gall and scores of Hunkpapas, who, unfortunately, dispatched him slowly. The *Army and Navy Journal* wrote: "[I]n opposition to the advice of friends, he pursued [an antelope] over a bluff but a few hundred feet from the command, when he was surprised by Indians, who were waiting for just such a chance as this, and killed, scalped and horribly mutilated [him]. It was done so stealthily that it was not known by the officers of the camp, till, being absent longer than they thought necessary a [search party was sent]."[15]

In fact, Crosby wandered off farther than anybody wished to admit, about four miles. When his body was finally discovered the next day, it had nine bullet wounds and three arrows in it, and his remaining arm had been hacked off. Linda Slaughter wrote that nobody knew he was missing until "[Gall rode up and] displayed some object on a pole, which by the aid of glasses was discovered by the soldiers to be . . . [Crosby's] scalp. . . . So dreadful was the mutilation of his features, that none of his lady friends at the fort was suffered to look upon his face." After finding Crosby, Crofton marched to Fort Rice, reaching it on October 6. Surprisingly, he did not inform Stanley, perhaps feeling that a messenger could not get through. In 1932 Stanley Vestal wrote: "It is said that Gall collected his [Crosby's] remaining arm and took it home as a trophy."[16]

On the evening of October 4, Rosser wrote in his diary: "After . . . [lunch] I went ahead to examine the line and ran onto a party of 80 hostile Indians and came near losing my scalp. Killed one. Lt. [Louis Dent] Adair and a Negro [Stephen Harris, Stanley's servant] killed. A narrow escape for me." Adair, in Stanley's 22nd Regiment, was the first cousin of Julia Dent Grant, the wife of President Grant. The NP Journal stated:

> About three . . . Gen. Rosser had a very narrow escape as he was two miles ahead of the line party when he discovered the Indians . . . They did not rush on him as they evidently thought they had a sure thing of it. Lt. Adair . . . was a mile away from the command on foot hunting. Gen. Rosser saw him and motioned him to run. Eckelson joined the Gen. just then, and

they turned back to help Adair . . . When they reached him they found he was [mortally] wounded and had wounded one of the Indians. There were three Indians within five hundred feet of him when Rosser got there, and he killed the one Adair had wounded and got all his trappings off of him. The fight occurred six miles from camp. The ambulance and a company of soldiers were sent out to bring Adair in. Steve (Gen. Stanley's mulatto cook) was caught by the Indians while out hunting and when found had three arrows in his body and five gun shot wounds in his head and neck.[17]

The next morning Adair died at 4:40 A.M. Ned Jordan's remembrance, likely written for the 1906 surveyors' reunion, described the events of October 4 slightly differently:

[A]bout 40 Indians appeared in front of . . . [Rosser]. His first thought was that they were our own mounted scouts, but after a few moments saw they were hostile . . . [He] retreated, but did not dare to let them see how slow his horse could run from the fact it was one of the [wagon] team horses . . . The Indians did not hurry as they thought they had him sure . . . [F]our or five galloped off on one side out of sight intending to get ahead of the General and come up in front of him and then whoop him up. The Gen. was retreating as fast as he dared to thinking that he would never come in sight of us when looking off on the right he saw a solitary man and rode toward him and motioned him back.

Just at that moment [the] four Indians came up from the other side of the hill as they supposed to head off Rosser when they stumbled right on Adair and shot him and jumped off their horses to scalp him. Eckelson and myself, who alone had horses, galloped to a little knoll, saw Rosser, gave the alarm, and then galloped to the rescue. Rosser, who was a beautiful shot, hopped off his horse for a steadier aim and shot the foremost Indian as dead as a herring. . . . It was a poor swap, a dead officer for a dead Indian Chief. It is against the rules for a soldier to remove a scalp but . . . [n]ot being a soldier I removed his scalp lock, which I still have, and on the sly a soldier took off the top of his head.[18]

Did the college-educated Jordan really take and keep the Indian's scalp lock? It appears that Jordan—in defiance of present-day sensibilities—did just that. In any case, the Indian, whom Rosser later identified as Little Red Horn, was definitely scalped and mutilated. At Adair's funeral each member of his company had a piece of the Indian's scalp hanging on his rifle. Stanley wrote that Adair was shot through the spleen with a Henry repeating rifle. Like Crosby, he had been hunting; but, probably for the family's sake, Stanley covered it up by saying he was looking for a campsite. Stanley, who was responsible for the command's safety, vehemently wrote: "All the deaths . . . come from the fatal mistake of going alone out of sight

of the command, a fault, my orders, my warnings, and displeasure, had not succeeded in entirely suppressing."[19]

Harris (the cook) and his wife had been in Stanley's employ for years, although
no dates are known. They did not realize that he was missing until an ambulance,
sent for Adair, saw his body in a ravine. Swipes wrote: "The poor fellow, it seems
fought to the last, as the cartridge shells around where his body was lying would
testify. His legs, arms, and breast were cut and hacked in a horrible manner. . . .
Stanley felt the loss of his cook, who was very much attached to him, not a little."
Reflecting the era's prejudices, most comments remark that Harris was not scalped
because his hair was curly. Harris's white bulldog was also killed, and the Indians
left the two side by side. Stanley wrote in his report that "Stephen Harris, (mulatto)
had served in the army and was a very excellent and upright man. . . . We buried
[him] at the crossing of the Heart River and brought the remains of the officers to
[Fort Rice]."[20]

Six nights later Rosser began a routine report to Linsley but suddenly switched
subjects, cathartically describing the events. Why Rosser wrote to Linsley, whom he
disliked, is not known, but the letter's structure suggests that his emotions simply
gushed out. Ironically, it is unlikely that Linsley (or anyone else) ever read the letter.[21]

> Since the [Indian] scout horses broke down I have done my exploring alone
> and on the 4th inst. came near making my last reconnaissance for life. The
> country was considerably chopped up and I had been ahead all day looking
> up the line. About 4 P.M. I was riding alone about three miles in advance of
> the party and its escort, when a party of about one hundred Indians rushed
> out from behind a hill, their ponies at full speed, their lances flourishing and
> came at me with all the fury in their savage nature. When I first saw them
> they were not over a thousand feet away. If you will indulge me I will
> attempt to picture the situation; but to give it the life in which I saw it, is
> beyond human expression, and [I] sincerely hope that you may never witness
> a scene so akin to it, as to enable you to appreciate my situation. My eyes
> swept over the prairie in vain for friendly support [but] none was to be
> seen. A few antelope stood on the hill close by apparently amazed at this
> strange conduct of human creatures. I was wretchedly mounted and knew it
> would be useless to run, as their ponies would soon overtake me, and there
> appeared but little possibility of escape from a horrible death at their hands.
> I was well armed with an army musket and had a belt of cartridges around
> me, and made up my mind that there was nothing for me to do but fight. At
> the first shot I fired they immediately dropped down behind their ponies
> and began circling around.[22] . . . This evident fear of my gun on their part
> gave me great confidence and hope. I *suppose* I maneuvered with great skill
> until we had skirmished about two miles, which occupied a very short time.
> Here I saw off to my right about a quarter of a mile [away] a soldier who

had just come into view and appeared not to understand what was going on. The Indians were nearer him than I was. I could not join [him] but motioned him back. He at once started back at a double quick towards the escort and party which were then about a mile back, and over a hill and out of sight from him and the Indians. As soon as the Indians saw this dismounted man they turned off from me and went in pursuit of the soldier. As soon as I was liberated I ran my horse at full speed to the crest of the hill, a few hundred yards ahead, where I could see the party. I was soon observed by the *gallant Eckelson* who, seeing the Indians galloping around me, snatched a musket from the hands of a soldier and in a moment was at my side. The Indians were then very near the soldier and we rode back to help him. The few scattering Indians fled before us, but just as we reached the soldier he was shot and fatally wounded, but we jumped off our horses at his side, drove the Indians away and held his body [illegible word or two]. [I shot] one of the Indians dead in face of the entire cowardly, savage band for at least half an hour [*sic*], until the company came at a run to the spot. The soldier for whom we risked so much to save, was Lt. Adair. As soon as the company came up, the savages went off to the hills whence they kept up the usual skirmishing until we finished work for the day and started to camp; then they came on the field and carried off their dead. Adair was taken into camp in our wagon where he soon died. He is a cousin of Mrs. President Grant [and] leaves a wife and several children in destitute circumstances.

A few moments before the Indians made a dash at me, they had killed General Stanley's servant who had straggled out of camp on a hunt, and when they saw me I suppose they took me for a straggler from camp also, and [as] I retreated [away] from camp they doubtless concluded that they had me safe, and hence the leisurely manner in which they pursued me. This circumstance was likely all that saved my life, for they could easily have rushed on me and killed me in the first half mile. Before they came on me they had come upon Lieut. Crosby who was out hunting and killed and scalped him. During our skirmish with them, one of them would occasionally ride out from the others and flourish over his head a long pole with a scalp on the end of it, which we knew had been taken from some of our friends. We soon learned that it was poor Crosby's. These Indians were evidently hanging around camp for the purpose of picking off stragglers, and I assure you they have proven a most efficient set of *file closers*. No man gets behind and no one asks permission to go hunting now. [Rosser's emphasis]

Despite the losses, work continued on October 5; the surveyors mapped seven more miles. The next day the column neared the Heart, and Harris was buried. Gall's Hunkpapas continued to follow them and mounted one brief "attack" (possibly part of a trap), to which the soldiers did not respond. Jordan described another incident a few days later:

> A few miles further on we came upon a place where a large Indian village had formerly existed. There were several graves and as I had promised a specimen to a young doctor, I availed myself of the opportunity . . . The one that I obtained had been drying over 20 years. He was a big brave. Nothing but the skeleton remained enclosed in what must have been an elegant buckskin suit beautifully wrought with beads. Pinned upon his breast was [sic] seven scalps, three of them blonde in color showing that they must have been white scalps and perhaps all of them. There were half a dozen pewter spoons and etc. which he probably obtained at the same time he did the scalps by murdering settlers or robbing an emigrant train. . . . I [also] found a red sandstone pipe. This material is very highly prized by all Indians and found in only one place in the whole world.[23]

Stanley received word of Crosby's death on October 9, another shock. It had taken six days to get the news, reflecting the obvious fear of sending out small parties. On October 10 the War Department released the report of Captain Kellogg, Sheridan's observer with Stanley through August. Numerous papers reprinted (sometimes in full) Kellogg's stolid findings, which cast the surveying expedition in positive light. But newspapers wanted readers, not a limp report placing greater emphasis on the discovery of coal than on Indian fighting. The *New York Herald* typically added color by subheadlining Kellogg's report: "The Red Men Hostile—Frequent Attacks on the Expedition." But Gall's ambushes negated Kellogg's report. A relative of the president, with a wife and small children, had been killed, vividly illustrating the dangers of the plains, the "barbarity" of the Indians, and the risks associated with the Northern Pacific.[24]

Stanley, perhaps feeling that his career was over, could not cope with the added news of Crosby's death. Rosser's October 11 diary noted: "The old man on a spree." At the site where Big Muddy Creek joins the Heart, Stanley and Crittenden began to shuffle troops, bringing fresh companies out and sending exhausted ones back to Fort Rice. On October 13 Stanley and Rosser stayed in camp; the surveyors were finishing maps and reports. The next day the two parted: the surveyors and a small escort headed to Fort McKeen to finish their work, and Stanley headed toward Fort Rice.

As the surveyors arrived at Fort McKeen, they saw Hunkpapas fighting the army's Ree scouts. In an October 2 fight, two Rees (Red Bear and a son) were killed, scalped, and mutilated a few hundred feet from the fort. McKeen's commandant, William P. Carlin, refused to come to the aid of his scouts or to permit the post's civilians to assist, for fear of causing an Indian war. McKenzie wrote disgustedly: "These military fellows at this post are the worst frightened men on the Indian subject that I have ever seen." Jordan later wrote:

> Below us on the river was a large band of Sioux. . . . Our scouts were brave and reckless and having plenty of ammunition, 40 of them dashed out against more than double their number. The fight was entirely by horseback and of the most thrilling nature as they dashed back and forth sometimes right under the stockade of the fort. There was a great deal of firing but they screened themselves so well behind their horses that for a long time no one was killed although several horses were. Finally one of our scouts was shot and fell from his horse . . . There was a great whoop on the part of the Sioux and a party of them galloped up to scalp him when a 15 year old son of the scout who had fallen was seen running . . . straight to his father. The Sioux ignored him but he reached his father first, seized his carbine, and shot two of them dead, wounded a third and with the help that arrived captured the scalps and bore his father's body into the fort.[25]

When Stanley heard of the Fort McKeen fighting, he immediately sent reinforcements to guard Rosser's engineers. McKenzie said that Rosser had asked for 15 more men, but Stanley, fearful of surveyor casualties, sent 75 infantry, 14 wagons, and the one-inch Gatling gun.[26]

Adair and Crosby's deaths made the surveying expedition another public relations disaster. The survey was also an engineering failure: besides not meeting Haydon, Rosser was unable to find a shorter route to the Yellowstone. Rosser's inability to find a shortcut soon leaked out, and the *New York Herald* stated that it was "believed not to have been an entirely successful expedition so far as permanently locating the exact line of grade for the railroad."[27]

Despite Rosser's frustration, nothing suggests that the result would have been different had Stanley stayed sober. Rosser's complaints about lost time seem unfair; Stanley acquiesced to his work in Montana long after it was clear that there was no shortcut. Stanley also displayed his wartime skills: without cavalry and with infantry of limited ability, he completed a difficult mission, bringing his command home with moderate loss. In all, the total march was likely about 625 to 650 miles. The three pairs of shoes issued to each enlisted man illustrated the corruption in the procurement process. Stanley wrote disgustedly that "some [of the shoes] that we examined had pressed paper for insoles and middle soles." As Grant had likely instructed (chapter 9), Stanley returned to Fort Rice on October 15 with Lt. Col. Henry Wallen.[28]

Ultimately, Gall's ambushes were too successful. As the presidential campaign came to an end, Grant wrote: "I do not believe our Creator ever placed different races of man on this earth with the view of having the stronger exert all his energies in exterminating the weaker." But after his election, Grant's relatively benign Indian policy was replaced by an iron glove.[29]

On returning to Minnesota, Rosser and most of the surveyors were laid off. While Rosser was rehired in early 1873, he had aged. Years later he wrote: "[A]lthough I have been in more than a hundred battles, I never dream of fighting or of war except with Indians, and for years after the death of Adair, I often cried out in my sleep—Indians! Indians!"[30]

For Jay Cooke, the two 1872 Yellowstone surveys proved to be the beginning of the end.

CHAPTER 12

"20,000 Hostile Indians"

During the winter of 1871–72 Jay Cooke reached the firm decision that the Northern Pacific could not succeed until Gregory Smith was removed. Cooke was fully aware that if Smith fought back, it could cause immense damage to the NP's operations, to say nothing of his bond sales. Given nineteenth-century sensibilities about disagreements among gentlemen and the congressional clout of Gregory's brother, Worthington, to say nothing of the collateral damage that would be caused by public accusations, Cooke had to proceed cautiously toward forcing Smith's "voluntary" resignation.

Cooke, increasingly weary, resented what he saw as Smith's greed, Smith's Northern Pacific salary increase to $20,000, his refusal to acknowledge Cooke's sales problems, continued large capital purchases, and the lack of attention to economy. For example, in addition to 48 locomotives already purchased, Smith ordered 50 new "first class" Baldwin locomotives, a suspiciously high number. One bizarre item, yet not atypical, was the procurement of a Missouri steamboat in early 1872, which arrived a year earlier than it could possibly be used.[1]

In Brainerd alone in 1871–72, Smith built a hotel, a roundhouse, two machine shops (one 60 by 260 feet), a milling and fabricating shop, and a combined headquarters-depot; many of these buildings were *replacements*. Brainerd's train depot illustrates Smith's cavalier financial attitude in 1872. The 1870–71 station was wood, 30 by 100 feet, and two and a half stories high. The new station, finished in September 1872, was brick, 50 by 150 feet, and three stories high. The *Minneapolis Tribune* said: "Architecturally [it] will eclipse any station in Minnesota, and is in pleasing contrast to the old niggardly accommodations [of] older railroad corporations." The *Brainerd Tribune* wrote that it had "the heaviest, richest cornices and bracket-work . . . a Mansard roof, with heavy dormer windows, and an immense [60-foot] tower . . . with an observatory of the richest finish. . . . We Brainerdites are as proud of it as a little boy with a new knife."[2]

Simultaneously, Smith's financial exposure and losses at home mounted. In 1872 the Vermont Central acquired a fleet of steamers plying the Great Lakes from Buffalo to Duluth. The venture demonstrated Smith's weak understanding of market forces: by summer he had to cut his prices by a third. Smith was also building a $500,000 state-of-the-art iron and steel rolling mill in St. Albans, requiring further attention and cash. Where the cash came from is unknown, but it could *not* have come from money-losing Vermont Central operations.[3]

The Cooke-Smith conflict was exacerbated by continual charges from Cooke's associates and investors concerning lax, dishonest field operations. In December 1871 Cooke instructed Smith to have somebody supervise Minnesota construction: "I beg you, dear Governor, to take the bull by the horns and to see whether we cannot . . . [build] the Northern Pacific as economically as it can be done in Iowa and other parts of the country." But Cooke closed his letter on a pleading note, saying that he was thinking of resigning if management did not improve. Milnor Roberts later wrote Cooke that the situation would not improve unless Smith "gave his whole time to the road . . . [or] that others have authority to make and keep up systematic instead of spasmodic action."[4]

Cooke's pleas went unheeded, and he all but gave up writing Smith. On March 8, 1872, he wrote NP treasurer A. H. Barney: "I must have some cooperation in regard to finances, or I shall feel like giving up"; and a month later: "Please do not buy anything or make any contracts where money is required without full consultation with me." As late as July 22 Barney wrote to Smith: "There is the usual growl from Philadelphia [but] otherwise all is serene." That nothing came of Cooke's complaints is seen by Cooke's April note to Smith commenting that he was spending $50,000 a month "for the fun of running a railroad without any receipts." Some of the fun that Cooke likely did not know about was a primitive tractor ("steam wagon") that towed wagons over open ground. The tractor, 25 feet long, had wide-tread wheels and a grappling device to pull itself out of ditches; it was designed by chief engineer Linsley and actually worked a few times before breaking down.[5]

One might ask what the Northern Pacific's blue-ribbon directors and its large investors were thinking. Men like George W. Cass, Ogden, Fargo, Wright, and Moorhead's brothers all had records of business accomplishment and were knowledgeable about the NP's problems yet did nothing to curb Smith. Henrietta Larson wrote that the failure came from their being physically distant and that the NP was a "minor consideration in their business activities." But this seems to miss the mark; in fact, most of the board members had made significant investments—some in the hundreds of thousands—in the NP or its related companies. Part of the problem lay with Cooke's image: his character and wealth were so legendary that, as Robert E. Riegel wrote, "no one doubted that if Cooke took hold of the project its success was assured." Yet if the directors left the problems to Cooke, they still continued to rubber-stamp Smith's requests. Not until March 1872 did the board establish an executive committee (Moorhead as chairman and Wright, Cass, Billings, and Smith) that was committed to Cooke. Despite seeing the handwriting on the wall, Smith and his stalwarts defiantly continued to make purchases and act with passive aggressiveness.[6]

By August 1872 Northern Pacific overdrafts reached $1.5 million—cash advanced by Jay Cooke & Co., sometimes secured by personal notes from Cooke or his partners. Rumors of Smith's "retirement," however, circulated in a *Brainerd Tribune* article but were quickly denied. After maneuvering between the Cooke and Smith forces (which included one of Moorhead's brothers), William Ogden threw his weight behind Cooke. Perhaps fearing a personal confrontation, in June Cooke sent Abe Nettleton with a letter "to demand, receive, and accept Governor Smith's resignation." Smith, getting wind of the mission, tried to avoid Nettleton; but Nettleton tracked him down, forcing him to sign a letter of resignation, which was accepted at the board's June 12 meeting.[7]

Not giving up, Smith postponed his resignation until November 1. He had hoped to reverse Cooke's action that summer, but "when he discovered . . . he had no one at his back he 'came down most gracefully and manfully.'" Richard Rice, Smith's ally, kept his board seat and vice presidency but was sent back to the West Coast in 1873. The resignation was not announced until September, and the "Vermont clique" continued its parasitic management for the rest of the summer. The board was still so split that the vote for Smith's replacement was postponed until August 20; when it was taken, George W. Cass—Cooke's first choice—beat Rice by only seven to four. Smith, consumed by his Vermont Central problems, was gone by late September; but the NP was virtually rudderless in the fall, as Cass was unable to take office until December.[8]

A further drain on Cooke and Northern Pacific finances was Thomas Canfield's Lake Superior and Puget Sound Land Company. Under Canfield's management the LSPS was a disaster. Charles L. Brace, in the *New York Times,* called it a "Crédit Mobilier affair of a small kind." Harnsberger wrote that its "bad reputation" and "methods it used handicapped the actual construction of the railroad and interfered with the sales of [NP] Securities [by] Jay Cooke & Co." Larson felt that of all NP activities, "none proved more disappointing . . . [as Cooke] was continually called upon to settle one problem after another arising out of the affairs of that concern." More recently, Professor Carroll Englehardt stated that, in addition to public criticism for its questionable land policies, "[s]ettlers, editors, and politicians also complained about the company's secrecy, speculative windfalls for insiders, and high lot prices."⁹

Canfield put the cart (insider profits) before the horse (rapid settlement). The LSPS's problems included conflicting land applications, quarrels with the surveyors (including Rosser) over routes, fake surveys, poor town platting, and sky-high prices that discouraged settlement, including some of the Billings plans. Canfield's money lust was so great that he was fighting Billings in disputes between Fargo (backed by Billings) and Moorhead (supported by Canfield). But at his worst Canfield was no monster; reasonable parcels of land were set aside for schools, churches, cemeteries, and newspapers (for example, the *Red River Star*), and other activities were supported. Sometimes Canfield was caught in ironic conflicts not of his own making. New businesses and residents wanted to buy lots at low prices but, on becoming property owners, pressured Canfield to make unsold lots more expensive, thereby raising the value of their new land.

Canfield's fight against speculators near Bismarck was almost slapstick. The railroad's survey stopped 15 miles from the Missouri to keep speculators from knowing the town's site; but, as the route would follow the Heart River, it took little imagination to guess the final location. In early 1872 speculators began camping along the Missouri, waiting to pounce. Canfield hired a "Colonel Smith" to stake claims and sell lots. Then one evening Canfield pulled out the marking stakes, walked three miles south, and replanted them, giving him the land he really wanted. As 1872 came to an end, Cooke made Canfield's removal and shutting down the LSPS a priority, but Canfield and his investors, for whom he had made considerable profits, dug in for a fight.¹⁰

Billings's land company had its own problems in 1872, as its work fell behind schedule. His surveys gave promise of faster sales by including not just topographical features but also soil and subsoil depth, drainage, and even suggestions concerning the best agricultural use of each section. Senator William Windom estimated that Red River Valley sales "will pay for the construction of the entire road from . . . [Duluth] to . . . the Sheyenne." Yet pricing each parcel was complex, bringing various subjective calculations into play: year-round weather, distance from railroad stops, and the cost of privately held adjacent land. And then Billings had to choose between a policy of large land sales with lower initial fees or a policy of higher up-front cash and fewer buyers. To his credit, he adopted a flexible strategy, giving buyers a series of options, but all this took time to evolve and put into practice.¹¹

Another unforeseen problem developed: many Scandinavians who arrived had no agricultural skills. While the NP might bring settlers, those without basic farming skills were unprepared to live off 160 acres and face the region's winters. A winter's sunset most often meant a weak sun, low on the horizon, that gave little comfort from gusty winds as the thermometer dipped to minus 25 degrees and a child began coughing.

But that was the future. Well into 1872, Northern Pacific chessboard generals moved phantom armies of immigrants, fighting fiercely over jurisdictional turf. One example: Billings and Smith quarreled over transporting immigrants when they reached NP track. Smith, fearing a flood of the unwashed, traded new NP passenger cars for old ones to the St. Paul & Pacific Railroad, blithely writing Cooke: "[A] portion of [the] old cars would be just as serviceable to us . . . [rather than] let immigrants come into and deteriorate our good cars." Smith's bigotry aside, it is difficult to believe that *nothing* else factored into his decision.[12]

The relationship between Smith and Billings became so strained that in April the frustrated Billings submitted his resignation to Cooke—even though he technically reported to Smith. Cooke, responding with patrician grace, noted that he had received the resignation but that "I cannot possibly consent to it and shall feel that my right hand has been taken off. . . . Go out with me in June and catch some fish in Lake Erie and have a good rest." Billings, reassured, jumped back into the trenches. The incident also illustrates that, as remarkable and independent as Billings was, he was, like so many others, mesmerized by Cooke's vision and force of character.[13]

The Northern Pacific's finances were further strained by the delay in certification—the release of lands that would boost the NP's value by more than $10 million. The certification issue, so damaging in 1871, was no better in 1872, again with not a single acre filed under Smith. The NP's Minnesota land was 2,925,000 acres; combined with partially overlapping St. Paul & Pacific and Lake Superior & Mississippi grants, this represented a total of some 4 million acres, or roughly one-twelfth of the state. Even subtracting wetlands and lakes, the figure included huge agricultural, timber, and mineral reserves. No one suggests that all this could have been sold rapidly, but others had started selling adjacent acreage. Billings could have sold some of it if Smith had not blocked him with one delaying tactic after another. Smith's procrastination makes little sense unless he feared that federal certification would undercut Canfield's efforts and his insider LSPS profits, some of which were likely used for his Vermont obligations and investments.[14]

Not until December 1872 was the Minnesota track certified. Henry Cooke had done his homework and wrote Jay that all three certification commissioners were "entirely friendly . . . able and respectable." The December 10, 1872, report was predictably favorable. It was filled with minutiae: grades and curves, embankments, ballasting, sidings, and telegraph lines were among the items noted. Minnesota track was measured as 228.793 miles, with 15 passenger and 9 freight stations, 20 water towers, three engine houses, and three repair shops (in Duluth, Brainerd, and Fargo). Every mile of track had 2,640 ties, and track iron was 56 pounds to the yard—not high, but a weight in common usage. There were 68 locomotives (high); some 1,100 platform and 350 boxcars; 25 passenger and observation and baggage cars; 52 hand cars; 36 rubble cars; 6 cabooses; 2 pay cars; a pile driver; and a wrecking car.[15]

With federal certification, the Minnesota land became available for Northern Pacific sale, varying in value from $2.50 to $8.00 an acre. While the land east of Brainerd held only low-grade timber, the rich, black, almost oily–looking alluvial soil in the Red River Valley ran an amazing two to four feet deep and was expected to fetch premium prices. The valley's some 20,000 square miles cut across (versus paralleling) the NP's land grant, but all agricultural production would travel over company track. Minnesota's acreage, even with a conservative average price of $3.50 per acre, added $10 million to the NP's value, giving the NP bonds an extra level of security. In addition, over 7.5 million acres in Dakota, Washington, and Oregon were slated for 1873 certification. Although they had a lower average value than Minnesota's land, NP assets would increase by another $15 million.

In 1872 track laying began optimistically. Nothing could be as bad as 1871's sinkages, as the land west of the Red River posed no great surprises. Yet construction soon slowed, not because of Dakota problems, but again due to Minnesota sinkages. Between Duluth and Brainerd, "[a] large crew labored unceasingly . . . hundreds of tons of gravel and logs were put in and finally the bottom was reached, at a depth of from 30 to 40 feet." On May 31 Rosser wrote Linsley: "There are several very bad places in the swamps . . . [and] some have never been fathomed." Numerous sections had to be rebuilt, at one point inserting fill for 65 feet—another testimonial to overall weak supervision, lax construction standards, and likely graft in 1871.[16]

Major personnel changes also occurred in 1872. Ira Spaulding resigned in the spring and was likely forced out. The surveyors gave him a $575 gold watch and decades later remembered him with affection. Dakota's Red, Sheyenne, and James Rivers presented no engineering obstacles, and the Red River bridge was officially completed June 7. The distance from there to Edwinton (also called the Crossing, Carlton, and Burleigh until finally named Bismarck in 1873) was 195 miles, not a daunting figure. By June construction was said to be 25 percent ahead of schedule, grading was "getting along nicely" for nearly a hundred miles, and track was expected at the James by August 1. More than 1,200 men were working, their numbers growing weekly.[17]

Behind the scenes, however, there were major problems. Rosser wrote Linsley on June 3 that workers had not arrived at Bismarck and that "contractors are running about over the light work and are not doing anything with the heavy work in the vicinity of the Sheyenne." In mid-July the problems became public; the *Sioux City Daily Journal* said that Burleigh & Evans (winners of a too-lucrative 50-mile contract) had subcontracted its work to a third party. Nonetheless, the NP insisted that track would reach the Missouri by October 31. A September *Railroad Gazette* story noted: "At least 100 car loads per day are sent to the front, with . . . [track] and similar material, to say nothing about the food and supply trains for the army of workmen."[18]

While construction continued toward Bismarck, by about October 10 the numbers had dropped to some 500 men and 300 mule teams, and track was 78 miles shy of the Missouri. On October 18 the *St. Paul Weekly Pioneer* quoted a confident George Brackett: "[T]rack will be laid through to . . . [the Missouri] as early as November 10." Three day later, an optimistic *Philadelphia Inquirer* correspondent on the Missouri wrote that "the locomotive is already nearly within hearing distance." The writer stated that grading and track laying was averaging almost three miles a day and "with average good weather could reach the Missouri in mid-November." In reality there was no margin for error, for the concept of "average good weather" was based on faith, not previous Dakota weather conditions.[19]

The *Minneapolis Tribune* wrote on November 14 that grading had reached the Missouri, track was 22 miles from Bismarck, and men, horses, and equipment were returning to Minnesota. Yet in the tense atmosphere, the crews' arrival, instead of being seen as good news, only fueled rumors that the NP was out of cash. The *Tribune's* optimistic figures denoted both good progress and the potential to reach the Missouri if the weather held. It did not. Track laying may have continued briefly; but then winter set in, bringing construction to a halt, with track actually 30 to 35 miles from Bismarck. The predictable finger-pointing soon followed. What had actually happened, how far the track was from the Missouri, and when construction was suspended were all immaterial: Jay Cooke had another disaster on his hands.[20]

Shortly after the return of the Stanley-Rosser column in October (the exact date is unknown), the Northern Pacific unceremoniously laid off most of its surveyors. Tom Rosser made sure his surveyors were paid, but by mid-November was unemployed himself. Meigs, because of his father's standing, was one of the few exceptions. Even Milnor Roberts's headquarters staff was cut, although a handful of draftsmen were retained to complete the summer's mapping.

On December 3 Montgomery Meigs led a team from Fargo on sleighs on a 20-day, 350-mile trip to inspect the road for 1873 construction requirements. As he crossed the treeless landscape, he noted that there were "many days when the thermometer was 20°." Fully aware of the NP's "tight fix," Meigs felt that he would soon be laid off, like Rosser and most of the other surveyors. "They have so disbanded the fine engineering corps we had and were so proud of that I scarcely care whether I stay or go," he wrote dejectedly. Railroad morale was at rock bottom, and the *New York Times* noted that "the disappointment felt along the whole line is great."[21]

In addition to construction delays and cash problems, questions about the value of the NP's land grants were to affect the Northern Pacific throughout 1872. In February

Senator Henry Wilson of Massachusetts (Grant's 1872 running mate), who took Crédit Mobilier bribes and $10,000 from Cooke, stated that the NP's land was worth only five cents an acre. Cooke, justifiably furious, wrote that "if he does not correct [the statement,] we will smash him flatter than a pancake." Cooke also wrote directly to Wilson. The senator, after receiving his note, immediately backtracked and "hastily made an acceptable [public] explanation."[22]

Cooke's enemies also persuaded congressman and ex-general Nathaniel P. Banks, the Pacific Railroads committee chairman, to investigate rumors of shoddy construction. The good-looking, square-jawed Banks began hearings in February, but the Cooke brothers chewed him up as rapidly as Stonewall Jackson had ten years earlier. The congressman soon said that "he had no charges to make, and knew of no facts reflecting upon the honesty and efficiency of the management." By April he was so docile that he allowed Sam Wilkeson to write his committee's report. Yet the inquiry broke 1872's early sales momentum, which Cooke felt resulted in over $2 million in lost sales. By June sales were back to $900,000; in his typical style, Cooke purchased another $100,000, so that he could say the figure was over a million.[23]

In addition to the Northern Pacific's construction issues, other problems gushed out, like a dike springing multiple leaks. Jay Cooke & Co. had invested $2 million in the Lake Superior & Mississippi. By early 1872 it needed $750,000 for interest payments and operations. The problem was solved through a third-party leasing agreement but led to the rival St. Paul & Sioux City Railroad's alignment with Wisconsin interests to fight the NP in Minnesota.

Meanwhile the St. Paul & Pacific hemorrhaged cash. If 1871's St. Paul to Breckenridge run made little sense, scarcer 1872 dollars were wasted on the 150-mile St. Vincent extension. Harnsberger wrote: "[H]ad the line been built honestly, the [SP&P's] revenues might have carried the indebtedness," but furious Dutch investors withheld further contributions. Cooke advanced a million, but construction costs rose faster. In May the Brainerd to Sauk Rapids run was again postponed: Moorhead, the SP&P's executive committee chairman, was unaware that under *its* congressional land grant the route had to be completed in early 1873. Work began again in midsummer, but by September Cooke was so low on cash that all SP&P construction stopped. Some 1,800 men were laid off without pay and, enraged, began destroying property. To get cash, Moorhead sold $300,000 worth of track from the NP's Minnesota reserve of 3,700 tons of track, slated for Dakota. The SP&P ended 1872 with 426 miles of track, but over half was on lines that had limited traffic or were incomplete.[24]

Montana competition also developed, with track planned by two railroads from Corrine and Logan, Utah. Northern Pacific statements spoke of cooperation, but everyone understood that either line would have been a transcontinental feeder. The *Helena Daily Herald,* a former NP ally, wrote: "Instead, therefore, of idly folding our hands and waiting for the Northern Pacific to do for us what it has not been able to do for itself, we will show our wisdom by looking elsewhere." Except for Governor Potts, who was on Cooke's payroll, NP support in Montana vanished.[25]

Additional competition resulted from the completion of the Sioux City & St. Paul, which made its first 270-mile run between the two cities on September 25, taking 23 hours. Regular service began in October, with 13-hour "express" passenger trains. While opinions varied as to whether the line would compete with or complement the Northern Pacific (a major destination was Duluth), nevertheless the SCSP had linked St. Paul and the Missouri River before the NP.

During the year Cooke attempted to form an alliance with British railroad magnate Sir Hugh Allen. Cooke would have invested in and played a prominent role in constructing track from Montreal to Vancouver, with the NP being linked at the Red River. But the idea left the British and Canadian governments even more determined to build the Canadian Pacific.[26]

Another opportunity arose when the Oregon Steam Navigation Company came up for sale. After internal debate, Cooke & Co. decided to purchase the stock with Northern Pacific bonds. Interestingly, Cooke was against but did not veto this new obligation, which was favored by Fahnestock. Cooke acquiesced, likely knowing that it would be good for company morale, as well as being a sound decision under normal conditions. But a huge blow came when Grant decided not to sell government bonds in 1872. His decision was due to hostility from banking and political interests (led by Drexel, Morgan & Co.), combined with election-year caution. The result was a stinging loss of income to Cooke and his partners and lower corporate cash reserves with which to assist the NP.[27]

Nevertheless, there was light—albeit dim—at the end of the tunnel. Three steamers shuttled between Moorhead and present-day Winnipeg on the Red River. Freight exceeded 3,000 tons, and two more steamers were ordered. A Northern Pacific contract with the Hudson Bay Company resulted in thousands of tons of freight, bales of fur, and passengers during the year, all on NP track. A *New York Times* writer stated that "to stand in the steam-boat warehouse . . . at Moorhead, and see what immense quantities of buffalo robes . . . of skins of the bear, the wolf, the fox [and] the beaver . . . is to be astonished again and again." It was a small beginning but represented far more traffic than in the ox-cart, light steamer, and stagecoach days.[28]

With its freight a third cheaper to the eastern states by steamer than by rail, Duluth grew rapidly. By 1873 there were three 60-by-900-foot warehouses and two and a half miles of docks (with room for 18 ships); the harbor was cleared by four $100,000 dredges, courtesy of federal pork barrel funds. Duluth's infrastructure included grain elevators, flour mills, dry docks, rail lines, iron manufacturing, blast furnaces, slate shipping (the area had the only formations west of Pennsylvania), and lumber yards. Duluth even promoted its freezing weather: a booster wrote that, unlike Chicago, which had occasional winter warm spells that caused meat spoilage, "The steady cold of our winters will prevent any anxiety on that ground."[29]

Despite weakening bond sales Sam Wilkeson tried to stem the tide with a variety of "good news" articles, letters, and reports. Newspapers and magazines carried his news and announcements, fulfilling the quid pro quo for Cooke's advertising. While Wilkeson had little trouble generating lengthy, enthusiastic copy, no subject elicited higher interest than Indian stories. Wide coverage was given to the 1872 eastern journey of a dozen Lakota chiefs who visited Grant, dined with Cooke, spoke at Cooper Union, and shopped in Manhattan's huge stores. But these were upbeat Indian stories; what really boosted newspaper circulation was the anticipation of fighting or, even better, the gory details of frontier warfare.

Unfortunately for Cooke, there was no shortage of Yellowstone survey stories, many untrue. The *Sioux City Daily Journal*, feeling that the livelihood of its city was at stake, was fast to repeat rumors. None was more damaging than the September 9 snafu at Sheridan's Chicago headquarters that resulted in a statement being released that "the fight was very severe and the troops have lost heavily, 40 being killed and wounded." The War Department's September 10 "correction" left the image of the fighting being caused by private business interests and stated outright that "the expedition is a failure." Both announcements were terrible blows to Cooke. The public had the impression of a Sioux victory and the railroad being blocked by (as the hysterical *New York Herald* estimated) "[n]ot fewer than 20,000 hostile Indians well armed and ready for the fray."[30]

Any reader had to wonder: if soldiers were not safe, how could a railroad be built or maintained? Compounding Cooke's problem, wire services telegraphed these and similar stories to hundreds of papers around the country. Wilkeson could do nothing to combat these articles. For three months, Sheridan and the War Department had released news about Baker's "defeat," the Stanley-Gall meeting, the O'Fallon Creek fight, Gall's ambushes of Adair, Crosby, and Rosser, and the Fort McKeen skirmishing. The stories were especially damaging when contrasted with widely circulated earlier letters by Roberts and Rosser downplaying Indian hostility. While there were other newspaper stories of Indian fighting, they were not in conjunction with a railroad under construction.[31]

The Northern Pacific's board of directors met with Cooke on August 21, and he reviewed with them at length the increasingly distressed financial condition of Jay Cooke & Co. Cooke's rare meeting with the board members and the news he brought undoubtedly left most of them in a state of shock. They quickly approved steps to distance the Northern Pacific from the St. Paul & Pacific. They also formed a committee to "examine the present financial condition" of the railroad. The minutes indicate that the committee was instructed to "recommend such changes and modifications" as to place the NP "on the most economical and efficient basis."[32]

In fact, little could be done. With Smith—who had never been able to delegate meaningfully and was now swamped by his Vermont Central problems—all but gone, the Northern Pacific was thoroughly leaderless. Cooke also must share in the blame. In retrospect and considering his still towering reputation, he should immediately have begun taking a more active role in the company's operations or supporting someone who could.

Cooke's October statement that the SP&P problem was "occasioned wholly by a temporary misunderstanding" was probably not believed. Yet what he did next was worse. After years of emphasizing the benefits from the alliance of Minnesota rail interests, Cooke and the Northern Pacific attempted to downplay the interrelationship of the NP and SP&P, which they had bragged about for two years. Cooke's next announcement stated: "The finances of the St. Paul & Pacific are wholly distinct from, and independent of, the finances of the . . . [NP, which] has no financial liabilities or responsibility in connection with the interest on SP&P bonds, or the construction of SP&P branch lines."[33]

The announcement of Smith's resignation was further seen as an admission of major problems. On September 22 the public discovered that his Vermont Central was out of cash; the *New York Herald* told "How the [VC] Has Become Bankrupt." The story said the VC was reeling in debt, obligations were twice as high as income, and bond sales receipts were missing. How Smith had kept it afloat was unknown, but it undoubtedly involved the abuse of his NP position. The *Railroad Gazette* wrote that the VC's "appetite seemed to grow by what it fed upon, until at last it swallowed its old rival, the Rutland apparently being tempted by [more than what it was worth]." For the first time Cooke understood not only Smith's motivations but that he had also treated his VC shareholders with equal contempt. Smith fended off the first round of creditors with various business economies, promises to restructure the debt, and personnel cuts—one VC engineer, James B. Dimock, "fastened 60 pounds of railroad iron to his body and then jumped off from a wharf." In 1873 Smith's problems would continue to grow, and he gave up any attempts to influence the NP.[34]

In 1872 the unthinkable occurred in Cooke's fiefdom: Fahnestock, the firm's best banker, questioned his leadership. Fahnestock was cosmopolitan, fastidious, a member of elite clubs, and involved in numerous charitable and civic activities. Some, such as the planned American Museum of Natural History, the Metropolitan Museum of Art, and various Episcopalian causes, were led by J. P. Morgan, who lived a few blocks from Fahnestock. The two men developed close philanthropic ties. While Fahnestock continued to recognize his fealty to Cooke, with each passing year he was drawn more into Morgan's orbit. Oberholtzer, writing cautiously in 1906, when Fahnestock was still alive, made it clear that "[i]t was Mr. Fahnestock's peculiar delight to make money . . . [He] saw that money was not to be made rapidly, if at all out of the [NP] Railroad, and his interest in it waned." On June 8 Fahnestock sent Cooke a 16-page letter about the Northern Pacific's problems, pleading with him to stop advancing the company money:

> Radical and immediate changes are necessary to save the company from ingloriously breaking down within the next year and involving us in discredit if not in ruin . . . The purpose of this letter is to impress upon you the precarious present situation and to set you to think about the best method of accomplishing what I regard as indispensably necessary . . . The road can be finished to the Missouri, but beyond that point I think it <u>must</u> depend upon an <u>entire</u> <u>rearrangement</u> [with the NP]. [Fahnestock's emphasis][35]

Cooke did not realize, probably because of the letter's supplicatory tone ("I beg you will not regard any of my views or criticisms as personal reflections"), that Fahnestock had issued an ultimatum. Although Cooke perhaps still regarded him as junior partner, Fahnestock had made the company's New York office its most profitable and had become his own man. It was one thing, Fahnestock said, to complete NP construction to the Missouri, but crossing the river was unacceptable. Cooke missed the letter's purpose and defiant frame of mind and disdainfully considered the comments "croaking" (the pejorative term for unjustifiable prophecies of disaster).[36]

Moreover, and unbeknownst to Cooke, Fahnestock was not acting alone. For years the cautious Moorhead had lobbied Cooke to reduce Northern Pacific advances and now, fearful of losing everything at 61, he joined those who were against the NP. To make matters worse, Moorhead, reeling from the pressure, spilled out the NP's woes to a friend with whom he rode each morning: Anthony Drexel, Morgan's partner. One can only speculate whether Moorhead's overwhelming stupidity was his unconscious way of getting even with Cooke, who so dominated his life. Moorhead also primed McCulloch, who bombarded Cooke with letters and telegrams from London during the year.[37]

Less vocal but also against the Northern Pacific were two New York junior partners, James A. Garland, 32, and Francis O. French, 35. Garland came to Cooke's attention when he taught a class in which Jay Cooke's son was a student and later headed the important New York bond division. Larson wrote that he "was an excellent broker—said to have been one of the best on the street." In 1870 French, whose father was one of Cooke's original Washington partners and who had become independently wealthy after marrying Amos Tuck's daughter, joined the New York branch.[38]

Cooke realized that he needed to review the firm's contract with the Northern Pacific when the Missouri was reached—or at least he told that to a number of people in late 1872. To Cooke's friends and associates, Smith's resignation was proof of his sincerity about change: he *had* rid the company of Smith; he *would* stop at the Missouri. Cooke was willing to make changes but was not about to walk away from the NP. Oberholtzer attributes this refusal to Cooke's feelings of obligation and fiduciary responsibility for tens of thousands of small bondholders who would have been wiped out as well as to his sense of "invincible power."[39]

Although sharp-eyed observers began to suspect the extent of Cooke's problems, his reputation and civic leadership were not affected. As 1872 began, Cooke was in Washington, testifying before the House Ways and Means Committee on American bond payments in Europe—time-consuming but still a responsibility for one of his standing. Cooke was delighted to play a key role as planning for the 1876 Philadelphia Centennial began and, quite naturally, was entrusted with its finances. He was continually credited with stupendous wealth. One story noted that he paid $4,000 to have five teeth filled. Normally Cooke did not comment, but this upset him; "I have no teeth but sound ones," he noted grumpily, "and am [still] able to crack hickory nuts."[40]

Nevertheless, there was one group that Cooke found it impossible to negotiate with: the Republican Party. He made two $5,000 contributions in February. After the second solicitation, he sent with his check a disgusted response that the fundraiser was an "Oliver Twist." Proving that fundraisers had no pride even then, the letter was thought humorous and was passed around at a Grant cabinet meeting. Cooke feared that Horace Greeley's election might result in the Northern Pacific's land grants being rescinded. In September, as Wall Street prices and Republican Party hopes sank, Cooke purchased $3 million in bonds to prop up the market. All told, the contributions from Cooke and his partners exceeded $50,000, a huge sum and perhaps 5 percent of Grant's total contributions.[41]

As 1872 came to its unhappy end, Northern Pacific prospects were bleak; track had not reached Bismarck, land certification did not occur until December, control of the St. Paul & Pacific and Lake Superior & Mississippi Railroads was slipping, bonds sales were negligible, and Cooke and his partners were all but out of cash. Cooke could have withdrawn at any time, but he refused. Had he walked away from the NP or firmly announced that construction would end at the Missouri, the history of the American West would have been entirely different. But Cooke and the NP staggered forward in 1873, thereby triggering the action that brought one of the nation's most renowned soldiers to the northern plains: George Armstrong Custer.

CHAPTER 13

"Looks Like War!"

Despite innumerable setbacks in late 1872, Jay Cooke and Northern Pacific president George W. Cass decided to finish the railroad's engineering. For 1873 the NP's primary eastern goals were first to complete track to Bismarck and then, once and for all, finish the Yellowstone mapping to have a "line of survey" from Lake Superior to Puget Sound. Secondary objectives were to find a shortcut west of Bismarck, thus avoiding potentially expensive construction along the east half of the Heart River, and to complete the Musselshell surveying.

Sheridan, fully supported by Grant, saw an opportunity to awe and, they hoped, to punish the Sioux, even though the army was tethered to a line of march determined by surveying requirements. Sheridan wrote Cass on January 27, 1873, to ask "as to the intentions of the company in reference to the progress of the road west of the Missouri River." He noted: "[W]e now have under consideration the changes . . . [necessary] to give adequate protection [to your surveyors and plan] . . . the construction of one or more military posts between the crossing of the Missouri and the mouth of Powder River on the line of the railroad."[1]

Meeting with the just-rehired Thomas Rosser in Chicago on February 16, Sheridan outlined his plans, which Rosser quickly passed on to Milnor Roberts. The army, Rosser wrote, would assemble 2,000 men at Forts Rice and Buford. On reaching the Yellowstone at Glendive, the column would march upriver to Pompeys Pillar, cross to the Musselshell, loop back east to the Yellowstone, and return, selecting the site for a new fort along the way. "The supplies and materials for constructing this post on the Yellowstone will be shipped [this] spring to Fort Buford," he noted. "Sheridan is very earnest and his preparations to protect our surveying parties during the summer are very elaborate."[2]

On February 24 Sheridan wrote Cass, saying that he had met with the secretary of war (and likely Grant) and asked for $250,000 for a new fort, and that "in contemplation of your road being pushed west of the Missouri, [I] succeeded in getting the 7th Cavalry transferred to the Department of the Dakota." As to the Yellowstone's rapids, he noted that boats could be assembled near Livingston, floated down, and then used to ferry troops across. When the ice broke, he would send a steamer "up the Yellowstone as far as the rapids and [see] if it is possible for her to pass as far as Powder River." Sheridan repeated his intention to build a fort; but, perhaps nervous about the NP's finances, he emphasized that "no work on these posts can be commenced until the points of crossing by the railroad are absolutely fixed."[3]

Although Custer may have been Sheridan's first choice, Stanley was placed in command, reflecting Grant's wishes and Stanley's 1872 performance. One thing that Sheridan did not see, or chose not to, was that Stanley was not up to the challenge. Some sources suggest that Rosser complained to Sheridan about Stanley, but the odds are against it. Rosser and Sheridan disliked each other, and Rosser had just been rehired. Only a request by Cooke or Cass would have carried weight. Stanley was fully aware that his career was going nowhere and wanted no part of another survey; moreover, his marriage was troubled and his infant son sickly. But he could not refuse, especially after Sheridan apparently promised that he would finally receive an eastern posting. Sheridan also had an unstated goal: the president's son, Frederick Grant, wanted to go on the survey, and it was imperative to protect him. Sheridan needed cavalry to protect Grant and confront the Sioux. Major Baker had proved unreliable, and Grant's wife had lost a first cousin. With Frederick Grant at risk, Sheridan could request the man he really wanted. Thus Grant must have given one of his characteristic grunts when he heard Sheridan's suggestion— a man Grant disliked more than most but who was arguably the best cavalryman in the army: George Armstrong Custer.

Over 125 years after his death, the names of Custer and the Little Bighorn still resonate. For generations Custer was idolized by most of the American public; however, by the Vietnam era he had become symbolic of all that was wrong with the military and this country's treatment of Native Americans. In fact Custer's personal stock had fallen so low that in the mid-1970s one writer stated: "By almost any rational definition, Custer was a fool. He was [also] a bad commander." But despite Custer's personal failings and overblown bravado, he was an inherently able, bright, and multifaceted individual. Certainly his Civil War and Great Plains record under fire is a continuing example of shrewd observation, understanding the art of the possible, aggressive personal leadership, unfailing determination, and—of course—a little bit of luck. Custer was not just a good Northern cavalry commander during the Civil War; the real question should be: was there a better cavalryman on either side?[4]

Born December 5, 1839, in New Rumley, Ohio, Custer was raised in Monroe, Michigan. A lifelong Democrat, Custer wanted to attend West Point but was disliked by the district's Republican congressman for "picketing" at a political rally. However, the congressman had a wealthy contributor whose attractive daughter was in love with Custer. In 1857 the nervous father quietly persuaded the reluctant congressman to appoint the hot-blooded suitor to far-away West Point. Custer, with no way to channel his energies, had horrific grades and racked up 726 demerits; but when just one demerit from expulsion, he held himself in check and never got another. Because of the start of the Civil War, he graduated (last) a year early (June 24, 1861). He was to enjoy exactly 15 years—not a day more—of good fortune, "Custer's Luck" as it was called.[5]

Combat brought Custer's skills, intelligence, and imagination to the fore. He was the first officer to go up in an observation balloon. (A few days later Tom Rosser became the first person to shoot down a balloon.) As George McClellan pushed toward Richmond in 1862, Custer's logical and analytical abilities were so praised that McClellan appointed him to his staff. The staff also included wealthy New York Democrat John Jacob Astor (40), who, like so many others, was impressed by and later befriended Custer. When McClellan was fired, Custer joined the staff of Alfred Pleasonton, who commanded the Army of the Potomac's cavalry. On June 28, 1863, he jumped Custer, a captain, to brigadier general, commanding a 2,300-man brigade of four Michigan cavalry regiments. One trooper soon noted: "[Custer] is a bully general and brave too. He is a very odd man but he understands his business."[6]

Custer, a resplendent target in his self-designed uniform, went into action east of Gettysburg against Jeb Stuart's cavalry. Custer's "Wolverines," as he dubbed them on taking command (thereby reinforcing their *esprit de corps*), played a key role in blocking Stuart from reaching Lee. On July 3, outnumbered and bearing the brunt of the cavalry fighting, he kept his brigade intact, staying between Stuart and thousands of exposed Union supply wagons. Two months later Custer, lightly wounded, rushed home on leave. On an earlier visit he had fallen in love with Elizabeth "Libbie" C. Bacon, from a prominent Monroe family. Now a general, Custer proposed and was accepted, marrying Libbie on February 9, 1864.

Sheridan took command of the Army of the Potomac's cavalry in March 1864. In May, with Custer's brigade leading a raid on Richmond, one of his men mortally shot Jeb Stuart at Yellow Tavern. Custer soon followed Sheridan into the Shenandoah Valley, where his combat skill and energy led to his promotion as division commander. At Tom's Brook (October 9), he and Rosser saw each other. "With my field glasses," Rosser wrote, "I easily recognized Custer as he rode along in front of his line and he evidently recognized me about the same time, for he wheeled his horse around facing me and gallantly raised his hat and made me a profound bow, which I returned as the men sent up a deafening cheer." When Custer—who had more men—overran Rosser's line, Rosser lost his baggage. Finding Rosser's uniform, Custer strutted around in the oversized jacket and sent him a note, telling him to get a better tailor.[7]

In Grant's 1865 offensive, Custer's cavalry closed the circle at Appomattox; but in the campaign's final hours his ego resulted in an act of incredible stupidity. Under a flag of truce, he met with James Longstreet and asked him to surrender unconditionally to Sheridan, with Custer accepting for Sheridan. "I am not the commander of the army and if I were I would not surrender it to General Sheridan," Longstreet replied. Custer's violation of military etiquette, which could have undercut both Lee and Grant, enraged Longstreet, a good friend of Grant at West Point. The act also must have infuriated Grant, who remembered friends and enemies for decades: Custer suddenly had an unerasable black mark.[8]

Custer's next eight years were ones of frequent frustration. Despite public lionization, he found that he had few friends, except for Sheridan. When the size of the army was cut after the war, instead of leading a dozen regiments he became a lieutenant colonel (Grant's revenge), the number two man in the 7th Cavalry, posted at Fort Riley, Kansas. In 1867, depressed and missing marriage's conjugal pleasures, he deserted his command to be with Libbie, for which he was court-martialed and convicted. The sentence was mild: a year's suspension and loss of pay.

At Sheridan's request, Custer was reinstated months early for an Indian campaign. On November 26, 1868, Custer's scouts discovered 50 Cheyenne lodges along the Washita River. At dawn the next morning he led a charge into a village at peace with the United States and flying the American flag. Over 100 Cheyennes died, and Custer's 21 dead included a 17-man detachment under Maj. Joel Elliott. Outnumbered by Cheyennes in adjacent villages, Custer made only a cursory search for Elliott. When Capt. Frederick Benteen wrote anonymously to a St. Louis paper that Custer had abandoned Elliott, Custer met with his officers, saying he would horsewhip the man who wrote the letter. The tough if unpleasant Benteen stepped forward, his hand on his pistol. Custer, livid, stomped out of the room, an act that some have interpreted as cowardice but that more likely represented his fear of another court-martial.[9]

When the 7th Cavalry's colonel retired. Sheridan tried to help Custer; but due to Grant's animosity the command went to Samuel D. Sturgis. In 1871 the regiment was assigned to Reconstruction duty and scattered over nine states. Custer was sent to a backwater assignment in Elizabethtown, Kentucky. Disgusted, he went to New York, unsuccessfully seeking work and hobnobbing with many of Grant's political enemies. Custer was socially lionized, as he had probably anticipated, for he had left Libbie in Monroe and openly "escorted ladies to opera and plays." While in Kentucky he began writing for *Galaxy* magazine; the $100 per article added a third to his monthly salary and kept him in the public's eye.[10]

In 1873 Custer was a gifted horseman, crack shot, sparkling conversationalist, facile writer, and to his contemporaries, a man's man. He had a keen sense of humor, was well read, and had developed an appreciation for music, theater, and the Hudson River school of painting. But Custer's life was increasingly contradictory: he was an army officer unsuited for a peacetime duty. He hated injustice in the abstract but punished outside acceptable norms; fought against graft but expected and accepted gifts; and, despite being a lover of horses, dogs, and even a field mouse, hunted so compulsively that some might feel that his actions came close to or crossed the line into slaughter. Within the military, Custer was disliked and feared: with Sheridan's unquestioning support his modus operandi included undermining and disregarding immediate superiors, leaving in his wake a slew of destroyed or damaged careers.

Custer's flaws were never as a military tactician, or at least not until his final hours. Men who successfully led cavalry charges had to be outstanding motivators, with good peripheral vision, an instinct for terrain, the ability to recover after a setback, and an instinctive, highly sophisticated understanding of combat. If Custer's military skills were exceptional, his personal flaws were certainly not insignificant. While his ambitiousness has perhaps been overstated, his huge ego soured relations with most of his fellow officers. At times his ego or impatience (the two often seem interchangeable with him) clearly got the better of him, wrecking his relationship with Grant and eleven years later quite likely costing him his life. Custer also did not listen well (see chapter 16 for the Braden incident on the morning of August 11), and the Cheyennes who came upon his body at the Little Bighorn symbolically expressed this by punching holes in his ears so that he could hear better.

After four and a half years of combat inactivity, Custer, at 33, was excited by his 1873 assignment, fully understanding that his opportunities for advancement and public recognition were dwindling. Thus, while he sincerely sympathized with the plight of Native Americans, he needed the stimulus of combat and public recognition even more.

None of the previous Yellowstone surveys equaled 1873's logistical effort. Given the 1,500-plus troops, to say nothing of the huge supply train that would be necessary, Sheridan realized that, if steamboats could be sent up the Yellowstone, troops could be ferried across at Glendive and supplies transported from Bismarck. As soon as it was practical, Sheridan sent the 200-foot-long, 33-foot-wide steamer *Key West* on a reconnaissance up the Yellowstone to see if it was navigable. Playing key roles were a trio of legendary western figures: Grant Marsh, the *Key West*'s captain; Major George A. "Sandy" Forsyth, the hero of the battle of Beecher's Island and a longtime Sheridan friend; and Yellowstone Kelly, chief scout and hunter.[11]

On May 6, with large chunks of ice finally gone from the Yellowstone, the *Key West* steamed out of Fort Buford with over 100 troops, 15 Indian scouts, a three-inch rifled cannon, and 6 horses. Despite men, supplies, and ammunition, the load was light; the steamer drew just 26 inches of water. While it made 28 miles the first day, from the second day on progress was slowed by rapids and shoals, all made more difficult by the low water. Forsyth noted that it took more than four hours to clear the first shoals, most likely by a combination of redistributing the *Key West's* weight, digging through sand and loose rock, using ropes, and perhaps even setting up a "grasshopper," a wooden device that lifted the boat and moved it forward a few feet at a time. The steamer passed Glendive Creek on May 10 and three days later was a few miles below the Powder River, averaging under three miles an hour after the first day's run.[12]

On May 11, after 225 miles, low water and two sandstone rocks halted the *Key West* 4 miles below the Powder River. Forsyth wrote: "With proper appliances these two rocks can be easily removed . . . and the channel opened . . . 80 miles further." No one had thought to bring the appliances or explosives, however, so the *Key West* returned to Fort Buford. Forsyth wrote that, with the channel known, the trip could be made in five days and that Marsh said the Yellowstone was easier to navigate than the Missouri west of Buford. No Indians were seen; but an "American" horse was spotted on the shore, thought to be a trick to ambush anyone attempting to recapture it. The expedition was thoroughly successful, received national publicity, and proved that a fort could be established on the Yellowstone and supplied by steamer.[13]

The 7th Cavalry left Memphis on March 11 (its trip is well documented in Roger Darling's definitive *Custer's Seventh Cavalry Comes to Dakota*). Sheridan then ordered Sturgis to St. Paul for administrative duties, leaving Custer in command of the regiment. The journey was highlighted by a ferocious April snowstorm and anger over Custer's correct but too-rigorous training methods and marching. On Friday, May 22, Custer reached Fort Sully, where he and Stanley met, likely for the first time.

One cavalry officer was Lt. Charles W. Larned (West Point, '70), a graceful writer earning pocket money as a *Chicago Inter-Ocean* correspondent. He wrote that Stanley "seems to be very much liked and impressed me very favorably when I met him. Large, handsome, and dignified." However, as Darling notes, this opinion might also have reflected Larned's anger at Custer. Custer genuinely liked Larned but also wanted favorable *Inter-Ocean* coverage and chose him as judge advocate for some routine desertion cases. Because the desertions made him look bad, Custer heavy-handedly tried to move the court from Fort Sully to the 7th Cavalry's campsite, where he could exercise more control. Larned, wet behind the ears, took his temporary role seriously and (for reasons he did not understand) easily got all 11 officers to sign a complaint against Custer. Sounding like Stanley a month later (see chapter 14), Larned wrote his mother in June: "[Custer] is making himself utterly detested by every line officer of the command, with the exception of one

or two toadies, by his selfish, capricious, arbitrary, and unjust conduct." Custer
backed off, perhaps wryly amused at Larned's success in fending him off, for he
continued giving the young officer plum assignments.[14]

After Fort Sully, the 7th Cavalry marched upriver and was south of Fort Rice
when Custer again became mired in controversy. At Rice was the steamer *DeSmet*,
owned and operated by the crusty Joseph LaBarge, 58, one of the best of the
Upper Missouri boatmen. LaBarge recalled that Stanley, a good friend, arranged for
him to ferry the 7th Cavalry across to Rice. LaBarge landed and went out to meet
Custer, who did not dismount or shake hands.

> I showed him my order for the transportation of the command and told
> him that if he would have the wagons brought down I would see to their
> proper disposition on the boat. "Stand aside, sir," he replied, "my wagon-
> master will take charge of the boat and see to ferrying the command over."
> "Not if I know myself," I replied, and started for the boat. Custer sent a
> guard to arrest me, but I took time by the forelock, drew in the stage, and
> steamed across the river and reported to General Stanley.[15]

In Darling's account, Custer had flagged LaBarge down 10 miles south of Rice,
and the two agreed on a price. When the *DeSmet* docked, Custer told LaBarge that
his wagon master would supervise the loading. LaBarge, who could curse in at least
three languages, emphatically refused. Custer lost his temper, saying that he would
arrest him. LaBarge excused himself, went to his engine room, and suddenly threw
the boat's gears into reverse. Custer was left on shore fuming. Many of his officers,
wet and perplexed, had been thrown or jumped off when the steamer jerked backward. Ultimately, the *Miner* ferried Custer across.[16]

Custer historian Edgar I. Stewart wrote that "General Terry warned Stanley . . .
that he could expect trouble from Custer, a prediction that was fulfilled." Darling says
that "source material reveals Custer in deep trouble all during the Dakota transfer—
impetuously exceeding his normal authority, unnecessarily entangling himself in
controversy." Custer's march to Fort Rice was characterized by altercations, confrontations, or evasions of authority involving his brother Tom, Benteen, LaBarge,
Larned, Sturgis, and Terry as well as the accidental death of some reservation Indians.
Stanley likely knew about most of these and that he would be spending months with
a man in a determinedly foul attitude, who was unresponsive to authority.[17]

Javan B. Irvine excitedly wrote his wife in April: "Telegraphic orders from General
Terry prohibits [*sic*] leave of absence during active operations. . . . The Government
has ordered troops to the front, reinforcing all posts along the frontier. . . . Looks
like war!" In the spring of 1873 the plains near Fort Rice slowly filled with troops,
wagons, supplies, horses, mules, and cattle. Adding to the confusion, with track

completed to Bismarck, the Northern Pacific had laid off some 1,500 workers; and many had walked the 25 miles to Rice, penniless and looking for work.[18]

Among the infantry officers was, again, Maj. R. E. A. Crofton, as well as the respected Lt. Col. Luther P. Bradley, 51, who had spent the past few years on the frontier. Bradley's letters and diaries indicate a dry sense of humor and wide-ranging interests; he had risen from a prewar bookstore owner to a brigadier general, being badly wounded at Chickamauga and Franklin. Bradley's rank and date of commission (July 28, 1866) were the same as Custer's. But in the event of Stanley's incapacitation—not a moot issue, given his drinking—the command would pass to the senior officer. Here the "tiebreakers" (including Civil War rank) gave it to Custer.[19]

Bradley and ten infantry companies were squeezed on board the steamer *Western* on May 24 at Yankton. A soldier named Hoffman soon fell off. "Every time we carry troops up [the Missouri] some of them get lost," an officer angrily told a *New York Herald* reporter, also noting that there was not "a single rope guard along the sides of the boat." On May 27 a soldier was felled by smallpox. Two more cases broke out, but somehow the disease was checked. The *Western* passed Custer and the *Miner*, on which the 7th Cavalry's officers' wives slept. Bradley noted: "[The] Steamer camps alongside them every night, rather a nice way of campaigning." When the *Western* reached Fort Rice on June 4, everyone was promptly quarantined because of the smallpox.[20]

On June 8 Bradley noted the increasingly hot, humid weather and "mosquitoes enough to eat us up." The next day the first mail, newspapers, and mosquito netting arrived. Bradley reported to his wife: "[B]attalion drill in the afternoon . . . [and] drilling every day, principally in 'skirmish.'" Despite the netting, he wrote: "I am tired of laying [*sic*] in camp to be eaten up by mosquitoes and shall strike tents gladly anytime." Everyone anticipated fighting. Newspaper articles, fed by rumors, had the Sioux gathering in large numbers. Hostile Indians were frequently seen, and light skirmishing occurred in late April and May just outside Fort Lincoln.[21]

The 1873 force included a "Scientific Corps." The *New York Tribune* editorialized: "All that anybody now recollects about Napoleon's being in Egypt is the successful exploration of the scientific corps." The group included Joel A. Allen (Harvard zoologist and mineralogist), Charles Bennett (Allen's assistant), Edward M. Konopicky (an Austrian artist at Harvard), Lionel Nettre (geologist, affiliation unknown), and a photographer, William R. Pywell, whose equipment did not reach them until late July. Escorting them was Capt. Henry M. Lazelle, a veteran of the 1872 survey who had just published a book (poorly reviewed) about "natural philosophy."[22]

Stanley furnished each member with an officer's tent and horse. The corps also had officer's rations, two two-horse "springwagons" (army buckboards), two six-mule wagons, a cook, and a guard unit. Konopicky complained about having three meals a day containing salted pork, but his worst comments were reserved for the Missouri's water, which was "warm and thick [and] has to stand for several hours before most of the sediment settles."[23]

On May 21, as Rosser was finalizing his plans, he wrote Jordan (who had been laid off the previous fall) and invited him back, noting: "The boys often speak of you and would rejoice to have you back with us." In addition to himself, he told Jordan that the team included Eckelson as chief of survey at $175 a month; Meigs, first assistant, $150; mapmakers, transitmen, and levelers, $125 each; three rodmen, $75; two picketmen, rodmen and axemen, and a cook, $60 each; one assistant, $40; a hunter; and at least four teamsters. Rosser's crew grew to between 26 and 28, likely costing some $12,000.[24]

Rosser's 1873 responsibilities included managing the final phase of railroad construction to Bismarck, a position well suited to his leadership abilities. After settling a strike on May 23, he was hampered by rain, humidity, mosquitoes, and water that sickened hundreds of the workers. To reach Bismarck, the track had to cross Apple Creek seven times; each crossing resulted in an 80- to 100-foot bridge. Nevertheless, the track was completed on June 3 with a final push of 3.79 miles. "As might be expected," Milnor Roberts wrote, "Bismarck was lively during the night and yesterday morning the killed and wounded far outnumbered live working men." Roberts noted that a contractor, "a Mr. Winston" (Rosser's brother-in-law), helped him round up workers on June 4. But Rosser's state of mind concerned Roberts: "From the tenor of telegrams he has received from his wife, I think his decision to go even part of the way will be very painful." Annoyed at Lizzy Rosser and the distraction she was causing, Roberts wrote Cass: "The last telegram from . . . [Rosser's] wife was in effect she could not be reconciled to the idea of his crossing the Missouri. It has been rumored that Indians have said 'if they could kill big General Rosser they could stop the railroad.' Whether any such rumor has reached Mrs. Rosser I know not. Very likely it originated with some white Ass. They are plentiful [here]."[25]

That same day Rosser returned to Minneapolis. He and Lizzy checked into the Metropolitan Hotel to be away from his mother-in-law, who was now living with them. Rosser met with General Terry, NP personnel, and Brackett (about side businesses), had photos taken of his family, and returned to Bismarck on June 12. In June Roberts chose Eckelson to replace Rosser so that there would be a smooth transition when Rosser left the surveyors at the Yellowstone. Later Custer wrote his wife that Eckelson was a "most agreeable young man." Meigs, who was passed over and became his assistant, generously wrote: "He is a noble fellow . . . full of fun and high spirits, energetic and bold, the very man for such work as ours."[26]

General Terry left Fargo at 5 A.M. on June 11, reaching Bismarck in twelve and a half hours—a trip that had taken a week in 1872. Roberts joined Terry, and the two reached Fort Rice early on June 12. Roberts was briefly reunited with his daughter and infant grandson at Rice and met Stanley and Custer. Those who have a low opinion of Custer's intelligence might note that Roberts, 63, did not suffer fools gladly; but he and Custer, 33, appear to have gotten along famously, beginning a friendship that survived the failure of the Northern Pacific and lasted until Custer's death.[27]

When Roberts and the military met on June 12, 200 new six-mule wagons, each capable of carrying 5,000 pounds of supplies, had not arrived. Teamsters had to be hired, and mule teams leased or purchased. The man apparently in charge was Maj. Eugene M. Baker, ex-commandant of Fort Ellis. Capt. Edward D. Baker was assigned to the survey as quartermaster; to make matters more difficult in reconstructing events, the newspapers confused the two. By June 11 Stanley was so frustrated that he sent a detachment of Indian scouts to search for the wagons. On June 14 everyone gave up; Stanley, consulting with Roberts, decided to send 5 companies of infantry and 25 cavalrymen to Fort Lincoln so that the surveyors might begin.[28]

The revised plan was for the escort to accompany the surveyors from Mandan on June 17. Stanley and Custer would wait at Fort Rice until the wagons arrived then head northwest "and intercept the engineering party some days out." As irony would have it, the wagons arrived on the Missouri's east bank on the afternoon of June 15. No specific location for the meeting was set, but it would be near present-day Glen Ullin.[29]

The surveyors left their Mandan campsite on the morning of June 17. They had marched less than an hour when they were attacked by 75 to 100 Hunkpapas. Rosser instinctively took over, galloped to the front, ordered the escort to follow him, and screamed: "Engineers to the rear!" (One of Rosser's brothers-in-law, meanwhile, was frantically—and unsuccessfully—trying to yank off a "mosquito head net.") The gunfire was so heavy that it could be heard in Bismarck and lasted long enough (perhaps two hours) that men in Bismarck had time to row across the Missouri and be in on the end of the fighting. William P. Carlin, commanding Fort Abraham Lincoln (the former Fort McKeen), wrote: "[T]he Sioux attacked us . . . just as the railroad engineers had started on their survey. I sent out my scouts and took two companies. . . . The Sioux fought obstinately, and held the ridge until forced to retreat. We have two Sioux dead in our possession, who were scalped and mangled by the scouts."[30]

For a week following the attack, the survey went uneventfully. Happily, Rosser had found a shortcut north of the Heart River that promised to save dozens of miles of difficult construction. The Indians were gone, and everyone was in good spirits. The afternoon of June 24 saw the surveyors 35 miles west of Bismarck when the sky began to darken rapidly. Cavalryman Lt. James Calhoun, Custer's brother-in-law, was 25 miles away and noted that "the sky became overcast with thick heavy clouds which assumed a greenish hue and caused all surrounding objects to have a most ghastly appearance." Meigs said that the sky blackened and hailstones fell faster and faster, "sting[ing] considerably." The horses were already nervous when three huge bolts of lighting crashed into the ground near them. When a cavalrymen shouted: "Go for the timber like hell!" almost everybody started a mad dash downhill toward some woods along a small stream—later named Hailstone Creek.[31]

The hailstones were "the size of large marbles and every one that struck raised a lump on the flesh." Most horses bolted, throwing their riders, and those who dismounted could not control them. Meigs's horse was "frantic with pain." As two riderless horses dashed by, his horse gave a tremendous jerk, sending him tumbling. Meigs sprinted to a small brush but discovered that two troopers were already hiding under it. Meigs pulled down his hat, protecting his head "from all but the sidelong stones," and shielded his body "by stretching my coat over my arm and holding that up high." He received numerous welts on his elbow, and his arm was black and blue.

While the storm lasted for no more than ten minutes, its violence destroyed the felt hats that many troopers wore and "even penetrated the brims of thick straw hats." Meigs said that Eckelson's horse bolted, his hat blew away, and his "head was completely covered with lumps as big as the end of one's finger, and his back and shoulders looked as if someone had been beating him with a tack hammer." Decades later a surveyor recalled being thrown off a wagon. He managed to find a bucket, raced to a tree, and with "the bucket over my head escaped any serious injury. My hands and back were, however, covered with bruises."[32]

Horses drawing the wagons panicked and ran over rocks, "smashing army [and surveyor] wagons almost to toothpicks and breaking their harnesses." Capt. Augustus W. Corliss wrote years later that the surveyors' wagons were "most admirably fitted for their use and were wonders of labor-saving and space-economizing expedients, most of them the result of General Rosser's experience during the war." Specially made tents, folding chairs and tables, drawing stands, and field supplies and equipment were also damaged. The hill was littered with untold numbers of dead antelope and some 30 mules; half a dozen horses either were dead or needed to be destroyed. Lt. Edward Lynch was so badly hurt that he had to be taken back to Fort Lincoln. Meigs expressed what many felt: "I think [had Stanley been with us,] the Yellowstone Expedition would have had to return." Rosser wrote to his wife on June 28:

> [W]e encountered the most violent hail storm which I ever witnessed which stampeded all of our horses and mules, broke our wagons, wounded the men and placed our entire detachment "hors de combat" . . . unable to move, waiting for General Stanley. [T]o give you some idea of its intensity . . . my hands were cut and bleeding by the ice, my head and back was

bruised, and when I stopped to change my clothing, my body looked like it had been beaten with a tack hammer. Many of the officers and men were knocked down by the ice and badly hurt, we had a large dog with us that was killed by the hail and the prairie is covered with antelope that were killed by the hail stones . . . [T]he hail was about the size of hickory nuts and fell to the depth of three inches and drifted in places [to] one and a half feet deep [and] did not all melt until the next day. I held onto my horse for I expected when it was over if I should survive it, that I perhaps would be the only man who could . . . report the disaster.[33]

Four days later Custer joined the surveyors. While Custer and Rosser had enjoyed a close, boisterous relationship at West Point, Rosser was apprehensive as to how Custer, his 1864 adversary, would act toward him; other friends from his West Point days had apparently snubbed him after the war. He need not have worried. "Gen. Rosser," a surveyor wrote in 1906, "had me write a message to Gen. Custer . . . and Gen. Custer [warmly] responded to the invitation."[34]

Custer soon developed a close relationship with the surveyors. Enthusiastic, easy-going, with high self-confidence and above-average education, they were demographically akin to his Wolverines. Their high regard for Custer is reflected in correspondence relating to the 1906 reunion. They also idolized Rosser, and his special relationship with the war hero only added to their feelings about both. To their delight, Custer soon spent most evenings with them, away from Stanley, the infantry, and even his own officers and men. For the surveyors, Custer was a breath of fresh air compared with the conservative Stanley, whose 1872 drinking could only have been disillusioning, no matter what his military virtues might have been.

CHAPTER 14

"Under the Whiskey Curse"

Reveille was sounded at 3:00 A.M. on the morning of June 20. The day was blustery and cool, the previous week's humidity gone, as enlisted men finished their breakfast of bacon, potato balls, biscuits, and coffee. In the age-old ritual, last-second packing was completed and the men lined up, waiting patiently for sleepy officers. Just after 5:30, "advance" was played. In careful order, the army marched west from Fort Rice. At Stanley's invitation to "gallop to the top of the hill and take a look at the column," officers, correspondents, and the Scientific Corps viewed the army's might. Even without the surveyors' escort, the 1,300-man force was huge by plains standards, comprising infantry, cavalry, and artillerymen with two three-inch rifled Rodman guns, which Stanley had chosen instead of smooth-bore Napoleons.[1]

The military included mixed-blood ("half-breed" in the rough vernacular of the frontier) scouts led by Basil Clement, 27 Indian scouts under Daniel Brush, staff, observers (including Fred Grant), quartermasters, sutlers, and Charley Reynolds's hunters. There were 353 civilians, mostly teamsters but also beef herders, correspondents, the Scientific Corps, and servants for some officers. Transport included some 275 six-mule wagons and 5 to 10 ambulances—all told, and including the surveyors, their escort, and civilians, more than 2,400 mules and horses. Some officers had hunting dogs, partially to warn against Indians, although there is no instance of dogs alerting soldiers on any of the surveys.[2]

Enlisted men had an overcoat, blanket, poncho, two shirts, two pair of shoes, and socks and drawers. They wore wool flannel pants, linen shirts, and hats of their own choosing and carried a rifle, 40 rounds of ammunition, a canteen, and a haversack for personal items. Each company had two six-mule wagons with five days' rations, extra shoes, pup tents, and other items. Sutlers' wagons were miniature general stores, carrying clothing, toilet items, writing materials, and other supplies as well as whiskey for the cavalry. The cavalry's sutler had two wagons, and the infantry's sutler presumably more, as he served twice as many. There were six blacksmith forges, 3,500 horseshoes, "an ample supply of mule shoes," nails, and coal for the forges. The column carried wheelwright tools as well as extra canvas and spare parts; a broken wheel, axle, or wagon tongue could be replaced immediately and later repaired.[3]

It was impossible to carry the 12 pounds of grain that horses and mules normally ate, so the quartermaster allotted an inadequate 5 pounds per day. Once they were underway, however, Stanley angrily discovered that "[t]he oats sent . . . [were] invoiced at 168 pounds to the sack, but by trial only averaged 130 pounds to the sack. The great discrepancy cannot be accounted for by wastage in handling." Two weeks later 45 empty wagons went back to Fort Lincoln for more supplies. Additionally, the army had hired steamers to bring further supplies up the Yellowstone.[4]

As they left Rice, Brush's scouts fanned out a mile in front. Stanley led the column, followed by ten infantry companies, the Rodman guns, and then quarter-master wagons flanked by the cavalry. The wagons were followed by the remaining infantry companies and the cattle. Three miles long, the column took an hour to pass a specific point. Luther Bradley wrote: "We had one of the prettiest sights I ever saw: the columns moving out together as the sun rose over the hills, and the music of the 7th Cavalry band cheering up the drooping." The *New York Tribune*'s Samuel June Barrows called the music "a little rough, but whatever its deficiencies . . . [it] has a tonic effect on the mind, which soothes the nerves and strengthens the muscles." Charles Larned wrote that the column did not "move with the ease and precision which only comes from habit . . . [But this] will wear off and each component will [soon] understand its time, place, and function." He was too optimistic, however: the column never fused.[5]

The spring of 1873 was exceptionally wet. April's snow and rain was followed by a gloomy May, in which it rained nearly half the time. The rains were both short, violent afternoon thunderstorms that typify the plains and also heavy, drenching rains lasting for hours. Milnor Roberts wrote George Cass on June 3 that it had rained 14 of the previous 31 days. Mosquitoes were so abundant that Larned noted: "At [the dinner] table they transform us into active windmills, one arm being con-stantly on the swing while the other shovels the eatables in anxious haste down our throats." Heavy rain resumed the evening of June 20. Barrows wrote:

> The felicity of camp life was assailed the very first night . . . [by] thunder and lightning, wind and rain. Sleep was arrested, tents blown down, bedding flooded, and our night's rest completely broken up. The only consolation for

this very bad night was that the next one might be better. The premise was hopeful; the conclusion false . . . only one night could be worse than the first one, and that was the second.[6]

Bradley's June 21 diary recorded "one of the severest thunder storms I have ever witnessed . . . the rain was in full proportion." He also noted storms on nine different dates and on June 28 that the rain "flooded the tent and sat me roosting on my camp chair chicken fashion until it stopped and the water ran out." Stanley, while often prone to exaggeration, was probably accurate when he wrote that it rained 14 of 17 days. He also noted that and the army's tents were so poor that "there is little difference in a tent [or] outside of it." Barrows regretted only "that no provision was made . . . for recording the amount of rain-fall."[7]

Lt. James Calhoun wrote that one storm blasted the camp around 2 A.M., uprooting the pegs in Custer's tent and forcing him to stand out in the driving rain, "*sans everything*" (Calhoun's emphasis), hammering his tent pegs back in. The terrain, the nature of the column, and the rains would have caused delays and personal frustration for even the most sober and patient commanders, which could not be said respectively for either Stanley or Custer. Younger men might shrug off the storms' impact; but for Stanley (whose tent also blew over), older and feeling the pressures of leadership, the storms caused sleep deprivation, always a weakening agent. Stanley's drinking can be traced from the June 20–22 thunderstorms. The lack of sleep caused tempers to flare within days between infantry (who viewed the cavalry as Johnny-come-latelies) and cavalry (always contemptuous of infantry). The *Chicago Post* stated: "It is well understood that an unpleasant feeling existed between these officers from the start." Throughout the command, frustration, backbiting, tension, and disrespect rose with the lack of sleep.[8]

Rain, humidity (eight men collapsed on June 21), the custom of marching 50 minutes and resting 10, with a 30-minute lunch, and Indians dictated the daily pace. When a warning was sounded, wagons galloped into a "corral" formation, with only their backs exposed, leaving an opening for the cattle. Soldiers would then tie a rope fence across the opening, as designated companies double-timed in front of the wagons in skirmish formation. Hunkpapas were tracking Stanley and undoubtedly took great pleasure at firing on the scouts, watching the column go into its defensive posture and then fleeing. It took almost an hour for the column to get underway again. Custer was not allowed to pursue, which undoubtedly frustrated him.[9]

Major delays were caused by the treeless prairie, which could absorb only so much water. The ground became soft, often unable to support the 5,000-pound wagons. Despite this, the column made 69 miles in the first six days. They crossed the Heart River on June 25 and found a good campsite. Stanley made June 26, their seventh day out, a rest day; Larned noted: "[R]eveled in laziness all day." Stanley's drinking probably had begun on June 22, when the march was only four miles. Adding to this likelihood is the contradiction between the normally supportive Bradley, whose diary states that the column stopped at noon, and Stanley's report, which states that "the entire day was spent making four miles on a level prairie."[10]

Late on June 26 Charley Reynolds rode into camp and told Stanley of the havoc caused among the surveyors by the hailstorm. To reach Rosser rapidly, Stanley set reveille for 2 A.M.; but Bradley disgustedly wrote in his diary the next night: "[M]en delayed by Custer . . . we did not get out of camp till after 5." Custer historian Lawrence A. Frost states that the delay was because some "cavalry officers played poker until the early morning hours, then overslept long enough to delay breakfast." He defends Custer by saying that while he knew his men were up late, "The men in the field had too few pleasures as it was"—a perplexing argument considering Rosser's distress.[11]

Despite the delay, Stanley marched 16 miles on June 27, camping some 6 miles from Big Muddy Creek. Custer rode ahead of him, taking with him Stanley's bridging equipment. On reaching the stream, he found it high but built a bridge that his horses and wagons could pass over and spent the evening north of Big Muddy Creek. Normally placid, with lazy S-curves across a half-mile-wide valley, the creek was penned in by a steep plateau over 50 feet high. Adding to Stanley's problems, his maps were literally blank concerning Big Muddy and the area where Rosser was stranded; he simply did not know where they were or how to reach them.

Stanley was marching, often in heavy rain, by 5:30 A.M., but on reaching Big Muddy, he was horrified to discover that the stream was rising rapidly, clearly endangering Custer's bridge. Stanley thought that the Big Muddy was 60 feet wide and 20 feet deep, and Larned wrote that the stream had risen 10 feet, calling it "viciously deep and rapid." The creek was likely 45 to 60 feet wide and about 10 to 15 feet deep, but its velocity made crossing impossible. The column stopped just south of present-day Almont, south of where Hailstone Creek and Sims Creek merge with Big Muddy Creek. About a mile to the south the enlarged Big Muddy literally smashed into a steep hill, making a 90-degree turn. Stanley's scouts had placed the column in front of a rampaging stream that drained 500 to 600 square miles, half the size of Rhode Island.[12]

Barrows wrote that Stanley took an active role: "[He] is not a Micawber. He never waits for anything to turn up if there is a chance of turning it up himself." But that afternoon Stanley (who was, of course, partially to blame because of June 22's four miles) could only watch the boiling water rise, sweeping away the bridge and equipment. Wild with frustration, he whipped off an angry letter, among the most controversial ever written about Custer. "I have had no trouble with Custer," he wrote his wife disingenuously, "and will try to avoid any, but I have seen enough of him to convince me that he is a cold blooded, untruthful, and unprincipled man. He is universally despised by all the officers of his regiment excepting his relatives and one or two sycophants. . . . As I said, I will try, but am not sure I can avoid trouble with him."[13]

Stanley had to resupply Rosser and get his 5,000-pound wagons across. Scouts looking for other crossings found none. As Stanley fumed, Lt. Philip H. Ray, 31, an 1872 survey veteran and the 8th Infantry's commissary officer, stepped forward. Ray, an 1861 enlistee, was rising slowly through the ranks despite obvious bravery and creativity. His plan was to turn a wagon into a rope ferry. Two volunteers, with ropes tied to them, waded into the raging creek, nearly drowned, but made it across. Once they were there, heavier ropes were tied to lighter ones and attached to a wagon frame. The ferry worked efficiently; each trip carried a thousand pounds of supplies or men, Stanley and Ray being among the first to cross. Soon supplies for Rosser, including blacksmith equipment, were on their way.

However, Ray's ferry could not take animals or wagons. With the water still high on June 30, Ray again came to the rescue. Dozens of wagons were stripped, and empty water kegs were lashed together and placed in their upside-down bottoms. Larned called them "a bouncing pontoon bridge of eccentric but sound proportions." The difficult part was hand-pulling 5,000-pound wagons. As the first one crossed, held in place by ropes and 100 men, the bridge swayed and sank lower, with rushing water slightly covering it. But the bridge held; and one by one the wagons, animals, men, and Rodmans crossed over a two-day period. Barrows wrote of Stanley: "I doubt if there is an officer . . . better qualified for [this] difficult work." Stanley generously thanked Ray in his report, thus sending Ray along on what proved to be a remarkable, adventurous career.[14]

Yet, in the cavalry's eyes, Stanley caused the delay. Custer wrote his wife: "Stanley is acting very badly [and] drinking." Custer's brother-in-law James Calhoun believed that "Stanley could easily have crossed the day we did . . . I am thoroughly disgusted with him and his entire outfit of infantry." Unfortunately, Frost's attitude remains the norm in far too many Custer biographies, but he still needs to be quoted: "Stanley was still back there drinking, and wishing, and drinking. The great procrastinator could have crossed the creek previously with the rest of the command but elected to cross leisurely and regally, all because he was in his cups again. . . . There is little question that the delay was unnecessary and the result costly," and, Frost continued, Stanley "delayed progress for a week."[15]

But should Stanley be blamed for June 27? Was he drunk, did he procrastinate, could he have crossed "leisurely and regally," was the result costly, and was a week lost? The answers to these questions usually appear to favor Stanley and certainly contradict Frost's interpretation. With the 2 A.M. reveille, Stanley's fault lay in not leaving the cavalry, which would soon have caught up. But even so, could his column have marched 22 miles over soggy ground, through three hours of "drenching rain," built a sturdy bridge, and had the entire column cross? Unless Barrows's account was a fabrication—and he had no motivation to lie—Stanley was sober and exercised effective leadership.

Meigs called the country "a sea of liquid mud." The main problem that Barrows noted was "[an] insidious enemy . . . an enemy the more which it is trodden on the more dangerous it becomes. I refer to Dakota mud." Wagons stalled on level ground, the men were exhausted, and "to save our mules we have been obliged to make but short marches." Every gully or incline had to be cut or filled by hand. Apparently firm ground often broke up; as Barrows wrote: "A bridge or filling that has to support 2,000,000 pounds in the course of an afternoon needs to be well made." Everybody was not working simultaneously: "frequently, 200 or 300 soldiers [are] watching the result [and] form a jury." The decisions were accompanied by loud heckling, clapping, and earsplitting whistles. Sometimes the result was hilarious: "I have seen a team pull on a stalled wagon until the rope broke . . . and 200 men were orderly piled one on top of another [in the mud] like a row of fallen bricks. [A]ll idea of gloom immediately vanished. . . . If one good laugh does not pull the wagon out of the mud . . . another laugh certainly will."[16]

A morale booster was Custer's band, led by Italian-born Felix Vinatieri, 39. Weather permitting, his band gave daily serenades and, besides playing "Garry Owen" (once a day for Custer), also played works by Schubert, Beethoven, and Strauss, among others. Konopicky, with a guard, would leave the column and ride to a nearby hill, making much admired sketches. He epitomized the word "tenderfoot": he was unable to ride for long periods and was so easily fatigued that he became the butt of numerous jokes. Fred Grant at one point handed him a not-quite-dead rattlesnake.[17]

Stanley's wagons linked up with Rosser on July 5; their first camp was at Gladstone, where the Green and Heart Rivers meet. By then, with dry weather and firm ground, Stanley averaged 19 miles a day. He called a day's halt on July 6, affording a welcome rest, notwithstanding the mosquitoes. Bradley noted: "[S]ome days you can hardly tell the color of [my] horse, they are so thick . . . [He is] covered with lumps as large as marbles." The Sabbath was celebrated by infantry officers who got so drunk that Stanley had to arrest them. Calhoun grumbled that "[Stanley] sets the example, his officers follow him, and . . . he goes unpunished."[18]

When the columns met, Rosser announced that he had found a route from Bismarck. When connected to the 1871 survey, it gave the Northern Pacific a path to the Yellowstone that saved dozens of miles of difficult construction along the Heart River. It also meant that the column could march directly to the Yellowstone, saving weeks of time. Stanley's reaction to Rosser's discovery, however, reflected his peevish side; he became angry over the extra supplies that the column had carried and remained angry in his report. The anger was unjustified, but Stanley likely was subconsciously hurt by Rosser's literally moving his surveyors into Custer's camp, the Rosser-Custer camaraderie, and the surveyors themselves, who now probably all but ignored him.

Many newspapers, to add to their prestige and ensure summer sales, annually covered some exploration or similar adventure with a good, albeit expendable correspondent. The *New York Tribune,* the country's leading newspaper, hired Samuel June Barrows, 28. Brilliant but sickly (he was not allowed to enlist), he was Secretary of State Seward's personal secretary, married one of the country's first female medical students, entered Harvard Divinity School (1871), and to pay his way wrote for the *Tribune* in the summers. In 1873 his health improved with the rigors of outdoor life, and he knew shorthand, which explains why his quotations ring true. He was friendly with Custer on the 1874 Black Hills expedition, but in 1876 reluctantly decided not to join him. Bradley wrote his wife: "[G]et the *New York Tribune* for the summer. Barrow [*sic*] . . . is a smart fellow and I think his letters will be worth reading, save them 'till I get home." Although his articles were never published in book form, he and Konopicky discussed collaborating on a book, and the letters remain the survey's most comprehensive source of information.[19]

Another writer was the president of the Winona, Minnesota, normal school (two-year teacher college) and an early National Education Association president, William F. Phelps, 51. In Auburn, New York, he taught 140 children in a one-room schoolhouse, catching the eye of a neighbor, William Seward, who sent him to Union College and helped him with jobs. Rosser called him "Fagin," and he was later recalled as "a tall, gaunt man with long legs, deep set eyes, with little tufts of [a] bristling beard sticking out of his face . . . [H]is ears were large and set out from his head. He rode a small pony and [his] long legs dangled almost to the ground. He slept in our tent, never took off his shoes, and snored like a Turk." The *St. Paul Pioneer* published his letter describing Custer and Rosser, a symbolic coupling that caught the public's fancy. Phelps described Custer as "slightly inclined forward in walking," with his hair "hanging in slight curls on the shoulder," and continued:

> [H]e wore a black, broad-brimmed, low-crowned hat, a dark blue, short sack-coat, light blue pants, and red shirt with collar turned over the vest. In talking he is intensely earnest and lively, and during this interview he sat leaning forward with his arms crossed and resting on his knees, which were also crossed . . . His manner is quick and nervous, and somewhat eccentric . . . Were he a religionist, you would expect him to be a first class fanatic, for it is impossible for such a man to do anything by halves. He is a good soldier, but has a reputation of being rather reckless in his style of life. . . .
>
> Rosser is a man about six feet two inches in height, broad and erect, with a well knit frame and weighing about 220 pounds. His face is round and full, his hair black, his complexion fair, with a ruddy tinge. He impresses

you in his physical presence as a man of great strength and endurance. In conversation his voice is never pitched on a high key, but is deliberate without being slow, energetic without being demonstrative. He is one who is eminently fitted to exert great influence over men and retain a hold on their confidence. He is a growing man.[20]

Stanley's contentious relationship with Custer over the cavalry's whiskey in mid-June fully illustrates character flaws in both men. John Carroll, a Custer authority, asked: "Was . . . [Stanley] afraid of his own weakness? Did . . . [the whiskey] represent a temptation which [he] felt he could not face or overcome?" Both answers appear to be yes. Stanley's attempt to fight his alcoholism—albeit ineffectively—by destroying the cavalry's liquor about June 22, if draconian, was his only way to ensure sobriety. In turn, Custer's attempt to hide the liquor was so uncharacteristic that it can only lead to the conclusion that he was doing it to upset and/or undermine Stanley. Indirectly confirming Custer's motivation is an account by Milnor Roberts's son Richard, Custer's secretary, who was with him in June 1876. Custer reached the Powder River on June 11: "[After] we were encamped the officers and men made a beeline for the proverbial sutler's store, but a majority of the men were doomed to disappointment as by order of General Custer no liquor was allowed to be sold, as he abhorred it, and never permitted soldiers to be supplied with it on any campaign if he could stop it."[21]

A frequently cited source is Marguerite Merington, a good friend of Elizabeth Custer. Merington, the spinster author of romantic books and "drawing room" plays, finished *The Custer Story: The Life and Intimate Letters of General George A. Custer* when she was over 90. Unfortunately she destroyed the letters, one of which Custer wrote after crossing Big Muddy Creek. In it Custer wrote that Rosser told him about Stanley's 1872 drinking and said that Rosser told Stanley in St. Paul (1873) that if he drank heavily, Custer would arrest him. But Rosser was unsure how Custer would greet him until they met in late June. Having just been rehired when he met with Stanley, Rosser was not about to endanger his career and family by threatening him. The "threat" likely did not happen. If Custer's letter accurately reflected a Rosser comment, Rosser might have reported something that he wished he had said or Custer might have written something that he wished Rosser had said.[22]

Once at the Yellowstone, Stanley let himself go. Larned wrote that "Stanley is under the whiskey curse and gets on periodical tears of two and three days duration during which he manages to disgrace himself and insult everyone who happens to displease him." The negative impact of alcoholic leadership on morale and performance cannot be measured, especially because Stanley was a mean drunk. Given the difficult conditions and constant Indian fears, Stanley's drinking was a psychological millstone around the neck of the entire command.[23]

After leaving Fort Rice, there were numerous petty misunderstandings and incidents, including one over Custer's "Dutch stove." Custer and his cavalry despised Stanley and the infantry and the sutler Augustus Baliran's whiskey. Stanley's anger erupted on July 8 over a minor issue: an army horse that technically had been improperly loaned to surveyor Fred Calhoun, the brother of Lt. James Calhoun. The incident, convoluted and filled with petty legalities, was the type of issue that proved so self-destructive to Stanley throughout his career. Stanley ordered Custer to his tent and placed him "in arrest," symbolically making him ride at the column's rear. Custer carried off his punishment with his usual flair but was outraged and hugely embarrassed. That night, after meeting with Rosser, Stanley "released" Custer and apologized to him. Rosser's July 8 diary simply notes: "I effected a reconciliation between Stanley and Custer." Stanley had not been drinking when the incident occurred; but he was mortified, almost despondent, at his loss of self-control and was effectively submissive to Custer for the duration of the survey.[24]

The *Sioux City Daily Journal* correspondent took no sides, writing: "Custer's men denounce his arrest as an act of tyranny, while Stanley's men on the other hand justify their chief in the matter. I have no opinion." The *Chicago Post* wrote: "The sympathy for . . . [Custer] was deep and universal outside of Stanley's head-quarters. . . . But there was no disguising the fact that Custer had used language disrespectful towards his superior officer." Bradley made no comment in his diary or his surviving letters. Merington has Custer stating: "With [Stanley's] subsequent faithful observance of his promise to begin anew in his intercourse with me, I banished the affair from my mind." But, regardless of what Custer wrote, he was still seething.[25]

From July 7 to July 15, when the wagons reached the Yellowstone, the party covered 130 miles, a good figure considering the difficulties faced. For three days the progress was outstanding: 58 miles. While the land rose slightly, there was ample water from the Heart and the ground was firm. July 7 saw the first fatality when John Mulloy, a teamster riding on a mule, slipped, fell under his wagon, and was crushed. That night he was wrapped in a blanket and buried in an unmarked grave. After setting up camp on July 9, Bradley wrote that he was in:

> a most picturesque spot surrounded by high buttes and ranges affording one of the prettiest views we have had. Somebody ought to give this country a better name than Bad Lands. The soil in the valleys is good, grass and timber abundant, and scenery not surpassed. . . . For grandeur and beauty of mountain scenes, they surpass anything I've seen, the Big Horn Canyon doesn't equal this, and I don't believe the Garden of the Gods in Colorado surpasses it.[26]

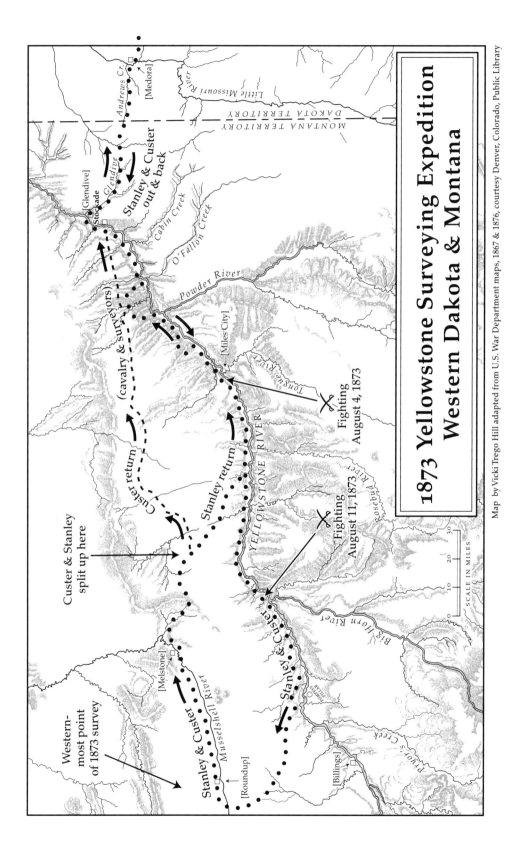

1873 Yellowstone Surveying Expedition
Western Dakota & Montana

Map by Vicki Trego Hill adapted from U.S. War Department maps, 1867 & 1876, courtesy Denver, Colorado, Public Library

The next day, in scorching weather, they reached Davis Creek; but it had to be crossed six times. About 8:30 A.M. on July 11 the column reached the Little Missouri, whose banks were covered with fine dirt and a high water, a mix similar to quicksand. The problem was solved by a covering of branches, brush, and wood, which the cavalry and beef herd crossed and recrossed, firming up the ground. As the backed-up wagons entered the river, teamsters cursed, bullwhips cracked, and soldiers stood stripped to the waist in the water, ready to push or pull as wagon-masters and officers shouted orders and encouragement. Everyone suffered, as the hills acted as sun reflectors, increasing the heat. The process was so slow that by evening the column was still strung out for miles. Not everyone worked hard, of course; Bradley and the Scientific Corps went exploring and "found the remains of lizards, 30 or 40 feet in length."[27]

The following day was cooler, the ground hard, and progress good. Stanley entered Montana on July 13; his men built a bridge and crossed Beaver Creek. After the Big Muddy, Stanley refused to camp on the "wrong" side of a stream if at all possible. July 14 saw the column crest the nearly imperceptible divide between the Yellowstone and Little Missouri and begin gradually descending. On July 15 every-one was on the march before 5 A.M. and finally halted, exhausted, 13 hours later atop a low hill a few hundred feet from the river. Their feet had kicked up a continual cloud of alkali dust, and there had been no water. But it was all worth it. Bradley wrote: "Here we are at last on the prettiest river I have ever seen in the west . . . with its rapid current, green trees, and pretty islands." Konopicky noted: "The Yellow-stone is a picturesque, large, fast flowing stream, that . . . reminds me of the left bank of the Danube at Nussdorf, with its wooded islands and meadows." But at this idyllic location, with ample supplies and no hostile Indians, all hell was about to break loose.

Glendive Creek's junction with the Yellowstone was selected for a supply depot, Camp Canby. Nine trips were made on the *Josephine, Peninah, Far West,* and *Key West* as four Fort Buford infantry companies unloaded and guarded the supplies. A *Peninah* passenger wrote: "The [infantry soldiers] . . . were encamped on a low point of land beside the creek and had made a very formidable looking fort." On June 30 a *Peninah* guard thought he saw an Indian. In seconds, scores of men were shooting into the darkness. As the gunfire increased, out of one cabin ran a distraught and disheveled "lady of the evening . . . [who] had no more wearing apparel than the law allowed, and appealed to a certain officer on the boat, not to leave her *now.*"[28]

Canby was at the base of a 40-foot bluff. On July 15 Custer and Rosser, riding to the Yellowstone together, inspected it and discovered that the bluff's steep slopes prohibited wagons from going down it to reach their supplies and that spring rains had turned adjacent bottomlands into an impassable swamp. The situation was, in short, a classic army snafu. Riding upriver, the two found a site for a camp and supply depot a dozen river miles away. The location, between Sand and Cedar Creeks, was on relatively flat land, had large cottonwood stands, was accessible to both the army wagons and the steamers, and became known as "Stanley's Stockade."

The new site, however, meant that all the supplies had to be reloaded, placed on the steamers, sent upstream, and again unloaded. With only two steamers available, the work took at least five days in hot, humid weather, frequently above 100 degrees, as large mosquitoes were joined by swarms of grasshoppers. The infantry and cavalry each had their own camp, a quarter-mile apart. Benteen wrote his wife that the infantry had a "stockade of logs," while the cavalry was in a wooded area, "40 to 50 yards from the bank of the river where there is a fine pebbly bottom—just the thing for bathing." In the stockade the blacksmiths set up their equipment. "We have *2,000 mules to shoe*" (Bradley's emphasis), Bradley wrote. With horses also being shod, the work could not have been completed in less than a week; there were only eight known forges, the weather was stifling, and it takes an hour and a half to shoe a horse or mule.[29]

On July 25 officers were flabbergasted to see a horse and buggy in the eastern hills. In it was Father Valentin Sommerheisen, a Jesuit who had lived on the plains since 1853 and had driven from Fort Rice. He had followed Stanley's trail with limited food, water, and a hunting rifle but without grain for his horse, his only protection a crucifix mounted on his buggy. The *New York Herald* said: "His object in following the expedition . . . seems to have been the desire to be first on the field." Sommerheisen was brave but no fool; on reaching the Yellowstone, he "felt relieved to find himself in a friendly camp." Later it was learned that Indians had seen him and had debated his fate, but because of the cross he was allowed to pass.

For Stanley, there was bad news from home. After six years on the plains, his wife was exhausted. Their son David, ten months old, had an unexplained illness, and other children were dying. Irvine wrote in August: "If Mrs. Stanley does not succeed in procuring servants, she will leave [him] . . . this fall." There was nothing for Stanley to do until the blacksmiths finished and the supplies moved. Unfortunately, one boat brought whiskey, the last thing he needed.[30]

On July 20 Stanley went on a binge lasting through July 23. A surveyor recalled that "a number of officers and soldiers proceeded on a big spree, including [Stanley] . . . [but] Rosser and several of the officers managed to have the balance . . . emptied out on the ground." The *Sioux City Daily Journal* stated: "The sutler to the infantry command lost six barrels and the cavalry sutler, seven." This was confirmed by the expedition's surgeon, who wrote: "Thirteen barrels of whiskey destroyed today Thank God!" Thus the issue was moot for the rest of the summer, except for hard-core drinkers, who were reduced to mixing Worcestershire sauce, Jamaican ginger, and vinegar bitters.[31]

Rosser wrote in his diary on July 21: "Stanley is very drunk, and I fear Custer will arrest him and assume command." Rosser's concern undoubtedly reflected a just-concluded meeting with Custer. Regardless of Stanley's logic or motivation when he had placed Custer "in arrest" earlier, it was his prerogative as commanding officer. If Custer had arrested Stanley, however, it would have been mutiny. Given cavalry-infantry tensions, it is unlikely that Bradley, Crofton, and other capable, strong-willed veterans would have accepted Custer's act. How would he have arrested Stanley, and what would he have done when Stanley sobered up? Who would have been blamed if a shot had been fired during a confrontation, as men screamed at each other and slowly reached for their weapons? Would Benteen and other cavalry officers have supported Custer? And, ultimately, what would President Grant have done? Custer knew the answers to these questions and, as a credit to his underlying common sense, did nothing after venting his feelings to Rosser.[32]

Not making things easier for Stanley was Frederick Grant's decision on July 23 to leave for Fort Buford without telling him, although he informed Custer. Other cavalry officers knew of the boat's leaving. "Information of a strictly confidential character has just reached me," Larned wrote, "that a small boat leaves the steamer tonight . . . carrying a limited quantity of mail." Taking a yawl (a large, curve-bottomed rowboat) from the *Josephine,* Grant was joined by a 6th Infantry officer, a *Sioux City Journal* correspondent, and six men from the quartermaster's unit.[33]

In midafternoon they piled into the yawl. Daylight proved uneventful, as they watched game, drank, and floated merrily along under a strong sun. At dusk, rather than risk camping, they stayed on the river. About 10 P.M. black clouds rapidly formed, the wind started to blow, and an "awe inspiring roar came over the prairies from out of those clouds." Huge bolts of lightning and large thunder claps burst nearby, and the yawl was "tossed about like a thistle on a summer breeze." Everyone dove to the bottom of the yawl. The *Journal's* correspondent (anticipating Winston Churchill) wrote: "So much confusion was never before gotten up by so small a crowd in such a brief lapse of time. . . . Everybody was a captain . . . [and] the captains were all looking out for No. 1." Then the yawl crashed into the shore, but the worst was over.[34]

The next morning, "wet and exhausted," they reached Buford after 126 miles. Everyone liked Grant ("he is lively, yet modest [and] puts on no airs"), but his lack of common sense was inexcusable. The river was particularly high, seven hours were spent floating in the dark, and—lightly armed—for over a dozen daylight hours they drifted through Sioux hunting grounds. One can imagine Stanley's shock when he learned that Grant had gone. Indeed, Barrows's comments in the *New York Tribune* make it clear that Grant's actions were thought to have crossed a line. Grant's "prank" went too far, but, of course, there were no repercussions.[35]

Rosser spent his last days with his surveyors at work on the Yellowstone's east bank to O'Fallon Creek, finishing maps and reports, robbing Indian graves, swimming three miles in the dangerous Yellowstone, and reluctantly boarding the *Josephine* on July 29. He reached Minneapolis on August 2 and then left for New York to meet with the Northern Pacific's executive committee.

With supplies moved and horses shod, the first elements of Stanley's column were ferried across the Yellowstone on July 26. Left behind to guard large amounts of supplies were an infantry and two cavalry companies under Benteen. While the only fighting he saw was against flies and mosquitoes, at the time an Indian attack was thought possible. In any case, after being in camp eleven days, the army was again on the move, escorting the surveyors but also hoping to find Sitting Bull and his followers. Their wait would be short.

Ulysses S. Grant (1822–85). As president, Grant closely followed the Northern Pacific's progress and the military efforts in support of the surveying expeditions. Grant made numerous behind-the-scenes decisions that helped Cooke and the Northern Pacific in 1870–71, but after this was privately and publicly circumspect. The photograph, taken by Matthew Brady ca. 1869, shows a reticent Grant and would accurately reflect his ambivalence toward Cooke's political requests. Courtesy National Archives.

Henry D. Cooke (1825–81), Jay's able younger brother. After the war, Henry became a card-playing crony of Grant, led the lobbying efforts of Jay Cooke & Co., and was the District of Columbia's first governor (mayor). Photograph by Matthew Brady (subsequently retouched). Courtesy National Archives.

William G. Moorhead (1811–95), Cooke's brother-in-law. Moorhead gave Cooke his first job in Philadelphia in 1838. One of Cooke's leading partners, he was cautious to the point of defeatism as well as ineffectual and cracked under the Northern Pacific's bad news. Author's collection.

Ogontz, Cooke's palatial Philadelphia suburban mansion. Built and partially designed by Cooke in 1865–66 and named after a Wyandot Indian chief that he had known, Ogontz had 53 rooms and more than 75,000 square feet. It cost well over a million dollars and was sited on 200 carefully landscaped acres. Author's collection.

W. Milnor Roberts (1810–81). Roberts was one of the era's leading civil engineers, and his 1869 reconnaissance and report gave Cooke the final proof of the Northern Pacific's efficacy. When Roberts became the railroad's chief engineer (1870), Cooke wrote him: "[I] consider you an *Honest man* as well as capable" (Cooke's emphasis). Courtesy Burlingame Special Collections Library, Montana State University–Bozeman.

Thomas H. Canfield (1822–97). Intelligent, dapper, and an outstanding lobbyist, Canfield was more responsible than anyone else in the mid-1860s for congressional passage of authorization for the Northern Pacific and its survival in the late 1860s. Yet he was shortsighted, greedy to actively dishonest, and a financial disaster both to himself and to the NP. Courtesy Vermont Historical Society.

Samuel Wilkeson (1817–89). A publisher and then a leading war correspondent, Wilkeson wrote an article about his son's death at Gettysburg that caught Cooke's eye. He soon joined Cooke's bond sales effort and was its leading publicist. Later he was the Northern Pacific's secretary for over two decades. Photograph by Matthew Brady, ca. 1865. Courtesy National Archives.

Five participants in the 1869 reconnaissance of the NP's Washington-Idaho-Montana route, possibly at Deer Lodge, Montana. *Left to right,* William E. C. Moorhead (Cooke's nephew), Wilkeson, Canfield, Roberts, and William Johnson (son of NP chief engineer Edwin Johnson). Courtesy Burlingame Special Collections Library, Montana State University–Bozeman.

J. Gregory Smith (1818–91), the Northern Pacific's president (1865–72). Smith was followed all his life by allegations, likely accurate, of financial irregularities. Making matters worse, his inability to plan, manage large-scale operations, or understand market forces was textbook-bad. Photo ca. 1864, when Smith was governor of Vermont. Courtesy Vermont Historical Society.

Edward C. Jordan (1846–1935), possibly the only Northern Pacific surveyor formally trained in civil and railroad engineering. Some of Jordan's 1870–72 correspondence and diaries survive, offering unique insights into the surveyors' daily lives. Photo from his 1868 yearbook. Courtesy Union College Special Collections Library, Schenectady, New York.

Ira Spaulding (*standing fourth from the left*) and surveyors, 1871. Spaulding was the Northern Pacific manager responsible for engineering and construction in Minnesota from 1868 to 1870. Rosser is sitting to his immediate right (in a white hat). Well liked by surveyors, Spaulding proved ineffectual—perhaps for reasons beyond his control—and "resigned" in 1872. Courtesy Albert H. Small Special Collections Library, University of Virginia.

Official ground-breaking ceremony at Carlton (Thomson Junction), Minnesota. The identity of the individuals is unknown. Photograph taken February 15, 1870. Courtesy Minnesota Historical Society.

This 1850 Vermont Central Railroad stock certificate was printed ca. 1847, and the locomotive depicted represents state-of-the-art technology. In late 1851 it was discovered that the treasurer, Josiah Quincy, Jr., was embezzling funds and selling nonexistent stock and that the president, Charles Paine, was drastically inflating certain expenses. Severely weakened, the railroad became prey for John Smith and his son Gregory. Author's collection.

The 1869 Minnesota-Dakota reconnaissance of the Northern Pacific had no technical importance but was undertaken to generate publicity for the railroad. The most interesting aspect of the picture is the body language of Gregory Smith, seated third from the left (white hat, white beard). Unlike any other participant, he resolutely refused to look at the camera. One person on the reconnaissance who was already in Jay Cooke's orbit was Nathaniel P. Langford, who would codiscover Yellowstone Park the next year. Courtesy Minnesota Historical Society.

Railroad operations were never easy. Whether this spectacular 1864 Vermont Central wreck was caused by lax management under president J. Gregory Smith or was simply bad luck is unknown. Courtesy Vermont Historical Society.

Two sketches by Northern Pacific surveyor Montgomery Meigs (1847–1931), the son of the Union army's quartermaster general. The canoeists are on the swollen Red River at Georgetown, Minnesota (1871). The man sitting is marking surveyor's stakes. Some of Meigs's letters and sketches between 1870 and 1873 survive and offer valuable insight into the lives of the surveyors. Courtesy Montgomery Meigs Orr Family Archive.

Northern Pacific locomotive engines were purchased almost exclusively from the reputable Baldwin Locomotive Works of Philadelphia. Engine no. 9, an "American" type locomotive that the NP used to pull freight trains, was photographed at Spokane Falls, Washington Territory, February 1888, by F. Jay Haynes. Courtesy Haynes Foundation Collection, Montana Historical Society.

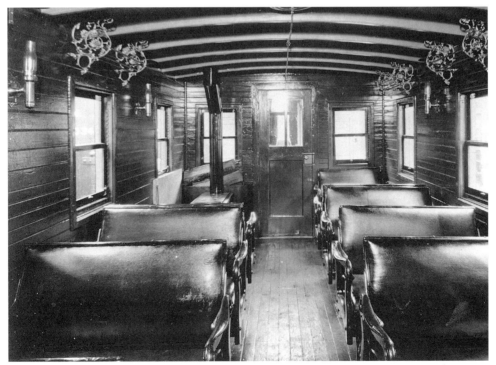

Interior of a St. Paul & Pacific Railroad passenger car, ca. 1875. Courtesy Minnesota Historical Society.

Opposite page: A train chugs into the west while a buffalo flees and Indians look on in fear and amazement (from a stock certificate of the Peoria and Bureau Valley Railroad.). *Above:* "Progress": as surveyors begin their work, Indians flee, followed by railroad construction crews (*left*) and commerce (*right*)(from a Fort Wayne, Cincinnati & Louisville Railroad stock certificate, ca. 1850). Author's collection.

Rosser (*third from left*) and surveyors at Fargo, North Dakota, 1872. The group's informality and camaraderie are apparent. The surveyor with his hat at a jaunty angle to the right of Rosser might be Jordan. Courtesy Albert H. Small Special Collections Library, University of Virginia.

Capt. Javan B. Irvine (1831–1904). Irvine was a failed businessman who stayed in the army after the war. He was an officer on the 1871 eastern survey and provided the most detailed description of daily life from any of the Yellowstone surveys (ca. 1880s). The Irvine and Stanley families were very close, and Irvine's diary and many letters provide an excellent picture of Stanley. Courtesy South Dakota State Historical Society.

Basil Clement, head scout on all three eastern surveys (1824–1910). A prototype scout, Clement was of French, Spanish, and Indian blood. He was raised in St. Louis and joined the American Fur Company as a teenager. Clement's long career included working for years under the legendary Jim Bridger. He was unable to get along with Custer, however, and appears to have "retired" after 1873. Courtesy South Dakota State Historical Society.

Joseph N. G. Whistler (1822–99), military commander of the 1871 Eastern Yellowstone Survey. Although he was a decent person, his leadership was generally ineffectual, marred by his self-indulgence, likely drinking, and inability to read a compass. Roger D. Hunt Collection, U.S. Army Military History Institute, Carlisle, Pa.

Sketch of Heart Butte by Charles "Shorty" Graham (1852–1911), a surveyor on the 1872 eastern expedition. Graham likely had been employed by the Northern Pacific since 1870 and was a self-taught artist. Later he was hired by *Harper's Weekly* and became one of the magazine's lead artists and in 1883 covered the NP's final spike ceremonies. Courtesy Albert H. Small Special Collections Library, University of Virginia.

Heart Butte.

Because of the badlands, the picturesque Little Missouri River (shown here five miles south of present-day Medora) was considered a potential barrier in 1871. In quickly finding two streams that fed into the river along which track could be constructed, Rosser's surveying efforts were considered a total success. Author's photograph.

Upper Yellowstone River near Greycliff, between Columbus and Big Timber, looking west. Before NP surveyors entered the Yellowstone Valley, the plan had been to build track on the north side (right) of the river. As soon as Milnor Roberts reached the area, he knew track would be prohibitively expensive to build and wrote that construction would have to be on the south side, where it is today. Author's photograph.

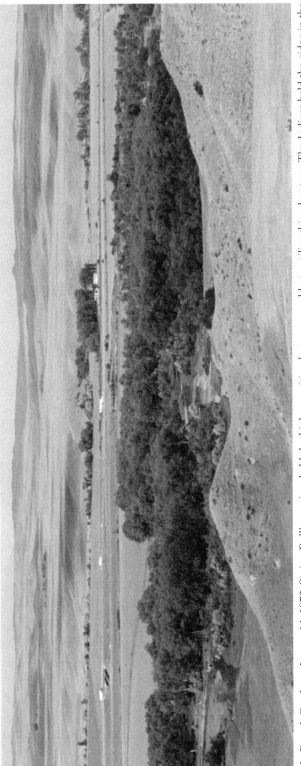

At Pryor's Creek on August 14, 1872, Sitting Bull's warriors held the higher position but were unable to utilize this advantage. The Indians held the ridge in the foreground and fired into a U-shaped area in the center and right of the picture. Author's photograph.

The Brainerd roundhouse, ca. 1872–73. A number of locomotives can be seen. Courtesy Minnesota Historical Society.

An NP work train crossing the Red River at Fargo-Moorhead in 1872. Courtesy Minnesota Historical Society.

The controversial "new" Brainerd depot was built in 1872, when the Northern Pacific was all but out of cash. It was half again as large as the two-story 1871 wooden depot that it replaced. Photo probably from the 1870s or 1880s. Courtesy Minnesota Historical Society.

Northern Pacific construction photographs (*also opposite page*), both likely taken in western Dakota, ca. 1878. Very few shots of NP construction crews exist, and these two accurately portray the manual effort required to cut through hills and lay track in the 1870s. Courtesy Haynes Foundation Collection, Montana Historical Society.

B-2193

George Armstrong Custer (1839–76). This full facial photograph taken by Matthew Brady ca. 1865 captures Custer's intensity and determination. Courtesy National Archives.

Col. David Sloane Stanley (1828–1902), commander of the 1872 Eastern Yellowstone Surveying Expedition and also the 1873 expedition. Stanley's commendable effort in 1872 was marred by his drinking, and his 1873 leadership remains controversial. Although William Pywell is known to have photographed Stanley during the 1873 survey, that picture is missing from the National Archives. This photograph was taken ca. 1880. Courtesy U.S. Army Military History Institute, Carlisle, Pa.

Rosser with his children, ca. 1873. This is easily the best photograph of Rosser. He is relaxed and at ease with his family, but his forcefulness and physical strength are on equal display. This is no "Papa Bear" to be trifled with. Courtesy Albert H. Small Special Collections Library, University of Virginia Library.

Hailstone Creek, where the surveyors were caught in a storm of golf ball–sized hailstones on June 24, 1873. Almost three dozen horses, mules, and a dog were killed or had to be destroyed. Every surveyor wagon was wrecked, and no one escaped injury. Author's photograph.

Gall or Pizi (1840–94). A Hunkpapa
Teton Sioux, Gall called himself
Man-Who-Goes-in-the-Middle, a
reference to being in the center of
the fighting. Brought up by Sitting
Bull's family after his parents died,
he was one of Sitting Bull's closest
associates in the 1860s and 1870s.
A renowned warrior, Gall played a
leading role in the 1872–73 fighting.
Courtesy National Archives.

Sitting Bull (1834–90). This photo, taken
ca. 1882, vividly captures Sitting Bull's
determination and intransigence. A
Hunkpapa, he took the lead in rallying
Arapaho, Cheyenne, and Sioux warriors
against the 1872 and 1873 Yellowstone
Surveying Expeditions. Courtesy National
Archives.

Big Hill from the south, showing the probable position where Baliran and Honsinger were ambushed by Rain-in-the-Face and a half-dozen Hunkpapas on August 4, 1873, and the location of the surveyors (and their escort) and the Yellowstone. Custer's actual position is unknown, but he was to the right. Author's photograph.

Pompey's Pillar in 1873. William Clark carved his initials on this landmark in 1806. William Pywell was the first to photograph it. Courtesy National Archives.

White Bull (ca. 1847–1947), a nephew of Sitting Bull. During the August 14, 1872, battle at Pryor's Creek, he joined Sitting Bull in smoking a pipe while seated between the Indians and soldiers; but he admitted decades later how frightened he had been. In 1926, at the 50th anniversary of the Battle of Little Big Horn, he led the surviving warriors. Photograph taken ca. 1926. Courtesy National Archives.

Rain-in-the-Face (ca. 1835–1905). Like Sitting Bull and Gall, Rain-in-the-Face was also a Hunkpapa Sioux. His name referred to his being splattered in the face with the blood of an enemy during his first fight. Rain-in-the-Face appears to have led the half-dozen warriors who killed Baliran, Honsinger, and Ball on August 4, 1873. Courtesy National Archives.

The army's Scientific Corps, pictured here, was to be the 1873 expedition's showpiece effort. But it was short-handed and plagued by mishaps, hot weather, and less-than-energetic personnel—and in truth there was little to be found other than lignite and small "petrifactions." Photograph by William Pywell, 1873. Courtesy National Archives.

The Northern Pacific intended to construct track from Bismarck to the Yellowstone (at present-day Glendive, Montana), as evidenced in this advertisement, which appeared in the August 16, 1873, *Philadelphia Inquirer* and other papers. The ad also convinced many of Cooke's partners that he had gone back on his promise not to finance the NP beyond the Missouri River. Author's collection.

Luther P. Bradley (1822–1910). Bradley was a bookstore owner and salesman before the Civil War, but he rose to brigadier general because of his ability and bravery in combat. Sheridan thought highly of him, and he was third in command in 1873. Bradley's diaries and letters offer an insightful overview of the survey. Courtesy U.S. Army Military History Institute, Carlisle, Pa.

Location of Custer's charge, August 11, 1873. The line of woods to the left is where Bradon was wounded. Shortly afterward Custer lined up six companies of cavalry stretching from the trees diagonally to the left. The Sioux and Cheyennes, nominally under Gall, were about in the position from which the photo was taken, diagonally to the right. Just beyond where the road dips and in back of the hill line is the Yellowstone. Custer charged from left to right. Author's photograph.

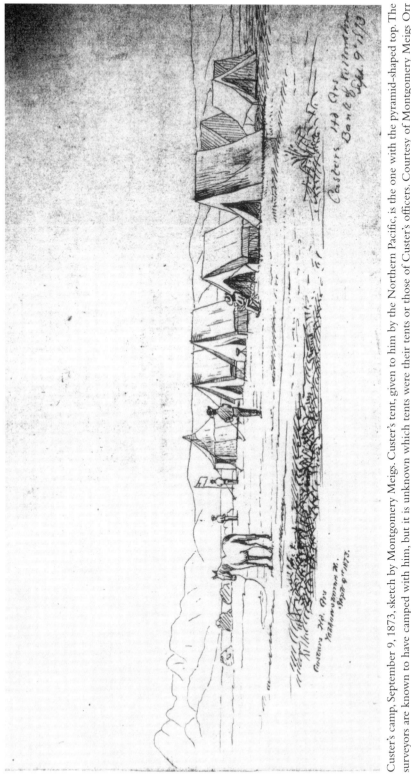

Custer's camp, September 9, 1873, sketch by Montgomery Meigs. Custer's tent, given to him by the Northern Pacific, is the one with the pyramid-shaped top. The surveyors are known to have camped with him, but it is unknown which tents were their tents or those of Custer's officers. Courtesy of Montgomery Meigs Orr Family Archive.

Harris Charles Fahnestock
(1835–1914). Fahnestock was a
bank teller until "loaned" to
Cooke in 1861. Cooke soon
made him the de facto manager
of the Washington office and
then placed him in charge of his
New York operations. Here
Fahnestock gradually fell under
Morgan's influence while simultaneously becoming convinced
that the Northern Pacific would
destroy Jay Cooke & Co. and
wipe out his fortune. Photograph taken ca. 1910. Courtesy
Baker Library, Harvard Business
School, Cambridge, Mass.

J. Pierpont Morgan (1837–1913).
Morgan, who actively specu-
lated *against* the Union during
the war, likely crossed swords
early with Cooke—and lost.
When Cooke established a
London branch, Morgan felt
threatened. He attacked Cooke's
Northern Pacific bond sales,
with the likely support of the
British government. Morgan's
alliance with Anthony Drexel
was caused in part by their
mutual fear of Cooke. Photograph taken in 1881. Courtesy
Archives of the Pierpont Morgan
Library, New York.

BROAD STREETS WITH WALL STREET—VIEW OF THE SUB-TREASURY, JAY COOKE & CO.'S BANK, PH OFFICE, FROM THE DREXEL BUILDING, ON FRIDAY, SEPT. 19TH.

September 18, 1873. Crowds filled the streets in front of Cooke's office in Philadelphia, and police had to be called in to prevent rioting. The same scene prevailed for three days on Wall Street (Cooke's building is the one with canopy poles), as shown in *Frank Leslie's Illustrated Weekly Newspaper*, October 11, 1873. Author's collection.

Surveyors' reunion in Minneapolis, January 1906. A major purpose of the event was to honor Rosser, who had been felled by a stroke the previous year. The reunion was well attended by surveyors from the eastern Yellowstone surveys and was given extensive coverage in Minneapolis and St. Paul newspapers. Among others the photo includes Montgomery Meigs (*fifth from left, standing*); Edward Jordan (*back row, third from left*); T. L. Rosser, Jr. (*back row, fifth from left*), H. C. Davis (*short beard, below right from Jordan*); Fendall G. Winston, Rosser's brother-in-law (*next to Davis on right*); Charles "Shorty" Graham (*seated, front row, fourth from left in light suit*); George Brackett (*seated, second row, below right from Winston, third from right*); and A. L. Berry (*seated, below and to right of Brackett*). Courtesy Albert H. Small Special Collections Library, University of Virginia.

Thomas Rosser at about 70. This was probably taken after a stroke left
him unable to speak. Nothing is known about his last years. Courtesy
Albert H. Small Special Collections Library, University of Virginia.

Gall's grave. Gall died in 1894, about 55. His last years were unhappy, and he likely suffered from his earlier wounds. For some reason, Gall's remains were temporarily disinterred about 1990. A new headstone, incompatible with its surroundings, was later placed over his grave. Author's photo.

Jay Cooke at 80. The last 25 years of Cooke's life were peaceful. After he made a second fortune and/or withdrew money he had hidden, Cooke repurchased Ogontz and Gibraltar. However, unable to maintain Ogontz, he gave it to a private girls' school and took an active role in the school's affairs. Author's collection.

CHAPTER 15

"All Down There Are Killed!"

Once they crossed the Yellowstone, the surveyors' goal was to reach Pompeys Pillar and the exact spot where the Baker-Haydon column had left the river and turned toward the Musselshell in 1872. By the evening of July 28, 1873, with everyone on the Yellowstone's west or north bank, the column marched 15 miles. The daily progress was determined by the exceptional heat on the baked and treeless ground, the availability of adequate campsites, and sometimes the ever-present wolves that "would come in large bodies during the night," stampeding the beef cattle. The Stanley-Custer relationship had somewhat improved, from outright hostility to military correctness; but on a practical basis Custer did as he wanted. Stanley, likely mortified by his drinking, seemed not to care about Custer or anything else for that matter.[1]

On Sunday, August 3, the column, on the march since 5 A.M., made one difficult detour before stopping just before noon at a stream they named Sunday Creek. Since leaving Stanley's Stockade, they had marched about 95 miles over difficult terrain. While they could have gone farther that day, the grass was good and the path up the creek's valley was obviously going to be a long uphill climb. The campsite was at the foot of a hill on the north side of Sunday Creek, at its junction with the Yellowstone, eight miles north of present-day Miles City.

Some men bathed, swam, fished, or napped, while others robbed and destroyed Indian graves they had found. To his credit, Stanley issued an order prohibiting the desecrations; yet even if it was not an effective deterrent, he was one of the few officers bothered by such practices. Many of the men also washed clothes, leaving their flannel pants and linen shirts to dry on rocks and low brushes. As cavalry lieutenant Charles Braden recalled: "A sudden whirlwind swept through the camp and carried off a number of garments. For a full minute the air was full of them. . . . It was a ludicrous sight, but proved a serious thing to [those] who lost an only shirt, with no way of getting another until the return of the expedition." Men without a linen shirt had to march with a flannel jacket or shirtless, either option a steep price to pay under a strong sun.[2]

On August 4 the column was on the march by 6 A.M.. Barrows wrote: "The coolness of the early morning, which had excited the hope of a relief from the oppression of the preceding days, soon disappeared and the sun rose without a single veil of a cloud." The day's route was determined by a steep, 300-foot bluff opposite Miles City. The bluff's eastern side was thickly wooded floodplain that narrowed and finally ended where the Yellowstone ran into the base of the steep bluff. The surveyors would follow the floodplain to this point, easily climb the bluff, and parallel the river until the floodplain reappeared a few miles later. The bluff, sometimes called Big Hill, is a boomerang-shaped ridge, 13 miles long where it parallels the Yellowstone and almost 2 miles wide at its center. The wagons had to follow the western side of the bluff along Sunday Creek, until the creek split. Following the southern branch and its tributaries, the climb became steeper until they reached the flat, dry crest. From there, a buffalo trail wandered down to the Yellowstone, offering numerous camping choices. The distance from Sunday Creek to a good campsite south of Big Hill was 18 miles, a difficult but not impossible day's march.[3]

Custer moved ahead with companies A and B: 86 men, 5 officers, and a few scouts, including Bloody Knife, whose cheerfully disrespectful "you can't hit the broad side of a barn" humor made him a Custer favorite. Capt. Myles Moylan (who had been captured by Rosser during the war) officially commanded the unit, thus giving Custer greater freedom of movement. The other officers were Tom Custer, brother-in-law James Calhoun, and Charles A. Varnum, who lived until 1936 and wrote a fascinating description of the day's action. By about 9:30 A.M. the cavalry had ridden 18 miles and was about 7 miles upriver from the confluence of the Tongue and Yellowstone. A half hour earlier, Bloody Knife had spotted the fresh tracks of nearly 20 Indian ponies, not enough to be a source of concern. On reaching the buffalo trail descending to the Yellowstone, the soldiers had a marvelous view. Custer wrote:

> Here and there the channel of the river was dotted with beautiful islands covered with . . . [thick grass] and shaded by groves of stately forest trees, while along the banks on either side could be seen for miles and miles clumps of trees varying in size from the familiar cottonwood to the waving osier, and covering a space in some instances no larger than a gentleman's garden, in others embracing thousands of acres.[4]

Looking upriver, they could see no signs of Sioux. Custer noted that it was nearly a mile directly to the river, where there were no trees. But another two miles or so upstream was a mid-sized copse of cottonwood with grass, an ideal campsite for Stanley. With most of the day to kill, Custer trotted over to the woods, unsaddling the horses and letting them graze. Two four-man "guard patrols" were posted. As the sun rose higher, some went fishing, while most cavalrymen, including Custer—who cheerfully admitted going to sleep—curled up in the thick grass, listened to the gurgling river, and with increasing lethargy swatted away insects before falling soundly asleep under the cottonwoods. Despite the idyllic surroundings, Custer had taken the precaution of having his trumpeter rest near him, for, as he told Barrows, "I had a presentiment that we were going to have an alarm." Precisely where Custer stopped is not known, and all efforts to pinpoint the exact location have been unsuccessful.[5]

Perhaps two miles away, watching motionless in another stand of cottonwood, were some of the Lakotas whose pony tracks Bloody Knife had seen. They had spotted Custer, Stanley's column, or both. Some of this scouting party, either Hunkpapas or Miniconjous, had raced back to their village, found Sitting Bull, gotten reinforcements, and were in the process of rushing back. A few days later Bloody Knife estimated that Sitting Bull's camp, about 20 miles from where Custer rested, held about 300 to 400 lodges. Under a less likely scenario—which Custer believed—hundreds of Indians hid in the woods all morning waiting for the opportunity to attack. Either way, despite the army's spring preparations and the June 16 attack on the surveyors, Sitting Bull's followers had been caught flatfooted by the army's presence on the Yellowstone's west bank. That summer he was also distracted by new external threats; the decline of the buffalo had brought large hunting parties of Métis from the Red River and a coalition of Crows and Nez Percés from the west. In defending their hunting grounds the Hunkpapas had already sustained considerable casualties.[6]

As Custer napped, Hunkpapas under Gall, Oglalas under Crazy Horse, Miniconjous, and Cheyennes rapidly drew up a plan to trap him. Reinforcements arrived silently from Sitting Bull's camp, staying out of sight and taking positions in the larger woods near Custer. By noon the Indians numbered between 150 and 200 warriors, although Robert Utley states the number as "about one hundred." Of the various Lakota war leaders, Gall and Rain-in-the-Face almost definitely participated. According to Indian historian Mari Sandoz and others, Crazy Horse was also there and helped plan the attack. Stephen E. Ambrose believed that Crazy Horse was in the decoy party and came so close that he literally saw Custer sleeping. One recent author has embellished the story by stating that "Crazy Horse's first look at Custer was of a white man in underwear and socks"—an unlikely event because of the sun's position, the shade of the trees, the speed at which Crazy Horse was riding, and Custer's claim that he took off only his hat and boots.[7]

About this same time, Dr. John Honsinger, the 7th Cavalry's veterinarian, rode to the front of Stanley's column. He talked briefly with Barrows, who described him as "a fine looking, portly man, about 55 years of age, dressed in a blue coat and buckskin pantaloons, mounted on his fine blooded horse, leisurely trotting along on the cavalry trail . . . When I saw him again, a few hours later, he was a corpse."[8]

Just before noon Custer's guard spotted six Indians dashing in the direction of the cavalry's grazing horses and woke Custer. According to Barrows, Custer instantly shouted, "Bring in your horses! Bring in your horses!" and ordered the bugler to sound "Boots and Saddles." As soon as Custer had all his men mounted, he rode out in front with John H. Tuttle (his orderly), Calhoun, and possibly Bloody Knife. He was closely followed by 20 men under Tom Custer, and they in turn by the remainder of the cavalrymen. With Custer leading, they quickly closed in on the large stand of cottonwood two miles upriver. However, Custer was immediately suspicious; after scores of battles and skirmishes, he knew that the Indians were not riding the way panic-stricken men should. "It was apparent from the first," he wrote, "that the Indians were resorting to [a] stratagem to accomplish that which they could not do by an open, direct attack." When Custer stopped after somewhat over a mile, the decoys also stopped. He moved again, and they retreated; but when Custer stopped, they did too.[9]

However impulsive Custer was by reputation, he was certainly aware of the tactic that had been employed against Fetterman. With his troopers coming up behind him, he again cautiously moved forward, looking carefully for Indians hiding in the cottonwoods, "an immense tract of timber . . . extending to the water's edge, but distant from our resting place . . . [by] about two miles." Calhoun wrote that Custer moved forward, attempting to tell the Indians in sign language that he wished to talk with them and indicating he was no longer certain that their intent was hostile, but Custer's instinct still said that the woods were full of Indians. As it happened, some of them were Cheyennes from Black Kettle's old band who knew Custer from having survived the Washita battle. Seeing him, they lost their self-control and charged out of the woods, ending whatever chance of success the ambush had. Varnum was amazed: "[A]bout 250 Indians in line, with war bonnets and stripped almost naked, rode up a bank out of the timber, yelling a war cry." Contrary to some accounts, they were generally well-armed, many with 16-shot Henry repeating rifles. The Sioux, however, were invariably short of ammunition, made some of it themselves, and saved gunpowder by limiting target practice. The result was that their bullets often had less striking power, and many were ineffective marksmen.[10]

Ambush of Custer, August 4, 1873

(MAPS NOT TO SCALE)

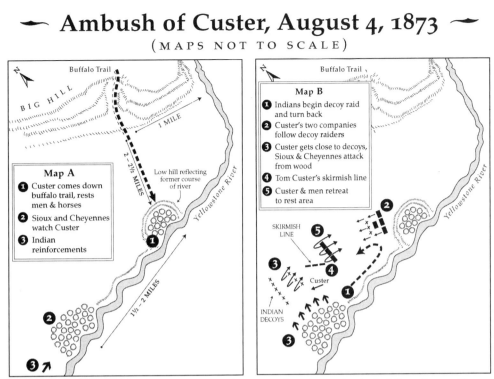

A. Custer arrives mid-morning and selects site for his men to rest and for the wagon train and column to camp in the evening. Becomes his defensive position in the afternoon.

B. Indian decoys begin "raid" on horses. Custer follows, avoids ambush, and retreats.

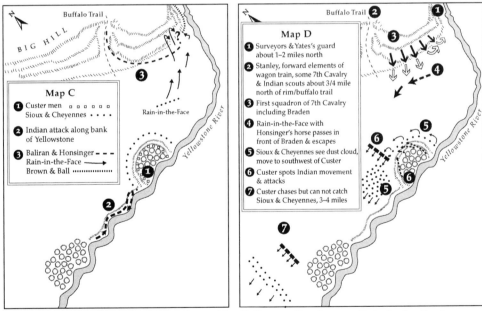

C. Fighting for three hours, failed Indian raid, Honsinger and Baliran route, and ambush site

D. Rescue force's route, Rain-in-the-Face's retreat, Indians' fall back, and Custer's charge

Maps by Vicki Trego Hill courtesy *Research Review: Journal of the Little Big Horn Associates*

As the Indians broke out of the woods, the attackers, Custer, and Tom Custer's 20 men formed a triangle. Custer, in danger of being cut off, instantly wheeled his horse around and dashed back, while his brother's troopers dismounted to form a skirmish line in the moderately high grass. Both the Indians and Custer raced toward the troopers. He was on a thoroughbred horse, but the Sioux had a better angle. Fortunately for Custer, the Sioux were concentrating so hard on him that they did not notice Tom Custer's men facing them. The instant Custer, his orderly, and Calhoun passed through, the skirmishers rose up in front of the startled Sioux and delivered two quick volleys. Calhoun noted that Tom Custer's orders were "executed . . . in a manner worthy of the highest praise, for they were mostly new men and had never been under fire before." No Indians were hit, but their attack came to a screeching halt.[11]

Custer, outnumbered, quickly realized that he needed to establish a defensive position. Ordering the remainder of his men to dismount and every fourth man to hold horses, he had the troopers form a wider and wider arc to avoid being flanked by the mounted Indians. For what was likely fifteen long minutes, his men half walked, half double-timed toward their original resting place adjacent to the river, firing occasional volleys to keep the Indians at bay. On reaching the woods, to avoid being flanked, Custer formed a defensive perimeter, trying to anchor both sides on the river. He soon realized that he needed more men and had every sixth man hold the horses, not the usual every fourth man. When this proved inadequate, he added two more horses per man, a total of eight each—a difficult battlefield task. Custer's position was strengthened by a low, circular embankment formed by the Yellowstone's previous course. "We found ourselves," he wrote, "deployed behind a natural parapet or bulwark from which the troopers could deliver a carefully directed fire . . . and at the same time be protected." As the positions stabilized, the Lakotas and Cheyennes also stretched their line, circling Custer to the river.[12]

Custer was aware only that they were fighting "Sioux," but Bloody Knife knew many of them well. Barrows correctly noted that they were "mainly Unkpapas [sic]." Robert Utley says that they also included Miniconjous, and Ben Innis places Gall on the scene. Thomas Marquis, who interviewed some surviving participants in the 1920s, makes a strong case for Oglalas being present, noting that they often hunted at the junction of the Yellowstone and Tongue and were likely the first Lakotas aware of Stanley's force. Thus it appears that Crazy Horse or other Oglalas were hunting near the Tongue, saw Stanley's column on August 2 or 3, swam the Yellowstone and alerted Sitting Bull, and then took part in the fighting.[13]

Although outnumbered, Custer had shorter interior lines but had no reserve other than his horse-holders. Surrounded as he was, there was no way a messenger could have broken through to Stanley. While Lakotas and Cheyennes were between Custer and Stanley, they themselves were in a dangerous position if Stanley arrived.

To prevent being surprised and to sound an early warning, a half-dozen warriors under Rain-in-the-Face rode toward Big Hill. Once the initial positions became firm, the Indians began taking casualties. At one point, as a warrior came riding within 200 yards, Bloody Knife and Custer fired simultaneously, hitting both man and horse. This Indian was likely a Cheyenne named Youngest Child; another Cheyenne, Tall White Man, was shot through the thigh, and a chief or medicine man was probably hit. Lakota casualties are not known, but apparently at least one was killed and a half-dozen wounded. Under the hot sun, despite being bloodied and unsuccessful, the well-armed Indians uncharacteristically refused to back off and stubbornly kept up the pressure.[14]

Unable to make frontal progress, after about an hour a 50-man war party attempted to stampede the horses by attacking Custer from the rear. The plan was to follow the river's dry bank, about ten feet below the level where the troops were deployed. The Indians had to advance in single file and were aware that they could be ambushed, so they had a lookout move forward at the same level as Custer. When the lookout was fired on, the main party fled, assuming they had been seen. In fact, no one knew that they were moving along the river. Custer later noted: "We learned how narrowly we had escaped a most serious if not a fatal disaster. . . . Had they been willing, as white men would have been, to assume greater risks their success would have been assured." After this tactic failed, the attackers tried another, setting a number of fires. The grass was too green to burn rapidly, however, and the fires spread slowly.[15]

Once the fires started, the smoke permitted both sides to move closer, attacking and counterattacking in small numbers, although nothing was accomplished other than using up ammunition. In the last hour of the fighting, firing virtually ceased, while both sides held their positions. Everyone was exhausted and covered with grime and sweat mixed with powder and war paint. In boxing idiom, they had both punched themselves out. The fighting had lasted three hours in 100-degree weather, the last hour made more difficult by the increasing smoke. Few of the participants had been in such a long battle; and as adrenaline wore off, more and more men would have found it difficult just to hold a rifle steady. The situation favored the side with greater numbers and the ability to withstand the heat. Custer, apprehensive as his front line ran low on ammunition, began taking the horse-holders' cartridges. Despite these problems, his sixth sense was still working; he suddenly spotted *something* going on among the Indians and instantly ordered his men to find their horses and mount up.

Throughout the morning Stanley's column had slowly marched up Sunday Creek Valley. Bradley noted that about 9 A.M. they stopped for an hour (likely where the stream split) in a "fine grove of trees and had a good rest, a rare chance in this country." Barrows felt that the temperature was 120 degrees in the sun. He quoted a scientist: "It is too warm to write, read, or think"; and an unhappy infantryman: "Curse the Jay Cookery that got up this expedition." Many, thinking that they would find more water later, marched with empty or half-filled canteens; but Sunday Creek's south branch was dry, and these men were soon to pay the price.

During the break, Stanley rode to the river's bluffs, taking in the gorgeous view of the wooded Tongue River Valley and its junction with the Yellowstone. Later he recommended the Tongue as the location for a new fort. Progress had been good, despite having to bridge Sunday Creek four times, but by noon the column was suffering from the heat, lack of water, and the increasingly steep trail. Enlisted men wore the same rough wool pants they had worn in winter—clothing that speeded dehydration, stuck to the skin, and caused sores on and between the legs. We can only imagine how bad it was for infantrymen (many of whom had lost their linen shirts the previous day), marching with rifles, ammunition, and knapsacks. The column now inched along at less than a mile an hour. Bradley wrote: "Men suffered terribly from [the] heat and some of the strongest broke down." Braden recalled scores of men collapsing and riding in ambulances. Even during the breaks, he wrote, "the horses would not graze; they stood motionless with their heads lowered, and their tongues protruded." Barrows noted that by 3 P.M. Stanley and the column's vanguard were "within three-quarters of a mile from the edge of the bluff." They were, in fact, two to three miles from where Custer was fighting, not the nine or ten miles stated by Frost.[16]

Meanwhile the surveyors were paralleling the Yellowstone. Including their escort of one company each of infantry and cavalry, both commanded by Captain Yates, they totaled about 120 men. Their work was difficult because of the heavy woods they had to transverse, but this was offset by the shade and being close to the river, whose 40-degree-colder water cooled the immediately adjacent areas. Although the surveyors were getting closer to the fighting, its sounds never reached them. There is no indication that they were aware of the battle or even the presence of Indians until the day ended. While their exact afternoon location is not known, they were a few miles "behind" Big Hill; and Custer's fighting was well to their right, outside their field of vision.[17]

If any of Stanley's scouts had spotted "hostiles" earlier, no one knew it. Stanley wrote that about 2 P.M. an Indian scout had ridden up and nonchalantly told him about gunfire in the valley, but the sporadic shooting had been attributed to Custer's spotting buffalo. The column marched on, clearly in a collective daze. Shortly after Stanley heard about the gunfire, Dr. John Honsinger and Augustus Baliran, both exhausted, decided to ride down the bluff to get water and rest. While Stanley had issued strict orders against straggling, there had been no sign of

Indians for over a month. Barrows said that, as the two rode forward, an Indian scout who spoke almost no English rode up and "stopped the Doctor and said 'Indians, Indians.' 'No, no,' said the Doctor; 'they are cavalry, cavalry.' The scout took hold of their bridle-reins and tried to turn their horses back. They refused to be convinced and the scout left them to their fate."[18]

At the base of the hill the two men cut left toward the river. Meanwhile two privates, John H. Ball and M. Brown, part of Yates's surveyor escort, decided to "goof off" and get some rest. With the surveyors strung out along the Yellowstone, the two slipped away—in frontaround the bluff's sharp bend and beyond anyone's line of sight. Here they split up. Brown unbridled his horse, took off his pistol belt, lay on the ground, and likely fell instantly asleep, as soldiers on break learn to do. As Brown lay down, Ball spotted Honsinger and Baliran and rode over to join them. Honsinger and Baliran were war veterans, known to be cautious; had they heard steady gunfire they presumably would have turned back. But the gunfire had become so irregular that it sounded like men hunting. The two must have seen the smoke and the burning grass but, apparently not considering it suspicious, rode forward. Both men were so exhausted and so intent on not slipping as they came down the slope that their minds did not register what they saw. Clearly the last thing they expected was to meet Indians as they made their way downhill, loosening gravel and stones. By frontier survival standards, they might as well have worn cowbells.[19]

Despite having little more than rocks and scrub brush to offer concealment, the half-dozen Hunkpapas quickly hid. One was Rain-in-the-Face, a veteran of the Fetterman and other Bozeman Trail fighting. As Honsinger and Baliran—likely half dazed and focusing on the Yellowstone—slowly rode toward the river, they were quietly surrounded. The Indians were so quiet and so close that one of them ran up and grabbed the bridle of Honsinger's horse and shot him, holding the horse as he rolled off. Or at least that was the story the terrified, incoherent Brown told Stanley a few minutes later. Clearly it is uncertain how much Brown really saw. Honsinger was found with his bald head smashed and numerous arrows in his body. Baliran was also quickly killed. He was found with his eyes open and his right hand in back of him, awkwardly clutching an arrow that had passed through his body. It is possible that Baliran's thighs were deeply slashed and his genitals mutilated. Ball must have briefly escaped; his body was not found until September and then by accident.[20]

About 3 P.M. Stanley and the officers with him heard some shots and a few minutes later saw Brown galloping toward the column, without his hat, belt, or revolver, his horse without a bridle. Terror-stricken and disheveled, he was screaming hysterically as he found Stanley at the head of the column. Brown was hampered by the fact that he could not tell the entire truth—that he saw what happened only because he and Ball had deserted Yates's command. Braden, riding near Stanley, remembered Brown's screaming, "All down there are killed!" Brown had been with Yates, so the officers who listened to his garbled story interpreted him to mean that Yates and the surveyors had been wiped out: a disaster of immense proportions.[21]

What Stanley thought is not known; but for a few seconds he likely swayed in his saddle, knowing that the implications included the end of his career. Certainly the surveyors and escort, strung out along the Yellowstone, could easily have been ambushed and, like Fetterman's command, killed to a man. Barrows wrote: "Gen. Stanley, who at this time had no knowledge of Gen. Custer's fight, immediately started all the cavalry in pursuit of the Indians." Stanley instinctively ordered his cavalry and scouts to the rescue, sending riders along the column to bring up the other cavalry companies and ordering the wagons to assume defensive positions. The execution was far from perfect, however. Edward Konopicky, near the end of the column and too exhausted to ride, wrote: "I was in [a] wagon when the adjutant came riding down from a hill toward the column in a full gallop shouting, 'Turn back! The Indians are here!' There was terrible confusion. The first wagons, including mine, turned around and raced into the cattle right behind us. . . . After about half an hour the column sorted itself out."[22]

Did Stanley personally lead the attack as he had in the heyday of his career, when he turned back Hood at Franklin? Barrows describes only the orders that Stanley gave, and Stanley himself makes no such claims, writing passively in his report: "I sent all the cavalry [and Indian scouts] to support Custer." In fact, as Barrows makes clear, when Stanley gave his orders, no one knew that Custer was in trouble.[23]

Five cavalry companies were spread out over the length of the three-mile wagon column; and by the time the orders reached the rear units, the first companies would have been on the valley floor. The cavalry and Indian scouts galloped in the direction from which Brown had ridden, away from the buffalo path. On reaching the hill's crest, they came to a screeching halt, finding themselves at the top of a steep, 200-foot gravel embankment. Dismounting, they scrambled down as best they could. Braden, who said he found a *good* route, noted that the horses had to be led down "and at times fairly slid on their haunches." As men and horses careened downhill, gravel, loose stones, and rocks bounced along with them; it was pure luck that no one was seriously injured. It is critical in reconstructing the scene to note that the men and horses kicked up a huge cloud of dust, which the Indians fighting Custer would quickly have spotted.[24]

Braden's company was down first. As the troopers mounted and realigned themselves, Rain-in-the-Face's half dozen Hunkpapas passed 100 yards in front, slowly trotting to the right, away from the river. "We could easily have fired on and probably killed some of their party," Braden noted; but on seeing Honsinger's large, distinctive horse, the troopers—also in a daze from the heat and for no logical reason—assumed that these Indians were their own Ree scouts. Not until the cavalry reassembled did Braden notice that the "scouts" had suddenly galloped away. Braden's men gave chase, but the Hunkpapas were lucky. The grass fires had spread, and Rain-in-the-Face escaped, zigzagging through the smoke and burning grass. Braden wrote that his men were "black as the ace of spades"; their horses were covered with lather, "and many a leg was badly singed while galloping through the patches of burning grass." Years later Braden remembered without embarrassment that when he reached the river at the end of the chase, "I crawled on all fours far enough into the Yellowstone to get my head under water."[25]

With the exception of Braden's contingent, the cavalry at the base of Big Hill galloped left toward the river, where they thought the surveyors were. Meanwhile Custer had his men line up in rough formation. It would have taken a few minutes to bring the horses from the woods and become organized; only then could he order them to charge, south, west, and away from Big Hill.

There are substantial differences of opinions, however, as to whether Custer charged independently of Stanley or waited until after the cavalry and Indian scouts had crested Big Hill. Most 1873 reports (including Custer's August 15 report, Barrows, Calhoun, and Larned) have Custer charging independently of Stanley. Even Stanley wrote: "[F]inding that the Indians had nothing new to develop, [Custer] mounted his squadron and charged, driving and dispersing the Indians." A number of excellent recent accounts, including those of Ambrose and Jeffry D. Wert, also tell the story without mentioning that Stanley came to Custer's rescue. In *Cavalier in Buckskin*, however, Utley writes: "Late in the day, with ammunition almost exhausted, the begrimed troopers glimpsed the rest of the cavalry galloping through the smoke to the rescue. Mounting, they joined the charge." In *The Lance and the Shield* Utley says that Custer "withdrew into a grove of timber and held off his assailants until Stanley came to the rescue."[26]

Custer certainly recognized that he needed rescuing, not mincing words in his *Galaxy* article:

> The reader can imagine how longingly and anxiously both officers and men constantly turned their eyes to the high ridges of hills, distant nearly two miles over which we knew we would catch the first glimpse of approaching succor. Our enemies seemed equally aware of our hopes and fears, and strange to say, their quick eyes . . . enabled them to detect the coming of our friends sooner than did we whose safety depended upon it.[27]

In fact, what actually happened reflected well on both Custer and Stanley. Braden, for example, specifically stated: "Our approach caused the Indians attacking Custer to withdraw"; and he noted that, after the Sioux attacks through the smoke failed, "[t]he Indians, abandoning this position, began to draw in their men." According to Barrows, Custer had his men mount and advance as skirmishers at a trot, but "finding this was not fast enough, a charge was ordered." The only plausible reason for a trot not being fast enough to close the distance was that the Indians were galloping away.[28]

There was no contemporary disagreement that no Lakotas or Cheyennes were caught between Custer and Stanley in the battle's final phase. The Indians fighting Custer heard bugle calls, saw cavalry coming down Big Hill, or both. Custer pursued them three or four miles, so some mention would have been made of Indians cut off between him and Stanley; the angle of Custer's pursuit should have trapped scores of them, but not a single one was caught. As he noted, the Indians saw "something" before he did and left the battlefield faster than Custer could attack. By the time Custer's men fully sorted their horses out, mounted, and fell into formation, the Indians had gained a precious few minutes' lead.

However, we also know that the Indians spotted the rescuers because Custer said so. The final two paragraphs in *Galaxy* offer a strikingly different perspective on the fight's final phase. Custer wrote that there was an unusual commotion in the Indians' ranks, and they began "a gradual withdrawal from in front of our right." The men in his center and right soon saw "an immense cloud of dust rising and rapidly approaching." As Custer watched, the cloud continued moving forward, the first horsemen and banners could be seen, and his men began shouting with relief. "It was a grand and welcome sight, but we waited not to enjoy it," Custer wrote, "[and] in a moment we were in our saddles and dashing after them."[29]

The irony that Stanley's charge was the result of Brown's incoherent story about the surveyors being attacked makes little difference. Stanley aggressively and properly ordered the cavalry forward. Even if Custer had not written the *Galaxy* article, there is a final piece of overwhelming circumstantial evidence pointing to Custer's awareness of the Indians' apprehension: he charged southwest, *away* from help. Otherwise Custer—low on ammunition and believing himself to be badly outnumbered, a truly desperate situation—would logically have stayed where he was, in a strong defensive position, or made a fighting retreat toward help as he had at Trevilian Station (1864).[30]

Given the frequent criticism of Custer's skills, did he perform well on August 4? A number of things could easily have gone wrong, especially with raw troops in their first action. While his field management looks easy, one has simply to place Samuel Sturgis (swept aside by Chief Joseph in 1877) or Marcus Reno (becoming unnerved at the Little Big Horn) in the same situation and the ending could have been far different, possibly disastrous.

CHAPTER 16

"Strike Up *Garry Owen*"

Custer's close call and the deaths of Baliran and Honsinger aroused Stanley from his lethargy. He began to encourage, if not actually push, Custer to pursue the Indians. On August 5, 1873, despite the previous day's fighting and hellish march, the energized Stanley sent everyone forward by 5 A.M. The marching was eased by the day's relative coolness and their route paralleling the river. At this point no one realized how close they had been to Sitting Bull's camp. When Stanley approached some steep bluffs and a good campsite about 4 P.M., having marched 11 miles, he halted the column to give the men a rest. Because it was believed that the Indians would dig up and mutilate white bodies, Honsinger's and Baliran's remains had been carried in the wagons all day. At dusk services were held. The two men were buried at a site marked on army maps, and horses were picketed all night over the graves so that by morning all signs of the burial had been obliterated.[1]

On August 6 the column slowly climbed a long hill and later made a steep descent to the floor of the valley (roughly opposite present-day Hathaway, exit 117 on I-94). Bradley wrote in his diary that the "sun came out as hot as ever," after a light rain, and the pioneers cut a "road down a long steep hill and had five hours hard work to get the train down." All told it had taken eleven hours to march six miles.

About noon on August 7, opposite the site where the Rosebud enters the Yellowstone, the party found Sitting Bull's previous camp, with large numbers of discarded lodge poles, axes, paddles, moccasins, food, personal items, and even war paint. The grass flattened by Indian travoises left a path 40 yards wide. Their discovery of the site greatly frustrated the more aggressive officers, who felt that they might have attacked the village on August 5 had they known of its existence. Sitting Bull was, of course, aware of his vulnerability—thus his hasty retreat. The findings were also an indication that the fighting on August 4 was essentially a blocking action.

On the morning of August 8 Custer's advance force found a second abandoned village, almost as large as the first. These Indians had joined the people leaving the first village. Bradley noted in his diary that they had "found rifles, axes, camp-kettles, and coffee, sugar, and bacon scattered along the trail." Barrows wrote that Stanley was now "determined to make an effort to punish them." When Custer asked permission to pursue them, Stanley quickly agreed. In the exchange of messages (they were riding some ten miles apart) Stanley first told Custer to take four days' rations but then increased it to seven and wrote the undoubtedly excited Custer that he should plan on taking all the cavalry companies as well as Lt. Brush's Indian scouts. While Stanley kept a handful of his Métis scouts, he was willing to entrust Custer with the surveying expedition's entire mounted force to accomplish his goal of punishing the Indians.

Custer, never one to wait, selected a campsite adjacent to Big Porcupine Creek, some eight miles upriver from current Forsyth. The wagon train had left Little Porcupine Creek shortly after 5 A.M. but was unable to cross the stream and had to take a time-consuming detour over some bluffs, in all taking 12 hours to cover 14 miles before finally reaching Custer's campsite. As soon as they arrived, the men of the 7th Cavalry began packing, taking with them a week of rations, overcoats, and blankets, and 100 extra rounds of ammunition each. Custer, possibly following the logic that in battle any surprise is a good one, brought his band with him.[2]

By 10 P.M. the cavalry was ready. "[I]n the silver moonlight" the bugler sounded the advance as some 485 men rode out: eight companies, Brush and the Indian scouts, the band, members of Stanley's staff, and Barrows. But at the last minute Custer made a perplexing decision, inexplicably taking a number of beef cattle, although surely aware that the slow-moving cattle could only delay him. Bradley wrote in his diary that evening: "Custer started after them tonight . . . but as he takes beef cattle on the hoof, I don't think he'll catch Indians." In the end, Custer's decision to take the small herd had no impact on trapping the fleeing Indians—they had too much of a lead—but it nevertheless remains startling. Clearly the question needs to be asked: had August 4's confrontation made him subconsciously hesitant about any upcoming, possibly more difficult fighting?[3]

The moonlight was ample for the scouts to follow Sitting Bull's trail. By 4:30 A.M. on August 9, having gone some 20 miles, with the sun rising and his men tired, Custer paused for a three-hour break. By 7:30 or 8 A.M. they were again giving chase and made 15 miles under an increasingly hot sun. Following a five- or six-hour midday break, Custer prepared for another long evening's march. But after riding another five or six miles along the Yellowstone, he came to the location where Sitting Bull's trail abruptly ended at the river. A scout volunteered to swim across—difficult enough but foolhardy if Lakotas were on the other side. The scout and his horse made slow headway in the strong current but finally reached the east bank and cautiously looked around. Upon returning, he reported finding the trail that the Indians from the two villages had made the previous day. But with the sun going down, Custer had no choice but to camp along the river.[4]

Barrows wrote that August 10 "was a day destined to failure and disappointment." Custer's camp was two to three miles below the Big Horn's junction with the Yellowstone, where the Yellowstone was over a quarter-mile wide and split by two parallel sandbars. Crossing to the first and second sandbars was easy enough, as the horses splashed through water two or three feet deep. But Custer was to get no farther. The main channel of the Yellowstone was some 150 yards wide, and the current strong. Scouts were sent to look for another crossing (whether upstream, downstream, or both is not known). Certainly Custer knew that he was just below the Big Horn and that, logically, going above its entry into the Yellowstone should have increased the odds of finding a crossing. Whether Custer's decisions to take the cattle and to try to cross downstream from the Big Horn are indicative of a man who is holding back is a question that cannot be answered more than 130 years later.

The logic for the crossing location was simple: it was the place where the Indians crossed and therefore it was a good location. Just about everybody made estimates of the Yellowstone's width but not necessarily from the same spot. Some sources indicate that a recent heavy rain upriver had caused the river to be high, but there is nothing to support or disprove this. Photos of the Yellowstone taken by Pywell a few days later, however, show that the river was far from its crest.

Throughout most of August 10 the cavalry stayed on or near the sandbars. Custer knew that Indian families had made the same crossing, but his men were stymied when they tried to swim their horses over. Braden wrote: "When the water reached half way between their bellies and their backs the strong current nearly carried them off their feet and the animals refused to go further, but turned around and started for shore." The next plan was to build a raft and get it to the other side then build larger rafts, setting up ferry operations. A handful of swimmers taking lariats but unable to carry arms swam the Yellowstone; but, according to Barrows, "the strength of the current snapped the rope several times and the plan was abandoned." Finally Custer asked Bloody Knife and some scouts to build two bullboats. "Two beeves were immediately killed and skinned," Barrows wrote. "When completed, this unique boat looked more like a large, raw-hide umbrella, three feet deep and about five in diameter . . . yet [able to] carry 1,000 pounds." By the time the second bullboat was finished, however, it was early evening.[5]

As dusk fell, an Indian came down to the river to water his horses; seeing Custer's camp, he fled in horror. His flabbergasted reaction, comical to those who saw him, suggested that Sitting Bull did not know he was being pursued, even though Custer had been at the Yellowstone for nearly a day. What nobody realized was that the Indian was either a great actor or the only person within 10,000 square miles who did not know Custer's location. Sitting Bull had sent messengers to nearby Oglala, Miniconjou, Sans Arc, and Cheyenne camps for help. That night, about 2 A.M., Braden awakened to what he thought was the sound of horses running over hard ground. A scout told him that Indians were gathering on the other side of the river and would attack at dawn. Braden woke Custer with the news, but "[Custer] replied that he did not believe the Indians were coming back. His manner indicated that he was annoyed at being awakened, [and] I was also annoyed at the manner of my early reception."[6]

If Custer could not reach the Indians, they could reach him. About 4 A.M., as cooks began breakfast and the mist on the Yellowstone rose, a handful of Indians fired at the troopers from across the river. As a cook in Braden's company held a pot of coffee over the fire, a bullet plowed into the hot coals, singeing the cook's hand and spilling the "precious" beverage. After a brief period of confusion, with yelling, milling around, and haphazard return fire, Custer ordered his men not to fire back with their carbines or untie the horses closest to the river, telling Barrows that he wanted "to furnish no cause of confidence to the Indians." But as more Lakotas came up to the river and began firing, Custer gave the order to untie the horses as his men gulped down breakfast.

Sitting Bull had developed a seemingly logical plan: keep pressure on Custer's center as mounted warriors swam the river, attacking from both sides. Despite the distance, light firing continued for two hours, coupled with insults between Custer's scouts and the Lakotas. The Lakotas wanted to know if Baliran and Honsinger had been officers, and they confirmed Ball's death. During a break in the firing, Barrows climbed a low hill, joining some men. "Do you see some of those black lookin' things in the river, Mister?" a trooper asked Barrows. "They are Indians." Barrows saw—a mile and a half away—Indians swimming the Yellowstone with their horses.

About 6:45 A.M. Barrows rejoined Custer and a small group along the river watching John Tuttle, the regiment's best shot, who carried a powerful Springfield hunting rifle. Tuttle wished "to drop a few more of them fellows." He then asked Barrows (a Harvard divinity student): "'Do you want to see me drop that Indian?' pointing to one on his pony who had come out of the wood. He brought his rifle to his shoulder and fired, the Indian dropped from his pony. Three or four other Indians ran to him. Tuttle took another shot and dropped another man." The men around Tuttle jumped with delight, and Louis Hills unabashedly wrote: "I laughed aloud when Tuttle shot the Indian." Custer warned Tuttle to get back, as the Indians would concentrate their fire at him, but Tuttle refused to stop. Barrows continued:

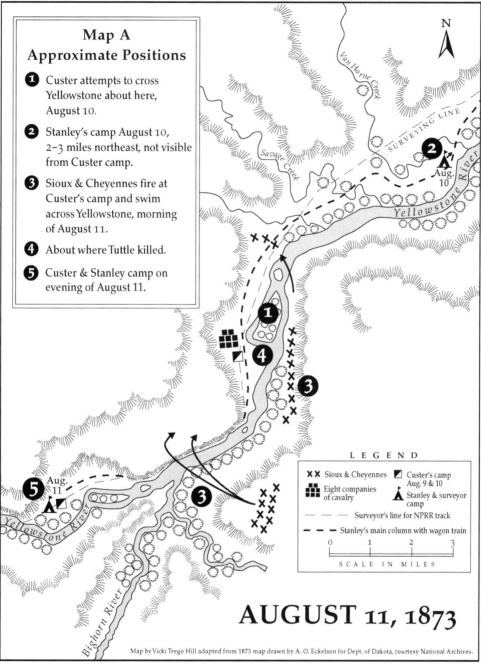

Map A
Approximate Positions

1 Custer attempts to cross Yellowstone about here, August 10.

2 Stanley's camp August 10, 2–3 miles northeast, not visible from Custer camp.

3 Sioux & Cheyennes fire at Custer's camp and swim across Yellowstone, morning of August 11.

4 About where Tuttle killed.

5 Custer & Stanley camp on evening of August 11.

LEGEND

XX Sioux & Cheyennes

◼ Eight companies of cavalry

◢ Custer's camp Aug. 9 & 10

⛑ Stanley & surveyor camp

–– Surveyor's line for NPRR track

- - - Stanley's main column with wagon train

```
0        1        2        3
SCALE IN MILES
```

AUGUST 11, 1873

Map by Vicki Trego Hill adapted from 1873 map drawn by A. O. Eckelson for Dept. of Dakota, courtesy National Archives.

Custer Position on August 10 and Morning of August 11

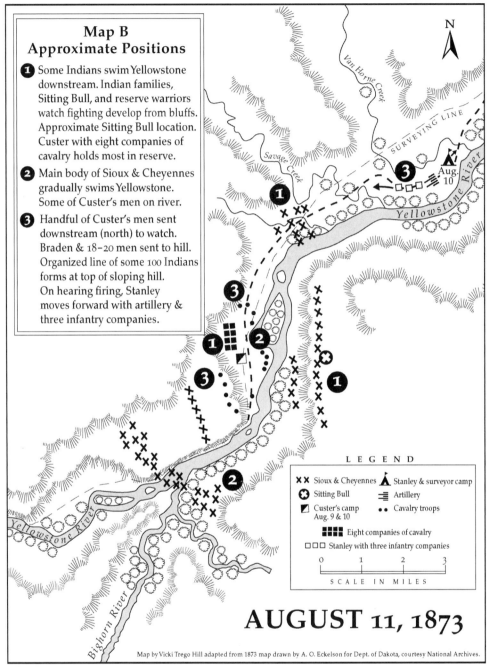

Map B
Approximate Positions

1 Some Indians swim Yellowstone downstream. Indian families, Sitting Bull, and reserve warriors watch fighting develop from bluffs. Approximate Sitting Bull location. Custer with eight companies of cavalry holds most in reserve.

2 Main body of Sioux & Cheyennes gradually swims Yellowstone. Some of Custer's men on river.

3 Handful of Custer's men sent downstream (north) to watch. Braden & 18–20 men sent to hill. Organized line of some 100 Indians forms at top of sloping hill. On hearing firing, Stanley moves forward with artillery & three infantry companies.

LEGEND

✗✗ Sioux & Cheyennes   ▲ Stanley & surveyor camp
✖ Sitting Bull   ≡ Artillery
◤ Custer's camp Aug. 9 & 10   •• Cavalry troops
▦ Eight companies of cavalry
□□□ Stanley with three infantry companies

0   1   2   3
SCALE IN MILES

AUGUST 11, 1873

Map by Vicki Trego Hill adapted from 1873 map drawn by A. O. Eckelson for Dept. of Dakota, courtesy National Archives.

Initial Sioux and Cheyenne Attacks

"[After] a short interval . . . [Tuttle fired again] and another man dropped from his pony. This was Tuttle's last shot. The Indians brought their best men forward and opened a cross fire on the tree behind which he was concealed . . . [Tuttle] turned his head to one side to take another sight[ing], when a shot struck him in the forehead and pierced his brain."[7]

Sitting Bull did not know it, but he was making things easy for Custer as his warriors swam the Yellowstone. A handful went to the bluffs to Custer's west, but most gathered in two groups, above and below him, forming large but uncoordinated pincers. Here their bravado betrayed them, as they began launching piecemeal attacks against the battle-experienced Custer. To the degree that the Indians had unified leadership, it was provided by Sitting Bull, who was shouting instructions and encouragement from a bluff across the river and actually could be heard on parts of the field. While Sitting Bull had a magnificent view of the field, the distance made most of his commands (if that was what they were) impossible to hear. Custer, in contrast, had interior lines of communication, and his men promptly executed their orders.[8]

Just after Tuttle's death Custer was told that Indians were advancing from the west. Not knowing their numbers, he sent Braden and about 20 men forward. They dismounted in a 30-foot, 45 degree–angle ravine and ran to the top, finding themselves on a gradual, upward-sloping plateau stretching west about a half-mile. Facing them were some 100 warriors, including Gall and possibly Crazy Horse. Forming two lines, in full war regalia, they launched the first of four charges. As Braden's men fired back, lying down or kneeling to present smaller targets, the Indians veered off each time. While some horses were hit, no Indians were wounded. But Braden was outnumbered, and his position was becoming indefensible. Each charge brought the Indians closer; some had swung around his left, between his men and the Yellowstone.[9]

At this point Braden got up for a better look—the last time in his 71-year life that he stood comfortably. A bullet shattered the bone in his left thigh, caused a compound fracture, and narrowly missed the femoral artery. For a split second, he remained erect, then the bullet's force and broken thigh tumbled him backward, down the 30-foot slope. Shortly afterward, as he was carried away on a stretcher, a man carrying him tripped, throwing him into a cactus bed and causing even more horrifying pain. Had Braden waited a minute, he might not have been hit; nearly three companies of reinforcements (E, K, and L) arrived. Faced with this larger force, the Indians quickly fell back.[10]

Seeing Indians crossing downstream, Custer ordered M company to push them back and prevent others from crossing. It was obvious, however, that the largest Indian force was assembling near where Braden had been shot. Sometime after 8 A.M. Custer decided to launch a counterattack, ordering G company to hold the ground between the river and the camp to prevent crossings there and to assist M company. Custer was watching the fighting develop as he sat on his horse in front of his troops when his horse and a nearby officer's horse were both killed. Taking another horse, Custer ordered companies E, K, and L forward; some of the men probably took the gap that runs through the area.

About this time Custer either heard the sound of Stanley's cannon or saw infantry coming upstream (or both), for he wrote in his August 15 report that "[t]he appearance of the main command in sight down the valley enabled me to . . ." and here Custer described his actions as he prepared to attack the Indians. With Stanley protecting him downriver, Custer decided to move up his reserve companies (A, B, and F), ordering them to clear the base of a hill. As Custer aligned his six companies, a wave of excitement swept through the ranks; they knew they were going into action, and those who could not see Stanley could probably hear the booming sounds of the Rodman guns.[11]

Stanley's appearance was the last thing anyone expected. "Owing to the bad country we had come over," Barrows wrote, "filled with creeks, ravines, and lofty hills, we did not expect the [wagon] train for a day." Cheers went up, Barrows reported. "Halloo," one man shouted, "Stanley's talking Dutch to them. Look at that!" A second cavalryman yelled, "Hurrah for old Stand-by!" (a pejorative rewording of Stanley's wartime nickname, "Our Stanley," and likely how the cavalrymen referred to him throughout the summer). As the other cavalry companies arrived, in his *pièce de résistance* Custer also ordered the 7th Cavalry's band forward. Barrows continued the story for his *New York Tribune* readers and hundreds of thousands of others around the country:

> "Strike up *Garry Owen*," said . . . [Custer] to the leader of the band [Vinatieri]. The familiar notes of that stirring Irish air acted like magic. If the commander had had a galvanic battery connecting with the solar plexus of every man in the field, he could hardly have electrified them more thoroughly. What matter if the cornet played a faltering note and the alto-horn was a little husky? There was no mistaking the tune and its meaning.[12]

The Lakotas and Cheyennes had to have been dumbfounded by the band and the six companies, each with horses of a different color, lined up as if on parade-ground formation. As the notes of "Garry Owen" faded, Custer, leading almost 300 men, ordered the charge. With trumpets blaring and troopers galloping toward them on the open field, the Indians wavered a second and then turned and fled. Gall, who had drawn attention to himself with a red blanket, unsuccessfully tried to rally the warriors. His horse was shot from under him; but another warrior quickly scooped him up, and he escaped. Custer chased the Indians for miles, through washes and gullies, across open meadows, and around three or four coulees. As

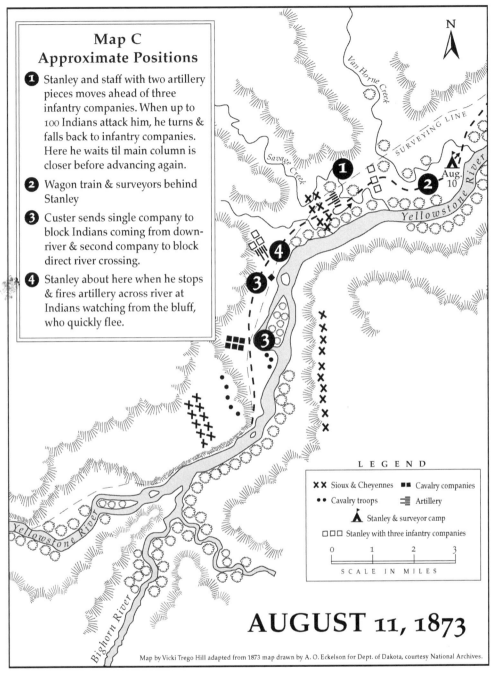

Map C
Approximate Positions

1 Stanley and staff with two artillery pieces moves ahead of three infantry companies. When up to 100 Indians attack him, he turns & falls back to infantry companies. Here he waits til main column is closer before advancing again.

2 Wagon train & surveyors behind Stanley

3 Custer sends single company to block Indians coming from down-river & second company to block direct river crossing.

4 Stanley about here when he stops & fires artillery across river at Indians watching from the bluff, who quickly flee.

LEGEND

✗✗ Sioux & Cheyennes   ■■ Cavalry companies

•• Cavalry troops   🢁 Artillery

🠷 Stanley & surveyor camp

☐☐☐ Stanley with three infantry companies

0   1   2   3

SCALE IN MILES

AUGUST 11, 1873

Map by Vicki Trego Hill adapted from 1873 map drawn by A. O. Eckelson for Dept. of Dakota, courtesy National Archives.

Stanley's Initial Arrival and Custer's First Moves

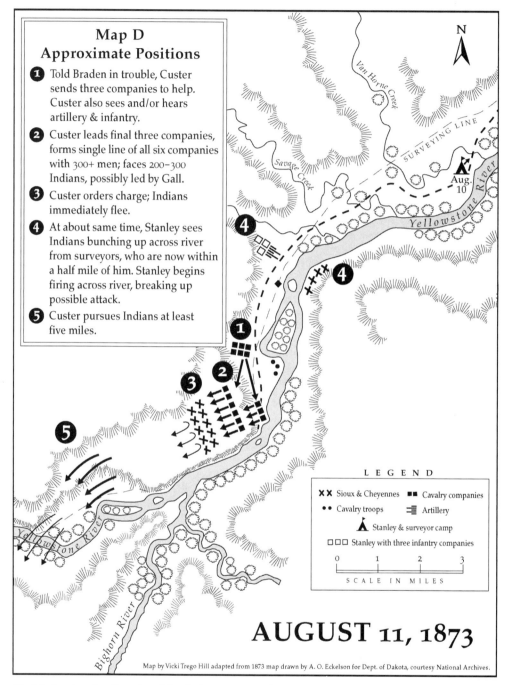

Map D
Approximate Positions

1 Told Braden in trouble, Custer sends three companies to help. Custer also sees and/or hears artillery & infantry.

2 Custer leads final three companies, forms single line of all six companies with 300+ men; faces 200–300 Indians, possibly led by Gall.

3 Custer orders charge; Indians immediately flee.

4 At about same time, Stanley sees Indians bunching up across river from surveyors, who are now within a half mile of him. Stanley begins firing across river, breaking up possible attack.

5 Custer pursues Indians at least five miles.

N

Van Horne Creek

SURVEYING LINE

Savage Creek

Yellowstone River

Aug. 10

LEGEND

X X Sioux & Cheyennes   **■■** Cavalry companies

● ● Cavalry troops   ⧻ Artillery

⛺ Stanley & surveyor camp

☐☐☐ Stanley with three infantry companies

0   1   2   3

SCALE IN MILES

Yellowstone River

Bighorn River

AUGUST 11, 1873

Map by Vicki Trego Hill adapted from 1873 map drawn by A. O. Eckelson for Dept. of Dakota, courtesy National Archives.

Final Indian Attacks; Custer's and Stanley's Counterattacks

soon as they safely could, one small band of Indians after another peeled off from the main body, most swinging left to the Yellowstone and swimming across, until, as Custer wrote, "they were completely dispersed." The action likely ended opposite the present-day community of Custer. No Indians were believed to have been killed in the chase, but some were probably wounded, and certainly a number of their ponies were shot.[13]

After Custer left, Stanley, the infantry, wagons, and surveyors—the tortoise to Custer's hare—marched 32 miles in two days. August 9 was typically difficult, as they "took to the bluffs again." The day was so clear that Bradley wrote at one point: "Saw Custer with our glasses some 20 miles ahead." August 10 was hot and dry; the main column kicked up a huge plume of dust that Sitting Bull or his scouts could easily see from the 150-foot, miles-long sandstone bluff across from the place where Custer was trying to cross the Yellowstone. Stanley's camp that night was opposite the present-day railroad crossing of Myers, Montana; had he gone another mile or so farther or had his Indian scouts, Custer's camp would easily have been seen.[14]

About 5 A.M. on August 11, just after the march began, Bradley heard "rapid firing four or five miles in advance." However, because of the Yellowstone's meandering course, thick woods along the banks, and some heavily wooded islands between the main command and Custer, nothing could be seen. Stanley, Bradley, the artillery, and three companies of infantry hurried to join Custer. The two mule-drawn Rodmans, mounted artillerymen, Stanley, and his staff had moved ahead of the infantry, who were probably soon huffing and puffing. Sometime after 7 A.M. they spotted Indians and Custer's camp. "Before we could hardly realize it," surveyor A. L. Berry later wrote, "a body of Indians galloped out of the gulch right in front of the artillery, and it looked as though we were going to lose both pieces of artillery as well as the men." Discretion being the better part of valor, Stanley and the artillery wheeled around and dashed for the safety of the three infantry companies. Once Stanley had reached them, they fired a volley, scattering his pursuers. However, as Berry wryly noted: "It was a very interesting chase."[15]

After the Sioux turned back, Stanley apparently waited until the lead companies with the main column could join him and then advanced with them and his artillery. In his report Stanley notes that he first came into sight of Custer's position about 7 A.M. Sometime between 7:30 and 8 A.M. and a mile or so from Custer's camp, he had the guns unlimbered after finding a low elevation. On the bluffs opposite the camp, Sioux families, older men, and reserve warriors—in all perhaps 1,000, including Sitting Bull—were watching. While Lt. John M. Webster was technically in charge, field artillery had always been Stanley's *forte,* and he was literally the one calling the shots. Berry recalled that a shell burst "about ten feet over their heads and carried down a great deal of stone, rock, and dirt into their very midst.

Some of them plunged off the rock into the water below [the top of the bluff was some 150 feet above the Yellowstone] while the balance made a wild scamper to get out of reach of our guns." By the time dust from the third shell had cleared, all sources agree, the Indians had vanished.[16]

Throughout the fighting, the well-guarded surveyors had continued their work. As they neared Stanley's position, a large group of Indian warriors on the opposite side of the river began to jeer and insult them, threatening to come across. Bradley wrote: "About ½ past 8 [sic] saw 100 [Indians] in a body on the south side of the Yellowstone, threw a couple of shells over and stampeded them." Decades later the surveyor Berry, likely without Bradley's combat experience, recalled the shelling lasting almost an hour, with the artillerymen "firing rapidly into the woods and other points wherever they could see the Indians moving." Nevertheless, the last shell fired signaled the end of the day's fighting.[17]

About 10:30 A.M. Custer returned from his chase and found that Stanley, the wagons, and the main infantry column had reached his camp. Quite possibly the band had also joined the charge, for Lt. Charles Larned wrote: "We rode back to the infantry after the charge, with the band playing in front of us [and] our pennons flying." Konopicky saw "the cavalry resting after the fight. General Custer came riding towards us with his band and a flag bearer with the American flag. He was on a white horse and wore a red shirt. He is a clear target and wears his hair long, but the Indians have not succeeded in getting him, even though he always rides in front leading his soldiers."[18]

Cavalry losses included Tuttle dead, Braden not expected to live, and three others with lesser wounds. Indian casualties were not known. One Indian source said that only one Indian was killed, but the most likely number was four. An Indian gave this number to Stanley, who noted: "My experience is that the Sioux generally give a pretty correct account of their losses." The *New York Times* correspondent estimated ten dead. Based on Custer's estimate, however, Barrows put Indian "casualties" at forty in a dispatch picked up by papers around the country. The number meant killed and wounded, but it is often misinterpreted as forty dead.[19]

Custer, not wishing to disclose that most of the Indians never crossed the Yellowstone, carefully wrote: "The number of Indians opposed to us has been estimated by the various officers engaged as from 800 to 1,000." The *Philadelphia Evening Bulletin* stated that Custer "was attacked by about 800 Indians who came down to the river and fired on his camp . . . 300 Indians then crossed the river." Larned and the *New York Times* estimated 500 to 600, implying that they all crossed. The 800 total seems reasonable, with possibly half swimming the Yellowstone. In short, Custer was never outnumbered on his side, although the Indian presence on the far side required his keeping reserves available. Sitting Bull's uncoordinated attacks had little chance; even if twice or three times as many warriors had crossed, the result would have been similar, especially considering Stanley's timely arrival. Bradley, who did not like Custer, wrote his wife: "You may see mention of this [fight] in the papers, but it was a small affair."[20]

Following the Indians' flight, the reunited column made good progress, marching five more miles that afternoon and reaching Pompeys Pillar on August 15. The surveyors soon found Haydon's stakes from 1872, and the Northern Pacific Railroad's goal of having a continuous line of survey from Lake Superior to Puget Sound was at long last achieved.

Unlike 1872, however, when Stanley and Rosser had reached the junction of the Yellowstone and Powder Rivers, there was no celebration. Any excitement that may have been generated by completing the engineering link was more than offset by the deaths that had been sustained, the necessity to march farther before they could even turn back, and the ruggedness of the side of the river that they were on, which would probably prevent railroad construction.

The next day half a dozen Indians fired at over 500 soldiers who were bathing or washing clothes in the Yellowstone. The incident was considered comical, as hundreds of men splashed out of the river in seconds. No one was hit. One story had a frightened infantryman leaving his clothes and sprinting naked half a mile through camp to his tent. On August 17 the column left for the Musselshell River, arriving three days later near present-day Roundup. From there Stanley sent a courier to Fort Benton with mail, Custer's report, and the correspondents' stories. Stanley, with time to reflect, had written his wife that it had been "the hardest summer's work he ever performed," according to Irvine. Stanley refused to rest at the Musselshell, pushing on and marching east 60 miles in four days. Not until Sunday, August 24, did he give everyone the day off.[21]

The tree-lined Musselshell was picturesque, and the valley filled with game and herds of 2,000 to 3,000 buffalo. The Musselshell's waters were clear, and for most of the men it was an idyllic day off: hunting, fishing, bathing, doing laundry, or just resting. As Stanley dourly noted, however, the river "has the peculiarity of having decided diuretic qualities." On August 25 the column reached the river's abrupt north turn at present-day Melstone. Custer and Eckelson scouted to the northeast but found the land unsuitable for a railroad. When Custer returned, he and Stanley decided to travel together for a few more days and then split up, to meet opposite Stanley's Stockade later. The wagon train and infantry roughly followed today's U.S. Route 12, and the cavalry and surveyors scouted a more direct route. Both routes proved so inhospitable, however, that they remain all but unsettled today.[22]

Because the gravely wounded Braden was not expected to live, his wish that his leg not be amputated was honored. A number of men volunteered to build a raft and float with him to the stockade, but Stanley felt that the idea was suicidal given the Indians' presence on the river. Litter bearers were tried, but heat and insects quickly ended this plan. A day's bouncing ride in an ambulance wagon proved unbearable; and the suggestion of an Indian travois was rejected precisely because Indians used them. Someone then remembered that a buggy with springs was stored in a wagon. The buggy was jerry-rigged into a one-man wheeled stretcher with a canvas top, pulled by a mule or in rugged country by enlisted men. Braden survived, but on his arrival at Fort Lincoln in September, it was discovered that his weight had fallen from 180 to 125 pounds and his left leg was an inch shorter than his right; his army career was over.[23]

Stanley reached the Yellowstone on August 31 at Little Porcupine Creek (opposite today's railroad stop at Flynn) and then retraced his route downstream. Even this was not easy, because heavy rains had swept away the roads built in August. On September 4 Ball's remains were found by accident. At 1 P.M. on September 9 the column finally reached the point on the Yellowstone opposite the stockade. Custer, despite following a more difficult route, had arrived five days earlier. The *Josephine* did not arrive until the same day as Stanley, because the river had dropped. Stanley and Custer soon parted: Custer escorted the surveyors to the Missouri, Stanley followed with the wagons, and other infantry companies boarded the *Josephine* for Omaha. All told, Stanley's report indicated a march of some 935 miles. Custer reached Fort Lincoln to discover that his report of the fighting had been widely published: he was again a national hero. When Stanley arrived, Custer was the model host. On Stanley's last evening before taking a steamer back to Fort Sully and obscurity, Custer, dominant and rehabilitated, had his band serenade Stanley.[24]

The contribution of the Scientific Corps proved modest. Konopicky wrote that Allen, Nettre, and Pywell had "mainly been practicing sleeping," and he was disgusted by Allen: "The scientific knowledge of this Cambridge trained gentleman does not extend a jot beyond his birds . . . [he] dares to pretend he is a botanist and mineralogist, and lets himself be called a professor." Allen and Bennett were unable to collect specimens, shooting nothing "despite the fact that they rode around with two flintlocks, revolvers, and knives like walking hardware stores." In an era when Charles Darwin's ideas were keenly debated, there were no discoveries or significant contributions. Allen's final report, which noted 2,000 rattlesnakes killed, was read to an audience of 31. Nettre never published. Konopicky's paintings are lost; his sketch books, which he took back to Vienna, did not survive the 1945–46 Russian occupation.[25]

Rosser had left his surveyors in late July, returned to Minneapolis for a week, and then traveled to New York. There he met with Milnor Roberts and the Northern

Pacific's executive committee on August 14, making a presentation on the less expensive, easier-to-build route between Bismarck and the Yellowstone. He briefed Sheridan in Chicago and, on returning to "the front," read numerous complimentary stories about his findings. The *Railroad Gazette* stated: "By the line just surveyed, which may be called 'Rosser's Line,' a saving in distance of 23.3 miles is effected over the line of 1871." By August 27 Rosser was back in Bismarck, readying materials to show bidders for 1874's construction. In September, blissfully unaware of Wall Street's rumblings and basking in well-deserved publicity, Rosser, 37, was confident, enjoying what proved to be the last happy days of his 71-year life.[26]

Milnor Roberts's year-end report in November reviewed the accomplishments of the 1873 survey, the Northern Pacific Railroad's longest and most efficient engineering effort. But by the time he submitted the report, Roberts, Jay Cooke, and the Northern Pacific Railroad were all bankrupt.[27]

CHAPTER 17

"We Do Not Anticipate Any Trouble"

George Washington Cass (West Point, '32), who replaced Gregory Smith as president of the Northern Pacific, had held key leadership roles in Pennsylvania canal, steamboat, railroad, and express freight operations. Cooke, who had known him for decades, needed his skills and reputation; but Cass was reluctant. Not wanting to manage a disaster, he asked Cooke if "there is any reasonable doubt of the ability of the company to meet its obligations and go forward with the work of construction." Cooke, courting him, offered reassurance, likely overstated the railroad's financial position, and committed the full support of his banking house. In so doing, Cooke—inadvertently or not—broke the commitment he had given his partners about taking a tough stand with the NP after it reached the Missouri. But once on board, Cass refused to participate in bond sales, one of the reasons Cooke had hired him. Cooke's partners wanted the NP to assume a greater bond sales role, but he felt constrained or had lost the will to push Cass and continued to shoulder the full responsibility for the NP's finances.[1]

Cass assumed the presidency in December and (once in office) was a whirlwind, enacting a host of economies. In March he wrote Cooke: "There is nothing like poverty to bring about close settlements"; and if he was frugal, there was much to be frugal about. With Cass taking a firm hand, Smith's team began leaving. Treasurer A. H. Barney resigned. "My duty has been to make enormous expenditures over which I had no control," he disingenuously wrote. Cooke was delighted with Cass's performance but probably kicked himself for waiting so long.[2]

As the new year began, Cass and Cooke faced huge problems. Bond sales had collapsed, Billings's land company had just had its Minnesota lands certified and could not be counted on to bring in much cash for some months, competition for government bonds was increasing, and Cooke's cash reserves were almost exhausted. Fortunately, the Northern Pacific's new construction requirements were limited to 40 miles in Washington and completing the line to Bismarck. In the spring Rosser began managing Dakota construction and over a thousand workers. However, instead of needing just 20 miles to reach Bismarck, the distance was closer to 35. In 1872, besides shoddy work, the NP had paid for at least 15 "ghost" miles of track, another sign of the graft and mismanagement. Additionally, the roadbed was in such terrible condition that it took some members of the Scientific Corps three days to go from Fargo to Bismarck on one of the first trains.[3]

Despite continued rumors about its finances, the Northern Pacific was publicly confident. On February 14 Secretary of War William W. Belknap released a telegram from Cass stating that the Northern Pacific "intend[ed] to put their road, from the Missouri River to the Yellowstone, under contract this spring." The only mention of anything similar is in the February 27 minutes, however: "President [Cass] was directed to cause a [surveying] party to be organized to commence the final location of the road between the Missouri River and the Yellowstone." In short, letting contracts was a public relations sham, clearly understood by all insiders and certainly by Cooke's partners, who were adamantly opposed to new financial commitments.[4]

In February Cooke began his drive to remove Canfield as president of the Lake Superior and Puget Sound Land Company as relations disintegrated over disputed land. Cooke angrily and imperiously wrote Canfield: "I now understand that through some arrangement all the [Duluth] lands fronting the Bay . . . which we understood was [sic] donated to the Northern Pacific has been seized by the Puget Sound Co. [sic]. This is the first I ever heard of that disposition of the property & it will have to be undone." Cooke then wrote Cass: "I will cooperate with you at once in changing the possession of that property from the L. S. & Puget Sound Co. to the Northern Pacific Co. *where it belongs"* (Cooke's emphasis). Despite the pressure, Canfield, whose life savings were tied up in the LSPS, refused to budge. Cooke wrote Canfield that his company had not worked "in harmony" with the NP. In defending himself, Canfield pointed to his Brainerd accomplishments. But board member Charles B. Wright, a one-time Canfield associate, now scornfully wrote Cooke that it was "conceded" that the LSPS "has with its narrow-minded policy driven more people out of Brainerd than it has kept in."[5]

Canfield refused to resign; while Cooke was horrified to discover that he did not have the legal power to replace him, a Cooke ally was elected vice president and made "himself a thorn in the side of [Canfield]." Cooke then developed a plan to close down the LSPS and roll it into Billings's operations. Canfield's friends, however, many of whom were associated with Moorhead's brother, J. Kennedy

Moorhead, held both LSPS and NP bonds. In essence, they blackmailed Cooke by saying that if he shut down the LSPS they would go public with the NP's problems. Canfield retained his position, albeit with diminished responsibilities.

Billings's land company still faced enormous difficulties, although by the spring of 1873 it had 2,925,000 acres to sell in Minnesota. Squatters occupied the Dakota side of the Red River, and the Northern Pacific did not have the wherewithal to evict them. American settlers were less inclined to accept authority than European immigrants were, and few would pay once they were on the frontier (and often well armed). Billings continued to emphasize large groups, but not until mid-1873 did this bear fruit, when families arrived from Great Britain, Sweden, Germany, and Russia in parties of 100 or more. Even if they all had purchased land, however, the numbers were insignificant. And, in fact, many of the families that arrived soon discovered that they could buy similar and sometimes better land less expensively from brokers offering both NP and public land. Nevertheless, the boom was dramatic. An article in the anti-NP *Cincinnati Commercial* placed population growth along the NP's track at 30,000.[6]

Billings also made a major effort to entice Americans, but many prospective purchasers soon left. One letter to Billings stated: "Hundreds of people are being turned [off] by the horrible smell and worse taste of the Glyndon water which has filtered through alkaline deposits." The NP's reception house had been built nearby, but its management seemed unable to find a solution. No 1873 land sales figures are known. As a base, the land company expenses from July 1, 1872, to June 30, 1873, when cash was very tight, were huge: $305,676. The NP's 1876 report and historian Sig Mickelson's analysis indicate that 695,072 acres were sold by September 29, 1875, mostly in the final two and a half years. The amount paid by September 18, 1873, is speculative; but if 125,000 acres had been sold at $4 per acre, and 15 percent deposited (slightly high assumptions), cash receipts would have been just $75,000. Even doubling these numbers leads to the same conclusion: cash from land sales came nowhere near expenditures.[7]

On December 9, 1872, Jay Cooke & Co. had come close to failing; its New York branch was overdrawn by $140,000. Fahnestock wrote Cooke: "[W]e are in a perfectly helpless position and we must have from you immediately either money or securities." Cooke was able to keep his company afloat, but in 1873 one financial cliffhanger followed another. Because of his enormous campaign contributions (financially and in propping up the bond market), Cooke expected to be the lead company in government bond sales despite the opposition led by Morgan and Drexel. But Grant refused to help, and Cooke and Morgan shared the lead. In the end the bonds sold poorly, perhaps sabotaged by Morgan. In 1873 the NP and the Southern Pacific jointly went to Congress to get federal subsidies for finished track. The effort went nowhere, however, because of the opposition of the Omaha-Chicago–New York axis, plus the Crédit Mobilier and Erie Railroad scandals. Close association with railroads became dangerous. Senator Windom, who had profited from the LSPS and other insider trading, now informed Cooke that he wanted to sever his NP ties, citing his chairmanship of the Select Committee on Transportation.[8]

Compounding Cooke's problems, currency became scarce. The April *Commercial and Financial Chronicle* stated that it was the "most protracted monetary pinch which has been known for a quarter of a century." European problems reduced foreign capital, interest rates rose, and business confidence declined, but some 20 new railroad bonds were being sold. While the NP paid 7 percent interest and was only one of two companies with land grants, it had the highest cost per mile of construction, was in the least-populated area, and had the longest mileage of any of its competitors. Ominously, more NP bondholders were selling, which put further pressure on Cooke, who did not have the resources to prop up the market. With bond sales anemic, Cooke grumbled to Cass that he wished "this Crédit Mobilier thing were out of the way." February 1873 sales were $320,000, which probably did not cover sales costs and interest payments.[9]

West Coast operations were another Northern Pacific drain: 60 miles of track had been constructed between Portland and Puget Sound, but cash receipts were negligible. Nevertheless, the NP moved ahead with construction in April to complete a line from Kalama, Washington (on the Columbia River, north of Portland), to Tacoma. Some problems were easier to resolve. After Horace Greeley died, it was discovered he held $10,000 in NP bonds. A fight ensued over their value, and Sam Wilkeson was subpoenaed. He wrote Cooke that whatever he testified would hurt the NP but that he felt it best to say, untruthfully, that the bonds were still worth $10,000. "Dear Uncle Samuel," Cooke began, in a response that cut through the conundrum: he would buy the bonds back for $10,000, and Wilkeson would not have to testify.[10]

Despite the flood of bad news, the Northern Pacific's overall picture was brightening. Bismarck replaced Sioux City as the disembarkation point for the Upper Missouri, and the army began routing supplies from there to its Dakota and Montana posts. Further traffic was anticipated after the Hudson Bay Company secured extensive Duluth dock space; the Canadian Pacific planned to ship all its equipment and track via Duluth. Now the city began assuming the role that Cooke had foreseen: trains arrived daily from the west, and east-bound freighters sailed five days a week. Besides the increased revenue, under Cass the NP's operations quickly improved. The *Railroad Gazette* showed a cost per mile 40 percent less for the NP than for the Central Pacific, for example, an indication that the NP was operating within industry norms. Other positive financial factors were the limited amount of new construction and the imminent certification of 10 million acres of prime West Coast timberland and valuable Dakota farmland. Further good news came from Rosser's discovery of potentially valuable coal deposits 50 miles from Bismarck.[11]

In mid-spring, however, Cooke gave up selling Northern Pacific bonds and decided to form a syndicate to sell the remaining $9 (of $30) million "7-30s." Cooke hoped to finish in late May, cleaning up both NP and Jay Cooke & Co. finances. As a sweetener, Cooke discounted the cost to 83 cents on the dollar, added other benefits, and announced that future bonds would bear only 6 percent interest. Harnsberger writes that Cooke "must have realized that the bankers and large investors would not be taken in, but perhaps the public would believe the explanation." Had the syndication succeeded, $8.47 million would have realized, paying back Cooke's advances, advertising, sales, and other costs, and the NP would have been received ample operational, construction, and reserve funds. It was also believed that construction would end at Bismarck; the *Railroad Gazette* noted: "This may indicate that the company does not purpose for some time to complete any more of its road than is now under contract."[12]

One investor viewing the NP's long-term prospects optimistically was Charlemagne Tower. Tower, the "Iron Millionaire," 64, who was possibly descended from *the* Charlemagne, was a longtime Cooke friend who believed in the NP land grants. Interested in Lake Superior's mineral resources, he purchased $56,000 in bonds in 1871 and continued investing, reaching $250,000. When Cooke offered his syndicate in April, Tower stepped up with another $250,000, and the NP was only too happy to give him a board seat for his support. Tower's purchase and another $250,000 purchase by Charles Wright set off a wave of jubilation, but it was to prove short-lived. Cooke's syndicate stalled at $2 million, with many of his longtime sales associates not participating.[13]

The bottom line was that U.S. economic problems were simply too great to overcome. As 7-30 sales declined and previous investors unloaded their shares, Cooke could no longer make up the difference, and NP prices began falling. By August 15 Northern Pacific and Lake Superior & Mississippi indebtedness to Jay Cooke & Co. was $6.96 million. Earlier, Cooke had decided to call in or have interest paid by James G. Blaine, Chase, Colfax, and others. Henry Cooke had to ask for the money, however, and he soon showed signs of cracking. Jay advised him to resign as governor of the District of Columbia and to ask Grant for a diplomatic post, writing on April 1, 1873: "Your health requires it . . . and you must, my dear brother, have instant relief from the cares and anxieties which perplex you." Publicly, Cooke was guardedly optimistic. "No one pretends to believe," he wrote one of his salesmen, M. C. Hazard, "that the road will earn enough money to pay its interest fully . . . [I]t will have to be raised just as all other roads raise their interest—from the sale of bonds, land sales, earnings, temporary loans, income bonds, second mortgages, stockholders, etc." But, he continued: "We do not anticipate any trouble on this score."[14]

The June 30 closing of the Northern Pacific's 1872–73 books, which showed revenues of half a million dollars, offered a glimmer of hope, clearly indicating better days ahead. Cooke was thoroughly exhausted, but his letters retain their intelligence and crispness. He again mustered up his bond sales force as best he could, although these efforts proved insufficient to meet cash needs. He also tried to drum up business for Duluth, but his progress was limited. A sign of 1873's desperation was Cass's effort to sell the NP's equity in the St. Paul & Pacific to a British group. With the breakdown of negotiations, two lines went into receivership in August: the incomplete Sauk Rapids–to–Brainerd link and the Moorhead-to-Canada (St. Vincent) line. Cass and Cooke redoubled their efforts to roll Canfield's LSPS into the NP, but they did not begin the formal process of taking control of the land company until September.

Throughout the spring and summer of 1873 potential Northern Pacific investors became more skittish, as stories about increased Indian hostilities appeared with greater frequency. The nation was transfixed by the Modoc "war," the murder of General E. R. S. Canby by Captain Jack (April 11), Jack's surrender (June 1), and his trial and execution. Illustrated weeklies were only too happy to increase circulation by "realistically" portraying scenes such as "Modocs scalping and torturing prisoners." But with Jack's capture, attention focused on the Yellowstone. On May 27 Sheridan announced the news of Forsyth's successful Yellowstone trip and that Fred Grant would accompany the survey "through the country of the warlike Sioux."[15]

In June newspapers carried stories of skirmishing between Ree scouts and the Sioux at Fort Lincoln, initiating a stream of Indian-fighting stories relating to the Northern Pacific. When Rosser was attacked at Mandan, word of the skirmish was telegraphed around the country. As described earlier, various papers assigned correspondents to the 1873 survey. Adding to these articles were nationally circulated War Department stories that included predictions of severe fighting. Not a week went by without newspaper rumors of hostile Indians and imagined or actual fighting. In September the public became riveted by the August 4 and 11 fighting, which it had not known about in detail until the *New York Tribune* printed Custer's official report on September 6. It did not matter that the accounts were invariably overstated or that the Sioux had been defeated with relative ease: Cooke and the Northern Pacific were the losers.[16]

In addition to the Indian stories, the business problems of the Northern Pacific slowly became public. Mid-July headlines such as "Railroad Troubles: Proceedings in Equity against the Northern Pacific" detailed NP and St. Paul & Pacific difficulties as their problems lurched into a U.S. District Court. The details were predictably complex, but the bottom line to any observer was that the plaintiffs in "[t]he[ir] complaint and accompanying affidavits set forth that the two last-named companies [NP and SP&P] are unable to pay their debts."[17]

Of all the correspondents writing about the Northern Pacific, none was as well known as Charles Loring Brace, 47, a graduate of Yale and Union Theological Seminary. Brace was a minister, philanthropist, leader of the Children's Aid Society, activist with the U.S. Sanitary Commission during the war, master of languages, sophisticated traveler, pragmatic economist, and prolific author. During the summer of 1873 he traveled through Minnesota and Dakota for the *New York Times,* writing a series of five articles entitled "The New North-West."[18]

Writing on July 29, Brace described Minnesota's timberlands and the Red River Valley, "the best wheat land in the country . . . the soil a black loam nearly 24 inches deep . . . nothing can exceed the agricultural capacities of this vast stretch of country." Brace felt that Billings's colonization plans would not work, as "individuals are never satisfied with the land allocated to them," but was excited by the new agricultural communities. "[C]hurches are erected in the smallest village. Everywhere the effort is to . . . lay the foundations on a moral structure." In words that were likely music to Cooke's ears, Brace wrote: "The railroad does much to aid this influence. . . . The result is already a better type of community than one often sees in the old States."

Brace did not enjoy the country between Fargo and Bismarck: "Lord deliver me from ever living on it." On the daylong ride, with passengers amusing themselves by shooting at birds and rabbits from the windows, the train was filled by 70 carpenters on their way to build the cavalry barracks at Fort Lincoln. Also on board was a gambler, a "quiet, reflective-looking, inoffensive man . . . but powerfully built," who had a "somewhat gaudily-dressed woman with [him]"; but Brace reported with relief that the two "behaved with the most perfect decorum." He wrote that the Northern Pacific's track needed ballasting: "the cars sway[ed] like a boat at sea."

Brace was generally pleased by the Northern Pacific's facilities: "consequent[ly] the traveler gets comfortable rooms and good meals in every place of importance." The NP had built first-class hotels in Duluth, Brainerd, and Fargo, which were leased to third parties after construction, an ideal formula for graft. Brace noted that "[t]he rolling stock is the very best," and "digging machines do the work of 75 men each day." There was a land boom in Bismarck, with choice lots selling for $8,000 an acre. As Brace arrived, the steamboat *Montana* docked, loaded with furs. He delightedly reported that ground for a Congregational church had been broken on the Tuesday prior to his arrival; by Sunday it had been completed and services held.[19]

Returning to Minnesota, Brace cited the problems with Canfield's land company ("a Crédit Mobilier of a small kind") but noted: "This, however, has already been broken up." He was enthusiastic about Canadian and western trade, supplying army posts, Dakota coal, Washington lumber, millions of acres of grazing land, Yellowstone tourism, and immigration. "In ten years if it is constructed, [perhaps] in five, the business will be large and remunerative. But to judge of its future as an investment there are many points on which it is extremely difficult to form a sound opinion." Brace was concerned as to "how far the Indians will let the road alone" and worried that with the NP "held by great numbers of small investors . . . any calamity to the company would be a national misfortune."

Brace discussed the Northern Pacific's potential and whether its land grants could cover its costs until the line was profitable. The answer, he felt, lay in how rapidly immigration occurred. The entire nation was interested in the NP because "a railroad into the heart of this country must open up great sources of wealth to our people." In contrast to other new railroad towns, he pointedly noted that the NP "has recognized its moral duties to the [new] communit[ies]" (thus reflecting Cooke's influence) and thought that Minnesota's "remarkable attention to education" boded well for the state's future. As to who would "handle the great [wheat] crop," Brace correctly predicted that while "St. Paul controls a great deal of the wheat traffic . . . [for] Milwaukee and Chicago [today] . . . cheapness of freights must prevail. Eventually all of the wheat export of Minnesota, during seven months of the year, must pass by Duluth and the branches" of the NP.

Brace's conclusion addressed 1873's economic problems and financial interests pitted against each other. Capital was "alarmed" and "produced a muddle in regard to transportation never before experienced." Business was "drawing in sail everywhere, discharging men, and making ready for the storm. *Woe to the company now in the West which has to borrow money or place bonds!*" (emphasis added). While impressed by the Northern Pacific's potential and the character of its immigrants, Brace thought the railroad perilously situated for the immediate future. He did not say that the NP was in trouble; but in accurately discussing the contracting economy, he made it clear that—within a larger context—major problems lay ahead. What he did not know, of course, was the extent of the company's financial weakness.[20]

As the summer progressed, the national economic picture worsened; nevertheless, on August 14 the Northern Pacific's executive committee met with Rosser and that same day decided to let bids for building to the Yellowstone. Within two days Milnor Roberts had placed advertisements for bids for 205 miles of track between Bismarck and the Yellowstone. The *Railroad Gazette* stated that there were "moderate grades . . . only one mile of bad clay lands . . . [and] with few exceptions the country is a rolling prairie." While a bridge was needed at the Little Missouri, cash could be saved by having a ferry service across the Missouri.[21]

With a cost of $5 million and given the Northern Pacific's finances, was the call for bids a "white lie" designed to attract investor dollars or was the executive committee carried away by Rosser's optimism? At first one believes that the announcement was a charade, designed to build public and governmental confidence. And, if conditions improved, the NP could always extend the road. But was it a deception? Cooke's New York partners and Moorhead, a board member, did not think so. Had the NP's announcement been a sham, Fahnestock, Francis French, and James Garland presumably would have known; instead they felt that they had been betrayed. Cooke also appears to have been suddenly invigorated by the possibility of building to the Yellowstone, writing Wilkeson about traffic down the Yellowstone by bateaux and steamers coming upriver. While Cooke's idea seemed impossible, two years later Grant Marsh took the *Josephine* just past present-day Billings.[22]

Bad news began in September; the Post Office had decided, despite Cooke's lobbying, to continue sending its mail to Helena via Corrine. The NP's bid, worth $150,000 a year, had been to send the mail via Bismarck and Missouri steamer—slower, riskier, and properly rejected; but Cooke's enemies publicized the defeat. Wall Street's mood was bleaker, economic interests were becoming jittery, and cash was increasingly "stringent" as eastern bank reserves began declining, partially reflecting the seasonal westward movement of money. Efforts by Cooke and others to release $40 million in Treasury greenbacks came to nothing. *Harper's Weekly* asked on September 6: "Shall We Have Another Black Friday?" The article blamed "bold, reckless speculators who have gradually possessed themselves of all the gold in the country" and worried that "the discovery of [the Treasury's] powerlessness could hardly fail to create a panic." Five days later the *Nation* noted: "Wall Street has been quite eventful, the principal features having been the collapse of the 'gold corner' [and] numerous rumors of trouble among speculators in the gold room."[23]

On September 6 the *New York Tribune* threw a combustible into the volatile investment community: Custer's dramatic account of the Yellowstone fighting. The *Army and Navy Journal* called it a "spirited narrative," noting that Custer "has gained an enviable reputation as an interesting writer and graphic describer." With unerring instinct Custer understated his role, credited subordinates, overstated Indian prowess, magnified dangers, and left the reader with the knowledge—without ever stating it—that victory had been achieved only through exceptional leadership: his. But for him, Custer implied, the "savage" foe would have been successful. That Baker (while dead drunk) and Stanley had brushed aside Indian attacks in 1872 was immaterial and not understood by the public. Custer's facile writing damned the Northern Pacific. A September 11, 1873, *New York Times* editorial illustrated

Cooke's problem. Referencing a previous story, "[which] shows that difficulties lie before the construction" of the NP, the *Times* wrote:

> The truth is, we have now struck upon the last and bravest of the old Indian races of the plain. The Sioux beyond the Missouri is a very different Indian from the stupid, peaceful, vagabond creatures who haunt the neighborhood of white settlement in the north-west, or who are learning agriculture on reservations. . . . If several thousand of our best soldiers, with all of the arms of the service, under some of our most dashing officers, can only hold the ground on their narrow line of march for 150 or 200 miles west of the Upper Missouri, [what] will peaceful bodies of railroad workmen be able to do, or what can emigrants accomplish in such a dangerous region?[24]

The *Times* answered its own question: "[F]irst of all the . . . [Sioux] must be taught a lesson by force. They must learn to submit." The response, regardless of ethical merit, registered with the public, defined the policy of Grant's second term, but was too late to help Cooke. How much Custer's report (all the more powerful because it was "official"), similar editorials, and innumerable Indian fighting stories eroded confidence in NP bonds is impossible to measure after so many years. But it frightened the financial community in general and Cooke's partners in particular. On Monday, September 8, gold plunged, and stocks, including "blue chips" like Western Union, went on a roller-coaster ride. Two firms associated with sugar brokerage (Sheppard Gandy & Co. and Francis Skiddy & Co.), already in distress from earlier speculation, and a third company (New York Warehouse & Security) appeared to be in trouble; they all had large holdings in the shaky Missouri, Kansas & Texas Railroad. Yet, even with this and a decline in gold prices, the market did not buckle. The *New York Times* wrote the next morning: "The Wall Street public was disposed to take an altogether cheerful view of the situation, although trouble is predicted in branches of the importing trade in consequence of the rapid and severe fall of gold."

The Northern Pacific's board of directors met in New York on September 9 for a two-day meeting. The board approved bonds paying lower interest and the selection of Tacoma for the railroad's western terminus and referred a sales offer from Canfield—in essence folding up his land company—to its executive committee. But the minutes do not indicate the directors' state of mind in the wake of the barrage of Yellowstone stories. Given the market, conversations likely focused on whether there would be a run on NP bonds and what Cooke could do to help. The *Herald* summarized Wall Street's mood: "It is an impossibility to diagnose the condition of the stock market at the present moment, as it has no foundation . . . [It] is tremulous, uneasy and quickly affected by rumors. It acts as if calamity were impending or expected, and invites rather than repels discouragement."[25]

On Friday, September 12, the *Herald*'s subheadlines read "Railroad Bonds and United States Securities Strong," but it also noted: "There have been few occasions during the year when so much difficulty attended a fair description of the market." The *Times* reported that gold had again dropped, the government selling $1 to $1½ million, and that "we discover no new element to disturb confidence or to discourage the hopes of a very early improvement in the Stock exchange [and] . . . railroads." Saturday's papers carried the news of a turnaround; the *Herald* wrote: "A smart and not unhealthy rally today followed the [week's] decline." The *Times* reported gold steady and blue-chip railroad and telegraph stocks advancing, noting with relief that the week's business "is done with much more ease and satisfaction than for some time past." Had the stock market been closed on Saturday, the week would have ended on an upbeat note.

Henry Cooke, all but broken, resigned as the District of Columbia's governor on September 12 and quickly received Grant's polite acceptance. The regrets were undercut, however, by Grant's immediate appointment of Alexander R. Shepard to replace him. Cooke graciously had Shepard inaugurated at his home, but a waiting period had been required to show that his resignation was real. Thus it *appeared* as if Henry had been forced out, another blow to Jay. Whether the resignation reflected political pressure from what the *New York Tribune* called Shepherd's "ring," Henry's emotional state, or both is unknown, but it could not have come at a worse time.[26]

On Saturday came stunning Wall Street news: the prestigious firm of Kenyon Cox & Co. had suspended. The *Herald* said that the company "owned a reputation equal to the best," and the *Times* that "Wall Street was thrown into a fever." Most sources blamed railroad speculator Daniel Drew, as most major stocks fell. But while the markets weakened, there was no panic. Monday morning's stories included the *Herald*'s somber "The Financial Lessons of the Past." The *Tribune* focused on Drew: "It was generally suspected that . . . [he] was 'short' of stocks, and that it was part of his scheme to allow his own [Kenyon-Cox] to fail in order to depress prices."[27]

Grant spent the evening of Monday, September 15, with Cooke at Ogontz. The planned overnight visit allowed him to drop off his son Jesse at a boarding school in Chelten Hills that Cooke had recommended. Grant had written a sister, Mary Grant Cramer, about his plans, and on September 10 he wrote a friend: "On Monday I go to Phila. with Jessie to put him at school. We will go out and spend the night with Jay Cooke, near the school . . . and leave [Tuesday] evening for Pittsburgh to meet the Society of the Army of the Cumberland on Wednesday evening."[28]

On Tuesday morning, after leaving Grant, Cooke returned to his office to discover an increasingly uneasy market. While financial stories were mostly pushed off the front pages by the sinking of the steamer *Ironsides* in Lake Michigan, the *New York Herald* wrote that the markets were "more or less brooding over the possibilities of [a] disaster." Stories on Wednesday, September 17, carried mixed news. The *New York Times* wrote that gold was steady and stated with obvious relief: "Money and Stock affairs in Wall Street are again reported free of exciting rumors." Contrary to the *Times*, however, the increasingly apprehensive *Herald* reported: "A contemplation of the stock market in its present condition is like 'looking through a glass darkly' . . . without finding a single hopeful feature."

The Northern Pacific's executive committee met on Wednesday. At the meeting the committee discussed the sale of land in Tacoma and Superior, Wisconsin, selling its interest in the St. Paul & Pacific, finalizing its offer to Canfield, and taking possession of $9 million in bonds that Cooke had been unable to sell. Yet, even as the committee met, the market began dumping western railroad stocks, based on false rumors concerning the dividend-paying Rock Island Railroad, and short-selling increased as the overall mood became gloomier.[29]

Thursday morning papers headlined "Heavy Raid," "Wall Street Alarmed," and "Panic in Stocks." The *Herald* noted: "[P]rices went down with a trend more emphatic than had been heard in weeks. . . . That a stringency exists . . . must be conceded." A major issue was the lack of cash to meet agricultural requirements in the South and Midwest. The problem was magnified by rumors of failures, another Chicago fire (not major, but still spooking a jittery market), what appeared to be a planned effort by Jay Gould to drive markets down, and the overall weakness of American and Canadian railroads. The Northern Pacific was not mentioned in any Thursday articles, and had not been for days, showing the public's confidence that, Indians or not, its dividends were secure with Cooke's support.

Leaving Philadelphia on Tuesday, Grant arrived in Pittsburgh in time for the Army of the Cumberland's Wednesday evening session. As a band played "Hail to the Chief," he joined Sherman, Sheridan, and others on the podium. The program included prayers, a welcome address, patriotic songs, and an "oration," before Grant, "being loudly called for," made some brief remarks. Grant then sat through more speeches until a minister, mercifully, gave the final prayer near midnight.[30]

Harris Fahnestock had to have been apprehensive as he entered his Wall Street office the morning of Thursday, September 18. He probably had met with Moorhead Wednesday evening and was about to take steps that would shut down Jay Cooke & Co. But if he miscalculated, his own career would be over. He knew that he had risen because of Cooke's patronage, but now he feared that all he had worked for would be lost. Fahnestock strongly believed that "Cooke had gone back on his promise [in September 1872] when he agreed not to advance the Northern Pacific a large sum." William Fahnestock, then 16, thus justified his father's actions; although he did not know the full details, he was told that they included putting

$100,000 in his mother's name, safe from creditors. What is important is not the actual amount, but rather that Harris Fahnestock told his children that he had begun setting aside cash a year before the crash.[31]

In describing Jay Cooke's activities that morning, a popular story first told by Oberholtzer would later take hold. As best described by Matthew Josephson in *The Robber Barons,* Grant spent Wednesday evening, September 17, with Cooke at Ogontz, enjoying fine wine, dinner, and the cigars that Cooke ordered specially rolled for him. On Thursday morning Cooke began receiving telegrams over his private line, informing him of problems at his New York office. Always the perfect host and unflappable, he kept a poker face, finished breakfasting with Grant, drove the president to his train, and only then dashed to his office. The descriptions of Grant's visit have continued into the twenty-first century and understandably vary in detail, because, as Oberholtzer learned to his chagrin years later, the incident never happened.[32]

It is most likely that on the morning of Thursday, September 18, Cooke hurried directly to his Philadelphia office. With the business news from the previous day being inherently bad, he would have arrived early, although years later he said that he was unaware that the market could be in such serious trouble. In New York, John Thompson and two other bankers walked over to Cooke's Wall Street offices. Thompson, 72, had played a key Wall Street role (*Thompson's Bank Note and Commercial Reporter*) for decades and knew Cooke through their mutual association with Treasury Secretary Chase and war bond sales. He had founded the First National Bank in New York in 1863 and was its president in September 1873. Speaking in 1881, Thompson described his activities that September 18:

> Early one morning the active managers of three of the New York City banks were invited to the offices of Jay Cooke & Co. We were informed that $1 million was necessary by 10 o'clock to save the house from protest. What security do you offer? was asked. Answer—None; our securities are all used. It is needless to say that the million was not forthcoming. We left. In fifteen minutes, Wall Street was in a panic.[33]

The names of the bankers with Thompson are not known, but Cooke's partners at the meeting were Fahnestock, Francis O. French, James Garland, and possibly a fourth individual. Two years earlier Edward H. Dodge, Enoch Clarke's Philadelphia partner, who had known Cooke since 1839 and would have blocked what was about to happen, had been discharged after a disagreement with Fahnestock and given a Northern Pacific sinecure. Cooke's older brother, Pitt, was at sea, expected to return from Europe any day. Whatever his deficiencies, had he been in New York he would have demanded that Jay be told; but without Pitt or Dodge there was no one to block Fahnestock.[34]

Larson charitably characterized the meeting as Fahnestock's asking the bankers "to advise him on what should be done." The advice of Thompson, who was secretly Fahnestock's employee, was that the New York offices should close their doors, because nothing could be done. In 1873 this was a literal act: doors were shut, customers were asked to leave, and business was suspended. Other than Thompson, no source mentions that the New York offices needed $1 million in an hour. Oberholtzer thought that the meeting was a charade. When his biography of Cooke was published, Fahnestock was still alive; but in 1937, with Fahnestock long dead, Oberholtzer wrote:

> Fahnestock took the subject into his own hands . . . [A]s far as available evidence appears, he might have acted a month or six weeks earlier. He could have waited awhile longer . . . [But Cooke] would not consent either to disassociate himself [from the Northern Pacific] or to the confession of failure . . . therefore the indomitable head of the firm was not told of the intention of his juniors.[35]

Fahnestock, Garland, French, and George F. Baker of First National were close friends of similar age. In the summer of 1873 the four entered into negotiations with Thompson, soon purchasing control of First National. By February 1874 the ex–Cooke employees were publicly working "for" First National but, in fact, privately controlled the bank. Fahnestock led the bank's bond division, with Garland and French also holding high positions. Their ownership, however, did not become known until 1877. Their association with Thompson was surely not coincidental, begun just after the Panic, when anyone associated with Cooke was in disrepute. The September 18 putsch was clearly an option planned in advance but likely agreed to and implemented because of the Yellowstone fighting and Custer's report. By then, or within days, the three had wrapped up their purchase of the First National and had transferred their cash and securities to safe havens.[36]

Shortly after Thompson and his associates concluded the meeting, Fahnestock told Garland and French that he would carry a written announcement over to the stock exchange. As he was leaving, he sent a telegram to Cooke informing him of what he had done. Meanwhile Garland and French cleared the bank and shut the front doors of the office. The market's nervousness and heavy selling on Wednesday meant that Wall Street was jammed. Fahnestock, carrying the announcement of Jay Cooke & Co.'s suspension, walked the short distance over to the crowded New York Stock Exchange. As custom required, he gave the message to the clerk, who in turn gave it to the president to read to the members. The president took one look then refused to read it. The correct procedures, he said, had not been followed; Fahnestock had written the notice in pencil, not ink. By the time Fahnestock rewrote and submitted the announcement, the floor was empty except for Fahne-stock, the clerk, and the Stock Exchange president.[37]

Cooke received the news in Philadelphia by his private telegraph. Could Jay Cooke somehow have saved his company? Clearly Fahnestock thought it was possible. His action, taken in concert with Moorhead, French, and Garland, was a carefully planned and carried out strike that gave Cooke no time to respond. Cooke himself may have hidden a few million dollars in cash or securities, which, with warning, he might have used to save his company and the Northern Pacific, although this is speculation. Additionally, the company's assets were twice as high as its liabilities. But on September 18, 1873, Fahnestock made sure that Cooke was never given the option. Cooke may have maintained his façade of composure for a while, but then he began crying. All *was* lost; there was to be no last-minute miracle. Sobbing in front of stunned employees, he gave his final orders.

By the time perplexed customers were ushered out and the massive bronze doors closed with a heavy thud, Cooke's career was over, a national panic had begun, the NP's strategy for domination of the Northwest had been damaged beyond repair, and Sitting Bull and his followers found themselves—ever so briefly—able to continue their traditional way of life.

CHAPTER 18

"Get Out, Gentlemen, Get Out"

At Washington's premier hotel, the Willard, a "testimonial" lunch was about to begin on Thursday, September 18. The guests were Washington's elite; General Sherman was to preside at the lunch honoring Henry Cooke, who had submitted his resignation as the District of Columbia's governor a week earlier. At 12:15 P.M. Cooke, perplexed and confused, read a telegram, telling him of the day's events in New York and Philadelphia. Like others at the Willard, he thought the telegram a hoax—at best, a bad joke.

A block away at Jay Cooke & Co.'s Washington branch, people were at the tellers' cages, some with checks in hand, when a midlevel manager named Macgowan walked over, loudly saying, "Get out, gentlemen, get out—the orders are to close our doors!" Minutes later Washington's largest bank, the First National, closed its doors. Henry Cooke was also its president. Jay Cooke & Co. was the financial agent for fourteen other banks, including five Freedman's Savings & Trust Company banks in the deep South. All soon shut their doors.[1]

On Wall Street people poured out into the street in large, frenzied crowds. In Philadelphia the crush was so great that police rushed to Cooke's office. Stocks and bonds began falling, and many banks simply shut their doors. The panic, a desperate run to find cash, reverberated from city to city. Tens of thousands lost everything, including Milnor Roberts, whose holdings were with Cooke. In Minneapolis Tom Rosser wrote in his diary: "Learned that Jay Cooke & Co. had failed and the future of our company is dark and uncertain." Rosser laid off the contractors he had just hired, somehow got his men paid, and packed his reports and maps—which were not to be needed until the end of the decade.

That afternoon Fahnestock invited reporters of the morning papers to his office for an interview, part of which was carried in Friday's *New York Herald:*

> Q. From this [written] statement it appears, then, Mr. Fahnestock, is [*sic*] that the failure of the Philadelphia [branch of Jay Cooke & Co.] is the cause of your downfall?
>
> A. Yes. For a long time past the Philadelphia house has been drawing upon us for large sums, and all this money went . . . to the coffers of the [Northern Pacific]. We went on lending money in this manner until we could stand it no longer. So we had to suspend.
>
> Q. Is it true that you have been taking the money placed in your bank by depositors to lend it to the Philadelphia house, which in turn loaned it to the Northern Pacific?
>
> A. This is true, quite true. Where else could we get the money?
>
> Q. Can you tell the sum . . . [needed] the last two weeks to lend to the Northern Pacific?
>
> A. No; I cannot tell you exactly the sum, but it is very large.
>
> Q. [For] how long did you anticipate this suspension [of business]?
>
> A. We did not anticipate it at all—that is we thought we would get over it, but since last Monday [September 8] matters have grown worse. . . . We found we could stand it no longer.
>
> Q. Do you have any idea of your liabilities?
>
> A. No; not as yet. We shall prepare a public statement as soon as possible. . . .
>
> Q. Do you hope to resume?
>
> A. We may; but I cannot tell. Of course it will depend on after-developments.
>
> Q. Do you know the . . . [amount] which the Northern Pacific is indebted to you?
>
> A. I cannot tell just at the present, and prefer not to make a guess.[2]

Fahnestock said they owed no money to the government but did not say that the government owed them between $100,000 and $250,000 for 1873 bond sales. A *New York Herald* reporter discovered that Moorhead had been visiting Fahnestock frequently. In the custom of the day, when he knocked on the door, Fahnestock met him on the steps of his house. Fahnestock admitted the visits, blandly stating that "he visits here very often." The reporter, clearly not in the Bob Woodward/Carl Bernstein league, left, satisfied. On September 26 Jay Cooke & Co. released a statement of its assets and liabilities, accurately indicating that total assets, including loans and miscellaneous holdings, were twice as high as liabilities.[3]

In Pittsburgh, on September 18, Grant quickly learned of the banking failures. Canceling his plans to return to Washington, he took an afternoon train to Philadelphia, arriving late Friday morning. The next day a *Philadelphia Inquirer* article stated:

President Grant arrived in this city yesterday and took a room at the Continental Hotel . . . [He] left early in the afternoon in the company of some personal friends among whom were gentlemen prominent in the banking business in this city. It being the general belief that the visit had an *intimate connection* with the financial disturbances in this city for the last few days. . . . All efforts made last night to find the whereabouts of President Grant or those with whom he was said to be in consultation . . . failed. [emphasis added][4]

Whether Grant met Cooke is not known, but the president had slept at Ogontz four nights earlier, and he and family members had borrowed considerable sums from Cooke. Grant also knew his financial limitations and would have wanted to hear from Cooke what had happened and what could be expected to happen. And, of course, he needed to be sure that there would be no unpleasantries concerning the loans. If the two met, it was likely for the last time; theirs had been a friendship of mutual convenience, and Grant had little time for those who were no longer of use.[5]

In the months and years that followed, despite some lulls and temporary market rises, the nation's economy slid downhill, complete with deflation and industrial unemployment. The country would not recover for six years, and the Panic of 1873 has been described by economic historian Robert Sobel as "second only to that of 1929–32."[6]

For a week or so Cooke lived in a daze, receiving the sympathies of friends and associates like Roberts, Rosser, Charlemagne Tower, and others. Cooke's secretary wrote Sam Wilkeson that "Mr. Cooke wishes me to express to you his thorough appreciation of your good letter of the 20th and to say to you that it is just what he should have expected from you . . . The kindness of his friends in this terrible hour is of great comfort to him." In October Cooke tried to put the pieces back together, but his effort to take control of the Northern Pacific was rebuffed by the mortified and angry George Cass, who felt that Cooke had misled him into accepting the NP's presidency. Cooke soon realized that he had few friends and no political support. Without options, he braced himself for years of litigation. Ogontz was closed in 1874, and Cooke moved into the home of a married daughter who lived nearby. For the next 31 years, he stayed in a child's bedroom, from which he could see the grounds of Ogontz.[7]

Cooke's business and political demise created a power vacuum that J. P. Morgan would fill. The person who recognized this best, with barely hidden jealousy, was Harris Fahnestock. His son wrote in 1915: "There is no question, however, that

Drexel, Morgan . . . never came into great prominence until after the failure of Jay Cooke & Co. It seems fair, then, to presume that had . . . [Cooke] lasted with [the] important changes . . . [that were "quite evident to" my father, it] would have occupied the position now taken by J. P. Morgan & Co."[8]

To the surprise of many, the Northern Pacific did not collapse. Wilkeson, in a widely reported September 19 interview, said that the NP's operations would continue but that construction to the Yellowstone "had [been] deferred." Rosser, who was not laid off, never saw how bad things were. In February 1874 he wrote Custer: "We expect to resume work west of the Missouri [this] summer and I shall look forward to meeting you again." (He concluded: "Mrs. R desires to be remembered to Mrs. C and yourself." The letter also confirms that the Custers visited them in Minneapolis.) Despite its problems, the Dakota and Oregon track was certified in 1873, thus adding 7.8 million acres to sell. Much of this was along the Red, James, and Sheyenne Rivers, and West Coast timberland, and the NP kept its financial solvency by exchanging land for bonds.[9]

The Northern Pacific's transcontinental construction resumed on May 31, 1879. In general, the route to the Yellowstone followed Rosser's 1873 survey, reaching the river in 1881. With Sitting Bull no longer a problem (he surrendered that year), the NP decided not to cross the Yellowstone where Glendive Creek enters it but rather to build on the south side of the river for some 225 miles to just east of present-day Billings. Ultimately, virtually none of the other work of the 1872–73 surveys along the Yellowstone was ever used.

On September 8, 1883, the last spike was driven along Montana's Clark Fork River near Gold Creek (between Deer Lodge and Missoula). Rather than using a golden spike, the first spike driven in 1870 was "found" and used. Northern Pacific president Villard handed the sledge hammer to a man who had helped drive the first spike: Henry C. Davis, who had been chased by Gall while hunting agates along the Yellowstone in 1872.[10]

The Northern Pacific never dominated regional traffic. James J. Hill took control of the St. Paul & Pacific, eventually transforming it into the Great Northern. Hill believed the "lost" Marias Pass story; after a series of dramatic adventures, the engineer John Stevens "discovered" the pass in 1889. Hill's route from the Great Lakes to Puget Sound was 150 miles shorter and had only one easy pass to cross. For decades the two railroads battled it out fairly evenly, each with its own competitive advantages. On March 3, 1970, however, both the Northern Pacific and the Great Northern became part of the Burlington Northern system and ceased to exist.

The *Bismarck Tribune* interviewed Custer on his arrival at Fort Lincoln. Clearly thankful to be out of the clothes he had worn all summer, he had on his wartime outfit that had "so often startled the corn-fed Johnnies . . . the well remembered plain blue pants, with their yellow stripe, the blue flannel shirt, with its wide collar and cuffs, loose at the throat, the black slouch and the jingling spurs." If the interview was bland, the attention was the message for the thoroughly happy Custer. On leave a month later, as if to confirm his renewed status, he joined Grant, Sherman, and Sheridan at a Toledo reception. Here the four formed a receiving line; to everyone's surprise, Sheridan kissed a particularly attractive young lady. When Grant did the same, the reception turned into a kissing contest: the masters of the universe (or at least of the Confederacy) bussed babies, grandmothers, and all between. Custer won the frantic contest by kissing 13 babies, 43 little girls, and 67 ladies, many more than once.[11]

Why did Fahnestock shut down Jay Cooke & Co.? Fahnestock, Moorhead, Garland, and French believed that Cooke had agreed not to cross the Missouri until the Northern Pacific's financing was renegotiated. When the NP's executive committee called for Bismarck-to-the-Yellowstone bids on August 14, Fahnestock felt that Cooke had gone back on his word. Nonetheless, the NP's action remains perplexing: given its lack of cash, it has the bravado of a public relations sham. Yet Cooke and Fahnestock, looking at it so very differently, were both taken by surprise. While this is admittedly a guess, perhaps it was Cass, acting independently, who made the decision—which everyone assumed was Cooke's handiwork. Then Custer's report, coupled with other articles and editorials, probably proved to be the triggering agent that scared Fahnestock and the others into action. Indeed, the NP, with Cooke's name behind it, stood firm in the weakened market and might have survived had it not been for Fahnestock's actions.

Hours after the crash, Cornelius Vanderbilt told a reporter: "Building railroads from nowhere to nowhere at public expense is not a legitimate undertaking"; while delightfully hypercritical from a man who had taken subsidies for *not* running shipping routes, this missed the point. Jay Cooke's gamble failed for other reasons. First, events beyond his control whipsawed him, including the Franco-Prussian War, railroad speculation, and the Crédit Mobilier scandal. Second, he never realized that British fears for Canada would lead them to oppose him actively. Third, Cooke failed to see that the Northern Pacific would create a backlash within the United States, forging a broad alliance of business and political interests that attacked at every opportunity. Most importantly, Cooke and the army underestimated Indian determination. The NP's 1872 annual report says it best: "Our men and their escort have been resisted and fought by armed forces of Indians, in such numbers and with such spirit as to stop our work. The company's engineers have in effect been driven by Indians out of the Yellowstone Valley."[12]

As Cooke and Smith completed their 1870 agreement, neither could know that by the year's end Smith's shortsightedness would place his Vermont Central in a financial vise. Yet Cooke knew Smith from the 1850s, was aware that he did not come with clean hands, and must have known his management limitations. Cooke's rueful admission decades later that he should have installed his own management team immediately makes his mistake all the worse, a reflection of ego and avoidance prevailing over common sense. Smith's stewardship of Cooke's money became a rainbow of inexcusably poor planning, weak personnel, cronyism, kickbacks, lack of financial controls, questionable purchases, "creative" bookkeeping, absentee decision-making, woeful ethics, and a bureaucratic chain of command characterized by evasion and buck-passing.

Cooke's failure was not because the Northern Pacific concept was illusory, as Vanderbilt and the German bankers thought. The area's growth became so dynamic that the NP's land began filling, and trade developed almost as fast as track was built. By the third quarter of 1873, the NP had a positive cash flow, 7.8 million acres of land were months from certification, and railroad traffic was growing exponentially. Cooke's gamble failed, but he was not wrong.

Only a handful of American business leaders ever had Cooke's intelligence, optimism, and sense of purpose. While derided as little more than an able salesman, he became dominant by force of intellect and character. Cooke understood one business category after another better than its specialists. Yet he was reclusive, peculiar in dress, authoritarian ("imperious though kindly," Oberholtzer said), and had a towering ego—probably not uncommon for those who believe they are "God's chosen instrument." These flaws, likely magnified by his wife's death, made it difficult for him to exchange ideas: he could listen, but he could not debate.[13]

Cooke later wrote that in 1869 "I was entirely too careful and conservative in expending so much time and money in [Roberts's] examination, but I felt that I could not conscientiously undertake the financial agency . . . unless fully satisfied." In 1870–71 he involved himself with facets of the Northern Pacific that he enjoyed (for example, immigration), not those critical to the NP's success. Nowhere is this better seen than in the case of the St. Paul & Pacific: instead of personally participating in key strategic decisions, he let poor Moorhead lead. Unimaginative, negative, and defeatist, Moorhead wanted "to be a contender" in Cooke's eyes—to prove how good he really was. He succeeded. Under Moorhead's leadership the SP&P completed unneeded track paralleling the Brainerd-to-Fargo route and began a 160-mile line to Canada. By chewing up precious 1871–72 resources, Moorhead let the vital Sauk Rapids to Brainerd route lapse and significantly contributed to the NP's failure to reach the Missouri in 1872.[14]

While Cooke was considered an exceptional promoter, in his sale of Northern Pacific bonds he refused to modify his successful wartime formula. The "7-30s" were not based on railroad reality but rather on pleasant memories. NP bonds were too high for safe investments and too low for risky ones. In 1872 at least 34 companies paid 10 percent or higher (four paid over 12 percent), and 39 others paid 7 to 10 percent. Although one cannot say for sure what the interest should have been, the return that Cooke chose for his NP bonds simply was not right for the 1870–73 market.[15]

Cooke never realized the importance of his personal presence. Increasingly reclusive, he limited his travel and refused to go to Europe when his standing was highest. Gibraltar fishing came ahead of "Pig Iron" Kelly's huge Philadelphia rally; and until it was too late he failed to meet with Boston and New York bankers, as he had during the war. It is most surprising and inexcusable that Cooke never visited Minnesota or Dakota between 1869 and 1873. Such trips would have been enormously beneficial to employee morale, his own understanding, and demonstration of his control. If Smith was an absentee manager, Cooke was even more an absentee owner.

Some contemporaries blamed the Northern Pacific for the fall of Jay Cooke & Co., while others cited poor investments. Smalley's 1883 NP history states that Cooke "could have stood up under its heavy loans to the Northern Pacific if it had not recklessly thrown its money and credit out in many other directions." This charge has been repeated over the years; but there was never a huge, under-performing portfolio, and Cooke was always the country's *largest* private banker. As important to the failure was Grant's lack of support for Cooke. In 1872 he did not allow federal bond sales, and in 1873 he blocked Cooke's exclusive sale of them. The 1873 collapse was, in part, due to the NP's drain on Cooke and Grant's cutting of a critical revenue stream.[16]

By late 1872 Moorhead had cracked under the pressure, telling Drexel his woes and plotting with Fahnestock. As for Fahnestock, his son wrote: "He was never wild on the [Northern Pacific and] . . . thought it was ahead of its time." Fahnestock felt that he had reached an agreement with Cooke; greedy, easily frightened, and fearful that all would be lost, however, he shut the company down. McCulloch was too far away to join the plotters, but his angry letters contributed to the troubled company's unrest. Thus Cooke's comment in his *Memoirs* becomes a remarkable understatement: "I did not receive from some of my most prominent partners that cooperation toward the close of 1872–73 that seemed necessary."[17]

Sitting Bull gained little from Cooke's fall. Sheridan, without the Northern Pacific to guard, sent Custer into the Black Hills in 1874. Rumors of gold proved true, and by 1875 thousands of heavily armed miners had pushed Sitting Bull farther north. In early 1876 the War Department initiated a policy to place Sitting Bull and his followers on reservations. Despite his June 25, 1876, victory against Custer's command, sixteen months later all of Sitting Bull's followers were either on reservations or in Canada. Afterward there was a spectacular increase in buffalo; but when the NP reached the Yellowstone, hunters quickly "harvested" the remaining herds.

Taking all the competition, Smith's mismanagement, Cooke's errors, and other factors into consideration, in the end what brought everything down was the impact of the "Indian problem" on the safety of Northern Pacific bonds—especially for Cooke's partners. The wild card in bond sales had always been Sitting Bull and his followers. While their numbers and prowess were invariably overestimated, the drumbeat of publicity was a red flag for many investors. In the end, the NP wanted to build a railroad in a "war zone." Sitting Bull also fully understood the purpose of Cooke's surveys; if his leadership did not win any battles in 1872, he achieved huge public relations victories with Baker's retreat, Adair's death, and Rosser's narrow escape. Bond sales, weak but acceptable in the first half of 1872, never recovered.

In 1873 the army fielded a huge force led by its most glamorous officer and encouraged newspaper participation. The result was that everything written represented a lose-lose situation for Cooke's bond sales. Even if nothing happened, the public had to ask why the large force was necessary. Fortunately for the press, there was ample fighting. Most damaging, however, was Custer's account of two incidents in which a total of two civilians and two soldiers died. Custer's rousing description of events that would not have merited coverage during the Civil War was so vivid, and the colorful enemy so valiant and determined, that most of the public and NP bondholders likely believed that it was too dangerous to build a railroad through the Yellowstone Valley.

On January 10, 1906, a number of ex-surveyors gathered for a reunion. "The Northern Pacific Pioneers of 1873 and Earlier" had been on or were associated with the eastern Yellowstone surveys and were again "going into camp." There was considerable last-minute scrambling to find a site; shockingly, their original venue, the prestigious West Hotel in Minneapolis, had burned down that morning, killing a fire captain, a West Point cadet, and six others.[18]

The purpose of the reunion and dinner (in addition to getting reacquainted) was to honor Rosser, now felled by a stroke. Rosser's brothers-in-law (Edward T., Fendall G., and William O. Winston) and his old friend George A. Brackett, all living in Minneapolis, had taken the lead in planning the reunion, assisted by New York financier Henry C. Davis. Davis, who arrived in his own railroad car, brought with him "Shorty" Graham and Ned Jordan.

The dinner itself appears to have been exceptional fun. Newspaper accounts speak of rounds of toasts and increasingly relaxed attendees as one humorous story followed another. There were, of course, solemn moments. A letter that Rosser had written to Brackett was read: "My physical condition and great affliction which deprives me of my speech also deprives me of my social pleasures . . . [If I were with you] I could but feebly express the esteem and affection in which you are still held, and the great deprivation it is to me that I can not be with you."

The next day the group toured St. Paul as guests of the Northern Pacific. Some of the ex-surveyors made presentations about their surveying experiences, a common theme being the Indian fighting. On Friday, in a remarkable coincidence, the papers noted that Hump, one of the last Lakota war chiefs, who had participated in the 1872–73 fighting, had passed through the city to meet with Theodore Roosevelt in Washington. Davis told reporters that they would issue a souvenir booklet, publish a book of their reminiscences and Graham's drawings, compile a list of ex-surveyors, and meet annually. Some "remembrances" were submitted; but most were short, and the quality was uneven. Rosser was sent a loving cup (a photo survives) and the souvenir booklet, but the book that Davis envisioned was never published, the list of ex-surveyors was not compiled, and there was never another reunion.

Despite Tom Rosser's fame, his life after 1873 was an ongoing struggle. He stayed with the Northern Pacific, where his jerry-rigging abilities culminated in his famous "ice bridge" across the Missouri at Bismarck (1878–79). But when construction was renewed in 1879, his lack of engineering skills (covered up by his surveyors) became apparent. Billings released him in 1881, albeit amicably. Sadly, Rosser was never given the opportunity to manage construction, an ideal fit for a person of his skills. He worked briefly for the Canadian Pacific but was fired for "using inside knowledge of future railway locations to speculate in real estate." In 1885 he returned to Virginia, buying an $8,000 house in Charlottesville that he named Rugby Hall.[19]

Rosser tried railway consulting, land speculation, Nicaragua canal construction, and lobbying. He lectured, wrote (a July 1876 letter began the Little Big Horn controversy), tried new businesses, and invariably failed. During the Panic of 1893 the family kept up appearances on Lizzy Rosser's income from a small dairy (she milked the cows herself) and "loans" from her brothers, whose railroad construction business continued to grow.

When the Spanish-American War broke out, President William McKinley appointed Rosser and other ex-Confederates as brigadier generals. But Rosser, overweight and ill, did little more than troop training. His politics—an ugly mix of racism and populism—attracted few. Without a future as a Democrat, he supported McKinley and then Roosevelt, who in 1905 gave him the Charlottesville postmastership. That fall a stroke paralyzed his vocal cords, leaving him unable to travel and forcing Lizzy to perform the postmaster's duties until his death, at 74, on March 29, 1910. Nothing is known about him after the 1906 reunion. Lizzy Rosser died on February 6, 1915.

In late 1873 Jay Cooke declared personal bankruptcy, losing Ogontz and Gibraltar. He was vilified by the press for vaingloriousness and greed, for swindling the public with worthless Northern Pacific land (although he owned more than anyone), and for being too powerful. Many of the charges were, of course, contradictory. Yet from Cooke's era to ours, *no one* has taken fiduciary responsibilities more seriously than he did. He was fully aware of the tens of thousands of middle-income families who had invested in NP bonds solely because of his endorsement, and the suffering that he caused was to him undoubtedly the most painful aspect of his failure.

When Ogontz was shut in 1874, Cooke moved in with his daughter's family (the Charles Barneys). Stories had it that he would walk the grounds like a ghost and peep into the empty rooms that were gathering dust. After his creditors were paid (in 1878–79), and in partnership with Jay Gould, he made a quick $2 million syndicating a Utah gold mine. One has the nagging suspicion, however, that he had hidden money from his creditors and that the story was mostly a cover. Regardless, he repurchased Gibraltar then Ogontz. Finding he could not afford to maintain Ogontz, Cooke converted it into school grounds for the Chestnut Street Seminary for young girls, took an active role in the school's affairs, and continued living with his daughter.

The repurchase of Gibraltar gave Cooke the opportunity to return to the area that had been his boyhood home. The caretaker of Gibraltar for 30 years was Mrs. Anna McMeens, the widow of a doctor who had died in the Civil War. A photograph of the two taken in the late 1880s shows an astonishingly relaxed Cooke; the almost intimate body language between the two leaps out from the otherwise carefully staged photograph.

In 1883 Smalley, with some anger, wrote: "After the crash he lived for a long time in retirement in a little cottage . . . to all appearances a broken man. But, after getting through the bankruptcy courts, he reappeared in business circles in Philadelphia, occupied his old offices on South Third Street and [built] a second fortune." But Jay Cooke was content, writing: "I have gone up in the tower and looked around, and it will not be necessary to do so again." In 1883 he was invited by Villard, who admired him, to join the Northern Pacific's final spike ceremonies. Cooke first said yes then vacillated and finally declined, instinctively knowing he would be treated condescendingly by Grant and others. In 1891 he decided to travel the entire NP route, including Yellowstone Park. A private car was placed at his disposal, and he was delighted to find himself venerated and honored from Duluth to Tacoma. In his sunset years Cooke came to terms with the NP's failure— in fact, taking considerable pride in his efforts:

> To my mind the enterprise was a legitimate and noble undertaking. . . . Naught but Indians, buffaloes, etc. existed where now stand great cities and villages . . . with thousands of churches and schools. Next to my great financial work during the war, I considered would be [*sic*] the successful opening

of this grand route from the lakes to the Pacific Ocean . . . As the years have passed on, I cannot but feel a great satisfaction in *having been the instrument* in opening and adding . . . millions of people, so many churches, schools, and colleges . . . wheat fields and mines to our country. [emphasis added][20]

Jay Cooke's last years were characterized by fishing trips, Gibraltar vacations, small-scale farming, Sunday School teaching, assisting the Ogontz seminary, and visiting his old bank (now owned by a son and his son-in-law), where he kept a desk. In 1900 he was thrown from a pony carriage driven by a great-grandson and badly bruised. The next year he experienced a fainting spell and was soon frail. On February 13, 1905, he held his annual reception and dinner at the Ogontz school but, exhausted, fell ill and began to fail. Three days later his family gathered around him. As the minister finished reading the prayers for the dying, Cooke, his mind clear, said "Amen" in a strong voice and then "That was the right prayer," his last words. His remains were placed in the Ogontz mausoleum with those of his wife and parents.[21]

"Ho Hechetu!" (It Is Well!)

John A. Haydon's fate is unknown. After being humiliated by Major Baker in 1872, he disappeared. His name does not appear in the 1880 census.

Ira Spaulding, 56, who had hired Rosser and other surveyors, died in Philadelphia on October 2, 1875. Nothing is known of his life after mid-1872.

On June 25, 1876, some 115 officers, enlisted men, scouts, and a correspondent associated with the 1871, 1872, or 1873 surveys died at the Little Big Horn. In addition to George and Tom Custer, their brother-in-law James Calhoun, and Milnor Roberts's son-in-law George Yates, they included the scouts Bloody Knife, Mitch Boyer, Isaiah Dorman, and Charley Reynolds. Many Sioux and Cheyennes who had tried to block the surveys in 1872–73 also were killed. The following year, during the Nez Percé campaign, at least nine officers and men associated with the surveys died.

Pitt Cooke, 60, Jay's ineffectual older brother, died in Sandusky on December 9, 1879. His *New York Tribune* obituary speaks of his "modest retirement."

Henry Cooke, 55, Jay's able younger brother, died in Washington of kidney and liver ailments on February 24, 1881. He had lived lavishly; but with few friends and limited resources after the crash, he was unable to start a new career. His emotional state after 1873 is also suspect.

George W. Cass, 78, died March 21, 1881. His 1873–74 Northern Pacific presidency reflected honesty and common sense. No one believed he was responsible for the railroad's problems, and under a less able individual the railroad's survival would have been unlikely.

W. Milnor Roberts had banked with Cooke and lost most of his money in the Panic. While he continued as the Northern Pacific's chief engineer, this income was negligible. At 64, he took consultancies in the United States, Canada, and Europe. A son, Richard, graduated from Lafayette College in 1875 and became Custer's secretary. When Custer's column left Fort Lincoln in 1876, Richard was hired as a beef herder, but fortunately was left behind when Custer set off on his ill-fated ride. After Roberts's son-in-law, Capt. G. W. Yates, died with Custer, Roberts became responsible not only for his three young children but also for three grand-children. In 1879 he was hired by the Brazilian government at $25,000 a year. Unbeknownst to Roberts, at the same time, Billings was refinancing the NP to renew construction, the work Roberts most wanted. On July 14, 1881, while on the Amazon, Roberts, 71 and virtually alone, succumbed to fever.

Edward Ball, 60, the able and respected 2nd Cavalry captain, died October 22, 1884. He had retired just that April and ended his career as a major.

Eugene M. Baker, 47, died at Fort Walla Walla on December 19, 1884. After 1872 his career had more downs than ups. Sheridan, who liked him, give him decent but physically taxing assignments. His death was caused by his drinking.

Sam Wilkeson, 71, died December 2, 1888. Wilkeson survived the Panic finan-cially but never again worked with Cooke. In October 1888 Wilkeson, still the Northern Pacific's secretary, became ill and took a fully paid "leave of absence," a generous charade by the railroad. Among others at his funeral were Billings, Fahnestock, and Villard, but not Cooke.

Frederick Billings, 67, died September 30, 1890. More than anyone else he restored the Northern Pacific's finances, permitting construction to resume in 1879. While Villard acquired the NP in 1881, Billings was fully honored at the "final spike" ceremonies. Billings's *New York Times* obituary noted that he had left $50,000 to "Moody's school for boys" (the Mount Hermon School in Massachusetts, which the author attended many decades later).

J. Gregory Smith, 73, died November 6, 1891, having weathered every investiga-tion and continuing to be a force in Vermont politics. By 1874 he was so financially strapped that he sold his NP stock to Charlemagne Tower at ten cents on the dollar. One of Smith's pallbearers was John B. Page, the cagey Rutland president whose 1870 contract triggered so many of Smith's problems.

Francis O. French, 55, died February 26, 1893. At First National Bank he and Fahnestock soon quarreled. French amicably sold out, wrote, traveled, and returned to banking, being president of Manhattan Trust at the time of his death.

Gall, about 54, died December 4, 1894. After two of his wives and three children were killed by Reno's men at the Little Bighorn, the enraged Gall played a key role. He fled to Canada with Sitting Bull; but in 1881, with his followers starving, Gall returned to the United States and surrendered. In his reservation years Gall, still suffering from his bayonet wounds, distanced himself from Sitting Bull, became a Christian, supported Indian education by whites, and agreed to the contraction of the Sioux reservation. Today some regard him as an Indian "Uncle Tom"; but, in truth, numerous issues concerning assimilation and acculturation remain unresolved. Gall is buried in Wakpala, South Dakota, overlooking Lake Oahe, a dammed section of the Missouri River. Walking through the unkempt cemetery on a cold, blustery Labor Day in 1997 was a reminder of the despair and poverty that typify so many reservations. Yellowstone historian Mark H. Brown wrote: "Gall, that rugged warrior who stood out from among his comrades, was buried in a prosaic grave like a white man. . . . Perhaps it would have been more fitting that he be placed on a scaffold . . . with the sun and moon to stand guard over him, and with the wind to tug at his wrappings and whistle and murmur past the scaffold poles."[1]

William G. Moorhead, 83, died January 13, 1895. Moorhead had hidden some of his money but after the Panic lived aimlessly. Oberholtzer wrote: "His mind failing, his closing years were entirely miserable." His passing was marked by no obituaries and the briefest of death notices.[2]

Thomas H. Canfield was 74 when he died on January 24, 1897. He had become active in promoting what eventually became the St. Lawrence Seaway. That mid-morning he was seated at a writing desk in a hotel lobby talking to a friend when his heart stopped. He proved to be as much a financial menace to himself as to the Northern Pacific; it took his children 20 years to pay off his debts.

Robert E. A. Crofton, the able but rakish Irish immigrant who had married into the DuPont family and had been with Stanley on the 1872 and 1873 expeditions, died after a brief illness on June 21, 1898, at 63. The 1890s had proven to be a publicly turbulent decade for Crofton, then a full colonel, as he led the troops that broke the 1894 Pullman railroad car strike in Chicago. In 1895 he was slapped in the face by lieutenant over a matter of "honor"—the officer was not court-martialed. Later that year three shots were fired at him (two hitting but not gravely wounding him) by another lieutenant, who was "said to have found Col. Crofton talking with [his wife]." At this officer's court-martial it was found that he was "irresponsible and [it was] recommended that he be confined to an asylum." Crofton retired in February 1897.[3]

Joseph N. G. Whistler, 77, died April 20, 1899. He retired in 1886 after a career marked by slow advancement in isolated western assignments; his wife left or divorced him. One obituary, however, noted that "to those who served under him he was like a father."[4]

Henry Inman was cashiered from the army in 1872. He become a western writer (*Stories of the Old Santa Fe Trail*) and collaborated with Buffalo Bill on a book. Decent but eccentric, he prematurely spent royalties and died deeply in debt on November 13, 1899, at the age of 62.

James A. Garland died July 26, 1900, at 62, having stayed with First National Bank for 25 years until retiring. He donated the first gift ever received by the

Metropolitan Museum of Art (the Garland Sarcophagus) and became the country's expert on Chinese porcelains.

David S. Stanley, 73, died in Washington on March 13, 1902, from a liver ailment. Despite Sheridan's promise, Sherman blocked Stanley's return east. With crocodile tears Sherman told Congress: "[Stanley's] regiment has been there ever since [1867] . . . I have promised them myself to bring them out . . . , but I have not been able to." Stanley was finally sent to Detroit's Fort Wayne—where, with no Canadian invasion imminent, there was little to do. In 1879 he brought to a head a longtime dispute with Sheridan's enemy William B. Hazen (a Sherman protégé) over who had crested Missionary Ridge first at Chattanooga in 1863, Hazen or Sheridan. Stanley was court-martialed and found guilty, but only admonished. Sheridan won the infighting, Stanley's career picked up, and he became a brigadier general after Sherman's retirement. A bitterness permeates his posthumous memoirs, and his last years were likely unhappy. If one person on the surveys truly needed to rest in peace it was the able but self-tortured Stanley.[5]

Albert O. "Eck" Eckelson, 57, died June 17, 1902. After 1873 he drifted west, did railroad work, married, and had three children. In 1889 his health broke, and he was unable to do physical labor. By 1901 he was living in an Oregon soldiers' home, where he died.

Javan B. Irvine, 72, died January 20, 1904. His life permanently changed on December 19, 1872. While Irvine was riding alone outside of Fort Sully, a Sioux rode up and asked if he could join him. Irvine assented. Soon the Indian stopped his pony, let Irvine move forward, pulled out a pistol, and shot him in the head. The bullet passed through Irvine's skull and brain, partially emerging from his forehead. Amazingly, he was not even knocked out of his saddle. Whirling his horse around, his face covered with blood, bone, and brain tissue, Irvine charged the terrified Indian but, growing weak, returned to Fort Sully. Here the post surgeon removed the bullet and sent it to the army medical museum. Despite the wound, Irvine stayed in the military for 19 more years but was regarded as something of a curiosity. While lucky to be alive, he suffered some brain damage. In 1939 one of Stanley's daughters gave a luncheon address and remarked: "I have heard that sometime afterwards, when he was left in command of a post, he put every officer under arrest! It may have been the bullet!"[6]

Rain-in-the-Face, about 70, died September 14, 1905. He was badly wounded at the Little Big Horn and later fled with Sitting Bull to Canada. He became a popular figure and loved to give interviews, sprinkling some with facts. In 1893 he signed autographs at the fully lighted Chicago World's Fair, and one wonders what his thoughts were. Just before his death he said:

I have lived peacefully ever since we came to the reservation. No one can say that Rain-in-the-Face has broken the rules of the Great Father. I fought for my people and my country. When we were conquered I remained silent as a warrior should. Rain-in-the-Face was killed when [he] put down his weapons before the Great father. His spirit was gone then; only his body lived on, but now it is almost ready to lie down for the last time. Ho hechetu! (It is well!)[7]

Samuel J. Barrows, 63, died April 21, 1909. He became a religious publisher, won a term in Congress, but offended so many that the Senate rejected him when he was nominated for Librarian of Congress. His last decade was devoted to prison reform and Indian education.

Basil Clement, 86, died peacefully on November 23, 1910. Custer did not like him, and his scouting days ended with the 1873 survey. Clement appears to have spent the rest of his life quietly, if not always soberly, on a small ranch on the Missouri near Pierre, South Dakota.

Henry C. Davis, 71, who had helped drive the Northern Pacific's last spike in 1883, died a wealthy man in New York's Waldorf-Astoria on December 15, 1910. The *New York Times* noted on the day of his death that he "had been under the care of ten physicians and two trained nurses."

Charles "Shorty" Graham, 59, died August 9, 1911. He became a lead artist with *Harper's Weekly,* drawing the Northern Pacific's "last spike" ceremonies in 1883. Newspaper photographic reproduction left him stranded, however, and his last years were difficult.

Philip H. Ray, 69, died October 30, 1911. Ray emerged from the 1873 survey with a "can do" reputation and was assigned to Apache campaigns, the 1881 International Polar Expedition, and Klondike duty. He had enlisted as a private in 1861 and retired in 1906 as a brigadier general. Unfortunately, none of his private papers are known to have survived.

Harris C. Fahnestock, 79, died June 4, 1914. In the takeover of First National he had expected to be president, but the backlash from the Panic prevented it. Fahnestock forced Thompson out in 1877, quarreled with Baker and Garland, inhibited French, and was an associate, not a friend, of Morgan. When William Fahnestock wrote his father's memorial, he took the unusual step of listing his father's friends and acquaintances to "prove" that he was not cold-hearted (two of them were the author's great-great-grandparents). Fahnestock likely lived to regret his 1873 stab in the back, not because of the havoc and heartache it caused, but because it did him so little good. He certainly would have been infuriated by the headlines in his *New York Times* obituary on June 5, 1914: "H. C. Fahnestock, Banker Is Dead; Associate of Jay Cooke."

Annie Roberts Yates, 65, the widow of George Yates and daughter of Milnor Roberts, died December 9, 1914. She returned to Carlisle after 1876 but later moved to New York. Her death was gruesome; the *New York Times* headline read: "Col. Yate's [*sic*] Widow Killed in Subway; Elderly Woman Whose Husband Fought with Custer Crushed at 14th Street Station."[8]

Charles Braden died January 15, 1919, at 71. His 1873 wound forced him to leave the army, but he became a teacher at a military preparatory school near West Point. He was active in academy affairs, and West Point's entire corps of cadets participated in his funeral ceremonies.

Lafayette E. Campbell, 73, died in Denver on May 3, 1919. Campbell was on the 1873 survey and kept a diary, which is now lost. He married a niece of Julia Dent Grant and in the 1890s became rich from his investment in or ownership of two silver mines.

Daniel H. Brush, 72, died in Baltimore on March 8, 1920. He later fought Apaches and was in action in Cuba and in the Philippines under his classmate Fred Grant. In 1908 (44 years after he had enlisted in the Civil War at 16) he became a brigadier general.

George A. Brackett, 84, died in Minneapolis on May 15, 1921. By 1894 he had lost almost everything; attempting to restart his career, he unsuccessfully built a toll road from Skagway to the Yukon during the gold rush. His last decades were financially difficult but not oppressively so.

Montgomery Meigs, 84, died December 9, 1931. In 1874 Meigs joined the Corps of Engineers and was sent to Keokuk, Iowa, to design, build, and manage locks and other improvements on the Mississippi River. He spent the rest of a productive life there.

Lovell H. Jerome, 85, died on January 17, 1935. Winston Churchill was apparently told when he was a young boy that his mother's first cousin, Jerome, had won the Congressional Medal of Honor, when in fact he had been forced out of the army in the late 1870s. The unreliable Lovell lived long and well on his family's inheritance, dying in his expensive Park Avenue apartment.[9]

Edward C. Jordan, 89, possibly the last of the Yellowstone surveyors, died on September 15, 1935. After 1872 he began his own civil engineering firm in Portland, Maine. Long active in public affairs, he was described in a front-page obituary as the dean of local engineers and a former "locating engineer" for the Northern Pacific.[10]

Charles A. Varnum, 86, died February 26, 1936, the last surviving officer on the Yellowstone surveys. He fought at the Little Bighorn, at Wounded Knee, and in the Philippines. He retired in 1907 but was called back into service in 1917, teaching at West Point.

White Bull (Sitting Bull's nephew) died July 21, 1947, possibly in his 100th year. Besides being at Pryor's Creek, he was at the Little Big Horn; some sources indicate that he killed Custer. At the ceremonies marking the Little Big Horn's 50th anniversary, surviving Sioux and Cheyenne participants chose White Bull to lead them.

The last known survivor of any of the Yellowstone surveys died on March 11, 1950, at the age of 98. **Charles A. Windolph** was a private in the 7th Cavalry. He was on the Black Hills expedition and at the Little Bighorn, left the army in 1883, and worked for a South Dakota mining company for 49 years.

Lt. Edward J. McClernand's Account of the Rescue of the 1871 Western Yellowstone Survey

Half a century after the 1871 western Yellowstone survey (chapter 7), Lt. Edward J. McClernand wrote an account of the rescue of the surveyors and cavalrymen trapped by the November 17 blizzard. *On Time for Disaster: The Rescue of Custer's Command* was published posthumously in 1926, when key participants Edward Ball, Eugene Baker, Fellows Pease, and George Tyler were dead. The only known officer still alive was the discredited Lovell H. Jerome, who had been forced to resign his commission in 1879.[1]

McClernand's account begins with an error. "One night on the *return march*," he wrote, "a tent caught fire during a high wind . . . and in an incredibly short time the camp was destroyed" (emphasis added). McClernand places the October 10 fire in late November and suggests that most if not all of the camp was destroyed; but the error (in an account written 50 years after the event) is understandable. Next McClernand turns to the blizzard, stating: "I was in temporary command." This is factually wrong; Ball was in command. When Ball left for Fort Ellis to seek aid, he placed Capt. George Tyler in command. Not only was McClernand then a lieutenant, but he was not attached to the surveyors' escort.

In Ball's 1871 account, many parts of which are verified in contemporary newspapers, he left his command to get emergency supplies, reaching Fort Ellis on Thursday, November 16. With a storm ominously approaching, the post's *entire* garrison waited it out on Friday. Not until Saturday did all of Ellis's men begin digging a path over the Bozeman Pass. They were unable to finish, however, and returned to Ellis that evening because of the cold and high wind.

In stark contrast, however, McClernand states that he led the rescuers, leaving Fort Ellis Thursday evening; there is no mention of Ball in his rendition. McClernand's melodramatic description of that evening is another embellishment:

> [N]ight overtook us when only eight miles out; utterly exhausted we went into camp in a little grove of pines just below the summit of the divide . . . That night the thermometer at Ellis [4,765 feet above sea level], a thousand or more feet below us, fell to 48° below zero, and the wind blew a gale. . . . even the animals huddled around the fire.

If wind-chill indexes had been available in the 1920s, McClernand might have modified his story. The on-line National Weather Service wind-chill chart does not show temperatures below minus 45 degrees; but at minus 45 degrees, with a 30-mile wind, the index is below minus 85 degrees. This figure does not include the pass itself being 1,000 feet higher and the wind-chill index therefore being lower. Having "survived" this cold, McClernand would have us believe that on Friday morning his party finished shoveling across the pass, reached the Shields River, and then crossed the frozen Yellowstone. In all, he claims that they marched 30 miles before reaching the cavalry and surveyors by 2 P.M.

McClernand goes on to state that everyone had marched about two miles when the huge storm engulfed them. His account of being caught in the howling storm is indeed dramatic. He says that "after two hours of this desperate struggle it was ascertained that we had been going in a circle." But the terrain that the column was marching across was sandwiched between hills to the immediate left and the frozen Yellowstone just to the right. There were indeed problems, but 150 men going in a large circle was not one of them.

McClernand first wrote about the incident in 1896, but there are significant differences between this and his 1920s version. Incidents not in the 1896 account were the fire that destroyed the camp in November, mention of a rescue party (or McClernand leading it), spending the night atop Bozeman Pass, being caught in the storm, and marching in a circle. While McClernand's 1896 version noted that "[t]he thermometer marked forty degrees below zero," still-living participants probably would not have objected to this as a "fact."

McClernand's account of the 1872 western survey, in which he takes over the surveying duties for an ill John Haydon (chapter 10), raises similar questions. Yet, intriguingly, McClernand's career could not have appeared more successful. He received a Congressional Medal of Honor (Nez Percé campaign) and a Silver Star in Cuba (1898), obtained fascinating postings in the later part of his career, and retired as a brigadier general. In fact, McClernand was sufficiently well thought of that he was recalled to active (administrative) duty during World War I.[2]

We do not know why McClernand made up these stories or whether other parts of his memoir or career may have been based on similar charades. Nor do we know the motivations for McClernand's fabrications. It is not unrealistic to speculate, however, that at West Point he was whipsawed between his father's wartime military failings and political squabbles (with Lincoln and Grant) on the one hand and his unimpressive physique and countenance on the other. Yet instead of succumbing, he emerged all the more determined to prove himself to his army peers. In any case, the desire to puff up one's résumé is sadly common, and McClernand's 1871 account simply cannot be considered reliable.[3]

NOTES

INTRODUCTION

1. For purposes of geographic identification, the names of present-day communities are included.

CHAPTER 1. "GOD'S CHOSEN INSTRUMENT"

1. Flynn, *Men of Wealth,* p. 482.

2. Cooke, "Jay Cooke's Memoir," ca. 1894, p. 53; Oberholtzer, *Jay Cooke,* 1:2–3.

3. *New Catholic Encyclopedia* (Washington, D.C.: Catholic University Press, 1981), 5:265. For Eleutheros Cooke, see *Dictionary of American Biography* [*DAB*]; *The National Cyclopaedia of American Biography* [*NCAB*], 1:253; and Larson, *Jay Cooke,* p. 4. Union has no record of Cooke's attendance.

4. Cooke, "Jay Cooke's Memoir," p. 8.

5. Ibid., p. 59.

6. Ibid., p. 17; Jackson, *Voyages of the Steamboat Yellow Stone,* pp. xv, 2, 7, and 18.

7. Moorhead, *Whirling Spindle,* pp. 128–29; Larson, *Jay Cooke,* p. 19; Minnigerode, *Certain Rich Men,* p. 56.

8. Cooke, "Jay Cooke's Memoir," pp. 10–11; Oberholtzer, *Jay Cooke,* 1:77; Carl Sandburg, *Abraham Lincoln: The War Years,* 4 vols. (New York: Harcourt, Brace and Co., 1939), 2:604.

9. Larson, "Jay Cooke's Early Work in Transportation"; Sandburg, *Abraham Lincoln,* 2:603; for the Vermont Central: Larson, "Jay Cooke's Early Work," pp. 94–95; Cooke, "Jay Cooke's Memoir," pp. 22–24.

10. This paragraph and the following one: Grayson, *Leaders and Periods of American Finance,* pp. 237–40.

11. Pollard, *The Journal of Jay Cooke,* pp. 35, 48–49; Cooke, "Jay Cooke's Memoirs," p. 6. Cooke was probably more active in abolitionist activities than his family or Oberholtzer wished to state, perhaps because of prevailing attitudes toward African Americans at the time of Cooke's death.

12. Profiles of Henry David Cooke (1825–81) are in *DAB* and *NCAB,* 10:510.

13. Oberholtzer, *Jay Cooke,* 1:103–20; Larson, "Jay Cooke's Early Work," pp. 106–8; Rottenberg, *The Man Who Made Wall Street.*

14. Oberholtzer, *Jay Cooke,* 1:146–49; Josephson, *The Robber Barons,* pp. 54–55. The actual amount of the pledges was $1,737,500.

15. Grayson, *Leaders and Periods of American Finance,* p. 243; Josephson, *The Robber Barons,* p. 56; and Oberholtzer, *Jay Cooke,* 1:153–84.

16. *DAB*; *NCAB*, 30:552; Oberholtzer, *Jay Cooke,* 1:185; Fahnestock Papers, F-223, Box 4, Folder 9, Baker Library, Harvard Business School.

17. Oberholtzer, *Jay Cooke,* 1:185, 342; French, *Witness to the Young Republic.*

18. Josephson, *The Robber Barons,* p. 57; Oberholtzer, *Jay Cooke,* 1:187–91. For a harsh view of Cooke's bond sales and motivation, see Lawson, *Patriot Fires,* chapter 2.

19. Oberholtzer, *Jay Cooke,* 1:188–90.

20. Minnigerode, *Certain Rich Men,* p. 64.

21. This paragraph and the following one: Cooke, "Jay Cooke's Memoir," pp. 35–36, 107; Sandburg, *Abraham Lincoln,* 2:602.

22. *Richmond Examiner,* February 20, 1865; Oberholtzer, *Jay Cooke,* 1:489.

23. Oberholtzer, *Jay Cooke,* 1: chapter 12; Larson, *Jay Cooke,* pp. 173–74; Gordon, "Paying for the [Civil] War," p. 22.

24. Oberholtzer, *Jay Cooke,* 1:530–37.

25. Grayson, *Leaders and Periods of American Finance,* p. 253; Sandburg, *Abraham Lincoln,* 2:608.

26. Josephson, *The Robber Barons,* p. 58; Oberholtzer, *Jay Cooke,* 2:447–53; "Jay Cooke's Country Seat," *Philadelphia Inquirer,* August 18, 1873; "Jay Cooke's Home," *Helena Daily Herald,* October 21, 1873.

27. Oberholtzer, *Jay Cooke,* 2:458; "Spotted Tail," *Philadelphia Inquirer,* August 2, 1872.

28. Pollard, *The Journal of Jay Cooke,* pp. 9 and 21; Thorndale, *Sketches and Stories of the Lake Erie Islands* ("Castled Gibraltar and Its Lord"), pp. 271–78.

29. Pollard, *The Journal of Jay Cooke,* pp. 26, 32; "Sherman's Railroad Scheme," *St. Paul Press,* October 22, 1869.

30. Oberholtzer, *Jay Cooke,* 2:81–82.

31. Ibid. 1:266; Larson, *Jay Cooke,* pp. 186–87. Henry's position has since become the office of mayor.

32. Cooke, "Jay Cooke's Memoir," p. 2.

33. This paragraph and following one: Larson, *Jay Cooke,* p. 192; Grayson, *Leaders and Periods of American Finance,* p. 254; Oberholtzer, *Jay Cooke,* 2:176–77.

34. Larson, *Jay Cooke,* pp. 244–45; Oberholtzer, *Jay Cooke,* 2:109; Smith, "The First Visit to the Head of the Lakes of Jay Cooke in 1867." The story appears partially fictitious: the description and an 1867 photograph certainly do not match Cooke.

Chapter 2. "The Northern Pacific Must Be Built"

1. Badeau, *Grant in Peace,* pp. 159–69; McFeely, *Grant;* and Oberholtzer, *Jay Cooke,* 2:75–80.

2. Raffe, "The Significance of Thomas Hawley Canfield's Life," p. 53. Canfield's autobiography is written in the third person: *Life of Thomas Hawley Canfield;* Ullery, *Men of Vermont.*

3. For Cooke's initial interest in the NP: "Northern Pacific," *St. Paul Weekly Press,* April 8, 1869; quotations: "Reads Like a Fairy Tale: The Early History of the Northern Pacific," *Fargo Record,* June 1895, p. 11.

4. "Early Northern Pacific History," *Northwest* (April 1885).

5. See profiles of Roberts in *DAB* and *NCAB*, 29:182; T. P. Roberts (son), "Incidents Illustrating the Life and Character of Milnor Roberts," 1923, Box 1, File 8; Obituaries, Box 1; William F. Shunk, "William Milnor Roberts, Civil Engineer," *Engineering News,* July 30, 1881, p. 301, Box 1, Roberts Papers, Special Collections No. 783, Montana State University–Bozeman Library.

6. Quotations: Cooke wrote "Honest man" in large letters and then underlined the comment, in Cooke to Roberts, October 13, 1870, Box 2, File 4; and profile of Roberts, *Northwest* (January 1884).

7. Roberts, "Autobiography," p. 89; Kirby et al., *Engineering in History,* pp. 298–305.

8. Oberholtzer, *Jay Cooke,* 2:93–95; Roberts, "Autobiography," pp. 80–81; Larson, *Jay Cooke,* p. 95; and Roberts, *Special Report of a Reconnaissance of the Route for the Northern Pacific Railroad.*

9. Union College Special Collections files: Augspurger, "A Buffalo Lawyer Takes Greeley's Advice"; obituaries in various New York City papers, December 3, 1889; *DAB* and *NCAB*, 4:414.

10. Harry W. Pfanz, *Gettysburg: The First Day* (Chapel Hill: University of North Carolina Press, 2001), title page and pp. 232–35; quotation: Crozier, *Yankee Reporters, 1861–65,* pp. 360–61.

11. "Letter from Gotham," *Helena Daily Herald,* May 26, 1871.

12. Roberts, "Field Diary" and "Autobiography"; Yellowstone: Hobson, *The Cambridge Gazetteer of the United States and Canada.*

13. Roberts, "Autobiography," pp. 81–82; quotation: Rae, *Westward by Rail,* pp. 90, 95; "East and West," *New York Times,* August 7, 1869; bridge photos: Ambrose, *Nothing Like It in the World;* and Bain, *Empire Express.*

14. Oberholtzer, *Jay Cooke,* 2:116; quotation: Rae, *Westward by Rail,* pp. 222–26.

15. Ambrose, *Nothing Like It in the World,* pp. 92–93.

16. Roberts, *Special Report,* pp. 7–9 and 12–13; Wilkeson, July 11, 1869, Cooke Papers, Microfilm M-31, Minnesota Historical Society, St. Paul; quotation: Oberholtzer, *Jay Cooke,* 2:120.

17. Canfield, *Partial Report to the Board of Directors,* pp. 12–13, and *Life,* p. 30 (quotation); Roberts, *Special Report,* pp. 10–11.

18. Roberts to Cooke, July 16, 1869; Oberholtzer, *Jay Cooke,* 2:119—the newspaper was actually the *Walla Walla Statesman;* Canfield, *Life,* p. 32.

19. Canfield, *Life,* pp. 30–31; quotation: "Northern Pacific Reconnaissance," *Helena Weekly Herald,* August 18, 1871; Oberholtzer, *Jay Cooke,* 2:122; and Roberts, "Autobiography," pp. 85–86.

20. "Rapid trip" and "evangelists": "The Northern Pacific," *New North-West* (Deer Lodge), August 13, 1869; Roberts quotation: Oberholtzer, *Jay Cooke,* 2:122; Wilkeson to Cooke, August 19, 1869, NP, Secretary's Department.

21. Roberts quotation: Oberholtzer, *Jay Cooke*, 2:123; Ashley quotation: "Grand Reception . . . ," *Helena Weekly Herald*, August 19, 1869; Bill Taylor and Jan Taylor, *The Northern Pacific's Mullan Pass on the "Montana Short Line."* The author's own white-knuckle adventure by automobile need not be recounted here.

22. Wilkeson to Cooke, August 19, 1869, NP, Secretary's Department; Utley, *The Lance and the Shield*, p. 87.

23. Coffin, *The Seat of Empire*, pp. 26–30; Smalley, *History of the Northern Pacific Railroad*, p. 154; Oberholtzer, *Jay Cooke*, 2:125–28, 259; for Langford: "Local News: Northern Pacific Exploration," July 15, 1869, and "Northern Pacific," June 24 and July 8, 1869, *St. Paul Weekly Press*.

24. "Northern Pacific Exploration," August 12, 1869, and "Northern Pacific Reconnaissance," August 10, 1869, *St. Paul Weekly Press*; NP Clippings Scrapbook for period, Minnesota Historical Society, St. Paul.

25. Robberies: "Editorial Correspondence," *Helena Weekly Herald*, September 23, 1869; Roberts, "Autobiography," pp. 87–88; "Reconnaissance," *St. Paul Weekly Press*, September 16, 1869.

26. Roberts, *Special Report*, pp. 14, 36, 40; Bursack and Masters, "The Northern Pacific before the Last Spike," p. 22; Michael P. Malone, *James J. Hill* (Norman: University of Oklahoma Press, 1998), pp. 31–32.

27. Canfield, *Partial Report*, p. 5; Cooke, "Jay Cooke's Memoir," p. 134.

CHAPTER 3. "FREE FROM FATIGUE"

1. Kirby et al., *Engineering in History*, chapter 9; quotation: Kirby and Laurson, *The Early Years of Modern Civil Engineering*, pp. 88–89; Jensen, *American Heritage History of Railroads in America.*

2. Henry B. Comstock, *The Iron Horse: An Illustrated History of Steam Locomotives* (Waukesha, Wis.: Greenberg Publishing Co., 1993), p. 38.

3. Johnson obituary, *New York Times*, April 20, 1872; Hone, *The Diary of Philip Hone*, August 29, 1832,

4. This paragraph and the following two: Hone, *The Diary of Philip Hone*, February 15, 1838; "Early Railroading," *St. Paul Weekly Press*, August 27, 1871; "Railroads 32 Years Ago," *Philadelphia Inquirer*, September 4, 1871.

5. U.S. Department of Commerce, U.S. Bureau of the Census, *Historical Statistics of the United States*, p. 430; *Historical Atlas of the United States* (Washington, D.C.: National Geographic Society, 1988), p. 188; Gordon, *An Empire of Wealth*, chapter 6; Earle, *Stage Coach and Tavern Days*, chapter 10.

6. This paragraph and the following paragraphs are drawn from Hone, *The Diary of Philip Hone*, 2:310–20. Hone's editor noted (p. viii) that the two published volumes were just a quarter of the original diaries.

7. Thomas Weber, *The Northern Railroads in the Civil War* (1952; reprint, Westport, Conn.: Greenwood Press, 1970); Clark, *Railroads in the Civil War*; Bacon, *Sinews of War.*

8. Nighttime operations and headlights: White, *A History of the American Locomotive,* pp. 215–17.

9. Renz, *The History of the Northern Pacific Railroad,* pp. 11–14; Thrapp, *Encyclopedia of Frontier Biography;* and Warner, *Generals in Blue.*

10. For Johnson: Renz, *History,* pp. 12–13; *DAB;* Smalley, *History,* p. 76.

11. Smalley, *History,* chapter 9; Renz, *History,* pp. 17–19; Perham's *DAB* profile.

12. The NP's office was destroyed by fire in 1865: Smalley, *History,* pp. 129–31; quotation: *DAB.*

13. Jones, *The Central Vermont Railway,* p. 51; quotation: Frey, *Encyclopedia; NCAB,* 8:323; *DAB; New York Times* obituary, November 7, 1891.

14. Hungerford et al., *Vermont Central;* Brown, *The Baldwin Locomotive Works,* p. 65. Rottenberg, *The Man Who Made Wall Street,* p. 63, implies that Cooke's investment was in the late 1850s, but an earlier date is more likely.

15. Jones, *The Central Vermont Railway,* first quotation on p. 42, longer quotation on p. 41. It is unclear, however, *which* Josiah Quincy was the thief. Jones lays the blame on the Josiah Quincy (1772–1864) who was a congressman, state legislator, judge, Boston mayor, and Harvard president (for 16 years) before retiring in 1845 to devote himself to writing. The author has been unable to confirm that it was this Quincy, and his profiles in *American National Biography, DAB,* and *NCAB* (6:147) and his *New York Times* obituary on July 4, 1864 (which states that after his retirement "he lived a strictly private life") do not indicate a whiff of scandal. More likely it was his lesser-known cousin Josiah Quincy (1793–1875), who is known to have been active in the railroad business (see *Appleton's Cyclopaedia of American Biography* [New York: D. Appleton and Co., 1888], 5:153).

16. Jones, *The Central Vermont Railway,* pp. 25 and 38; Larson, *Jay Cooke,* pp. 94–95.

17. Hungerford et al., *Vermont Central,* p. 30; Shelby Foote, *The Civil War,* 3 vols. (1974; reprint, Norwalk, Conn.: Easton Press, 1991), 3:586–87 and 725; James D. Horan, *Confederate Agent* (New York: Crown, 1954), chapter 18; the movie is *The Raid* (1954). The author has not ascertained if Smith was in St. Albans at the time of the robbery.

18. Rutland, in Frey, *Encyclopedia;* Page: *NCAB,* 8:324; Shaughnessy, *The Rutland Road;* quotation: Hungerford et al., *Vermont Central,* p. 77.

19. Quotation: profile of Smith in *DAB.*

20. This paragraph and following one: Renz, *History,* pp. 22–26; Fawn F. Brodie, *Thaddeus Stevens: Scourge of the South* (1959; reprint, New York: W. W. Norton and Company, 1966), p. 185; Smalley, *History,* pp. 141–47 (quotation on p. 146).

21. This paragraph and the following one: Linklater, *Measuring America,* pp. 7 (quotation), 72, and appendix, "Units of Measurement."

22. Kirby and Laurson, *The Early Years of Modern Civil Engineering,* chapter 1.

23. Grasshoppers were a major problem: when they were squashed by the tens of thousands, the goo rendered braking systems useless. Screens became the practical answer. Latrobe, "Engineering," pp. 98–99.

24. Jensen, *American Heritage History of Railroads in America,* pp. 27, 186; accident figures: *Railroad Gazette,* January 25, 1873; Robert C. Reed, *Train Wrecks: A Pictorial History* (New York: Bonanza Books, 1974).

25. Jerry Masters and Bill Bursack, "A Brief Outline of Surveying: Tools of the Trade," unpublished, 1998.

26. Lewis T. Buckman, C.E., East Berne, N.Y., February 3, 2003, letter to the author; Milnor Roberts to Joseph Walker Flenniken, June 28, 1872, 134.L.14.1.B, Minnesota Historical Society, St. Paul.

27. Corliss, "The Yellowstone Expedition of 1873," pp. 6–7.

28. "How Railroads Are Built," *New York Times,* August 12, 1873; Lubetkin, *Union College's Class of 1868,* p. 167.

29. Quotations in this paragraph and the following paragraphs: Milnor Roberts, "General Arrangement of the Parties," July 11, 1871, NP, Secretary's Department; "How Railroads Are Built"; and Buckman letter, February 3, 2003.

30. The axeman: Thomas L. Rosser, Field Diary, October 7, 1872, Collection 1171-g-h-j, Box 16; Roberts to Flenniken, July 8, 1872, NP Records, 134.L.14.1.B.

31. "Division of the Missouri," *Army and Navy Journal,* September 30, 1871, describes the incident and subsequent court-martial.

CHAPTER 4. "THE BUFFALO WILL DWINDLE AWAY"

1. McNeill, *Plagues and Peoples,* p. 204. During the 1942–43 construction of the Alaskan-Canadian highway, even with the assistance of public health officials, some isolated tribes had mortality rates of 25 percent. Kennedy, *Hidden Cities,* pp. 161–62; and Krech, *The Ecological Indian,* chapter 3. Krech (p. 93) is more conservative than Kennedy or Thornton, *American Indian Holocaust and Survival.*

2. Cronon, *Changes in the Land,* p. 86. The present work was already in page proofs when the author read Charles C. Mann's *1491.* Mann devotes an entire fascinating chapter ("Why Billington Survived") to New England and Squanto's story.

3. Kvasnicka and Viola, *The Commissioners of Indian Affairs, 1824–1977,* pp. 123–33.

4. Bray, "Teton Sioux Population History, 1655–1881," pp. 169–77; U.S. Department of the Interior, *Annual Report, 1872,* p. 48; Denig, *Five Indian Tribes of the Upper Missouri;* Hodge, *Handbook of American Indians North of Mexico;* and Swanton, *The Indian Tribes of North America.*

5. Indian Affairs estimate by Ben Innis, *Bloody Knife,* p. 17; Bray, "Teton Sioux Population History," p. 175.

6. Secoy, *Changing Military Patterns of the Great Plains Indians,* chapter 6; Parkman, *The Oregon Trail,* pp. 163–64.

7. This figure is the author's estimate. John Keegan, *Fields of Battle: The Wars for North America* (New York: Alfred A. Knopf, 1996), p. 287, says that the 1868 Fort Laramie treaty resulted in 77,000 square miles of reservation land *and* 147,000 of unceded territory. Denig, *Five Indian Tribes of the Upper Missouri,* p. 19.

8. Clodfelter, *The Dakota War*, offers a thorough account. Good 1863–64 battle maps with brief descriptions are found in Snortland, *A Traveler's Companion to North Dakota State Historic Sites.*

9. Raynolds, *Report of Capt. W. F. Raynolds*, p. 11.

10. Utley, *Lance and the Shield*, p. 82. For a hard-line view, see Brown, "Who Broke the Treaty of 1868?"

11. U.S. Department of War, *Annual Report, 1869*, p. 65; Vestal, *Sitting Bull*, pp. 118–24. An 1871 *Bozeman Avant Courier* story mentions Flatheads riding east *through* the town, so the fight likely occurred about then. Utley, *Lance and the Shield*, pp. 84–91 (quotation on p. 91); Farr, "Going to Buffalo."

12. Innis, *Bloody Knife;* Topping, *Chronicles of the Yellowstone;* Crow warfare: Vestal, *Sitting Bull*, pp. 113–17; miners: U.S. Department of War, *Annual Report, 1869*, p. 62; Métis: Utley, *Lance and the Shield*, pp. 102–105.

13. Hutton, *Phil Sheridan and His Army*, p. 116.

14. U.S. Department of War, *Annual Report, 1869*, p. 56. Sherman to Hancock, April 14, 1870, in "General Hancock and the President," *Army and Navy Journal*, May 28, 1870.

15. Sheridan, *Record of Engagements with Hostile Indians;* U.S. Department of War, *Annual Report, 1869*, p. 66, *1870*, p. 27, *1871*, pp. 27, 58; Mattison, "Fort Rice."

16. Ege, *"Tell Baker to Strike Them Hard";* Hancock in U.S. Department of War, *Annual Report, 1870*, p. 29.

17. U.S. Department of War, *Annual Report, 1869*, pp. 61–62.

CHAPTER 5. "KNEE DEEP IN MUD"

1. Tim Brewer, *Moon Handbooks, Minnesota* (Emeryville, Calif.: Avalon Travel Handbooks, 2004); "Northern Pacific," *St. Paul Weekly Press*, January 6, 1870; Smalley, *The Great Northwest*, p. 323; quotation: Meigs, *Railroad West*, p. 12.

2. Malles, *Bridge Building in Wartime;* quotation: Relf, "Narrative of Richard Relf."

3. William L. Riordon, *Plunkitt of Tammany Hall* (1905; reprint, New York: E. P. Dutton, 1963), chapter 1, "Honest Graft and Dishonest Graft"; Harnsberger, *Jay Cooke and Minnesota*, p. 77.

4. Bushong and Bushong, *Fightin' Tom Rosser*, pp. 1–3; Beane, "Thomas L. Rosser"; Glasrud, *Roy Johnson's Red River Valley.*

5. For the battles, see an untitled article about the 1872 survey, signed by Rosser, Collection 1171-g-h-j, Box 12, Miscellaneous Writings, Small Special Collections Library, University of Virginia, Charlottesville.

6. Robert K. Krick, in *Encyclopedia of the Confederacy*, ed. Richard N. Current (New York: Simon and Schuster, 1993), p. 1347; quotation: Krick, "'The Cause of All My Disasters,'" pp. 92–96; Meigs to his parents, July 11, 1872; Jordan, "Account of Edward C. Jordan's Experiences."

7. See Bushong and Bushong, *Fightin' Tom Rosser*, pp. 41–43. No photographs of Lizzy before 1882 have survived; Rosser's diary at one point notes that personnel associated with the survey had asked for pictures of her.

8. Rosser to wife, December 24, 1869, Rosser Papers, Collection 1171-g-h-j, Box 1.

9. Eckelson information courtesy of Larry Schrenk, October 30, 1999, letter to the author.

10. Meigs family: *DAB*; *New York Times* obituary, December 10, 1931; Meigs, "Letters of Montgomery Meigs," ed. Atwater. Meigs was likely christened Montgomery Cunningham Meigs, but he came to dislike having the same name as his famous father. Certainly by the end of his life he had purposely dropped "Cunningham." However, numerous contemporary records and sources identify him with the middle name or confuse him with his father.

11. John Meigs is buried at the crest of Arlington National Cemetery; his grave is covered by his effigy, like an English medieval knight. Meigs, *Railroad West*, p. 18. In the novel the protagonist (Meigs) marries the general's sister, a Freudian conundrum that the author will let others interpret.

12. Jordan, *The Jordan Memorial*, pp. 73–74, 230–33.

13. Jordan's grades and the courses he took courtesy of Union College, Special Collections; Sinclair, *Development of the Locomotive Engine*, p. 592.

14. Diary, P-2245, Minnesota Historical Society, St. Paul; employment: Spaulding to Jordan, May 23, 1870, courtesy of Mark H. Jordan, Gorham, Maine.

15. Oberholtzer, *Jay Cooke*, 2:158–60 for agreement; Smalley, *History*, chapter 20. The estimate of 40 percent is the author's.

16. It is not known exactly when Smith submitted his $975,000 bill. Oberholtzer, *Jay Cooke*, 2:163–65; Larson, *Jay Cooke*, pp. 166, 287; "Jay Cooke," *Railroad Gazette*, May 28, 1870.

17. Oberholtzer, *Jay Cooke*, 2:167; Smalley, *Great Northwest*, pp. 185, 381–82; "Northern Pacific Inauguration . . . ," *St. Paul Weekly Press*, February 24, 1870; Hiram Hayes to O. D. Wheeler, October 23, 1911, and G. W. Cooley to Brackett, January 7, 1906, both in Brackett Papers.

18. "The Northern Pacific," *St. Paul Weekly Press*, January 6, 1870; Oberholtzer, *Jay Cooke*, 2:245–46; "Old and New Roads, Northern Pacific," *Railroad Gazette*, December 3, 1870; Renz, *History*, p. 35.

19. This paragraph and following one: Oberholtzer, *Jay Cooke*, 2:244–46.

20. Oberholtzer, *Jay Cooke*, 2:168, 181; "Sectional . . . ," *St. Paul Weekly* and *Daily Press*, May 12 and June 3, 1870, for congressional "yeas" and "nays" by state and name.

21. Oberholtzer, *Jay Cooke*, 2:176; Larson, *Jay Cooke*, p. 293.

22. "The Northern Pacific," *St. Paul Weekly Press*, January 27, 1870 (Relf's description was for 1869, but conditions were no different in 1870), Brackett Papers.

23. Quotations to the end of this section from Jordan letter, January 14, 1871, courtesy of Mark H. Jordan.

24. Latrobe, "Engineering"; "Progress of Construction," *Duluth Minnesotian*, November 19, 1870; Renz, *History*, p. 35.

25. Harnsberger, *Jay Cooke and Minnesota*, p. 72; Smalley, *Great Northwest*, p. 383.

26. Oberholtzer, *Jay Cooke*, 2:243; Harnsberger, *Jay Cooke and Minnesota*, p. 78; train: Meigs, *Railroad West*, pp. 13–17. At a 2001 Northern Pacific Railway Historical Association (NPRHA) conference in Duluth, Tim Schandel, director of the Lake Superior Railroad

Museum, told the author that he had heard the story numerous times but had never seen any documentation.

27. In the 1660s one of Brackett's ancestors testified that the Reverend Robert Jordan had been placed under a witch's spell. Although they had adjacent property and fought the French and Indians side by side, relations between the two families remained cold up to the twentieth century.

28. Brackett, *The Story of George Augustus Brackett;* "Northwestern Construction Co.," *Minneapolis Tribune,* July 2, 1870, Brackett Papers.

29. "A Canadian Pacific Railroad," *New York Times,* September 5, 1870; quotation: Harnsberger, *Jay Cooke and Minnesota,* p. 64.

30. "Great Excursion," *Duluth Minnesotian,* August 27, 1870; "Duluth . . . ," *Railway Gazette,* August 27, 1870.

31. Quoted in "Light Dawning," *Duluth Minnesotian,* October 22, 1870; *Railroad Gazette,* November 19 and November 26, 1870.

32. Harnsberger, *Jay Cooke and Minnesota,* p. 73; "Railroad Company vs. Liquor Dealers," *Duluth Minnesotian,* October 1, 1870; Renz, *History,* pp. 35–36. No one has done more thorough research on this subject than Renz.

33. DeLacy is a fascinating character in early Montana history, and his family's roots traced back to a knight with William the Conqueror. "A New Map of Montana," *Helena Daily Herald,* September 1, 1870; the two Roberts autobiographies differ slightly: 1:91–93, 2:28; Oberholtzer, *Jay Cooke,* 2:247.

34. "Light Dawning"; "Progress of Construction," *Duluth Minnesotian,* November 19, 1870; Oberholtzer, *Jay Cooke,* 2:247–50.

35. "Sale of St. Paul & Pacific," *St. Paul Weekly Press,* December 1, 1870; quotations: Harnsberger, *Jay Cooke and Minnesota,* pp. 80–81.

CHAPTER 6. "NO SYSTEM OBSERVED"

1. Roberts to Cooke, NP, Secretary's Department.

2. Oberholtzer, *Jay Cooke,* 2:263; "Vermont Central," *Duluth Minnesotian,* August 26, 1871; Harnsberger, *Jay Cooke and Minnesota,* pp. 80–81.

3. This paragraph and the following two paragraphs: Oberholtzer, *Jay Cooke,* 2:250, 257, 265; Winks, *Frederick Billings,* p. 193.

4. Oberholtzer, *Jay Cooke,* 2:162–63.

5. Brace, "The New North-West," *New York Times,* August 6, 1873; Harnsberger, *Jay Cooke and Minnesota,* pp. 85, 89–90.

6. Mickelson, *The Northern Pacific Railroad and the Selling of the West;* "Railroads as Colonizing Agencies," *St. Paul Weekly Press,* January 5, 1871.

7. For Billings, see *DAB, NCAB* 35:361, and Winks, *Frederick Billings;* "Land Commissioner," *Duluth Minnesotian,* June 3, 1871.

8. James B. Hedges, "The Colonization Work of the Northern Pacific Railroad"; Mickelson, *The Northern Pacific Railroad,* p. 83.

9. Hedges, "Colonization Work," p. 317; Mickelson, *The Northern Pacific Railroad,* pp. 17, 22–24; Winks, *Frederick Billings,* p. 206, gives a figure of $45,000. Loomis lost the trust of Billings and was later discharged. Gordon Gordon committed suicide in 1874.

10. "Northern Pacific, Efficient Medical Dept.," *St. Paul Pioneer,* June 3, 1871; Hedges, "Colonization Work," pp. 319–20.

11. "North Dakota," *St. Paul Pioneer,* July 15, 1871; "Settlements on Red River," *St. Paul Weekly Press,* June 8, 1871.

12. Mickelson, *The Northern Pacific Railroad,* p. 126, table 6; Winks, *Frederick Billings,* p. 194; quotation: George W. Cushing to M. C. Kimberly, January 6, 1906, Brackett Papers.

13. *Duluth Minnesotian,* September 9, 1871 (untitled, opposite "Norwegian Customs"); quotation: "Northern Pacific Land Grants," *Railroad Gazette,* December 23, 1871.

14. Henry Cooke to Jay Cooke, May 26, 1871, NP, Secretary's Department.

15. Harnsberger, *Jay Cooke and Minnesota,* pp. 90–91. The original plan had the SP&P take the east side of the Mississippi to Brainerd. In the spring it was changed to meet NP track at Staples, thus saving more than 20 miles.

16. "Riot," *St. Paul Weekly Press,* January 12, 1871; "Beheading," *Duluth Minnesotian,* November 4, 1871; "From the Northern Pacific," *St. Paul Pioneer,* August 1, 1871; "Red River," *Minneapolis Tribune,* October 12, 1871.

17. "Northern Pacific," in "General Railroad News," *Railroad Gazette,* January 28 and March 18, 1871 (quotation); Renz, *History,* p. 35; NP, Secretary's Department, August 14, 1871.

18. "Frontier," *St. Paul Pioneer,* March 29, 1871; "Extinction of Indian Title," *St. Paul Weekly Press,* September 7, 1871.

19. "Our Railroads," *St. Paul Press,* April 12, 1871; "Northern Pacific Line," *Duluth Minnesotian,* April 15, 1871.

20. Rosser to Linsley, June 23, 1871, NP, Secretary's Department; "Progress," *St. Paul Weekly Press,* June 1, 1871.

21. J. Kevin Graffagnino, in Frey, *Encyclopedia,* p. 366.

22. "Postponement," *St. Paul Weekly Press,* July 22, 1871; "Northern Pacific," *Railroad Gazette,* August 12, 1871; "Northern Pacific," *Philadelphia Inquirer,* August 22, 1871; "Northern Pacific," *St. Paul Pioneer,* September 11 and October 13, 1871. Some papers incorrectly give the date as July 1, 1873, to reach the Missouri, but it was *1872.*

23. Quotation: "Northern Pacific," *St. Paul Pioneer,* November 25, 1871; "R.R. Accident" and "Northern Pacific Accident," *Minneapolis Tribune,* December 12 and 14 (description of accident), 1871; "Westward Ho!" and "Moorhead," *St. Paul Pioneer,* October 6 and 12, 1871; Oberholtzer, *Jay Cooke,* 2:262; and "Northern Pacific," *Railroad Gazette,* January 6, 1872.

24. "St. Paul and Pacific," *Railway Gazette,* November 11, 1871. Today Breckenridge-Wahpeton's population is a tenth of Fargo-Moorhead's.

25. Larson, *Jay Cooke,* p. 331; Harnsberger, *Jay Cooke and Minnesota,* pp. 109, 117. Grant's take on McCulloch was better than Cooke's. McCulloch's autobiography, *Men and Measures of*

Half a Century, leaves out any mention of Cooke, the only person who would employ him after he left Johnson's cabinet.

26. Cooke to Wilkeson, July 17, 1871, NP, Secretary's Department; "Distinguished Visitors," *St. Paul Weekly Press,* August 10, 1871; "European Commissioners," *Duluth Minnesotian,* August 12, 1871; Stewart, *Penny-an-Acre Empire in the West,* chapter 10.

27. Bond sales: Larson, *Jay Cooke,* chapter 17; Oberholtzer, *Jay Cooke,* vol. 2, chapter 16; Smalley, *History,* chapter 21; Harnsberger, *Jay Cooke and Minnesota,* pp. 125–27; "'Our' Railroad," *Helena Daily Herald,* April 29, 1871; and Oberholtzer, *Jay Cooke,* 2:230, 236.

28. "The Great North-West," *New York Times,* June 13, 1871; Pollard, *The Journal of Jay Cooke,* p. 235; Charles A. Dana, *Impressions: 125 Years* (Duluth: Duluth News Tribune Co., 1994), p. 9.

29. Oberholtzer, *Jay Cooke,* 2:230, 236 (Colfax), 2:308–10 (Knott).

30. Quotation: "The Yellowstone Expedition," *Helena Daily Herald,* September 26, 1870; *New York Times,* October 14, 1870. Also Haines, *The Yellowstone Story,* 1:107, 127–41; Kinsey, *Thomas Moran and the Surveying of the American West,* chapter 4; Schullery and Whittlesey, *Myth and History in the Creation of Yellowstone National Park,* chapter 5; Winks, *Frederick Billings,* pp. 285–86; Burlingame, *The Montana Frontier,* p. 319.

31. Haines, *The Yellowstone Story,* vol. 1, p. 105; "Northern Pacific" and "Editorial Correspondence," *Helena Daily Herald,* April 13 and May 26, 1871.

32. Larson, *Jay Cooke,* p. 345; "Converting U.S. 5-20's," *Harper's Weekly,* September 30, 1871; Smith to Cooke, February 9, 1871, NP, Secretary's Department; Oberholtzer, *Jay Cooke,* 2:234, 239; Smalley, *History,* p. 172.

33. "What Jay Cooke Thinks," *Duluth Minnesotian,* October 21, 1871.

34. Winks, *Frederick Billings,* p. 192; "Cooke," *Duluth Minnesotian,* September 2, 1871; Renz, *History,* p. 41. Sales dollars not stated by Harnsberger, Larson, or Oberholtzer. "Third Railroad . . . ," *New York Tribune,* June 6, 1871.

35. "The Northern Pacific, Jay Cooke's Views," *Brooklyn [or New York] Evening Mail,* February 3, 1871. See NP Clippings Scrapbooks, 1866–1904, Microfilm 522, Minnesota Historical Society, St. Paul.

36. "The Northern Pacific, Jay Cooke's Views"; Larson, *Jay Cooke,* pp. 346–47.

37. Pollard, *The Journal of Jay Cooke,* pp. 235–37; Cooke to Wilkeson, July 17, 1871, NP, Secretary's Department; "Mrs. Jay Cooke," *Philadelphia Public Ledger,* July 25, 1871; "Decease of Mrs. Cooke," *Philadelphia Inquirer,* July 24, 1871.

38. Quotation: Larson, *Jay Cooke,* pp. 356–58; Cooke to Wilkeson, September 20 and 30, 1871; NP, Secretary's Department.

CHAPTER 7. "STOP FIRING AT ME"

1. Smith to Roberts, June 20, 1871, NP, Secretary's Department.

2. Wilkeson to Roberts, May 10, 1871, Roberts Papers, Box 2, File 4; Roberts to Mrs. T. L. Rosser, September 1, 1873, Box 1.

3. Smith to Roberts, June 20, 1871, NP, Secretary's Department; and Thomas Canfield, *Partial Report to the Board of Directors,* p. 5.

4. Pollard, *The Journal of Jay Cooke,* p. 237; Roberts, "Surveys and Explorations," December 1871, p. 2, Roberts Papers, Series 6, Box 10; "Mechanics and Engineering . . . ," *Railroad Gazette,* August 5, 1871; quotation: "Serenade . . . ," *Helena Daily Herald,* July 22, 1871.

5. Roberts, "Surveys and Explorations," pp. 2–4; "Progress of Northern Pacific Surveys," *Duluth Minnesotian,* October 7, 1871; Hoxie, *Parading through History,* p. 99.

6. 2nd draft of Roberts autobiography (Roberts Papers, Box 1, File 4) and "Surveys and Explorations."

7. "Northern Pacific Surveying Party," *Helena Daily Herald,* August 1, 1871; Roberts to headquarters, July 20, 1871, and Cameron to Roberts, February 28, 1876, NP, Secretary's Department.

8. Roberts to his wife, November 11, 1871, p. 7; and Roberts, "Down the Valley of the Yellowstone," Roberts Papers, Box 10, File 5; Roberts to Flenniken, March 19, 1872, NP, Secretary's Department.

9. Roberts to NP New York headquarters, July 28, 1871, NP, Secretary's Department.

10. Ball, Report (untitled), December 10, 1871:; obituary, *Army and Navy Journal,* November 8, 1884; Ball-Story affair: Brown, *Plainsmen of the Yellowstone,* pp. 436–38.

11. Ball Report, p. 1.

12. Ibid., pp. 8–9; Barlow, *The Report of Major J. W. Barlow, Who Accompanied a Surveying Party of the Northern Pacific Railroad,* p. 42.

13. Ball Report, p. 2.

14. Annin, *They Gazed on the Beartooths,* 2:66–68.

15. United States Military Academy, *Annual Reunion of the Association of the Graduates,* June 12, 1885, pp. 58–63.

16. White, *Custer, Cavalry and Crows,* pp. 32–34; Annin, *They Gazed on the Beartooths,* 2:63–65.

17. Quotations: Roberts, "Down the Valley," p. 1; Roberts, "Field Diary of 1871 Reconnaissance" (hereafter cited as "Field Diary").

18. Barlow, *Report,* pp. 2, 42; Hoxie, *Parading through History,* pp. 12, 83–84; Roberts, "Field Diary" (November 5) and "Down the Valley," p. 2 (quotations); Roberts to his wife, November 11, 1871, p. 1.

19. Roberts, "Down the Valley," pp. 2, 4; "Field Diary," November 5, 1871.

20. For this paragraph and the following one: Roberts, "Field Diary," November 4 and 6 (quotations). While his father became a lieutenant general, Schofield never rose above a captain's rank. To Roberts, "cheap" meant inexpensive, not shoddy, as it is often used today.

21. Jerome: West Point sources; *New York Times* obituary, January 18, 1935; Jerome-Churchill biographies. (His brother was the district attorney who prosecuted Harry Thaw for murdering the architect Stanford White.) This and the following paragraphs: Roberts to his wife, November 12, 1871, pp. 5, 7; Roberts, "Field Diary" for November 11; Roberts, "Down the Valley," pp. 5–7.

22. Roberts, "Down the Valley," p. 7; Roberts to his wife, November 12, 1871, p. 2; Roberts, "Down the Yellowstone," p. 6.

23. Milk River agent A. J. Simmons to J. A. Vialle, December 5, 1871, Office of Indian Affairs, 1872 Letters Received, A88–U297, No. 234, Roll 492, courtesy Dave Eckroth; Bradley, *The March of the Montana Column,* p. 57; Roberts to his wife, November 12, 1871, p. 5. "Place of the Skulls" is the Rimrock area of Billings.

24. Roberts, "Field Diary," November 13, 1871; letter to his wife, November 14, 1871, p. 10.

25. This paragraph and the following one: Roberts to his wife, November 14, 1871, p. 10.

26. Roberts, "Field Diary," November 15, 1871.

27. "A Card, Northern Pacific Railroad," *Helena Daily Herald*, November 22, 1871.

28. Ball Report, p. 5. Tyler, from Maryland, was possibly related to President John Tyler.

29. Ball Report, p. 6. Ball states that he left Ellis "with Lt. McClernand and twenty-eight men."

30. "Arrival of Surveying Party" and "News from the Yellowstone," *Bozeman Avant Courier,* November 30, 1871. A late 1990s *USA Today* story about the Bozeman Pass notes: "As wind blows over the Rockies and down passes . . . it is squeezed into the valleys and speeds up."

31. "Arrival of Surveying Party" and "News from the Yellowstone"; Sergeant Page: Rodenbough, *The Army of the United States*, p. 182.

32. Ball Report; "Army" column, *Army and Navy Journal,* December 2, 1871; *Bozeman Avant Courier,* November 30, 1871; "Soldiers Frozen Badly," *Philadelphia Inquirer*, November 27.

33. Fifty-five years later, with the key participants long dead, Lt. Edward J. McClernand described the events in his memoir *On Time for Disaster: The Rescue of Custer's Command,* pp. 24–26. See the appendix of the present work for details. Capt. George L. Tyler to J. W. Flenniken, December 5, 1871, NP, Secretary's Department. One suspects that in the end the NP reimbursed the officers.

34. Roberts, "Surveys and Explorations," pp. 6–7, 20–21; Roberts, "The Yellowstone Valley: A Preliminary Report," pp. 2, 4, 7–8, 10–11.

35. $25,000: Hoxie, *Parading through History,* pp. 119–21.

CHAPTER 8. "THE ARMY OF THE GLENDIVE"

1. "Indians," *New York Times,* August 3, 1871; "Fort Rice Expedition," *Helena Daily Herald,* September 8, 1871; "Probability of an Indian War," *Sioux City Daily Journal,* August 26, 1871.

2. The 1871 Rosser letters to his wife, a diary, and a "field journal" are in Collection 1171, Small Special Collections Library, University of Virginia, Charlottesville; William D. Hoyt, ed., "Rosser's Journal: Northern Pacific Survey, September, 1871," *North Dakota Historical Quarterly* 10, no. 1 (1926); Rosser, letters to his wife, Collection 1171-g-h-j, Box 1, "1867–1873," diary, Box 2; Rosser, "*Across Dakota and Up the Yellowstone* (1871 report); Roberts Papers No. 783,

Series 6, Box 10, Burlingame Library, Montana State University–Bozeman. Hereafter "Rosser letters," "Rosser Diary," "Rosser Journal," and "Rosser Report." To reduce notes, the sources of quotations from these documents are given in the text.

3. E. C. Winnie to Daniel Linsley, September 11, 1871, NP, Secretary's Department.

4. Rosser Report, p. 4.

5. Slaughter, *Fortress to Farm,* pp. 49–50. There are factual errors in Slaughter's account, but the basic story appears true.

6. Stanley's "Middle" or "Dakota" district included 1,213 men at Forts Randall, Rice, Stevenson, and Sully and the Cheyenne River, Grand River, Lower Brulé, and Whetstone Indian Agencies; U.S. Department of War, *Annual Report, 1871,* pp. 25–26.

7. Rosser Report, p. 7; and Rosser Diary, September 8, 1871.

8. Whistler: West Point data; *NCAB,* 9:48; *New York Times* obituary, April 22, 1899. De Trobriand, *Military Life in Dakota,* pp. 49, 52–53, 270, 328; Microfilm "Records of the War Dept., U.S. Army Commands, Whistler's Report of the Yellowstone Expedition," 751 MDM 1871, National Archives (1953); hereafter cited as "Whistler Report."

9. Inman: *DAB* and *NCAB* (9:247). Some of his father's paintings are on permanent exhibit at the Buffalo Bill museum, Cody, Wyoming; court-martial: untitled section, *Army and Navy Journal,* February 25, 1871; Inman's popularity: "The Yellowstone Expedition," *St. Paul Weekly Press,* November 9, 1871.

10. Irvine diaries, letters to his wife, and biographical materials are held by the South Dakota State Historical Society, Pierre. These is no reference or collection number.

11. Campbell, 1871 Diary.

12. Irvine letters, September 8, 1871. Dorman was wounded near the Hunkpapa camp, where he was known. For the rather unpleasant details, see Connell, *Son of the Morning Star,* pp. 25–28.

13. DeLand, "Basil Clement (Claymore)"; Stanley to Hancock, September 21, 1871, NP, Secretary's Department.

14. Hancock: U.S. Department of War, *Annual Report, 1871,* p. 27; Whistler Report, pp. 1–4; "The Army," *Army and Navy Journal,* August 26, 1871; "Northern Pacific," *Railroad Gazette,* September 2, 1871; "Yellowstone . . . ," *Sioux City Journal,* October 31; some 535 men: 7 companies at 45 each; 125 teamsters and cooks, 25 or 26 Indian scouts; Rosser Report, p. 2; 40–50 others: Whistler Report, staff, physicians, Gatling gun crews, scouts, quartermasters, and beef-herders. Whistler's report does not state the caliber of the Gatling guns.

15. The number of horses and mules is based on a *minimum* of 4 mules for each of the 122 wagons (488) and 75 to 100 horses for the scouts, officers, Gatling guns, surveyors, and others. If the 55 civilian-owned wagons had 6-mule teams, as is likely, the number jumps to over 670.

16. This paragraph and the following paragraphs are from the Campbell Diary, September 7, 1871; Irvine letters and Diary, September 6–10, 1871; and Rosser Diary (September 6–10, 1871) and Report, p. 8.

17. The sources cited in note 16 and "Yellowstone Expedition," *Sioux City Daily Journal,* October 31, 1871.

18. Rosser Report, pp. 8–9; Whistler Report, September 11, 1871; Rosser Diary, September 12, 1871.

19. Jordan, "The Yellowstone Expedition of 1871"; Patterson, "A Short Account of the Preliminary Survey of the Northern Pacific Railroad in 1871."

20. Campbell Diary, September 12, 1871.

21. This paragraph and remainder of this section: Rosser Diary and Journal, Irvine Diary, and Whistler Report, September 14–17, 1871; Irvine Diary, September 22–23, 1871.

22. "Yellowstone Expedition," *Sioux City Daily Journal*, September 21, 1871. Sioux City, with a railroad to Chicago, then dominated Upper Missouri trade and travel.

23. "Washington News," *Philadelphia Inquirer*, September 23, 1871; the *Herald*'s letter was reprinted in the *St. Paul Weekly Press*, October 5, 1871, as "Hostile Sioux."

24. "Indian Country: War on the Northern Pacific," *Minnesota Tribune*, September 30, 1871.

25. Rosser Journal, Irvine Diary, and Whistler Report, September 24, 1871.

26. Rosser report, p. 10. In 1880 NP track followed a stream a few miles north, Railroad Creek.

27. Irvine Diary, September 25, 1871; Whistler Report, p. 22.

28. Irvine Diary, September 28, 1871. Irvine has no quotation or punctuation marks in his depiction of the incident.

29. Rosser's Journal ends on September 26, 1871. His only September 30, October 1, and October 2 diary entry is "sick." Beaver Creek was also called the North Fork of the Little Missouri and Inman's Fork. Irvine Diary, October 3, 1871.

30. This paragraph and the remainder of this section: Whistler Report, October 1, 1871; Irvine Diary (and other diaries), October 3–4, 1871, and October 17, 1871, letter; Campbell Diary; Rosser Diary and Report, pp. 11–12; Jordan, "The Yellowstone Expedition of 1871"; Jordan, "The Yellowstone Expedition of 1871"; and Patterson, "A Short Account." For Bates, see the *DAB*.

31. "Surveying Party," *St. Paul Daily Pioneer*, October 15, 1871; "Expedition to the Yellowstone" and "Yellowstone Expedition Returning," *Sioux City Daily Journal*, October 7 and 8, 1871.

32. Irvine Diary, October 4 and 5, 1871.

33. Campbell Diary and Irvine Diary, October 12, 1871.

34. Rosser Diary and Irvine Diary, October 14, 1871.

35. Linda Slaughter incorrectly remembered that "a hop was given that night in honor of the engineers" (*Fortress to Farm,* p. 52) but correctly recalled the infantry company that escorted Rosser as well as their return to Fort Rice *after* Whistler.

36. "Yellowstone Expedition," *Sioux City Daily Journal*, October 31, 1871; "Yellowstone Expedition," *St. Paul Weekly Press*, November 9, 1871; quotation: Irvine letter, October 17, 1871.

37. Sitting Bull: Utley, *Lance and the Shield,* pp. 106–107; quotation: Jordan, "The Yellowstone Expedition of 1871"; Patterson, "A Short Account."

CHAPTER 9. "THE FEAR OF RED SKINS"

1. Stanley's 1872 report was not published until 1956; Stanley Report, p. 24; quotation: Slaughter, *Fortress to Farm*, p. 66.

2. "Indian War Brewing," *St. Paul Weekly Pioneer*, April 26, 1872; Stanley to Rosser, April 4, 1872, NP, Secretary's Department.

3. "Military Division of the Missouri," *Army and Navy Journal,* June 1, 1872; "Indian Affairs," *New York Tribune*, July 2, 1872.

4. Stanley, *Personal Memoirs,* p. 16; obituary, U.S. Military Academy, *Annual Reunion of the Association of the Graduates* (West Point, June 10, 1903), pp. 48–73; West-Stanley-Wright Papers, U.S. Army Military History Institute, Carlisle, Pa.; Wright profile in *DAB.*

5. Stanley, *Personal Memoirs,* pp. 16–17, 25; obituary, pp. 55–56; McKinney, *Education in Violence,* p. 479.

6. The Indian: Stanley, *Personal Memoirs*, pp. 52–53; anti-Semitism: "the day before, the troops had been paid and a big Jew firm [that] was taking in money very fast," p. 153; offer: p. 62.

7. Stanley in combat: Peter Cozzens, *The Darkest Days of the War: The Battles of Iuka and Corinth* (Chapel Hill: University of North Carolina Press, 1997); Welsh, *Medical Histories of Union Generals,* pp. 317–18.

8. Castel, *Decision in the West,* pp. 163–66. Stanley, with Thomas's strong support, became a corps commander following John McPherson's death on July 22.

9. Ibid., pp. 570–71 (appendix C); Stanley B. Hirshson, *The White Tecumseh: A Biography of General William T. Sherman* (New York: John Wiley and Sons, 1997), pp. 239, 250; spat with Sherman: Stanley, *Personal Memoirs,* p. 183; Sherman comment: Lloyd Lewis, *Sherman: Fighting Profit* (1932; reprint, Lincoln: University of Nebraska Press, 1993), p. 407.

10. Stanley, *Personal Memoirs*, p. 195; Fletcher Pratt, *Ordeal by Fire: An Informal History of the Civil War,* p. 419.

11. In *Personal Memoirs,* p. 203, Stanley paraphrases Adam Badeau's *Life of Grant.*

12. Carroll, *Custer in Texas,* p. 76.

13. Stephen R. Riggs, *Mary and I: Forty Years with the Sioux* (Chicago: W. H. Holmes, 1880), p. 299; Duffy and Pender: Irvine Diary, November 15–16, 1870; "A History of Fort Sully," *South Dakota Historical Collections* 26 (1952): 258–59 (author unknown).

14. Cavalry request: Robertson, "'We Are Going to Have a Big Sioux War,'" p. 9; Rosser, "The Death of Adair," pp. 2–3; escort size: Stanley report, pp. 1–5; Agard lived in Dakota for 30 years and spoke Sioux.

15. Wagons: Stanley Report, p. 5; Reynolds: Gray, "On the Trail of 'Lonesome Charley' Reynolds"; George B. Grinnell, "Recollections of Charley Reynolds," *New York Posse Brand Book* 3, no. 3 (1956); John Remsburg and George Remsburg, *Charley Reynolds: Soldier, Hunter, Scout and Guide* (1931; reprint, Mattituck, N.Y.: J. M. Carroll Co., 1978).

16. Wallen: Thrapp, *Encyclopedia of Frontier Biography*, West Point sources; "Eighth Infantry," *Sioux City Daily Journal,* July 10, 1872.

17.   Perret, *Ulysses S. Grant,* p. 83. The connection between the two incidents and "sly" are the author's inference, not Perret's. But Grant could never give Wallen's *family* a bad posting; their wives were best friends and schoolmates, and Mrs. Wallen was a Julia Grant bridesmaid. Wallen file, Archives—Special Collections, West Point, N.Y.

18.   See the epilogue for details.

19.   Brush, Sr.: *NCAB,* 11:460; Brush, Jr.: Thrapp, *Encyclopedia of Frontier Biography* (vol. 4) and standard West Point sources.

20.   Linsley profile: *NCAB,* 16:233.

21.   Meigs letters: first letter not dated, but April 1872; second letter July 11.

22.   Bismarck's letter: Northern Pacific "Minute" book, Minnesota Historical Society, St. Paul.

23.   Rather than make the guard company march the next day, Stanley normally let them ride in the wagons; Jordan, "Account," pp. 6–7. Jordan's "two months" is incorrect.

24.   Brown, *Bury My Heart at Wounded Knee,* p. 132; Crofton: letter on returning from the 1873 survey (October 28), Crofton-Shubrick Papers, Collection No. 1325, Hagley Museum and Library, Wilmington, Del.

25.   Quotation: Rosser Diary, Rosser Papers, Collection 1171-d-e-f, Box 2; hunger: Stanley Report, pp. 24–25. Indians added cactus to alkaline water to absorb the chemicals, something that most soldiers would not do.

26.   Cotter, *How the Northern Pacific Groped Its Way West,* p. 4.

27.   Northern Pacific Railroad, "Journal of N.P.R.R. Surveying Expedition from Missouri River to Powder River," Surveyors Records 137.K.13.3 (B) and also file 2703-12-149, both at the Minnesota Historical Society, St. Paul; August 9 and 13, 1872. Hereafter referred to as Surveyors' Journal.

28.   Baker-Yellowstone area: Raban, *Bad Land.*

29.   "Surveying Expedition to the Yellowstone," *Red River Star,* July 27, 1872; "Dakota Letter from Chief Engineer Roberts," *Philadelphia Inquirer,* August 6, 1872.

30.   Gall likely knew of the Sitting Bull/Baker fight (chapter 10), thus freeing him to attack. Stanley Report, p. 7; Rosser, "Death of Adair," p. 8; Surveyors' Journal, August 16, 1872; Shields, "Reminiscences of a Railroad Builder," p. 4.

31.   Betty Rosser Diary, Rosser Papers, 1171-g-h-j, Box 11. A photo of the dead infant survives.

32.   "Among the Reds," *Sioux City Daily Journal,* September 27, 1872.

33.   Ibid.; Elizabeth Custer, in Doane Robinson, "A History of the Dakota or Sioux Indians . . . ," *South Dakota History Collections* 1 (1902): 154. Some sources give Gall's birth as 1848, but this appears unlikely.

34.   Eastman, *Indian Heroes and Great Chieftains,* pp. 78–79; Innis, *Bloody Knife,* p. 22.

35.   Eastman, *Indian Heroes,* p. 3; Mangum, "Gall," p. 29; Praus, *The Sioux;* Vestal, *New Sources of Indian History,* pp. 221–24.

36. Bozeman Trail: Robinson, *A History of the Dakota,* p. 360; speech: Blackburn, *History of North and South Dakota*, pp. 151–52; quotation: W. C. Vanderwerth, *Indian Oratory: Famous Speeches by Noted Indian Chieftains* (Norman: University of Oklahoma Press, 1973), p. 184; wounds: Blackburn, *History of North and South Dakota,* p. 151.

37. Rosser, "Death of Adair," pp. 10–11; Bushong and Bushong, *Fightin' Tom Rosser,* p. 191, n. 15. Anecdotal accounts speak to stakes still being in place in the late 1870s.

38. Today three bridges cross the Powder River at this point: the old highway bridge, Interstate I-94, and a railroad bridge. Surveyors' Journal, August 18; Rosser, "Death of Adair," pp. 10–11; Stanley Report, p. 7; and Jordan, "Account of Edward C. Jordan's Experiences," p. 7.

39. Stanley Report, pp. 7–8; Davis, Journal; Davis profile: *NCAB,* 16:299.

40. Surveyor's Journal, August 18, 1872. Rosser, "Death of Adair," pp. 12–13. In a footnote (p. 13) that helps date "Death of Adair," Rosser states that Davis was the NP's passenger agent, a job he left in 1895.

41. Davis, Journal. There are numerous contemporary references to Gall as "The Gaul."

42. Rosser, "Death of Adair," pp. 13–14. In "Among the Reds," *Sioux City Journal*, September 27, 1872, the fighting is described as after, not before, Gall and Stanley met. Rosser's memory of Gall in a stovepipe hat is likely incorrect, a minor error after two decades.

43. Stanley Report, p. 8; Rosser, "Death of Adair," p. 14 (Rosser's emphasis). The Powder's width is an estimate; there is no way of telling how wide it was in August 1872.

44. Jordan, "Account," p. 7; Gall quotation: Rosser, "Death of Adair," p. 14; Stanley on Gall and Indian wounded: Stanley Report, p. 8; Ray quotation: "Among the Reds"; Davis, Journal. Rosser states that the Indians fired *after* Stanley withdrew: "Death of Adair," p. 15.

Chapter 10. The "Battle of Poker Flat"

1. Much of this chapter reflects the help of David Eckroth of Billings, Montana, who walked the author over the Pryor Creek battle site and shared numerous documents. U.S. Department of War, *The War of the Rebellion,* series 1, vol. 30, part 4, p. 489, and *Supplement to the Official Records,* part 2, vol. 67, serial no. 79, p. 574. For Haydon, the author is appreciative of the research of Paul M. Baltay of Arlington, Va.

2. Flenniken Letterpress book, 134.L.14.1 (B), Box 1, August 23 and September 9, 1872, Minnesota Historical Society, St. Paul. Flenniken indicates that he had made copies of a preliminary report.

3. Barlow, *Report.*

4. "Northern Pacific," *Railroad Gazette,* June 8 and September 7, 1872; Roberts to Flenniken, May 30, June 5 and 28, 1872, NP, Secretary's Department.

5. Roberts to Flenniken, June 5 and 28, NP, Secretary's Department.

6. Baker's *Report* states 369 men but is otherwise useless; see Barlow, *Report*, p. 2.; animals: over 200 for all cavalry and infantry officers, 65 six-mule wagons (390), other army and surveyor ambulances and wagons, horses for some surveyors, scouts, wolfers, and prospectors, and some 100 head of beef. "Our Military Defenses," *Bozeman Avant Courier,* July 30, 1872.

7. Barlow, *Report*, p. 2.

8. Ponsford, "Reminiscences," dated by Ponsford November 16, 1910; Gray, *Custer's Last Campaign,* p. 32.

9. Barlow quotations in this paragraph and the following paragraphs: Barlow, *Report*, pp. 4–6.

10. Barlow, *Report,* pp. 6–7; Bradley, *March of the Montana Column,* p. 57; Bradley not being on the survey: Brown, *Plainsmen of the Yellowstone*, p. 201.

11. Robinson, *History of the Dakota,* pp. 400–403; "Military Division of the Missouri," *Army and Navy Journal,* June 1, 1872; "Indian Wars, 1855–1875" file, Montana Room, Billings Public Library. These paragraphs follow Utley's *Lance and the Shield* outline, pp. 106–107. Vestal's account (*Sitting Bull*, p. 126) is too geographically convoluted to be plausible.

12. "Lower River Indian Affairs," *Helena Daily Herald,* January 11, 1873; Bradley, *March of the Montana Column*, pp. 56–57; Utley, *Lance and the Shield,* pp. 107–108.

13. Is Bradley (*March of the Montana Column*, pp. 56–62, 129) accurate? He was not at Pryor's Creek but was close to officers who were. Bradley was killed (1877 Nez Percé campaign) before he could edit his manuscript. Thus the candid, harsh language concerning Baker was likely written for his own enjoyment—something writers like to do. On the location: nobody wants to sleep downwind of 700 horses, mules, and cattle, so it is safe to assume that the animals were on the camp's northeastern side.

14. Ponsford, "Reminiscences," p. 2; McClernand, *On Time for Disaster*, pp. 28–29; and Bradley, *March of the Montana Column*, p. 60 (quotations here and in the next paragraph). Bradley, Ponsford, and Rodenbough (*Army of the United States,* p. 505) all say that Rawn commanded four companies. Barlow writes: "Capt. Bacon's battalion of infantry" (Report, p. 7), but the 1872 and 1873 *Army Register* shows no such officer with either regiment.

15. Marquis (as told by Leforge), *Memoirs of a White Crow Indian,* p. 83.

16. Barlow, *Report,* p. 7.

17. Utley, *Lance and the Shield*, pp. 107–10; quotation: Vestal, *Sitting Bull*, pp. 125–31.

18. See Sandoz, *Crazy Horse,* pp. 270–72; Bradley, *March of the Montana Column,* p. 62.

19. Barlow, *Report,* p. 7.

20. Gibbon to A. A. G., Maj. O. D. Greene, Department of Dakota, August 19, 1872, National Archives Record Group 393, Letters Received 2940.

21. Haydon dispatch, in ibid.; Hancock to Smith, August 23, 1872, and Smith to Hancock, August 27, 1872, both National Archives Record Group 393, Letters Received 2763.

22. "Local News," *Helena Daily Herald,* August 20, 1872; and "The Indian War," *Bozeman Avant Courier,* August 22, 1872.

23. Barlow, *Report,* p. 9; Schneider, *Montana's Yellowstone River,* charts on pp. 35 and 54.

24. Barlow, *Report,* pp. 8–10, is the primary source for the decision to turn back. Others include Bradley, *March of the Montana Column;* McClernand, *On Time for Disaster;* and contemporary newspaper accounts.

25. Barlow, *Report,* pp. 9–10 ("Colonel" was a courtesy title); Flenniken to Roberts, August 23, NP Letterpress book, Minnesota Historical Society, St. Paul.

26. McClernand, *On Time for Disaster,* pp. 30–31; Bradley, *March of the Montana Column,* p. 63; "Abandoned," *Bozeman Avant Courier,* September 5, 1872.

27. This paragraph and the previous paragraph and quotation: Barlow, *Report,* pp. 12–14.

28. "Gallatin County Items," *Helena Daily Herald*, September 13, 1872; Barlow, *Report,* p. 15. That the rider's story was shot through with discrepancies apparently bothered no one.

29. "A Brush with Indians," *New York Times*, September 30, 1872.

30. McClernand's story (*On Time for Disaster,* p. 31) has many elements similar to his 1871 fabrication.

31. "Washington Intelligence" and "Yellowstone Survey," *Helena Daily Herald*, September 11 and 25, 1872.

32. Barlow, *Report,* pp. 17–18.

33. September 10, 1872, stories: "Another Indian War," *New York Herald.* "Savages on the War-path," *New York Tribune;* "The Hostile Savages," *New York Times;* and "An Indian War," *Minnesota Tribune;* "Railroad Connection," *Helena Daily Herald,* September 9, 1872; "Indian Attack on Northern Pacific Surveying Party," *Sioux City Daily Journal,* September 7, 1872. Sheridan was in Dakota on September 9.

34. Among many September 11, 1872, papers: *Philadelphia Inquirer* and *Chicago Inter-Ocean;* also "Military Division of the Missouri," *Army and Navy Journal*, September 14, 1872.

35. "Lower River Indians," *Helena Daily Herald*, January 11, 1873.

36. Baker: "Local News" and editorial, *Helena Daily Herald*, January 6 and 13, 1873.

CHAPTER 11. "FALSTAFF'S RAGAMUFFINS"

1. Rosser Diary and Betty Rosser Diary, August 19, 1872.

2. W. A. Graham, *The Custer Myth: A Source Book of Custeriana* (1953; reprint, Machanicsburg, Pa.: Stackpole Books, 1995), pp. 99–100; Shirley L. Leckie, *Elizabeth Bacon Custer and the Making of a Myth* (Norman: University of Oklahoma Press, 1993), pp. 190–91; Stephen E. Ambrose, *Citizen Soldiers: The U.S. Army from the Normandy Beaches to the Bulge to the Surrender of Germany, June 7, 1944–May 7, 1945* (New York: Simon and Schuster, 1997), p. 355.

3. "Northern Pacific–Dakota Division," unsigned remembrance, ca. 1906, Rosser Papers, 1171-g-h-j, Box 12, "Miscellaneous Writings," pp. 4–5.

4. Surveyors' Journal, August 23, 1872; Robertson, "'We Are Going to Have a Big Sioux War,'" p. 12; Clarence E. Bennett Papers, MS 39, Mansfield Library, University of Montana, Missoula; Sitting Bull: "The Great North-West . . . Kellogg's Expedition," *Bozeman Avant Courier*, November 7, 1872.

5. Rosser, "Death of Adair," pp. 16–18 (Rosser's emphasis). Stanley's infantry mostly had "two-banded breech-loading rifled muskets" (Stanley Report, p. 25); some had Spencer carbines, but half this ammunition did not fire.

6. The site, on private property, was discovered in 2001 by David Eckroth of Billings and John Hawkins of Bozeman. The site's owner and Mr. Eckroth were kind enough to walk the

author over it on July 5, 2002. Utley (*Lance and the Shield,* p. 111) believes that Sitting Bull was with Gall in early October, but Vestal (*Sitting Bull,* pp. 130–31) does not. NP sources do not mention Sitting Bull, and the author has not included him in depicting the events of October 3–4.

7. "Yellowstone Expedition," *Sioux City Daily Journal,* October 19, 1872. The real name of Swipes is unknown.

8. Rosser, "Death of Adair," p. 19.

9. NP Journal, August 25, 1872, Minnesota Historical Society, St. Paul. The message went from Sheridan to Hancock to Rice's commandant, Thomas L. Crittenden, on August 19. The author has a photocopy of the telegram but not a citation.

10. Rosser Diary, September 1; Stanley Report, pp. 10 and 22; "Stanley . . . ," *Minneapolis Tribune,* September 7, 1872.

11. Sheridan's stop at Fort Sully is in "Dakota," *Sioux City Daily Journal,* September 18, 1872; baby story from Stanley's daughter: Rumbough, "'The Regular Army O!'" (the name of an army song). One wonders if Stanley's wife, brought up in the army, might not have had a little something to do with Josephine's response. Trivia: "The Regular Army O!" is sung in the middle third of John Ford's film *Fort Apache.*

12. Stanley Report, p. 24; Swipes, "Yellowstone Expedition," *Sioux City Daily Journal,* October 19 and 26, 1872. Swipes was well known. A November 11 *Yankton Herald* story by "Dolly V. Arden" (the Dolly Varden was a famous gold mine of that era) says that "everybody enjoyed themselves hugely, Nibsey Swipes . . . notwithstanding."

13. This paragraph and the following one: Rosser Diary, September 21–25, 1872; "Yellowstone Expedition" (October 19, 1872); Surveyors' Journal.

14. Indian chase: Stanley Report, pp. 11–12; Robertson, "'We Are Going to Have a Big Sioux War,'" p. 13.

15. James H. Mundy; *No Rich Man's Sons: The Sixth Maine Volunteer Infantry* (Cape Elizabeth, Maine: Harp Publications, 1994), p. 261; Stanley Report, p. 12; "Fort McKeen," *Army and Navy Journal,* November 2, 1872.

16. Slaughter, *Fortress to Farm,* p. 67; Robertson, "'We Are Going to Have a Big Sioux War,'" pp. 13–14; "Yellowstone: Interesting News from General Stanley Expedition," *Sioux City Daily Journal,* October 26, 1872; Vestal, *Sitting Bull,* p. 131. Vestal interviewed a number of the surviving Hunkpapas in the 1920s.

17. Surveyors' Journal, October 4, 1872, Minnesota Historical Society, St. Paul.

18. In "Death of Adair," pp. 19–20, Rosser notes: "As I rode leisurely along, I observed the heads of men just over a little 'swell' to my left and front, which I took at once to be [Stanley's] pickets . . . I rode on giving myself no concern about them." Jordan ("Account," p. 8) knew what Rosser was thinking because he had visited him about 1900. The two undoubtedly talked about the incident: there are numerous similarities (including errors) in both accounts.

19. Rosser, "Death of Adair," p. 25; Stanley Report, pp. 13–14.

20. "Yellowstone: Interesting News"; Bertram Adler, "Old Timer Tales—No. 4," *Railroad Man's Magazine,* ca. 1920s; Stanley Report, pp. 13–14. The exact location of the Heart River crossing is unknown.

21.   Rosser to Linsley, October 10, 1872, 134.L.13.8 (F), Minnesota Historical Society, St. Paul. Linsley resigned shortly after Smith left. Rosser's letter was a report, so it was filed and not forwarded. Considering the disarray that the NP was in that fall, it is amazing that the letter even survived.

22.   Here Rosser switches from 8-by-10-inch paper to a 10-by-16-inch sheet, replacing pages 6 and 7; this suggests that he removed and rewrote something of a highly personal nature after completing the letter.

23.   Jordan, "Account," p. 9.

24.   "Northern Pacific," *New York Herald*, October 11, 1872. The adjacent column described a baseball game between the Philadelphia Athletics (11) and Boston Red Stockings (3), played before 1,800 fans.

25.   Quotation: Surveyors' Journal, October 14, 1872; "Indians Fighting," *Minneapolis Tribune*, October 10, 1872; Irvine to his wife, October 5, 1872; Jordan, "Account," pp. 9–10.

26.   Irvine to his wife, October 17, 1872.

27.   "Two Battles with Sioux," *New York Herald*, October 28, 1872.

28.   Robertson, "'We Are Going to Have a Big Sioux War,'" p. 10; Stanley Report, pp. 24–27.

29.   "Indian Policy of the President," *Philadelphia Inquirer*, October 20, 1872.

30.   Quotation: undated and untitled, Rosser Papers, 1171-g-h-j, Box 12, "Misc. writings," p. 6.

CHAPTER 12. "20,000 HOSTILE INDIANS"

1.   "Northern Pacific Contracts in Pennsylvania," *Helena Daily Herald*, January 30, 1872. In a testament to the unnecessary expenditure, at least 24 of the locomotives were sold in 1874–75.

2.   "A Ramble over the Northern Pacific," *Minneapolis Tribune*, July 17, 1872; the *Brainerd Tribune* story was reprinted in "Northern Pacific Headquarters at Brainerd," *St. Paul Weekly Pioneer*, October 4, 1872.

3.   Steamship issues: "Reduction in Fares," *Minneapolis Tribune*, June 12, 1872; rolling mill: "Vermont Central," *Railroad Gazette*, August 17, 1872.

4.   Larson, *Jay Cooke*, pp. 349–51 and 375–76 (including Roberts to Cooke, June 3, 1872).

5.   Cooke to Barney, March 8, 1872, in Larson, *Jay Cooke*, p. 373; February 26, 1872: Oberholtzer, *Jay Cooke*, 2:224; Barney to Smith, July 22, 1872, in Larson, *Jay Cooke*, p. 375; Cooke to Smith, April 25, 1872, in Harnsberger, *Jay Cooke and Minnesota*, p. 138–39; "Dakota . . . a Prairie Steam Wagon," *Minneapolis Tribune*, September 15, 1872.

6.   Larson, *Jay Cooke*, pp. 375–78; Riegel, *The Story of the Western Railroads*, p. 122; executive committee: Larson, *Jay Cooke*, p. 387; Smalley, *Northern Pacific Railroad Book of Reference*, pp. 88–89. The NP's vice president was an ex-officio member of the committee.

7. Overdrafts: Larson, *Jay Cooke*, p. 374; "Retirement," *Brainerd Tribune*, February 24, 1872; voting Smith out: Oberholtzer, *Jay Cooke*, 2: 326; Smalley, *Northern Pacific Railroad Book of Reference*, p. 94.

8. Oberholtzer (*Jay Cooke*, 2:327) does not identify the source of Smith's "coming down"; Harnsberger, *Jay Cooke and Minnesota*, p. 141; Smalley, *Northern Pacific Railroad Book of Reference*, p. 95.

9. Brace, "The New North-West," *New York Times*, August 6, 1873; Harnsberger, *Jay Cooke and Minnesota*, pp. 89–90; Larson, *Jay Cooke*, p. 369. This paragraph and the following paragraph draw heavily from Englehardt, "The Incorporation of America," pp. 27–31 (quotation on p. 27).

10. "Up-River Notes," *Sioux City Journal*, September 7, 1872; and Oberholtzer, *Jay Cooke*, 2:231–32.

11. Harnsberger, *Jay Cooke and Minnesota*, pp. 250–51.

12. Smith to Cooke, September 30, 1871; Harnsberger, *Jay Cooke and Minnesota*, p. 259.

13. Cooke to Billings, April 27, 1872, in Oberholtzer, *Jay Cooke*, 2:325.

14. "Red River of the North," *Red River Star*, July 27, 1872; Oberholtzer, *Jay Cooke*, 2:305–306.

15. This paragraph and the next one: Henry to Jay Cooke, October 8, 1872, in Oberholtzer, *Jay Cooke*, 2:306–307; "Northern Pacific Report of the Examiners," *Philadelphia Inquirer*, December 12, 1872; Hedges, "Colonization Work," p. 321.

16. "The Sink," *Brainerd Tribune*, May 18, 1872; "Northern Pacific," *Minneapolis Tribune*, August 11, 1872; Rosser to Linsley, May 31, 1872, 134.L.13.8 (F), Minnesota Historical Society, St. Paul.

17. "Personal," *Railroad Gazette*, April 20, 1872; "Northern Pacific Steamboat Dock at Duluth," *St. Paul Weekly Pioneer*, June 28, 1872; "Northern Pacific Notes," *Minneapolis Tribune*, June 12, 1872.

18. Rosser to Linsley, June 3, 1872, 134.L.13.8 (F), Minnesota Historical Society, St. Paul; "Northern Pacific," *Sioux City Daily Journal*, July 19, 1872; "Northern Pacific," *Railroad Gazette*, August 3 and September 7, 1872.

19. "Facts regarding the Northern Pacific," *Brainerd Tribune*, November 23, 1872; track: Renz, *History*, p. 39; "From the Northern Pacific," *St. Paul Weekly Pioneer*, October 18, 1872; "Northern Pacific," *Philadelphia Inquirer*, October 21, 1872.

20. "Northern Pacific," *Minneapolis Tribune*, November 14, 1872; *Sioux City Daily Journal*, December 14, 1872; "Facts Regarding the Northern Pacific," *Brainerd Tribune*, November 23, 1872.

21. Meigs, "Letters," December 1872; "Northern Pacific," *Railroad Gazette*, January 11, 1873; Linsley to Cass, October 30, 1872, NP, Secretary's Department; "Dakota," *New York Times*, December 16, 1872.

22. Quotation: Larson, *Jay Cooke*, p. 362; Crédit Mobilier: Oberholtzer, *A History of the United States since the Civil War*, 2:545.

23. Oberholtzer, *Jay Cooke,* 2:322–23; Larson, *Jay Cooke,* p. 364; "Northern Pacific, Favorable . . . ," *New York Times,* June 13, 1872; and "How a Committee May Make a Report without Knowing It," *New York Herald,* June 22, 1872; quotation: "Northern Pacific," *Railroad Gazette,* February 17, 1872; detailed editorial ("Congress and the Northern Pacific") in the *Railroad Gazette,* August 3, 1872.

24. Harnsberger, *Jay Cooke and Minnesota,* pp. 313–17; Larson, *Jay Cooke,* pp. 369–70; "Saint Paul & Pacific," *Railroad Gazette,* June 1, October 12, and December 14, 1872. The sale of track could explain the NP's failure to reach Bismarck.

25. *Railroad Gazette,* April 6, June 15, and September 7, 1872; *Helena Daily Herald,* June 18 and 28, September 9, October 17, 1872.

26. "Sioux City and St. Paul," *Sioux City Daily Journal,* September 26 and 29, 1872; "Canada Pacific," *Railway Gazette,* June 22, 1872; two *Gazette* stories (October 12) state both 269 and 272 miles; Larson, *Jay Cooke,* pp. 365–71.

27. Larson, *Jay Cooke,* pp. 359–61.

28. "The Northwest," *New York Herald,* September 9, 1872; Smalley, *Northern Pacific Railroad Book of Reference,* p. 87; *New York Times,* December 16, 1872.

29. Johns, *Duluth,* p. 24; Renz, *History,* p. 38.

30. "Hostile Savages," *New York Times,* September 10, 1872 (a national wire service story); "Reported Failure of Yellowstone Expedition," *Chicago Inter-Ocean,* September 11, 1872 (also a wire service story); "What Is to Be Done with the Indians," editorial, *New York Herald,* September 12, 1872.

31. "Indian Raid on Northern Pacific Post," *New York Times,* November 11, 1872; "Killed by the Sioux," *St. Paul Weekly Press,* November 29, 1872; "From the Missouri," *St. Paul Weekly Pioneer,* December 6, 1872.

32. Smalley, *Northern Pacific Railroad Book of Reference,* p. 96, and *History of the Northern Pacific Railroad,* p. 188.

33. Quotation: "St. Paul & Pacific," *Railroad Gazette,* October 19, 1872; "The Northern Pacific," *Minneapolis Tribune,* November 19, 1872,; Oberholtzer, *Jay Cooke,* 2:392.

34. "The Vermont Central Railroad," *New York Herald,* September 22, 1872; "The Vermont Central Railroad and Its Troubles," *Railroad Gazette,* September 28, 1872; Dimock's suicide: "Personal," *Railroad Gazette,* November 9, 1872; follow-up articles appeared in the *New York Herald* on October 3, 1872 ("The Vermont Central Railroad"), and in the *Railroad Gazette,* October 19, October 26, and December 21, 1872 (all titled "Vermont Central").

35. Morgan's first love was the Metropolitan; Fahnestock was a trustee for decades and its treasurer from 1901 to 1914. Fahnestock to Cooke, June 8, 1872, Oberholtzer, *Jay Cooke,* 2:381–83.

36. Oberholtzer, *Jay Cooke,* 2:381; for "croak," see *The New Oxford American Dictionary* (2001).

37. Moorhead and Cooke: Harnsberger, *Jay Cooke and Minnesota,* p. 143; Drexel and McCulloch: Oberholtzer, *Jay Cooke,* 2:383–87.

38. Oberholtzer, *Jay Cooke,* 2:355; Larson, *Jay Cooke,* pp. 304, 420, and 497, n. 27; French: *NCAB,* 2:345.

39. Larson, *Jay Cooke,* p. 386; and Oberholtzer, *Jay Cooke,* 2:389.

40. "Washington News," *New York Times,* January 13, 1873; teeth: Oberholtzer, *Jay Cooke,* 2:358–59.

41. Oberholtzer, *Jay Cooke,* 2:352–58; 5 percent is the author's estimate; there are no hard figures for 1872.

CHAPTER 13. "LOOKS LIKE WAR!"

1. Sheridan to Cass, January 27, 1873, NP, Secretary's Department.

2. Rosser to Roberts, February 23, 1873, NP, Secretary's Department.

3. Sheridan to Cass, February 24, 1873, Folder SC-1889, Montana Historical Society, Helena. The handwriting is so sloppy that Sheridan likely wrote it himself.

4. David Nevin, *The Old West: The Soldiers* (New York: Time-Life Books, 1975), p. 181.

5. Wert, *Custer,* pp. 22–25. Custer clearly had many of the symptoms associated with Attention Deficit Hyperactivity Disorder. A study along these lines would be welcome.

6. See Longacre, *Custer and His Wolverines,* chapter 7; casualty figures for three of Custer's regiments: Fox, *Regimental Losses,* pp. 376–78; quotation: Wert, *Custer,* p. 110.

7. This paragraph draws from Wert, *Custer,* chapter 9: Libbie's letters to George Custer, p. 165; Rosser quotation: S. Roger Keller, ed., *Riding with Rosser* (Shippensburg, Penn.: White Mane Publishing, 1997), p. 47.

8. Quotation: Wert, *Custer,* pp. 224–26; Longacre, *The Cavalry at Appomattox,* p. 194.

9. Wert, *Custer,* pp. 275–79, sides with Custer concerning Elliott. The author believes that Custer instinctively knew that if he had touched Benteen, Benteen would have brought charges against him.

10. Escorting ladies: Wert, *Custer,* p. 294; posting: Darling, *Custer's Seventh Cavalry Comes to Dakota,* p. 27.

11. The *Key West* is often confused with its sister ship, the *Far West;* Way, *Way's Packet Directory, 1848–1983,* p. 271; Forsyth's being bumped: Darling, *Custer's Seventh Cavalry Comes to Dakota,* pp. 118–19.

12. Forsyth, "Expedition Up the Yellowstone River"; "Up the Missouri," *Sioux City Daily Journal,* May 27, 1873; Forsyth obituary, *New York Times,* September 13, 1915.

13. Forsyth, "Expedition Up the Yellow River," pp. 8–10; "Yellowstone," *Sioux City Journal,* May 25, 1873; "Navigation of the Yellowstone," *Helena Daily Herald,* May 23, 1873.

14. Larned to his mother, May 24 and June 11, 1873; Darling, *Custer's Seventh Cavalry Comes to Dakota,* p. 177.

15. Chittenden, *History of Early Steamboat Navigation on the Missouri River,* pp. 431–32. LaBarge called Stanley "a gentleman of rare qualities, one who never forgot to treat a civilian as a man—something many officers were little disposed to do."

16. Darling, *Custer's Seventh Cavalry Comes to Dakota,* pp. 183–84.

17. Stewart, "A Psychoanalytic Approach to Custer," p. 75; Darling, *Custer's Seventh Cavalry Comes to Dakota,* p. 2.

18. Irvine to his wife, April 11, 1873; workers: "Struggles for the Yellowstone," *Sioux City Daily Journal*, June 7, 1873.

19. Custer outranking Bradley: conversation with Dr. Richard Summers, U.S. Army Military History Institute, Carlisle, Pa., April 18, 2002.

20. Bradley 1873 Diary and letters; "A Soldier Drowned," *New York Herald*, June 16, 1873.

21. Bradley letters to his wife, June 12 and 15, and Diary, June 19, 1873; "Indian Fighting at the Crossing," *Sioux City Daily Journal*, June 3, 1873.

22. "Exploring the Yellowstone Region," *New York Tribune*, July 25, 1873; Frost, *Custer's 7th Cav*, p. 23; "Military Division of the Missouri," *Army and Navy Journal*, May 31, 1873; see the *Nation*, July 10, 1873, for a thoroughly negative but logical review of Lazelle's *One Law in Nature*.

23. Edward Konopicky to his parents, June 11 and 17, 1873, copies from Robert Pils, Austrian Museum of Natural History, Vienna, Austria, translated by Paul M. Baltay, Arlington, Va.

24. Original survey plans, Rosser to Milnor Roberts, March 1, 1873, NP, Secretary's Department; Rosser's letter to Jordan, in Lubetkin, *Union College's Class of 1868*, p. 168; "Organization of the Survey," *New York Tribune*, June 28, 1873; Frost, *Custer's 7th Cav*, p. 28.

25. This paragraph and quotations from Rosser's Diary: various newspaper accounts and Roberts to Cass, June 3 and 5, 1873, NP, Secretary's Department.

26. Custer quotation: Merington, *The Custer Story*, p. 257; Meigs quotation: letter to his father, July 25, 1873, in "Letters."

27. Contemporary estimates placed the mileage from Fargo to Bismarck between 197 and 202 miles. Various newspapers discussed Terry's train ride to Fargo; see also Konopicky's June 9, 1873, letter.

28. Wagons: Schuler, *Fort Sully*, pp. 39–40; Edward D. Baker's orders: "Yellowstone Expedition," *Army and Navy Journal*, May 17, 1873; Indian scouts: "From Fort Rice," *Sioux City Journal*, June 29, 1873.

29. Roberts to Cass, June 15, 1873, NP, Secretary's Department.

30. Rosser: P. W. Lewis to F. G. Winston, December 14, 1905, Brackett Papers; Corliss, "The Yellowstone Expedition of 1873"; "Yellowstone" and "Sioux Country," *Chicago Inter-Ocean*, June 19 and July 2, 1873; "Surveyors and Sioux," *New York Herald*, June 19, 1873; "Cavalry Post," *Bismarck Tribune*, July 16, 1873; Carlin: "Military Division of the Missouri," *Army and Navy Journal*, July 5, 1873.

31. Rosser Diary, June 24, 1873; Calhoun: Frost, *Some Observations on the Yellowstone Expedition of 1873*, pp. 43–44; Meigs to his father, June 28, 1873, in "Letters."

32. *Bismarck Tribune*, July 11, 1873; "The Land of the Sioux," *New York Tribune*, July 25, 1873; "Yellowstone Expedition of 1873," ca. 1906, Brackett Papers; Meigs, "Letters."

33. Corliss, "Yellowstone Expedition of 1873," pp. 6–7; Meigs, "Letters"; Rosser to his wife, June 28, 1873, p. 8. For a more complete text of this and other letters, see Lubetkin, "Thomas L. Rosser and the Yellowstone Surveying Expedition of 1873."

34. "Yellowstone Expedition of 1873," Brackett Papers, p. 5.

CHAPTER 14. "UNDER THE WHISKEY CURSE"

1. "Yellowstone Expedition," *New York Tribune*, July 25, 1873; "Into the Sioux Country," *Chicago Inter-Ocean*, July 2, 1873.

2. David S. Stanley, "Report of the Yellowstone Expedition of 1873," in *Personal Memoirs*, pp. 244–47; "Land of the Sioux," *New York Herald*, June 23, 1873; horse and mules: "Western Explorations: The Yellowstone Expeditions," *New York Tribune*, July 3, 1873, says 745 horses and 1,593 mules, but "The Army Mule and His Driver," *Atlantic Monthly* (May 1875): 550, gives 280 wagons and 1,680 draft mules.

3. Soldiers: "Land of the Sioux"; "Western Explorations"; Corliss, "Yellowstone Expedition of 1873," p. 8; Heski, "Soldiers, Surveyors, Steamboats and Stanley's Stockade," p. 20.

4. Grain: Heski, "Soldiers, Surveyors, Steamboats and Stanley's Stockade," p. 20; Stanley Report, p. 268; "Military Division of the Missouri," *Army and Navy Journal*, June 14, 1873.

5. Bradley Diary, June 21, 1873; Barrows, "Yellowstone Expedition," *New York Tribune*, July 25, 1873; Larned Diary, June 20, 1873; Larned to his mother, June 17, 1873.

6. Larned to his mother, June 17, 1873; Barrows, "Yellowstone Expedition."

7. Bradley Diary, June 21, 1873; Stanley Report, pp. 246, 268; Barrows, "Yellowstone Expedition." During the author's basic training in 1962, he shared a pup tent for five straight nights of heavy rain with another six-foot-five-inch individual, two rifles (the 1870 army also likely wanted its men to have dry weapons), and always damp clothing. The experience was thoroughly miserable but was surely less fun in 1873.

8. Frost, *Some Observations*, p. 45, n. 7; "Late Scandal in the Yellowstone Expedition," a *Chicago Post* story reprinted in the *Philadelphia Evening Bulletin*, September 9, 1873.

9. Corliss, "Yellowstone Expedition of 1873," pp. 9–10. Orders not to pursue are the author's assumption—it is impossible to believe that Custer was not willing.

10. Larned Diary, June 25, 1873; Bradley Diary, June 22, 1873; Stanley Report, pp. 245–46.

11. Bradley Diary, June 27, 1873; Frost, *Some Observations*, p. 61. Stanley, sober, was up at the 2 A.M. reveille, whereas the inability of many cavalry officers to get up then *was* apparently caused by drinking. About this time the column was delayed when the officers' breakfast was cooked in a slow-cooling Dutch oven. Whether this was the same date and caused the June 27 delay, as the author believes, is, however, unclear.

12. Larned Diary, June 30, 1873; Larned letter to his mother, July 6, 1873; Stanley Report, p. 246. The author's visual estimates favor Stanley's estimates of the depth and width.

13. Barrows, "Yellowstone Expedition," for this paragraph and the following paragraphs; Stanley, *Personal Memoirs,* p. 239.

14. Stanley Report, pp. 246–47; Larned, "Yellowstone," *Chicago Inter-Ocean*, August 6, 1873; Barrows, "Yellowstone Expedition."

15. Merington, *The Custer Story,* pp. 251–53; Frost, *Custer's 7th Cav,* pp. 55–56; Frost, *Some Observations*, pp. 22 (quotation) and 48, n. 11.

16. Meigs to his father, July 22, 1873, in "Letters"; Barrows, "Yellowstone Expedition."

17. Konopicky to his parents, June 21, 1873. Trivia: as football fans know, Vinatieri's great-grandson, Adam, kicked the winning field goals in the 2002 and 2004 Super Bowls.

18. This paragraph and the following one: Stanley Report, p. 247; Bradley, letter to his wife, July 6, 1873; Calhoun quotation: Frost, *Some Observations,* p. 49. Rosser suspected for some time that he knew a shortcut and, as a matter of courtesy, should have told Stanley. Stanley's calling Rosser "Mister," versus "General," in this report was a petty slap.

19. Bradley to his wife, July 1, 1873. Four of Bradley's letters are missing, three from when Stanley was drinking heavily—a coincidence?

20. Phelps profile: *DAB, NCAB* 12:480; quotations: Berry, "Yellowstone Expedition of 1873," p. 3; Phelps, "Custer and Rosser," *St. Paul Pioneer,* July 12, 1873.

21. Carroll, *Cavalry Bits,* p. 29; Frost, *Custer's 7th Cav,* pp 49–50; Mills, *Harvest of Barren Regrets,* p. 209; Roberts, "Custer's Last Battle," pp. 28–29.

22. Merington: *New York Times* obituary, May 21, 1951; *New York Times* interview, Book Review, February 12, 1950, p. 7; Rosser telling Custer: Merington, *The Custer Story,* pp. 251–53.

23. Larned Diary, July 28, 1873.

24. Frost, *Custer's 7th Cav,* p. 56; Rosser Diary, July 8, 1873; Ambrose, *Crazy Horse and Custer,* p. 360.

25. "Yellowstone," *Sioux City Daily Journal,* August 9, 1873; "Late Scandal in the Yellowstone Expedition"; Merington, *The Custer Story,* p. 265.

26. A month later Braden overheard men saying that they would build a coffin, not bury him in a blanket like the others. Bradley Diary, July 9, 1873; Bradley, July 16, 1873, to his wife.

27. This paragraph and the next: Bradley to his wife, July 16, 1873; Konopicky to his parents, July 20, 1873.

28. The *Far West* and *Key West* each made three trips, the *Peninah* two, and the *Josephine* one. "Yellowstone" ("lady of the evening," including the emphasis), *Sioux City Journal,* July 16 and 18, 1873.

29. This paragraph and the next: for Stanley's Stockade, see Heski, "Soldiers, Surveyors, Steamboats and Stanley's Stockade," pp. 27–30; Carroll, *Camp Talk,* pp. 7–9; Bradley to his wife, July 16, 1873; "Yellowstone," *New York Herald,* August 9, 1873.

30. Stanley's son lived until May 4, 1942; Irvine letters to his wife, August 9, 12, 25, and 28, 1873.

31. "Northern Pacific" (surveyor's narrative), p. 6; "Yellowstone," *Sioux City Daily Journal,* August 9, 1873; Maria Kimball, *A Soldier-Doctor of Our Army* . . . (Boston: Houghton Mifflin Co., 1917), p. 70.

32. Rosser Diary, July 21, 1873. The column was ahead of schedule and faced no threat to its survival, so Custer's legal case could not have been weaker.

33. Larned to his mother, July 21, 1873.

34. "Perilous Ride," *Sioux City Daily Journal,* August 17, 1873.

35. Miles: Frost, *Some Observations,* p. 137; quotation: "Yellowstone," *Sioux City Daily Journal,* August 9, 1873; "The Yellowstone Expeditions," *New York Tribune,* August 23, 1873.

CHAPTER 15. "ALL DOWN THERE ARE KILLED!"

1. Frost, *Some Observations,* p. 57.

2. Ibid., p. 55; Charles Braden, "The Yellowstone Expedition of 1873," p. 237.

3. Barrow, "Yellowstone War," *New York Tribune,* September 8, 1873. The location is identified on a U.S. Geological Survey Map as Big Hill.

4. Custer, "Battling with the Sioux on the Yellowstone," pp. 201–19, quotation on p. 206; Varnum, *Custer's Chief of Scouts;* Barrows, "Yellowstone War," mentions 9:30; Bradley Diary, 18 miles.

5. Barrows, "Yellowstone War"; Haynes, "Geoarcheological Survey of the Reservation Creek [Big Hill] Battlefield, Montana," and in various letters and conversations told the author that the river's changing path and ice acted as a scouring agent, destroying any evidence as to its location.

6. Distance: Barrows "Yellowstone War," combined with Bradley's daily mile count (Diary); 1873 fighting of Métis and Crows/Nez Percés with the Hunkpapas: Diessner, *There Are No Indians Left But Me!* (p. 62).

7. 200–250 warriors: Barrows "Yellowstone War"; Custer, *Boots and Saddles,* p. 238; see Custer, "Battling with the Sioux," p. 207; "about one hundred": Utley, *Lance and the Shield,* p. 112; Sandoz, *Crazy Horse,* p. 275; Ambrose, *Crazy Horse and Custer,* p. 362; Powell, *People of the Sacred Mountain,* p. 825; "first look" quotation: Welch and Stekler, *Killing Custer,* p. 91. As to Crazy Horse's presence and seeing Custer asleep, Sajna, *Crazy Horse,* p. 247, states that "there is nothing in the primary record to even vaguely support such a claim." The author believes that Crazy Horse was in the decoy party.

8. Frost, *Custer's 7th Cav,* p. 77, states that Honsinger was 49; Barrows, "Yellowstone War."

9. Custer, "Battling with the Sioux," p. 208; Calhoun in Frost, *Some Observations,* p. 60.

10. Custer, "Battling with the Sioux," pp. 208–209; sign language: Calhoun in Frost, *Some Observations,* p. 61; Sandoz, *Crazy Horse,* p. 275. Welch and Stekler, *Killing Custer,* p. 91, cite Indian impetuousness and "their lack of firearms" for Custer's escape. Contemporary accounts, however, describe them as well armed. The comments on Sioux ammunition are the author's interpretation.

11. Calhoun in Frost, *Some Observations,* p. 61; Custer, "Battling with the Sioux," p. 211, concerning Indian wounded.

12. Corroboration for Custer's fighting on foot: Varnum, *Custer's Chief of Scouts,* p. 45. There are obvious embellishments between 1873 and Custer's account in "Battling with the Sioux," pp. 213–14.

13. Barrows, "Yellowstone War"; Utley, *Lance and the Shield,* p. 112; Innis, *Bloody Knife,* p. 100; Marquis, *Rain-in-the-Face and Curley,* pp. 4–5.

14. Marquis, *Rain-in-the-Face,* p. 5; Powell, *People of the Sacred Mountain,* p. 826.

15. Along the river: Barrows, "Yellowstone War"; Custer, "Battling with the Sioux," pp. 216–17.

16. Bradley Diary, August 4, 1873; Braden, "The Yellowstone Expedition of 1873," p. 228; Barrows, "Yellowstone War"; inaccurate mileage: Frost, *Custer's 7th Cav,* p. 68.

17.   Barrows, "Yellowstone War," is the only contemporary source describing the approximate locations of Custer, the surveyors, Stanley, the wagons, and Honsinger and Baliran.

18.   Barrows, "Yellowstone War"; and Stanley Report, p. 249.

19.   Frost, *Custer's 7th Cav,* p. 68, states that Brown and Ball "struggled behind in a search for water." In fact the two were often just yards from the river and *between* Yates's two companies and Custer. If Yates had been ahead of them, he would have been where Rain-in-the-Face sprang his ambush.

20.   This paragraph and the next two paragraphs follow the general description in Barrows, "Yellowstone War"; D. A. Kinsley, *Custer: Favor the Bold, a Soldier's Story* (New York: Henry Holt, 1968), p. 457; Hills, "With General George A. Custer on the Northern Pacific Surveying Expedition in 1873," pp. 152–53. Barrows and Stanley (Report) say that the bodies were not mutilated, but this probably reflected concern for the families' feelings; Brown's first name is unknown.

21.   Braden, "The Yellowstone Expedition of 1873," p. 228.

22.   Barrows, "Yellowstone War"; Konopicky to his parents, undated, ca. August 16, 1873, letter 9.

23.   Stanley Report, p. 249.

24.   Braden, "The Yellowstone Expedition of 1873," p. 229.

25.   Ibid., pp. 229, 231.

26.   Stanley Report, p. 250; Utley, *Cavalier in Buckskin,* p. 120, and *Lance and the Shield,* p. 112. "Stanley came to the rescue" could mean either that Stanley personally led the cavalry or that the rescue forces were commanded by him.

27.   Custer, "Battling with the Sioux," pp. 218–19.

28.   Braden, "The Yellowstone Expedition of 1873," p. 230; Barrows, "Yellowstone War"; Custer, *Boots and Saddles,* p. 240.

29.   Parts of this paragraph closely follow or quote Custer, "Battling with the Sioux," pp. 218–19.

30.   Frost, *Custer's 7th Cav,* pp. 68–69, makes no mention of Stanley's role.

CHAPTER 16. "STRIKE UP GARRY OWEN"

1. This paragraph and the following paragraphs draw on Barrows, "The Yellowstone War," *New York Tribune,* September 9, 1873; Custer's "Official Report" and Stanley's Report; Bradley's Diary and letters; Braden, "The Yellowstone Expedition of 1873"; Konopicky's letters; and other contemporary sources. Some dates and sources are cited directly in the text.

2. Bradley's Diary, August 8, 1873, is the main source for this paragraph.

3. While few sources, including Custer, mention his taking the slow-moving beef cattle, virtually all sources and Custer himself mention the "bullboats" (Custer, "Official Report," p. 126: "I then caused some cattle to be killed and by stretching fresh hides over a kind of basket frame prepared by the Crow guide made what are known among the Indians as 'Bullboats'").

4. Barrows was likely the only correspondent with Custer. Frustratingly, not knowing what time the sun set makes the late afternoon or early evening times far less meaningful; for example, did Custer have three or four or perhaps even five hours of daylight left at 6 P.M.?

5. Braden, "The Yellowstone Expedition of 1873," pp. 232–33; Barrows, "The Yellowstone War."

6. Utley, *Lance and the Shield*, p. 112; Braden, "The Yellowstone Expedition of 1873," p. 233.

7. This paragraph and the preceding two: Braden, "The Yellowstone Expedition of 1873"; Barrows, "The Yellowstone War"; Hills, "With General George A. Custer," p. 157.

8. Numerous contemporary sources mentioned that Sitting Bull shouted instructions.

9. Ambrose, *Crazy Horse and Custer,* p. 366; Braden, "The Yellowstone Expedition of 1873," pp. 234–37; Custer, *Boots and Saddles,* p. 245. Utley, *Cavalier in Buckskin,* p. 121, says there were 100 Indians. Braden and Barrows ("The Yellowstone War") estimated 200 Indians.

10. Godfrey, handwritten memoir, p. 11.

11. Custer quotation in his formal report of August 15, 1873, reprinted in Frost's *Some Observations,* p. 130.

12. Exactly where Barrows was during the shelling and Custer's charge is not clear. All quotations: Barrows, "The Yellowstone War." The Barrows story was quickly reprinted in numerous other papers.

13. Custer, "Official Report," p. 130; Frost, *Some Observations,* pp. 75–76 and 126–32.

14. Bradley Diary, August 9 and 10, 1873.

15. Stanley Report, p. 251; Berry, "Yellowstone Expedition of 1873," p. 10. There is no corroboration of Berry's account, but it explains the delay until 7 A.M., when Stanley says he first saw Custer's camp.

16. Berry, "Yellowstone Expedition of 1873," pp. 10–11; Stanley Report, p. 251.

17. Bradley, Diary, August 11, 1873; Berry, "Yellowstone Expedition of 1873"; and Stanley Report.

18. Larned to his mother, September 6, 1873; Konopicky, undated, letter 9.

19. Tuttle: Joe De Barthe, *The Life and Adventures of Frank Grouard,* p. 116; "The Yellowstone Expedition," *New York Times,* September 10, 1873; Stanley quotation: "Military Division of the Missouri, the Big Horn Fight," *Army and Navy Journal,* November 8, 1873; Barrows, "The Yellowstone War."

20. Custer quotation: Custer, *Boots and Saddles,* p. 247; "The Yellowstone Expedition Twice Attacked" by Samuel Barrows, for the *New York Tribune, Philadelphia Evening Bulletin,* August 25, 1873; Larned to his mother, September 10, 1873; "The Yellowstone Expedition," *New York Times,* September 10, 1873; some other newspaper examples, all on August 26, 1873: "Indian Savagery," *Philadelphia Inquirer;* "Yellowstone Expedition," *Chicago Inter-Ocean;* and "Custer Chastising the Sioux," *Helena Daily Herald;* "The Yellowstone Expedition Attacked by Indians," *St. Paul Daily Pioneer;* Bradley to his wife, August 19, 1873.

21. Irvine to his wife, September 9, 1873. It can be assumed that Stanley's wife discussed the letter with Irvine, who paraphrased its contents.

22. Buffalo: Konopicky letter, ca. September 10–11, 1873; Stanley Report, p. 263.

23. Godfrey, handwritten memoir, pp. 11–12; and Braden (unsigned), "An Incident of the Yellowstone Expedition of 1873."

24. Miles: Stanley Report, p. 254; Bradley, Diary, September 9, 1873; Frost, *Some Observations,* p. 83.

25. Konopicky letters, July 20 and September 12, 1873. The National Archives has no record of the paintings; sketchbooks: conversations with Professor William E. Farr, University of Montana, 2002–2003; Allen, "Notes on the Natural History of Dakota and Montana Territories," p. 33.

26. "Northern Pacific," *Railroad Gazette,* August 16, 1873.

27. Roberts to Cass, "Report of the Chief Engineer," November 19, 1873.

CHAPTER 17. "WE DO NOT ANTICIPATE ANY TROUBLE"

1. Profiles of Cass in *American National Biography, DAB,* and West Point sources; Cass to Cooke, December 2, 1872, in Oberholtzer, *Jay Cooke,* 2:390; Cooke's response: Larson, *Jay Cooke,* p. 388; Cass and bond sales: Harnsberger, *Jay Cooke and Minnesota,* p. 142.

2. "President Cass and Party," *Brainerd Tribune,* November 2, 1872; Cass to Cooke, March 1873, in Oberholtzer, *Jay Cooke,* 2:329, 330 (Barney quotation).

3. G. M. Mead to Cass, April 11, 1873, NP, Secretary's Department; Konopicky to his parents, June 9, 1873.

4. "Army," *Army and Navy Journal,* February 22, 1873; "National Pacific," *Bozeman Avant Courier,* March 21, 1873; Smalley, *Northern Pacific Railroad Book of Reference,* pp. 101–10.

5. This paragraph and following one: Cooke to Canfield and Cooke to Cass, both February 10, 1873, NP, Secretary's Department; Wright quotation: Oberholtzer, *Jay Cooke,* 2:331; Englehardt, "The Incorporation of America," p. 33.

6. Hedges, "Colonization Work," pp. 325–26; Mickelson, *The Northern Pacific Railroad,* tables 9, 10, and 11; *Cincinnati Commercial,* June 20, 1873; Oberholtzer, *Jay Cooke,* 2:332 quotation), 339. The figure of 30,000 assumes zero population in 1869.

7. Harnsberger, *Jay Cooke and Minnesota,* pp. 300–301; Northern Pacific Railroad, *Annual Report, 1873,* and *1876,* p. 12; Mickelson, *The Northern Pacific Railroad,* table 6.

8. Larson, *Jay Cooke,* p. 390; sabotage: Sobel, *Panic on Wall Street,* p. 171; Oberholtzer, *Jay Cooke,* 2:392, 409–10.

9. *Financial Chronicle* and cost per mile: Larson, *Jay Cooke,* p. 397; foreign capital: Sobel, *Panic on Wall Street,* p. 162; Cooke to Cass, March 1, 1873, NP, Secretary's Department.

10. "Northern Pacific," *Railroad Gazette,* April 12, 1871; Oberholtzer, *Jay Cooke,* 2:414–15.

11. Oberholtzer, *Jay Cooke,* 2:243, 351; "For the East," *Minneapolis Tribune,* June 7, 1872; "Locomotive Returns," *Railroad Gazette,* April 19, 1873; Larson, *Jay Cooke,* p. 400; Smalley, *Northern Pacific Railroad Book of Reference,* pp. 112–13.

12. Larson, *Jay Cooke,* p. 401; Harnsberger, *Jay Cooke and Minnesota,* p. 319; "Northern Pacific," *Railroad Gazette,* May 31, 1873.

13. Bridges, *Iron Millionaire,* chapter 8.

14. Larson, *Jay Cooke,* p. 405 ($5,092,146 or 73 percent was NP debt); Oberholtzer, *Jay Cooke,* 2:411–12 (letter to Hazard) and 417 (letter to Henry).

15. Quotation: "The Modoc War," *Harper's Weekly,* May 17, 1873, p. 416; "The Country of the Warlike Sioux," *New York Times,* May 27, 1873; "Military Division of the Missouri," *Army and Navy Journal,* May 31, 1873.

16. "Indians," *Chicago Inter-Ocean;* and "Surveyors and Sioux," *New York Herald,* both June 19, 1873.

17. "More Railroad Trouble," *St. Paul Daily Pioneer,* July 15, 1873; "Railroad Troubles," *New York Times,* July 19, 1873; quotation: "St. Paul & Pacific," *Railroad Gazette,* July 26, 1873.

18. *New York Times,* July 17 and August 5, 6, 8, and 9, 1873.

19. The inference concerning graft is the author's, not Brace's.

20. "Decline in Railroad Construction," *Railroad Gazette,* August 9, 1873.

21. "Northern Pacific," *Railroad Gazette,* August 23, 1873; "Northern Pacific Road, Proposals," *St. Paul Daily Pioneer,* August 20, 1873.

22. Cooke to Wilkeson, August 19, 1873, NP, Secretary's Department. Had a fort been built at the Tongue and a railroad been under construction, the idea might have worked.

23. *Harper's Weekly* editorial ("Shall We Have Another Black Friday?"), September 6, 1873; "This Week in Trade and Finance," *Nation,* September 11, 1873; "Northern Pacific Contract for Carrying Mail Refused," *New York Times,* September 1, 1873; Larson, *Jay Cooke,* p. 406; "The Week in Trade and Finance," *Nation,* September 11, 1873; Sobel, *Panic on Wall Street,* pp. 172–75.

24. "The Yellowstone War," *New York Tribune,* September 6, 1873; editorial (untitled), *Army and Navy Journal,* September 13, 1873; "The Yellowstone Expedition," *New York Times,* September 11, 12, and 13, 1873.

25. Smalley, *Northern Pacific Railroad Book of Reference,* p. 113; "Financial and Commercial" (column), *New York Herald,* September 11, 1873.

26. "Financial Affairs" section, *New York Times,* September 12 and 13, 1873; Shepard-Cooke: *Philadelphia Evening Bulletin,* September 13, 1873; Grant, *Papers,* 24:212–13; "Washington," *New York Tribune,* September 15, 1873; *Philadelphia Inquirer* editorial, September 16, 1873.

27. *New York Herald, Times,* and *Tribune,* September 14 and 15, 1873.

28. Oberholtzer, *Jay Cooke,* 2:421; Grant, *Papers,* 24:210–11. Northern newspapers gave wide coverage to the September 17–18 reunion, usually headlined "Army of the Cumberland."

29. Smalley, *Northern Pacific Railroad Book of Reference,* pp. 114–15; Sobel, *Panic on Wall Street,* pp. 177–78.

30. "From the Interior: The Army of the Cumberland Re-unionReception of President Grant," *Philadelphia Evening Bulletin,* September 18, 1873; "Army of the Cumberland," *Army and Navy Journal,* September 27, 1873.

31. Quotations: Fahnestock, Memorial, p. 9. The actual amount was likely well over $100,000.

32. Oberholtzer wrote: "On the night of the 17th, President Grant arrived at 'Ogontz'" (*Jay Cooke,* 2:421). All writers accept this date and general outline (e.g., Josephson, *The Robber Barons,* pp. 169–70). However, in 1937 Oberholtzer backed off, stating: "Grant, *but a day or two since,* had been an overnight guest at 'Ogontz'" (emphasis added) (*History of the United States,* 3:84).

33. Larson, *Jay Cooke,* p. 407; quotation: "The Commercial Situation . . . ," *Bradstreet's: A Journal of Trade,* August 13, 1881, p. 101. Sobel (*Panic on Wall Street,* pp. 178–79) places the meeting at 10 A.M.

34. Oberholtzer, *Jay Cooke,* 2:201. Henry Cooke continued to socialize with Benjamin French long after French had lost his influence in Washington: French, *Witness to the Young Republic,* pp. 609 and 621.

35. Oberholtzer, *History of the United States,* 3:84.

36. Ibid., 3:84 and 92; Larson, *Jay Cooke,* p. 420; French's *New York Times* obituary and *NCAB* (2:345) give 1874 as the date when First National was taken over.

37. Fahnestock, Memorial, p. 10. It is unclear when, if ever, Fahnestock notified Cooke.

CHAPTER 18. "GET OUT, GENTLEMEN, GET OUT"

1. "Washington: The Suspension of Henry Cooke," *New York Herald,* September, 19, 1873.

2. "Cooke's Crash," *New York Herald,* September 19, 1873.

3. "Panic Past . . . Affairs of Jay Cooke & Co." and "Statements of Suspended Companies," both *New York Herald,* September 24 and 28, 1873.

4. "The Financial Storm . . . Grant in the City," *Philadelphia Inquirer,* September 20, 1873.

5. Oberholtzer, *History of the United States,* 2:543.

6. Sobel, *Panic on Wall Street,* p. 192.

7. Cooke to Wilkeson, NP, Secretary's Department, September 22, 1873.

8. Fahnestock, Memorial, p. 6.

9. Quotation: "Northern Pacific," *New York Times,* September 20, 1873; Rosser to Custer, February 16, 1874, courtesy John Doerner, Little Bighorn Battlefield National Monument; "Northern Pacific, Present Conditions," *St. Paul Weekly Press,* October 16, 1873. The certification included 5,120,000 acres in Dakota.

10. Spike: "Mr. Villard handed the sledge to H. C. Davis," *Northwest* (September 1883): 14.

11. "Home Again," *Bismarck Tribune,* September 24, 1873; "Toledo . . . Kissing the Ladies," *Frank Leslie's Illustrated Weekly Magazine,* November 11, 1873.

12. "Interview with . . . Vanderbilt," *New York Herald,* September 19, 1873; "Annual Report to the Secretary of the Interior," September 30, 1872, Microfilm 369, Minnesota Historical Society, St. Paul.

13. Oberholtzer, *History of the United States,* 3:82.

14. Cooke, "Jay Cooke's Memoir," p. 134.

15. "Railroad Investments," *Nation,* August 15, 1872. The analysis is the author's.

16. Smalley, *History,* p. 201; and Renz, *History,* p. 47.

17. Cooke, "Jay Cooke's Memoir," p. 142. Cooke called the opposition "two or three leading partners."

18. For the 1906 reunion: Brackett Papers; Rosser Papers, 1171-d-e-f, Box 2; various January 1906 Minneapolis/St. Paul newspapers; *Mainstreeter* 22, no. 2 (Summer 2003).

19. Pierre Berton, *The Great Railway* (Toronto: McClelland and Stewart, 1997), p. 242; Thomas, "'Under Indictment,'" pp. 225–30.

20. Smalley, *History,* p. 202; tower: Oberholtzer, *Jay Cooke,* 2:519; Cooke, "Jay Cooke's Memoir," p. 145.

21. Oberholtzer, *Jay Cooke,* 2:456–57; and Philadelphia, New York, and Washington, D.C., papers for the obituaries and funeral.

POSTSCRIPT: *"HO HECHETU!"* (IT IS WELL!)

1. Brown and Felton, *The Frontier Years,* p. 232.

2. Oberholtzer, *Jay Cooke,* 2:537.

3. Obituary, *New York Times,* June 23, 1898.

4. West Point obituary: U.S. Military Academy, *Annual Reunion,* June 7, 1899, p. 182.

5. Sherman quotation: *Army and Navy Journal,* February 4, 1874, p. 408; court-martial: Hutton, *Phil Sheridan and His Army,* p. 400, n. 75; Kroeker, *Great Plains Command,* chapter 10.

6. Rumbough, "'The Regular Army O!'"

7. Eastman, *Indian Heroes and Great Chieftains,* pp. 150–51.

8. *New York Times,* December 10, 1914; full obituary, *Carlisle [Pa.] Sentinel,* December 11, 1914; Pohanka, *A Summer on the Plains,* pp. 73–74.

9. See Martin, *Jennie,* 1:254; a long *New York Times* obituary, January 18, 1935; and *Annual Report of the Association of the Graduates of [West Point],* June 11, 1935.

10. *Portland Press-Herald,* September 16, 1935. Richard Relf was alive as late as 1931.

APPENDIX

1. An earlier account by McClernand appeared in Rodenbough, *The Army of the United States,* pp. 179–83; McClernand, *Cavalry Journal* 25 (October 1926): 506–508; *With the Indian and Buffalo in Montana* (Glendale, Calif.: Arthur Clarke Co., 1969), renamed *On Time for Disaster,* pp. 24–26.

2. 1872 surveying: McClernand, *On Time for Disaster,* p. 31. Also see the book's excellent introduction.

3. Information about General John A. McClernand can be found in numerous Civil War sources. Two photos of Edward McClernand appear in *On Time for Disaster.*

BIBLIOGRAPHY

PRIMARY SOURCES

Note: In order to facilitate further research on this period of American history, the author has turned over hard copies of more than 40 reports, diaries, longer letters, and related 1870s documents relating to the 1871, 1872, and 1873 Yellowstone Surveying Expeditions to the U.S. Army Military History Institute in Carlisle, Pa. The documents were selected primarily because of the difficulty that other researchers would have in accessing them.

Allen, Joel Asaph. "Notes on the Natural History of Dakota and Montana Territories . . . Made by the North [*sic*] Pacific Railroad Expedition of 1873 . . ." *Proceedings of the Boston Society of Natural History* (Boston) 17 (October 1874).

Baker, Eugene Mortimer. "Report of the Operations of the Escort to Surveyors of the N.P.R.R. Company Down the Yellowstone." Retyped copy, Montana Historical Society, Helena.

Ball, Edward. Untitled report concerning the 1871 Yellowstone Surveying Expedition from Fort Ellis, Montana, December 10, 1871. MF-339, Reel 1, Montana Historical Society, Helena.

Barlow, John Whitney. *The Report of Major J. W. Barlow, Who Accompanied a Surveying Party of the Northern Pacific Railroad, in Relation to Indian Interference with That Road.* U.S. Senate, Executive Document 16, 42nd Congress, 3rd Session, January 6, 1873.

Barrows, Samuel June. Articles concerning the Yellowstone Expedition of 1873. *New York Tribune*, June 28, July 3 and 25, August 5, 19, and 23, and September 6, 8, and 9, 1873.

———. "The Northwestern Mule and His Driver." *Atlantic Monthly* (May 1875).

Bennett, Clarence E. "August 26, 1872 Letter to Wife." Clarence Edmund Bennett Papers (MS 39). Mansfield Library, University of Montana, Missoula.

Benteen, Frederick W. "Letters" (relating to the 1873 Yellowstone Survey). Frederick W. Benteen–Theodore Goldin Papers/Correspondence 1895–96, U.S. Army Military History Institute, Carlisle, Pa.

Berry, A. L. "Yellowstone Expedition of 1873: The Narrative . . ." Ca. 1906. Rosser Collection 1171-g-h-j, Box 12. Small Special Collections Library, University of Virginia, Charlottesville.

Boston Board of Trade. *Report on the Northern Pacific Railroad, Made to the Government of the Board, and Unanimously Adopted, November 27, 1865.* Boston: J. H. Eastburn's Press, 1865.

Brace, Charles Loring. "The New North-West." A series of articles that appeared in the *New York Times,* July 29 and August 5, 6, 8, and 9, 1873.

Brackett, George Augustus. Correspondence, "Remembrances," etc., relating to 1906 surveyors' reunion (Brackett Papers). Miscellaneous Papers, Catalog No. P1547. Minnesota Historical Society, St. Paul.

Braden, Charles. "An Incident of the Yellowstone Expedition of 1873." *Journal of the United States Cavalry Association* 15, no. 54 (October 1904) (unsigned but written by Braden).

———. "The Yellowstone Expedition of 1873." *Journal of the United States Cavalry Association* 16 (October 1905).

Bradley, James H. *The March of the Montana Column: A Prelude to the Custer Disaster.* Ed. Edger I. Stewart. 1896; reprint, Norman: University of Oklahoma Press, 1991.

Bradley, Luther Prentiss. 1873 Diaries and Letters. U.S. Army Military History Institute, Carlisle, Pa.

Burr, James D. "A Method of Conducting a Railroad Survey in a New, Wooded Country." *Railroad Gazette* (Chicago), June 17 and June 24, 1871.

Campbell, Lafayette E. 1871 Diary. American Heritage Center, University of Wyoming, Collection No. 10435, Laramie.

Canfield, Thomas Hawley. *Life of Thomas Hawley Canfield . . . and His Connection with the Early History of the Northern Pacific Railroad.* Burlington, Vt.: privately printed, 1889.

———. *Partial Report to the Board of Directors of the Northern Pacific Railroad of a Portion of a Reconnaissance Made in the Summer of 1869, between Lake Superior and the Pacific Ocean.* New York: privately printed, 1870. Also includes Samuel Wilkeson's *Notes on Puget Sound.*

———. *Reads Like a Fairy Tale: The Early History of the Northern Pacific Railroad.* Fargo: North Dakota Institute for Regional Studies, North Dakota State University.

Coffin, Charles Carlton. *The Seat of Empire.* New York: John W. Lovell Company, 1870.

Cooke, Jay. "Jay Cooke's Memoir." Ca. 1894. Unpublished. Microfilm, Minnesota Historical Society, St. Paul.

Cooke, Jay, & Co. *The Northern Pacific Railroad: Its Route, Resources, Progress and Business.* Philadelphia: privately printed, ca. 1871.

———. *The Northern Pacific Railroad's Land Grant and the Future Business of the Road.* Philadelphia: privately printed, 1870.

Corliss, Augustus W. "The Yellowstone Expedition of 1873." Handwritten (part missing), May 7, 1896; Indian Wars Miscellaneous Collection folder, U.S. Army Military History Institute, Carlisle, Pa.

Cotter, James H. "How the Northern Pacific Groped Its Way West, Remembrances of a Northern Pacific Surveyor." (1872). Montana Historic Society, Helena.

Crofton, Major Robert Erskine Anderson, and Gabrielle Josephine [DuPont] Shubrick Crofton (wife). Letters and selected family papers, Hagley Museum and Library, Wilmington, Del.

Custer, George Armstrong. "Battling with the Sioux on the Yellowstone." *Galaxy Magazine* 22, no. 1 (July 1876). Also published in Paul Andrew Hutton, ed., *The Custer Reader.* Lincoln: University of Nebraska Press, 1992.

————. "Official Report of the Tongue River and Big Horn Fights." *New York Tribune*, September 6, 1873.

Davis, Henry Chandler. "Journal: July 26, 1872, through September 3, 1872." Microfilm 189. State Historical Society of Wisconsin, Madison.

De Trobriand, Philippe Régis. *Military Life in Dakota: The Journal of Philippe Régis De Trobriand.* Trans. Lucile M. Kane. St. Paul: Alvord Memorial Commission, 1951.

Drips, Joseph H. *Three Years among the Indians in Dakota.* 1894; reprint, New York: Sol Lewis, 1974.

Fahnestock, Harris Charles. Miscellaneous letters to Jay Cooke, October 1868–April 1874. F-223, Box 3, Folder 2. Baker Library, Harvard Business School, Cambridge, Mass.

Fahnestock, William. Memorial to his father, H. C. Fahnestock. 1915, F-223, Box 4, Folder 9. Baker Library, Harvard Business School, Cambridge, Mass.

Forsyth, George A. "Expedition Up the Yellowstone River to the Mouth of the Powder River." Report to Gen. Philip H. Sheridan, May 28, 1873. Microfilm. Montana Historical Society, Helena.

French, Benjamin Brown. *Witness to the Young Republic: A Yankee's Journal, 1828–1870.* Ed. Donald B. Cole and John J. McDonough. Hanover, N.H.: University Press of New England, 1989.

Godfrey, Edward S. Untitled handwritten memoir concerning Charles Braden. 1922. West Point Files, in Braden (likely) or Godfrey folders, possibly in both.

Grant, Ulysses S. *The Papers of Ulysses S. Grant.* Ed. John Y. Simon. 24 vols. Carbondale: University of Illinois Press, 2000.

Hayden, Ferdinand V. *Geological Report of the Exploration of the Yellowstone and Missouri Rivers . . . 1859–1860.* Washington, D.C.: U.S. Government Printing Office, 1869.

Hills, Louis E. "With General George A. Custer on the Northern Pacific Surveying Expedition in 1873." *Journal of History* 8, no. 2 (April 1915).

Hone, Philip. *The Diary of Philip Hone.* Ed. Bayard Tuckerman. 2 vols. New York: Dodd, Mead and Company, 1889.

Irvine, Javan Bradley. Correspondence, diaries, press clippings, obituary, letters, and miscellaneous. South Dakota State Archives, South Dakota Cultural Heritage Center, Pierre.

Johns, H. T. *Duluth.* Duluth, Minn.: privately printed, ca. 1872.

Jordan, Edward C. "Account of Edward C. Jordan's Experiences in [the] West during the Construction of the Central Pacific and the Northern Pacific Railroad." Ca. 1906. Courtesy of Mark Jordan, Gorham, Maine.

————. "Diary: May, 1870–May, 1871." P-2245. Minnesota Historical Society, St. Paul.

————. "Miscellaneous Letters, 1870–1873." Courtesy of Mark Jordan, Gorham, Maine.

————. "The Yellowstone Expedition of 1871." Ca. 1906. Courtesy of Mark Jordan, Gorham, Maine.

Kellogg, Sanford Cobb. "Report to Gen. Sheridan concerning Stanley's 1872 Yellowstone Expedition." *Bozeman Avant Courier,* November 7, 1872.

Konopicky, Edward. 1873 Letters. Trans. Paul M. Baltay. German editing by Robert Pils. Museum of Natural History, Vienna, Austria.

Larned, Charles W. "Expedition to the Yellowstone River in 1873: Letters of a Young Cavalry Officer." Ed. George F. Howe. *Mississippi Valley Historical Society Review* 39 (1952–53).

———. "Letters and Diary from 1873." Special Collections and Archives Division, United States Military Academy Library, West Point, N.Y.

Latrobe, Benjamin H. "Engineering: The Introduction of Railways." *Railroad Gazette,* April 30, 1870.

Linsley, David Chapman. "Diary, May 25 to August 3, 1870." Ed. F. W. DeGuire (656, L655d). Duluth, Minnesota, Public Library.

McClernand, Lt. Edward J. *On Time for Disaster: The Rescue of Custer's Command.* 1926; reprint, Lincoln: University of Nebraska Press, 1989.

McLaughlin, Daniel. *Chronicles of a Northern Pacific Veteran.* N.p.: Privately printed, 1930.

Meigs, Montgomery C. "Letters of Montgomery Meigs Written While Engaged in the Survey of the Northern Pacific Railroad, 1872–1873, edited by Elizabeth Rodgers Atwater." Master's thesis, State University of Montana, 1937. Microfilm 140. Montana Historical Society, Helena.

"Northern Pacific" (surveyor's narrative of 1871–73). Rosser Collection 1171-g-h-j, Box 12, Miscellaneous, Small Special Collections Library, University of Virginia, Charlottesville.

Northern Pacific Railroad. "Annual Reports, 1869–1876." (Microfilm) M-369. Minnesota Historical Society, St. Paul.

———. "Clippings and Scrapbooks, 1866–1904." Office of the Secretary of the Northern Pacific. (Microfilm) M-522. Minnesota Historical Society, St. Paul.

———. "Journal of N.P.R.R. Surveying Expedition from Missouri River to Powder River.*"* 137.k.13 (B). Minnesota Historical Society, St. Paul.

———. "Secretary's Department: Unregistered Letters Received and Related Records, Undated and 1864–1876." (Microfilm) M-459. Minnesota Historical Society, St. Paul.

"The Northern Pacific Railroad System." *Harper's Weekly,* January 21, 1871.

"Panic in Wall Street." *Harper's New Monthly Magazine,* December 1873.

Patterson, Robert Maskell. "A Short Account of the Preliminary Survey of the Northern Pacific Railroad in 1871." Ca. 1906. Manuscript 681, B-433. State Historical Society of North Dakota, Bismarck.

Phelps, William Franklin. "Notes on the Yellowstone." *National Teacher's Monthly* (serialized but not all issues) 1, no. 1 (November 1874) through 2, no. 5 (March 1876).

Ponsford, John W. "Reminiscences." Collection 659. Burlingame Special Collections Library, Montana State University, Bozeman.

———. "Statement of the Baker Fight on the Yellowstone River in '72." 1912. Burlingame Special Collections Library, Montana State University, Bozeman.

Raynolds, William F. *Report of Capt. W. F. Raynolds, U.S. Corps of Engineers, on the Exploration of the Yellowstone and Missouri Rivers in 1859–'60.* U.S. War Department, Corps of Engineers, 40th Congress, 1st session, Executive Document No. 77. Washington, D.C.: USGPO, 1867.

Relf, Richard. "Narrative of Richard Relf." George Augustus Brackett, Miscellaneous papers, Catalog No. P1547. Minnesota Historical Society, St. Paul.

Roberts, Richard A. "Custer's Last Battle: Reminiscences [about] General Custer." Ca. 1891, unpublished. George W. Yates Papers, U.S. Army Military History Institute, Carlisle, Pa.

Roberts, Thomas P. "Remembrances of William Milnor Roberts." Speech ca. 1922. Collection No. 783, Series 1, Box 1, File No. 8. Burlingame Special Collections Library, Montana State University, Bozeman.

———. *Report of a Reconnaissance of the Missouri River in 1872.* U.S. War Department, Corps of Engineers. Washington, D.C.: USGPO, 1875.

Roberts, William Milnor. "Autobiography." Two drafts, 1874. Collection No. 783 (Roberts Papers). Series 1, Box 1, Files 4 and 5; Burlingame Special Collections Library, Montana State University, Bozeman (hereafter Roberts Papers).

———. Correspondence, 1871–1874. Roberts Papers, Series 2, Box 2, Folders 4–5.

———. "Down the Valley of the Yellowstone: Extracts from the Fall [1871] Letters . . ." Roberts Papers. Series 6, Box 10.

———. "Field Diary of 1871 Reconnaissance." October 30–November 20, 1871. Roberts Papers, Series 3, Box 4, Folders 1–4.

———. "Journal." August 18–September 1, 1871. Roberts Papers, Series 3, Box 3, Folders 18–19.

———. "Report of the Chief Engineer on the Unfinished Portion of the Northern Pacific . . . April 27, 1874." Roberts Papers, Series 6, Box 10.

———. "Report of the Chief Engineer to the President of the Northern Pacific R. R. Co. on the Surveys of 1873 West of the Missouri River. Made November 19, 1873." NP Unregistered Letters.

———. *Special Report of a Reconnaissance of the Route for the Northern Pacific Railroad between Lake Superior and Puget Sound via the Columbia River.* Philadelphia: McLaughlin Brothers, 1869.

———. "Surveys and Explorations, Preliminary Report of [the] Engineer-in-Chief on [the] Montana Surveys." Roberts Papers, Series 6, Box 10.

———. "The Yellowstone Valley: A Preliminary Report." Roberts Papers, Series 6, Box 10.

Rosser, Betty Barbara (Mrs. Thomas L.). "1872 Diary." Collection 1171 g-h-j, Box 11. Small Special Collections Library, University of Virginia, Charlottesville.

Rosser, Thomas Lafayette. *Across Dakota and Up the Yellowstone, General Rosser's Report.* Collection 783 (Roberts Papers). Series 6, Box 10. Burlingame Special Collections Library, Montana State University, Bozeman.

———. "The Death of Adair." Unpublished, handwritten and signed, not dated, ca. 1895. Collection 1171-g-h-j, Box 12. Small Special Collections Library, University of Virginia, Charlottesville.

———. Diary for 1871, 1872, and 1873. Collection 1171-g-h-j, Box 16. Small Special Collections Library, University of Virginia, Charlottesville.

———. Letters, 1867–73. Collection 1171-g-h-j, Box 1. Small Special Collections Library, University of Virginia, Charlottesville.

———. "Report of Gen. Rosser to D. C. Linsley, Assistant Chief Engineer, October 10, 1872 . . ." 134.L13.8(F). Minnesota State Historical Society, St. Paul.

———. Untitled. Two handwritten, signed accounts of Charley Reynolds and 1872 Expedition. Collection No. 1171-g-h-j, Box 12. Small Special Collections Library, University of Virginia, Charlottesville.

Rumbough, Sarah Eliza Stanley. "'The Regular Army O!'" 1939. West-Stanley-Wright Family Papers. U.S. Army Military History Institute, Carlisle, Pa.

Sheridan, Philip Henry. *Record of Engagements with Hostile Indians within the Military Division of the Missouri from 1868 to 1882*. Chicago: Military Division of the Missouri, 1882.

Slaughter, Linda W. *Fortress to Farm or Twenty-three Years on the Frontier*. Ed. Helen Eastman. 1895; reprint, New York: Exposition Press, 1972.

Smalley, Eugene V., compiler. *Northern Pacific Railroad Book of Reference for the Use of the Directors and Officers of the Company*. New York: privately printed, 1883.

Stanley, David Sloan. *Personal Memoirs of Major-General David S. Stanley*. 1917; reprint, Gaithersburg, Md.: Olde Soldier Books, 1987.

———. "Report on the Yellowstone Expedition of 1872." No. 917.86 Sta. Montana Historical Society, Helena. Also *Westerners Posse New York Brand Book*, vol. 3, nos. 2 and 3 (1956).

United States Department of the Interior. *Annual Report of the Commissioner of Indian Affairs, U.S. Department of the Interior*. Washington, D.C.: U.S. Government Printing Office, 1867–74.

United States Department of War. *Annual Report*. Washington, D.C.: USGPO, 1866–74.

———. *Official Army Register* [for January of each year]. Washington, D.C.: USGPO, 1869–74.

———. *Outline Descriptions of the Posts and Stations of Troops . . . of the United States*. Washington, D.C.: USGPO, 1872.

———. *Outline Descriptions of the Posts in the Military Division of the Missouri Commanded by Lt. Gen. P. H. Sheridan*. Chicago: Division of the Missouri, 1876.

———. *The War of the Rebellion: A Compilation of the Official Records of the Union and Confederate Armies*. 128 vols. Washington, D.C.: USGPO, 1881–1901.

———. Corps of Engineers. *Annual Report*. Washington, D.C.: USGPO, 1870–74.

———. Surgeon General's Office. *A Report on Barracks and Hospitals with Descriptions of Military Posts*. Circular No. 4, December 5, 1870. Washington, D.C.: USGPO, 1870.

Varnum, Charles A. *Custer's Chief of Scouts: The Reminiscences of Charles A. Varnum.* Ed. John Melvin Carroll. 1982; reprint, Lincoln: University of Nebraska Press, 1987.

Wade, William V. "Reminiscences." B-38. North Dakota Historical Society Collections.

Warren, Gouverneur Kimble. *Preliminary Report of Explorations in Nebraska and Dakota in the Years 1855–56–57.* Ed. Frank N. Schubert. 1875; reprint, Washington, D.C.: USGPO, ca. 1983.

Whistler, Joseph Nelson Garland. "Report of the Expedition Accompanying the Engineers of the Northern Pacific Railroad." Microfilm 751 MMDM 1871. Montana Historical Society, Helena.

Wilkeson, Samuel. *Notes on Puget Sound* (1869). Included in Thomas Hawley Canfield, *Partial Report to the Board of Directors [of the Northern Pacific Railroad] of a Portion of a Reconnaissance Made in the Summer of 1869, between Lake Superior and the Pacific Ocean.* New York: privately printed, 1870.

"A Year in Montana." *Atlantic Monthly Magazine* (August 1866).

SECONDARY SOURCES

Adler, Dorothy R. *British Investment in American Railways, 1834–1898.* Charlottesville: University Press of Virginia, 1970.

Ambrose, Stephen E. *Crazy Horse and Custer: The Parallel Lives of Two American Warriors.* 1975; reprint, Garden City, N.Y.: Doubleday and Co., 1996.

———. *Nothing Like It in the World: The Men Who Built the Transcontinental Railroad.* New York: Simon and Schuster, 2000.

Ambruster, Kurt E. *Orphan Road: The Railroad Comes to Seattle.* Pullman: Washington State University Press, 1999.

American National Biography. 22 vols. New York: Oxford University Press, 1999.

Andrist, Ralph K. *The Long Death: The Last Days of the Plains Indian.* 1964; reprint, New York: Macmillan Publishing Co., 1993.

Annin, Jim. *They Gazed on the Beartooths.* 3 vols. Columbus, Mont.: privately printed, 1964.

Augspurger, Owen B. "A Buffalo Lawyer Takes Greeley's Advice." *Niagara Frontier* (Buffalo and Erie County [New York] Historical Society) 7, no. 1 (Spring 1960).

Bacon, Benjamin W. *Sinews of War: How Technology, Industry, and Transportation Won the Civil War.* Novato, Calif.: Presidio Press, 1997.

Badeau, Adam. *Grant in Peace, from Appomattox to Mount McGregor.* 1887; reprint, Freeport, N.Y.: Books for Libraries Press, 1971.

Bailey, John W. *Pacifying the Plains: General Alfred Terry and the Decline of the Sioux.* Westport, Conn.: Greenwood Press, 1979.

Bain, David Haward. *Empire Express: Building the First Transcontinental Railroad.* New York: Viking Press, 1999.

Barnard, Sandy. *I Go With Custer: The Life and Death of Reporter Mark Kellogg.* Bismarck: Bismarck Tribune, 1996.

————, ed. *Ten Years with Custer: A 7th Cavalryman's Memoirs.* Terre Haute, Ind.: AST Press, 1991.

Barnett, Louise. *Touched by Fire: The Life, Death, and Mystic Afterlife of George Armstrong Custer.* New York: Henry Holt and Company, 1996.

Barrows, Isabel C. *A Sunny Life: The Biography of Samuel June Barrows.* Boston: Little, Brown, and Company, 1913.

Bean, Geraldine. "General Alfred Sulley and the Northwest Indian Expedition." *North Dakota History* 33, no. 3 (Summer 1966).

Beane, Thomas O. "Thomas L. Rosser." *History: The Magazine of Albemarle County [Virginia].*

Bergmann, Kurt. *Brackett's Battalion, Minnesota Cavalry, 1861–66.* Minneapolis: Adeniram Publications, 1996.

Berton, Pierre. *The National Dream: The Great [Canadian Pacific] Railway* and t*he National Dream: The Last Spike.* 2 vols. 1970 and 1974; reprint, Toronto: Penguin Books, 1989.

Blackburn, William M. *History of North and South Dakota.* With notes by Doane Robinson. Pierre: South Dakota Historical Collections, 1902.

Blackstead, David J., ed. *Bismarck 100: Official Publication of the Bismarck Centennial Association.* Bismarck: Bismarck Centennial Association, 1972.

Bluemle, John P. *The Face of North Dakota.* Revised ed. Bismarck: North Dakota Geological Survey, 1991.

Bonney, Orrin H., and Lorraine Bonney. *Battle Drums and Geysers: The Life and Journals of Lt. Gustavus Cheney Doane, Soldier and Explorer of the Yellowstone and Snake River Regions.* Chicago: Sage Books, 1970.

Boyes, W. *Custer's Black White Man.* Washington, D.C.: South Capitol Press, 1972.

Brackett, Russell D. *The Story of George Augustus Brackett (1821–1921) and His Descendants: A Genealogy.* Minneapolis: privately printed, 1977.

Bray, Kingsley M. "Teton Sioux Population History, 1655–1881." *Nebraska History* (Summer 1994).

Bridges, Hal. *Iron Millionaire: Life of Charlemagne Tower.* Philadelphia: University of Pennsylvania Press, 1952.

Brown, Dee. *Bury My Heart at Wounded Knee.* Norwalk, Conn.: Easton Press, 1989.

————. *The Galvanized Yankees.* 1963; reprint, Lincoln: University of Nebraska Press, 1986.

————. *Hear That Lonesome Whistle Blow: Railroads in the West.* New York: Holt, Rinehart and Winston, 1977.

Brown, John K. *The Baldwin Locomotive Works, 1831–1915: A Study in American Industrial Practice.* 1995; reprint, Baltimore: Johns Hopkins University Press, 2001.

Brown, Mark H. "Frederick S. Calhoun: A Little-Known Member of the 'Custer Clique.'" *Greasy Grass* 10 (May 1994).

————. *The Plainsmen of the Yellowstone.* New York: G. P. Putnam's Sons, 1961.

————. *Who Broke the Treaty of 1868?* Presentation, June 21, 1975. "1855–1875" folder. Billings-Parmerly Library, Montana Room, Billings, Montana.

Brown, Mark H., and William R. Felton. *Before Barbed Wire* [and] *The Frontier Years: L. A. Huffman, Photographer on Horseback.* 2 vols. New York: Holt, Rinehart and Winston, 1955–56.

Burgum, Jessamine Slaughter. *Zezula or Pioneer Days in the Smoky Water Country: A Collection of Historical Sketches . . . of the Early and Romantic History of Dakota Territory along the Missouri River.* Valley City, N.Dak.: Getchell and Nielsen, n.d. (ca. 1930s).

Burlingame, Merrill G. *The Montana Frontier.* 1941; reprint, Bozeman: Montana State University Press, 1980.

Bursack, William W., with Jerry R. Masters. "The Northern Pacific before the Last Spike: Locating the Route." Unpublished. 2004.

Burt, Struthers. *Powder River: Let 'er Buck.* New York: Farrar and Rinehart, 1938.

Bushong, Millard K., and Dean M. Bushong. *Fightin' Tom Rosser, C.S.A.* Shippensburg, Pa.: Beidel Printing House, 1983.

Carley, Kenneth. *The Sioux Uprising of 1862.* St. Paul: Minnesota Historical Society, 1976.

Carroll, John Melvin, ed. *Camp Talk: The Very Private Letters of Frederick W. Benteen of the 7th U.S. Cavalry to His Wife, 1871–1888.* Mattituck, N.Y.: J. M. Carroll and Company, 1983.

———, general ed. *Cavalry Bits: The Yellowstone Expedition of 1873.* Mattituck, N.Y.: J. M. Carroll and Company, 1986.

———, ed. *The Custer Autograph Album.* College Station, Tex.: Creative Publishing Co., 1994.

———. *Custer in Texas: An Interrupted Narrative.* New York: Lewis-Liveright Publishers, 1975.

Castel, Albert. *Decision in the West: The Atlanta Campaign of 1864.* Lawrence: University Press of Kansas, 1992.

Chandler, Alfred D., Jr. *The Visible Hand: The Managerial Revolution in American Business.* Cambridge, Mass.: Harvard University Press, 1977.

Cheney, Roberta Carkeek. *Names on the Face of Montana: The Story of Montana's Place Names.* Missoula: Mountain Press Publishing Co., 1996.

Chernow, Ron. *The House of Morgan: An American Banking Dynasty and the Rise of Modern Finance.* 1990; reprint, New York: Simon and Schuster, 1991.

Chittenden, Hiram Martin. *The American Fur Trade of the Far West.* 2 vols. 1935; reprint, Lincoln: University of Nebraska Press, 1986.

———. *History of Early Steamboat Navigation on the Missouri River: Life and Adventures of Joseph La Barge.* 2 vols. New York: Francis P. Harper, 1903.

———. *The Yellowstone National Park.* Ed. Richard A. Bartlett. 1895; reprint, Norman: University of Oklahoma Press, 1964.

Clark, John E., Jr. *Railroads in the Civil War: The Impact of Management on Victory and Defeat.* Baton Rouge: Louisiana State University Press, 2001.

Clawson, Roger. *Pompey's Pillar: Crossroads of the West.* Billings, Mont.: Prose Works, 1992.

Clodfelter, Michael. *The Dakota War: The United States Army vs. the Sioux, 1862–1865.* Jefferson, N.C.: McFarland and Company, 1998.

Cochran, Thomas C. *Railroad Leaders, 1845–1890: The Business Mind in Action.* Cambridge, Mass.: Harvard University Press, 1953.

Connell, Evan S. *Son of the Morning Star: Custer and Little Big Horn.* San Francisco: North Point Press, 1984.

Cozzens, Peter. *General John Pope: A Life for the Nation.* Urbana: University of Illinois Press, 2000.

Crawford, Lewis F. *History of North Dakota.* Chicago: American Historical Society, 1931.

Cronon, William. *Changes in the Land: Indians, Colonists, and the Ecology of New England.* New York: Hill and Wang, 1983.

Crozier, Emmet. *Yankee Reporters, 1861–65.* 1956; reprint, Westport, Conn.: Greenwood Press, 1973.

Cullum, George W. *Biographical Register of the Officers and Graduates of the United States Military Academy . . .* Boston: Houghton, Mifflin and Company, 1891.

Custer, Elizabeth B. *Boots and Saddles, or Life in Dakota with General Custer.* 1885; reprint, Norman: University of Oklahoma Press, 1987.

Darling, Roger. *Custer's Seventh Cavalry Comes to Dakota.* El Segundo, Calif.: Upton and Sons, 1989.

De Barthe, Joe. *The Life and Adventures of Frank Grouard.* Ed. Edger I. Stewart. New York: Time-Life Books, 1980.

DeLand, Charles Edmond. "Basil Clement (Claymore): The Mountain Trappers." *South Dakota Historical Collections* (1922).

———. *The Sioux Wars.* South Dakota Historical Collections, vols. 15 and 17. Pierre, S.Dak.: State Publishing Company, 1930 and 1934.

Delo, David M. *The Yellowstone, Forever!* Helena, Mont.: Kingfisher Books, 1998.

Denig, Edwin Thompson. *Five Indian Tribes of the Upper Missouri: Sioux, Arikaras, Crees, Assiniboines, Crows.* Ed. John C. Ewers. 1961; reprint, Norman: University of Oklahoma Press, 1989.

Diamond, Jared. *Guns, Germs and Steel: The Fates of Human Societies.* New York: W. W. Norton and Company, 1997.

Dictionary of American Biography. Ed. Dumas Malone. 24 vols. (includes 2 supplements). New York: Charles Scribner's Sons, 1928–44.

Diessner, Don. *There Are No Indians Left But Me!: Sitting Bull's Story.* El Segundo, Calif.: Upton and Sons, Publishers, 1993.

Dixon, David. "The Sordid Side of the Seventh Cavalry." *Journal of the Little Big Horn Associates* (June 1987).

Donald, David, ed. *Inside Lincoln's Cabinet: The Civil War Diaries of Salmon P. Chase.* New York: Longmans, Green and Company, 1954.

Drache, Hiram M. "The Economic Aspects of the Northern Pacific Railroad in North Dakota." *North Dakota History* 34, no. 4 (Fall 1967).

Duffus, R. L. "Railway Epic of the Great Northwest: The Completion of the Northern

Pacific Fifty Years Ago." *New York Times Magazine*, September 3, 1933.

Earle, Alice Morse. *Stage Coach and Tavern Days.* 1900; reprint, New York: Dover Publications, 1969.

Eastman, Charles A. *Indian Heroes and Great Chieftains.* 1918; reprint, Lincoln: University of Nebraska Press, 1993.

———. *The Soul of the Indian: An Interpretation.* 1911; reprint, Lincoln: University of Nebraska Press, 1989.

Ege, Robert J. *"Tell Baker to Strike Them Hard": Incident on the Marias, 23 Jan. 1870.* Bellevue, Neb.: Old Army Press, 1970.

Elliott, Howard. "Jay Cooke, Duluth and the Northern Pacific Railway." Address at the unveiling of Jay Cooke's statue, October 15, 1921. Printed by the Northern Pacific Railroad, ca. 1921–22.

Ellis, Richard N. *General Pope and U.S. Indian Policy.* Albuquerque: University of New Mexico Press, 1972.

Englehardt, Carroll. "The Incorporation of America: The Northern Pacific, the Lake Superior and Puget Sound Company, and the Founding of Fargo-Moorhead." *North Dakota History* 68, no. 4 (Winter 2001–2002).

Ewers, John C. *Indian Life on the Upper Missouri.* 1968; reprint, Norman: University of Oklahoma Press, 1988.

Farr, William E. "Going to Buffalo: Indian Hunting Migrations across the Rocky Mountains." *Montana: The Magazine of Western History* 53–54, nos. 4 and 1 (Winter and Spring 2003–2004).

Faust, Patricia L., ed. *Historical Times Illustrated Encyclopedia of the Civil War.* New York: Harper and Row, 1986.

Fawley, Paul C. "A History of the Yellowstone River Basin, from the Earliest Explorations to 1865." Master's thesis. Bozeman: State University of Montana, 1934.

Flynn, John T. *Men of Wealth: The Story of Twelve Significant Fortunes from the Renaissance to the Present Day.* New York: Simon and Schuster, 1941.

Fox, William F. *Regimental Losses in the Civil War: A Treatise on the Extent and Nature of the Mortuary Losses in the Union Regiments . . .* 1898; reprint, Dayton, Ohio: Morningside Press, 1985.

Freedom, Gary S. "Moving Men and Supplies: Military Transportation on the Northern Great Plains, 1866–1891." *South Dakota History* 14, no. 2 (Summer 1984).

Freeman, Michael. *Railways and the Victorian Imagination.* New Haven: Yale University Press, 1999.

Frey, Robert Lovell, ed. *Encyclopedia of American Business History and Biography: Railroads in the Nineteenth Century.* New York: Facts on File, 1998.

———. "A Technological History of the Locomotives of the Northern Pacific Railway Company." Ph.D. dissertation, University of Minnesota, 1970; microfilm, University Microfilms, Ann Arbor, Mich.

Friendlander, Amy. *Emerging Infrastructure: The Growth of Railroads.* Reston, Va.: Corporation for National Research Initiatives, 1995.

Frost, Lawrence A. *Custer's 7th Cav and the Campaign of 1873.* El Segundo, Calif.: Upton and Sons, 1985.

———, ed. *Some Observations on the Yellowstone Expedition of 1873.* Glendale, Calif.: Arthur H. Clark Company, 1981.

Gerber, Max E. "The Steamboat and Indians of the Upper Missouri." *South Dakota History* 4, no. 1 (Winter 1973).

Glasrud, Clarence A., ed. *Roy Johnson's Red River Valley: A Selection of Historical Articles First Printed in the [Fargo] "Forum."* Moorhead, Minn.: Red River Valley Historical Society, 1982.

Goetzmann, William H. *Army Exploration in the American West, 1803–1863.* 1959; reprint, Austin: Texas State Historical Association, 1991.

———. *Exploration and Empire.* 1966; reprint, New York: Vintage Books, 1972.

Gordon, John Steele. *An Empire of Wealth: The Epic History of American Economic Power.* New York: HarperCollins, 2004.

———. "Paying for the [Civil] War." *American Heritage* (March 1990).

Gray, John S. "Bloody Knife, Ree Scout for Custer." *Westerners Brand Book* (Chicago) 17, no. 12 (February 1961).

———. *Custer's Last Campaign: Mitch Boyer and the Little Big Horn Reconstructed.* 1991; reprint, Lincoln: University of Nebraska Press, 1993.

——— "Custer Throws a Boomerang." *Montana* (Spring 1961).

———. "Frank Grouard: Kanaka Scout or Mulatto Renegade?" *Westerners Brand Book* (Chicago) 16, no. 8 (October 1959).

———. "Itinerant Frontier Photographers." *Montana* (Spring 1978).

———. "On the Trail of 'Lonesome Charley' Reynolds." *Westerners Brand Book* (Chicago) 14, no. 8 (October 1957).

Grayson, Theodore J. *Leaders and Periods of American Finance.* 1932; reprint, Freeport, N.Y.: Books for Libraries Press, 1969.

Grodinsky, Julius. *Transcontinental Railway Strategy, 1869–1893: A Study of Businessmen.* Philadelphia: University of Pennsylvania Press, 1962.

Grosvenor, W. N. "The Railroads and the Farms." *Atlantic Monthly* (November 1873).

Hadley, Arthur T. *Railroad Transportation: Its History and Laws.* New York: G. P. Putnam's Sons, 1897.

Haines, Aubrey L. *The Yellowstone Story: A History of Our First National Park.* Rev. ed. 2 vols. Niwot: University Press of Colorado, 1996.

Hamilton, James M. "History of Fort Ellis." Speech, May 12, 1933. Burlingame Library, Montana State University, Bozeman.

Hammer, Kenneth M. *Men with Custer: Biographies of the 7th Cavalry.* Ed. Ronald H. Nichols. Hardin, Mont.: Custer Battlefield and Historical Association, 1995.

———. "Railroads and the Frontier Garrisons of Dakota Territory." *North Dakota History* 46, no. 3 (Summer 1979).

———. "Territorial Towns and the Railroads." *North Dakota History* 4 (Fall 1969).

Hanson, Joseph Mills. *The Conquest of the Missouri: Being the Story of the Life and Exploits of Captain Grant Marsh.* 1916; reprint, Machanicsburg, Pa.: Stackpole Books, 2003.

———. "Thomas Lafayette Rosser." *Cavalry Journal* (March–April 1934).

Hanson, Victor Davis. *Carnage and Culture: Landmark Battles in the Rise of Western Culture.* New York: Doubleday, 2001.

Hardorff, Richard G. "Baliran, Honzinger, and the Custers: The Facts and Fictions of the Rain-in-the-Face Myth." *Journal of the Little Big Horn Associates* (December 1988).

Harnsberger, John L. *Jay Cooke and Minnesota: The Formative Years of the Northern Pacific Railroad, 1868–1873.* 1956; reprint, New York: Arno Press, 1981.

———. "Jay Cooke and the Financing of the Northern Pacific Railroad." *North Dakota Quarterly* (Autumn 1969).

———. "Jay Cooke, the Northern Pacific and the Founding of Bismarck. D.T." *North Dakota Quarterly* (Summer 1981).

———. "Railroads to the Northern Plains, 1870–1872." *North Dakota Quarterly* (Summer 1959).

Harnsberger, John L., and Robert P. Wilkins. "Transportation on the Northern Plains, I. The Genesis of Commerce; III. The Railroads Arrive." *North Dakota Quarterly* (Winter 1961; Summer 1961).

Hassrick, Royal B. *The Sioux.* 1964; reprint, Norman: University of Oklahoma Press, 1989.

Hatch, Thom. *Custer and the Battle of the Little Bighorn: An Encyclopedia.* Jefferson, N.C.: McFarland and Company, 1997.

Hatcher, Harlan. *The Great Lakes.* New York: Oxford University Press, 1944.

Haynes, C. Vance, Jr. "Geoarcheological Survey of the Reservation Creek Battlefield, Montana." Believed to be unpublished, ca. 1992.

Hedges, James B. "The Colonization Work of the Northern Pacific Railroad." *Mississippi Valley Historical Review* 13, no. 3 (December 1926).

Hedren, Paul L. *Traveler's Guide to the Great Sioux War.* Helena: Montana Historic Society Press, 1996.

Heitman, Francis B. *Historical Register and Dictionary of the United States Army . . . from September 29, 1789, to March 2, 1903.* 1903; reprint, Urbana: University of Illinois Press, 1965.

Heski, Thomas M. *The Little Shadow Catcher: D. F. Barry, Celebrated Photographer of Famous Indians.* Seattle: Superior Publishing Co., 1978.

———. "Soldiers, Surveyors, Steamboats and Stanley's Stockade." *Research & Review: Journal of the Little Big Horn Associates* (Summer 1999).

———. "The Trail to Heart River and the Rediscovery of James N. DeWolf." *Research & Review: Journal of the Little Big Horn Associates* (June 1995).

Hobson, Archie, ed. *The Cambridge Gazetteer of the United States and Canada: A Dictionary of Places.* New York: Cambridge University Press, 1995.

Hodge, Frederick W., ed. *Handbook of American Indians North of Mexico.* 2 vols. 1906; reprint, New York: Pageant Books, 1959.

Hoopes, Lorman L. *This Last West: Miles City, Montana Territory, 1876–1886—The People, the Geography, the Incredible History.* Miles City, Mont.: privately printed, 1990.

Houston, E. Lina. *Early History of Gallatin County.* Bozeman: privately printed, 1933.

Howard, Joseph Kinsey. *Strange Empire: A Narrative of the Northwest.* 1952; reprint, St. Paul: Minnesota Historical Society, 1994.

Hoxie, Frederick E. *Parading through History: The Making of the Crow Nation in America, 1805–1935.* Cambridge: Cambridge University Press, 1995.

Hungerford, Edward, et al. *Vermont Central—Central Vermont: A Study in Human Effort.* Boston: Railway and Locomotive Historic Society/Harvard Business School, 1942.

Hunt, Roger D. *Brevet Generals in Blue.* Gaithersburg, Md.: Olde Soldier Books, 1990.

Hunter, Louis C., and Beatrice Jones Hunter. *Steamboats on the Western Rivers: An Economic and Technological History.* Cambridge, Mass.: Harvard University Press, 1949.

Hutton, Paul Andrew, ed. *The Custer Reader.* Lincoln: University of Nebraska Press, 1992.

———. *Phil Sheridan and His Army.* 1985; reprint, Lincoln: University of Nebraska Press, 1989.

———. "Phil Sheridan's Frontier." *Montana* (Winter 1988).

———. "Phil Sheridan's Pyrrhic Victory: The Piegan Massacre, Army Politics, and the Transfer Debate." *Montana* (Spring 1982).

Hyde, George E. *Red Cloud's Folk: A History of the Oglala Sioux Indians.* 1937; reprint, Norman: University of Oklahoma Press, 1987.

———. *Spotted Tail's Folk: A History of the Brulé Sioux.* 1961; reprint, Norman: University of Oklahoma Press, 1987.

An Illustrated History of the Yellowstone Valley. Spokane: Western Historical Publishing Company, 1907.

Innis, Ben. *Bloody Knife: Custer's Favorite Scout.* 1973; reprint, Bismarck: Smokey Water Press, 1994.

———. *A Chronological Record of Events at the Missouri–Yellowstone Confluence Area from 1805 to 1895.* Williston, N.Dak.: Fort Buford 6th Infantry Regiment Association, 1971.

Iseminger, Gordon L. "Land and Emigration: A Northern Pacific Railroad Company Newspaper." *North Dakota Quarterly* (Summer 1981).

Jackson, Donald. *Voyages of the Steamboat Yellow Stone.* New York: Ticknor and Fields, 1985.

Jackson, W. Turrentine. *Wagon Roads West: A Study of Federal Road Surveys and Construction in the Trans-Mississippi West, 1846–1869.* Berkeley: University of California Press, 1952.

Jensen, Derrick, and George Draffen. *Railroads and Clearcuts: Legacy of Congress's 1864 Northern Pacific Railroad Land Grant.* Spokane: Inland Empire Public Lands Council, 1995.

Jensen, Oliver. *American Heritage History of Railroads in America.* 1975; reprint, New York: Random House, 1993.

Johnson, Roy P. "Maj. Gen. Thomas L. Rosser." *Fargo Forum.* 1950; reprinted April 2, 9, 16, 23, and 30 and May 7, 14, 21, and 28, 1978.

Jones, Robert C. *The Central Vermont Railway: A Yankee Tradition, Volume I, "The Early Years, 1830–1886."* Silverton, Colo.: Sundance Books, 1981.

Jordan, Tristam Frost. *The Jordan Memorial: Family Records of the Rev. Robert Jordan and His Descendants in America.* 1882; reprint, Camden, Maine: Picton Press, 1995.

Josephson, Matthew. *The Robber Barons: The Great American Capitalists, 1861–1901.* 1934; reprint, Norwalk, Conn.: Easton Press, 1987.

Kelsey, Vera. *Red River Runs North!* New York: Harper and Brothers, 1951.

Kennedy, Roger G. *Hidden Cities: The Discovery and Loss of Ancient North American Civilization.* New York: Macmillan, 1994.

Kingsbury, George Washington. *History of the Dakota Territory [and] South Dakota: Its History and Its People.* 5 vols. Chicago: S. J. Clarke Publishing Co., 1915.

Kinsey, Joni Louise. *Thomas Moran and the Surveying of the American West.* Washington, D.C.: Smithsonian Institution Press, 1992.

Kirby, Richard Shelton, and Philip Gustave Laurson. *The Early Years of Modern Civil Engineering.* New Haven: Yale University Press, 1932.

Kirby, Richard Shelton, Philip Gustave Laurson, Sidney Withington, Arthur B. Darling, and Frederick G. Kilgour. *Engineering in History.* 1956; reprint, New York: Dover Publications, 1990.

Koury, Michael J. *Military Posts of Montana.* Bellevue, Neb.: Olde Army Press, 1970.

Krech, Shepard, III. *The Ecological Indian: Myth and History.* New York: W. W. Norton and Company, 1999.

Krick, Robert K. "'The Cause of All My Disasters': Jubal A. Early and the Undisciplined Valley Cavalry." In *Struggle for the Shenandoah: Essays on the 1864 Valley Campaign,* ed. Gary W. Gallagher. Kent, Ohio: Kent State University Press, 1991.

Kroeker, Marvin E. *Great Plains Command: William B. Hazen in the Frontier West.* Norman: University of Oklahoma Press, 1975.

Kvasnicka, Robert M., and Herman J. Viola, eds. *The Commissioners of Indian Affairs, 1824–1977.* Lincoln: University of Nebraska Press, 1979.

Lamar, Howard R. *Dakota Territory 1861–1889: A Study of Frontier Politics.* New Haven: Yale University Press, 1966.

———. *The New Encyclopedia of the American West.* New Haven: Yale University Press, 1998.

Larson, Henrietta M. *Jay Cooke: Private Banker.* Cambridge, Mass.: Harvard University Press, 1936.

———. "Jay Cooke's Early Work in Transportation." *Pennsylvania Magazine of History and Biography* (Historic Society of Pennsylvania, Philadelphia) 59, no. 4 (October 1935).

Larson, Robert W. *Red Cloud: Warrior-Statesman of the Lakota Sioux.* Norman: University of Oklahoma Press, 1997.

Lass, William E. *A History of Steamboating on the Upper Missouri River.* Lincoln: University of Nebraska Press, 1962.

———. "Steamboats on the Yellowstone." *Montana* (Autumn 1985).

Lawson, Melinda. *Patriot Fires: Forging a New American Nationalism in the Civil War North.* Lawrence: University Press of Kansas, 2002.

Licht, Walter. *Working for the Railroad: The Organization of Work in the Nineteenth Century.* Princeton: Princeton University Press, 1983.

Liddic, Bruce R., and Paul Harbaugh, eds. *Custer and Company: Walter Camp's Notes on the Custer Fight.* 1995; reprint, Lincoln: University of Nebraska Press, 1998.

Linklater, Andro. *Measuring America: How an Untamed Wilderness Shaped the United States and Fulfilled the Promise of Democracy.* New York: Walker and Company, 2002.

Longacre, Edward G. *The Cavalry at Appomattox: A Tactical Study of Mounted Operations.* Mechanicsburg, Pa.: Stackpole Books, 2003.

———. *Custer and His Wolverines: The Michigan Cavalry Brigade, 1861–1865.* Conshoshocken, Pa.: Combined Publishing Co., 1997.

Lounsberry, Clement A. *Early History of North Dakota: Essential Outlines of American History* 1919; reprint, Ann Arbor, Mich.: University Microfilms International, 1978.

Lubetkin, M. John. "An Ambush That Changed History: Thomas Rosser, David Stanley, Gall and the 1872 Eastern Yellowstone Survey." *Journal of the West* 43, no. 1 (Winter 2004).

———. "Clash on the Yellowstone: Monday, August 4, 1873." *Research & Review: The Journal of the Little Big Horn Associates* 17, no. 2 (Summer 2003).

———. "The Forgotten Yellowstone Surveying Expeditions of 1871: W. Milnor Roberts and the Northern Pacific in Montana." *Montana: The Magazine of Western History* 52, no. 4 (Winter 2002).

———. "The 1906 Reunion: Thomas L. Rosser and the Northern Pacific Pioneers of 1873." *Mainstreeter* 22, no. 2 (Summer 2003).

———. "Thomas L. Rosser and the Yellowstone Surveying Expedition of 1873." *North Dakota History* 70, no. 3 (2003).

———. *Union College's Class of 1868: The Unique Experiences of Some Average Americans.* McLean, Va.: privately published, 1995.

MacDonald, John G. "History of Navigation on the Yellowstone River." Master's thesis, Montana State University–Bozeman, 1950.

Malles, Ed, ed. *Bridge Building in Wartime: Colonel Wesley Brainerd's Memoir of the 50th New York Volunteer Engineers.* Knoxville: University of Tennessee Press, 1997.

Malone, Michael P., Richard B. Roeder, and William B. Land. *Montana: A History of Two Centuries.* Seattle: University of Washington Press, 1988.

Mangum, Neil. "Gall: Sioux Gladiator or White Man's Pawn." 5th Annual Symposium, Custer Battlefield and Historical Museum Association, Hardin, Montana, 1991.

Mann, Charles C. *1491: New Revelations of the Americas before Columbus.* New York: Knopf, 2005.

Marquis, Thomas B. (as told to). *Memoirs of a White Crow Indian (Thomas H. Leforge)*. 1928; reprint, Lincoln: University of Nebraska Press, ca. 1995.

Martin, Ralph G. *Jennie: The Life of Lady Randolph Churchill*. Englewood Cliffs, N.J.: Prentice-Hall, 1969–71.

———. *Rain-in-the-Face and Curly: The Crow*. Hardin, Mont.: Custer Battle Museum, 1934.

———. *Sitting Bull and Gall: The Warrior*. Scottsdale, Ariz.: privately printed, 1934.

Masters, Jerry R. "The Bismarck Bridge." *Mainstreeter* 16, no. 2 (Spring 1997).

———. "Building the New Salem Cutoff." *Mainstreeter* 17, no. 3 (Summer 1998).

———. "Routes across the Rockies." *Mainstreeter* 21, no. 2 (Summer 2002).

Mattison, Ray H. "The Army Post on the Northern Plains, 1865–1885." Originally published in *Nebraska History* 35. Reprinted by the Oregon Trail Museum Association, Gering, Neb., 1962.

———. "Fort Rice: North Dakota's First Missouri River Military Post." *North Dakota History* 20 (1953).

McChristian, Douglas C. *The U.S. Army in the West, 1870–1880: Uniforms, Weapons, and Equipment*. Norman: University of Oklahoma Press, 1995.

McCulloch, Hugh. *Men and Measures of Half a Century: Sketches and Comments*. New York: Charles Scribner's Sons, 1888.

McDermott, John D. "The *Frontier Scout*: A View of Fort Rice in 1865." *North Dakota History* (Fall 1994).

McDonald, Capt. William N. *A History of the Laurel Brigade*. 1907; reprint, Arlington, Va.: Beatty Press, 1973.

McFeely, William S. *Grant: A Biography*. 1981; reprint, Norwalk, Conn.: Easton Press, 1987.

McKinney, Francis F. *Education in Violence: The Life of George H. Thomas and the History of the Army of the Cumberland*. 1961; reprint, Chicago: Americana House, 1991.

McLemore, Clyde. "Fort Pease: The First Attempted Settlement in Yellowstone Valley." *Montana Magazine of History* (January 1952).

McNeill, William H. *Plagues and Peoples*. Garden City, N.Y., Doubleday, 1976.

Meigs, Cornelia Lynde. *Railroad West: A Novel*. Boston: Little, Brown and Company, 1937.

Mercer, Lloyd J. *Railroads and Land Grant Policy*. New York: Academic Press, 1982.

Merington, Marguerite, ed. *The Custer Story: The Life and Intimate Letters of General George A. Custer and His Wife Elizabeth*. 1950; reprint, Lincoln: University of Nebraska Press, 1987.

Meyer, Roy W. *History of the Santee Sioux: United States Indian Policy on Trial*. Lincoln: University of Nebraska Press, 1967.

Mickelson, Sig. *The Northern Pacific Railroad and the Selling of the West*. Sioux Falls, S.Dak.: Center for Western Studies, Augustana College, 1993.

Mills, Charles K. *Harvest of Barren Regrets: The Army Career of Frederick William Benteen, 1834–1898*. Glendale, Calif.: Arthur H. Clark Company, 1985.

Minnigerode, Meade. *Certain Rich Men: Stephen Girard—John Jacob Astor—Jay Cooke—Daniel Drew—Cornelius Vanderbilt—Jay Gould—Jim Fisk.* New York: G. P. Putnam's Sons, 1927.

Moorhead, Elizabeth. *Whirling Spindle: The Story of a Pittsburgh Family.* Pittsburgh: University of Pittsburgh Press, 1942.

Murray, Robert A. *The Army Moves West: Supplying the Western Indian Wars Campaigns.* Fort Collins, Colo.: Old Army Press, 1981.

Myhra, Thomas J. "The Economic Influence of Steamboats on Early Bismarck." *North Dakota History* 29, no. 2 (April 1961).

The National Cyclopaedia of American Biography. 61 vols. New York: James T. White and Company, 1898–1982.

Nevins, Allan. *Hamilton Fish: The Inner History of the Grant Administration.* New York: Frederick Ungar Publishing Co., 1957.

Nordhoff, Charles. "The Columbia River and Puget Sound." *Harper's New Monthly Magazine* (February 1874).

Oberholtzer, Ellis Paxson. *A History of the United States since the Civil War.* 5 vols. New York: Macmillan Company, 1937.

———. *Jay Cooke: Financier of the Civil War.* 2 vols. 1907; reprint, New York: Augustus M. Kelley Publishers, 1968.

O'Connor, Richard. *Iron Wheels and Broken Men: The Railroad Barons and the Plunder of the West.* New York: G. P. Putnam's Sons, 1973.

Olson, James C. *Red Cloud and the Sioux Problem.* 1965; reprint, Lincoln: University of Nebraska Press, 1975.

Parkman, Francis. *The Oregon Trail.* 1847; reprint, New York: Literary Guild, 1945.

Parsons, John E. "Sioux Resistance on the Yellowstone, 1872." *Westerners New York Posse Brand Book* (New York) 3, no. 1 (1956).

Paul, R. Eli, ed. *Autobiography of Red Cloud, War Leader of the Oglalas.* Helena: Montana Historical Society Press, 1997.

Perret, Geoffrey. *Ulysses S. Grant: Soldier & President.* New York: Random House, 1997.

Pfaller, Louis, Reverend. "The Fort Keough to Bismarck Stage Route." *North Dakota History* 21, no. 3 (July 1954).

Pohanka, Brian, "George Yates: Captain of the Band Box Troop." *Greasy Grass* (May 1992).

———. *A Summer on the Plains, 1870: From the Diary of Annie Gibson Roberts.* Bryan, Tex.: J. M. Carroll and Company, 1983.

Pollard, James E. *The Journal of Jay Cooke, or The Gibraltar Records, 1865–1905.* Columbus: Ohio State University Press, 1935.

Popovich, John. "Incident along the Yellowstone: The Man Who Amazed the '73 Expedition." *Journal of the Yellowstone Corral of the Westerners* (Fall/Winter 1983).

Powell, Peter John. *People of the Sacred Mountain: A History of the Northern Cheyenne Chiefs and Warrior Societies, 1830–1879.* 2 vols. San Francisco: Harper and Row, 1981.

Powell, William H. *List of Officers of the Army of the United States from 1799 to 1900.* 1900; reprint, Detroit: Gale Research Company, 1967.

Pratt, Fletcher. *Ordeal by Fire: An Informal History of the Civil War.* New York: Harrison Smith and Robert Haas, 1935.

Praus, Alex. *The Sioux, 1798–1922: A Dakota Winter Count.* Bloomfield Hills, Mich.: Cranbrook Institute of Science, 1962.

Prucha, Francis Paul. *American Indian Policy in Crisis: Christian Reformers and the Indians, 1865–1900.* Norman: University of Oklahoma Press, 1976.

———. *American Indian Treaties: The History of a Political Anomaly.* 1994; reprint, Berkeley: University of California Press, 1997.

———. *Broadaxe and Bayonet: The Role of the United States Army in the Development of the Northwest, 1815–1860.* 1953; reprint, Lincoln: University of Nebraska Press, 1995.

———. *The Great Father: The United States Government and the American Indians.* Lincoln: University of Nebraska Press, 1984.

Raban, Jonathan. *Bad Land: An American Romance.* New York: Pantheon Press, 1996.

Rae, William Fraser. *Westward by Rail: The New Route to the East.* 1871; reprint, New York: Promontory Press, 1974.

Raffe, Deirdre N. "The Significance of Thomas Hawley Canfield's Life." Master's thesis, Burlington, University of Vermont, 1995.

Remele, Larry, ed. *Fort Buford and the Military Frontier on the Northern Plains.* Bismarck: State Historical Society of North Dakota, 1987.

Renz, Louis Tuck, *The Construction of the Northern Pacific Railroad.* Walla Walla, Wash.: privately printed, 1973.

———. *The History of the Northern Pacific Railroad.* Fairfield, Wash.: Ye Galleon Press, 1980.

Richland County Farmer-Globe (Wahpeton, N.Dak.). *Fort Abercrombie, 1862.* Special supplement of September 22, 1936; reprint, West Fargo, N.Dak.: Pioneer Enterprises, 1989.

Riegel, Robert Edgar. *The Story of the Western Railroads: From 1852 through the Reign of the Giants.* 1926; reprint, Lincoln: University of Nebraska Press, 1990.

Rister, Carl C. *Border Command: General Phil Sheridan in the West.* Norman: University of Oklahoma Press, 1944.

Robertson, Donald B. *Encyclopedia of Western Railroad History, Volume II: The Western States, Colorado, Idaho, Montana, Wyoming.* Dallas: Taylor Publishing Company, 1991.

———. *Encyclopedia of Western Railroad History, Volume III: Oregon, Washington.* Caldwell, Idaho: Caxton Printers, 1995.

Robertson, Francis B. "'We Are Going to Have a Big Sioux War': Colonel David S. Stanley's Yellowstone Expedition of 1872." *Montana* 34, no. 4 (Autumn 1984).

Robinson, Doane. *A History of the Dakota or Sioux Indians . . .* 1904; reprint, Minneapolis: Ross and Haines, 1956.

Robinson, Elwyn B. *History of North Dakota.* Lincoln: University of Nebraska Press, 1966.

Rodenbough, Theophilus F. *The Army of the United States . . .* New York: Maynard, Merrill Company, 1896.

Rolston, Alan. "The Yellowstone Expedition of 1873: Military-Civilian Contentions regarding Western Exploration and Indian Policy." *Montana* (Spring 1970).

Rottenberg, Dan. *The Man Who Made Wall Street: Anthony J. Drexel and the Rise of Modern Finance.* Philadelphia: University of Pennsylvania Press, 2001.

Sajna, Mike. *Crazy Horse: The Life behind the Legend.* New York: John Wiley and Sons, 2000.

Sandoz, Mari. *Crazy Horse: The Strange Man of the Oglalas.* 1942; reprint, Lincoln: University of Nebraska Press, 1992.

Schneider, Bill. *Montana's Yellowstone River.* Helena: Montana Magazine, 1985.

Schoenberger, Dale T. "Custer's Scouts." *Montana* (Spring 1966).

Schrenk, Lorenz P. "The Northern Pacific Pioneer Steam Era, 1870–1905." Manuscript.

Schubert, Frank N. *Vanguard of Expansion: Army Engineers in the Trans-Mississippi West, 1819–1879.* Washington, D.C.: U.S. Army Corps of Engineers, 1980.

Schuler, Harold H. *Fort Sully: Guns at Sunset.* Vermillion: University of South Dakota Press, 1992.

Schullery, Paul, and Lee Whittlesey. *Myth and History in the Creation of Yellowstone National Park.* Lincoln: University of Nebraska Press, 2003.

Secoy, Frank Raymond. *Changing Military Patterns of the Great Plains Indians: 17th Century through Early 19th Century.* 1953; reprint, Lincoln: University of Nebraska Press, 1992.

Selmeier, Lewis W. "First Camera on the Yellowstone." *Montana* (Summer 1972).

Sharp, Paul F. *Whoop-Up Country: The Canadian-American West, 1865–1885.* 1955; reprint, Norman: University of Oklahoma Press, 1973.

Shaughnessy, Jim. *The Rutland Road.* Berkeley, Calif.: Howell-North Books, 1964.

Sheldon, Robert C. "Surveying the Dakotas." *North Dakota Quarterly* (Winter 1961).

Shields, L. F. "Reminiscences of a Railroad Builder." *North Dakota Historical Quarterly* 1 (1927).

Sibbald, John R. "Frontier Inebriates with Epaulets." *Montana* (Summer 1969).

Sinclair, Angus. *Development of the Locomotive Engine: A History of the Growth of the Locomotive from Its Most Elementary Form.* 1907; reprint, Cambridge, Mass.: MIT Press, 1970.

Smalley, Eugene V. *The Great Northwest: A Guide Book and Itinerary for the Use of Tourists and Travelers over the Lines of the Northern Pacific Railroad.* St. Paul: Riley Brothers, 1886.

———. *History of the Northern Pacific Railroad.* 1883; reprint, New York: Arno Press, 1975.

Smith, George M. "The First Visit to the Head of the Lakes of Jay Cooke in 1867." American Exchange National Bank of Duluth, ca. 1920. Cooke file, Duluth Public Library.

Smith, Phyllis. *Bozeman and the Gallatin Valley: A History.* Helena, Mont.: Falcon Press, 1996.

Snortland, J. Signe, ed. *A Traveler's Companion to North Dakota State Historic Sites.* 2nd ed. Bismarck: State Historical Society of North Dakota, 2002.

Sobel, Robert. *Panic on Wall Street: A History of America's Financial Disasters.* New York: Macmillan Company, 1968.

Stearns, Harold G. "The Volunteer Hostage." *Montana* (Autumn 1968). Also see Mark H. Brown's "Letter to the Editor" concerning the Stearns article, *Montana* (Winter 1968).

Stearns, Harold Joseph. *A History of the Upper Musselshell Valley of Montana.* Harlowton, Mont.: Times-Clarion Publishers, 1966.

Stewart, Edgar I. *Custer's Luck.* 1955; reprint, Norman: University of Oklahoma Press, 1980.

————, ed. *Penny-an-Acre Empire in the West.* Norman: University of Oklahoma Press, 1968.

————. "A Psychoanalytic Approach to Custer." *Montana* (Summer 1971).

Straub, Hans. *A History of Civil Engineering: An Outline from Ancient to Modern Times.* Trans. Erwin Rockwell. London: Leonard Hill Limited, 1952.

Strouse, Jean. *Morgan: American Financier.* New York: Random House, 1999.

Sully, Langdon. *No Tears for the General: The Life of Alfred Sully, 1821–1879.* Palo Alto, Calif.: American West Publishing, 1974.

Swanton, John R. *The Indian Tribes of North America.* 1952; reprint, Washington, D.C.: Smithsonian Institution, ca. 1969.

Tapp, Hambleton. "James Proctor Knott and the Duluth Speech." *Register of the Kentucky Historical Society* 70, no. 2 (April 1972).

Tate, Michael L. *The Frontier Army and the Settlement of the West.* Norman: University of Oklahoma Press, 1999.

Taunton, Francis B. "Yellowstone Interlude: Custer's Fights with the Sioux." In *More Sidelights of the Sioux Wars.* Special Publication 10. London: English Westerners Society, 2004.

Taylor, Bill, and Jan Taylor. *The Northern Pacific's Mullan Pass on the "Montana Short Line."* Missoula: Pictorial Histories Publishing Company, 2002.

Taylor, Joseph Henry. "Bloody Knife and Gall." *North Dakota Historical Quarterly* 4, no. 3 (April 1930).

————. *Kaleidoscopic Lives: A Companion Book to "Frontier and Indian Life."* Washburn, N.Dak.: privately published, 1902.

————. *Sketches of Frontier and Indian Life on the Upper Missouri.* Bismarck: privately published, 1897. Also known as *Frontier and Indian Life.*

Thomas, William G., III. "'Under Indictment': Thomas Lafayette Rosser and the New South." *Virginia Magazine of History and Biography* 100, no. 2 (April 1992).

Thorndale, Theresa. *Sketches and Stories of the Lake Erie Islands.* Sandusky, Ohio: I. F. Mack and Brothers, Publishers, 1898.

Thornton, Russell. *American Indian Holocaust and Survival: A Population History since 1492.* Norman: University of Oklahoma Press, 1987.

Thrapp, Dan L. *Encyclopedia of Frontier Biography.* 3 vols. 1988; reprint, Lincoln: University of Nebraska Press, 1991.

Topping, E. S. *Chronicles of the Yellowstone.* 1884; reprint, Minneapolis: Ross and Haines, 1968.

Trimble, Michael K. *An Ethnohistorical Interpretation of the Spread of Smallpox in the Northern Plains Utilizing Concepts of Disease Ecology.* 1979; reprint, Lincoln, Neb.: J and L Reprint Company, 1986.

Tucker, Glen Edgar. *Hancock the Superb.* 1960; reprint, Dayton: Morningside Press, 1980.

———. *Victory Rode the Rails: The Strategic Place of Railroads in the Civil War.* 1953; reprint, Lincoln: University of Nebraska Press, 1992.

Ullery, Jacob G., ed. *Men of Vermont: An Illustrated Biographical History of Vermonters and Sons of Vermont.* Brattleboro, Vt.: Transcript Publishing Company, 1894.

United States Department of Commerce, U.S. Bureau of the Census. *Historical Statistics of the United States: Colonial Times to 1970.* Washington, D.C.: USGPO, 1975.

United States Department of Interior. *Biographical and Historical Index of American Indians and Persons Involved in Indian Affairs.* Boston: G. K. Hall, 1966.

———. U.S. Geological Survey. *Guidebook of the Western United States: Part A, The Northern Pacific Route . . .* Washington, D.C.: USGPO, 1916.

United States Military Academy. *Annual Reunion of the Association of the Graduates of the United States Military Academy.* West Point, N.Y., various annual issues.

United States Works Projects Administration (WPA). Federal Writers Project. *Minnesota: A State Guide.* 1938; reprint, New York: Hastings House, 1954.

———. *South Dakota, A Guide to the State.* 1938; reprint, New York: Hastings House, 1952.

———. *WPA Guide to 1930's Montana.* 1939; reprint, Tucson: University of Arizona Press, 1994.

———. *WPA Guide to 1930's North Dakota.* 1938; reprint, Bismarck: State Historical Society of North Dakota, 1990.

Utley, Robert M. *Cavalier in Buckskin: George Armstrong Custer and the Western Military Frontier.* Norman: University of Oklahoma Press, 1988.

———. *Frontier Regulars: The United States Army and the Indian, 1866–1891.* New York: Macmillan and Company, 1973.

———. *Frontiersmen in Blue: The United States Army and the Indian, 1848–1865.* 1967; reprint, Lincoln: University of Nebraska Press, 1981.

———. *The Indian Frontier and the American West.* 1983; reprint, Albuquerque: University of New Mexico Press, 1993.

———. *The Lance and the Shield: The Life and Times of Sitting Bull.* New York: Henry Holt and Company, 1993.

Van Brunt, Walter, ed. *Duluth and St. Louis County, Minnesota: Their Story and People.* Chicago: American Historical Society, 1921.

Van West, Carroll. *Capitalism on the Frontier: Billings and the Yellowstone Valley in the Nineteenth Century.* Lincoln: University of Nebraska Press, 1993.

Veenendaal, Augustus J., Jr. *The Saint Paul & Pacific Railroad: An Empire in the Making.* DeKalb: Northern Illinois University Press, 1999.

Vestal, Stanley. *The Missouri.* 1945; reprint, Norman: University of Oklahoma Press, 1996.

———. *New Sources of Indian History: 1850–1891, The Ghost Dance [and] The Prairie Sioux, A Miscellany.* Norman: University of Oklahoma Press, 1934.

———. *Sitting Bull: Champion of the Sioux.* 1932; reprint, Norman: University of Oklahoma Press, 1989.

———. "White Bull and One Bull: An Appreciation." *Chicago Westerners Brand Book* 4, no. 8 (October 1947).

Villard, Henry. *Memoirs of Henry Villard, Journalist and Financier, 1835–1900.* 1904; reprint, New York: Da Capo Press, 1969.

Warner, Ezra J. *Generals in Blue: Lives of the Union Commanders.* Baton Rouge: Louisiana State University Press, 1964.

Warren, Israel P. *The Stanley Families of America: As Descended from John, Timothy and Thomas Stanley.* Portland, Maine: B. Thurston and Co., 1887.

Way, Frederick, Jr. *Way's Packet Directory, 1848–1983: Passenger Steamboats of the Mississippi River System since the Advent of Photography . . .* Athens: Ohio University, 1983.

Weisberger, Bernard A. *Reporters for the Union.* Boston: Little Brown and Company, 1953.

Welch, James, with Paul Stekler. *Killing Custer: The Battle of the Little Bighorn and the Fate of the Plains Indians.* New York: W. W. Norton and Company, 1994.

Welsh, Dr. Jack D. *Medical Histories of Union Generals.* Kent, Ohio: Kent State University Press, 1996.

Wemett, W. E. "Making a Path to the Pacific: The Story of the Stevens Survey." *North Dakota History* 29, no. 4 (October 1962).

Wert, Jeffry D. *Custer: The Controversial Life of George Armstrong Custer.* New York: Simon and Schuster, 1996.

White, John H. *A History of the American Locomotive, Its Development: 1830–1880.* 1968; reprint, New York: Dover Publications, 1979.

White, William H. *Custer, Cavalry and Crows: The Story of William White as Told to Thomas Marquis.* Bellevue, Neb.: Old Army Press, 1975.

Windolph, Charles. *I Fought with Custer: The Story of Sergeant Windolph, Last Survivor of the Little Big Horn.* 1947; reprint, Lincoln: University of Nebraska Press, 1987.

Winks, Robin W. *Frederick Billings: A Life.* 1991; reprint, Berkeley: University of California Press, 1998.

Winser, Henry J. *The Great Northwest: A Guide-Book and Itinerary for the Use of Tourists and Travelers over the Lines of the Northern Pacific Railroad.* New York: G. P. Putnam's Sons, 1883.

Wissler, Clark. *Indians of the United States.* 1940; reprint, Garden City, N.Y.: Doubleday Anchor Books, 1966.

Wood, Charles R. *The Northern Pacific: Main Street of the Northwest*. Seattle: Superior Publishing Company, 1968.

Newspapers and Periodicals

Army and Navy Journal. Weekly; May 1869–July 1874.

Bismarck Tribune. Weekly; June 1873–September 1874.

Bozeman Avant Courier. Weekly; September 1871–December 1873.

Brainerd Tribune. Weekly; February 1872–September 1873.

Chicago Inter-Ocean. Daily; May–October 1872; June–September 1873.

Commercial and Financial Chronicle. Weekly; July 1871–December 1873.

Duluth Minnesotian. Weekly; January 1870–December 1871.

Frank Leslie's Illustrated Newspaper. Weekly; September 1870–mid-February 1874.

Greasy Grass. Custer Battlefield Historical and Museum Association. Annual, 1985 to present.

Harper's New Monthly Magazine. June 1870–May 1874.

Harper's Weekly. January 1871–December 1873.

Helena Herald. Daily and weekly; January 1869–November 1873.

Journal of the Little Big Horn Associates. Bi-annual, June 1987 to present.

Mainstreeter. Northern Pacific Railway Historical Association. Quarterly, 1995–2004.

Minneapolis Tribune. Daily, selected dates 1871–73.

Nation. Weekly; January 1872–October 1873.

New York Herald. Daily; June–October 1872; May–October 1873.

New York Times. Daily; spring 1869–winter 1873.

New York Tribune. Daily; July–October 1872; June–October 1873.

Northwest Magazine. Monthly; January 1883–December 1889.

Philadelphia Evening Bulletin. Daily; August–October 1872; August–September 1873.

Philadelphia Inquirer. Daily; July–December 1872; July–October 1873.

Railroad Gazette. Weekly; January 1870–December 1873.

Record (Fargo). Monthly and later quarterly; May 1895–2nd quarter 1905.

Red River Star (Moorhead). Weekly; July 1872–December 1873.

St. Paul Pioneer. Daily and weekly; April 1871–October 1873.

St. Paul Press. Daily and weekly; 1869 through 1873.

Sioux City Journal. Daily; June–December 1871; July 1872–September 1873.

ACKNOWLEDGMENTS

I would like to thank Mark Jordan of Gorham, Maine, who "introduced" me to his great-uncle, the surveyor Edward C. Jordan, and the Yellowstone Surveying Expeditions. I am most grateful (alphabetically) to two college friends and fraternity brothers, Paul M. Baltay of Arlington, Virginia, who researched numerous individuals in the book and discovered and translated Edward Konopicky's letters; and Lewis T. Buckman, a civil engineer, from East Berne, New York, who did his best to explain some of the mysteries of surveying and civil engineering. Dave Eckroth of Billings, Montana, generously shared with me his discoveries of and insights into the 1872 battle sites. Dr. C. Vance Haynes, Jr., Regents Professor emeritus, University of Arizona, generously shared his research concerning the 1873 fighting. Bruce Liddic, past president of the Little Big Horn Associates, went out of his way to be helpful and offer cogent advice. Jerry Masters of Kansas City and Larry Schrenk of Minneapolis, Northern Pacific Railway Historical Association (NPRHA) members, proofread a draft and have been exceptionally helpful over the years. Bill McConnachie of Hysham, Montana, lives on the August 11, 1873, battle site and was kind enough to describe it to me. Through the Internet I met and was immeasurably assisted by Margaret Prasthofer-Lewis of London, England, Lt. Lafayette Campbell's great-granddaughter. Dr. Richard J. Sommers of the U.S. Army Military History Institute, Carlisle, Pennsylvania, kindly took an interest when my research had just begun; in addition to his patience in answering numerous questions, I am appreciative of his wise counsel. Francis Taunton, vice chairman of the English Westerners Society, has written about the 1873 expedition and could not have been more helpful. And for years Dick Upton, Upton & Sons, El Segundo, California, has called invariably useful books to my attention.

Special thanks are also due to Betty Allen and Ellen H. Fladger, Union College Special Collections, Schenectady, New York; Walter L. Bailey, North Dakota State Historical Society, Bismarck; Sheila Biles, United States Military Academy Archives and Library, West Point; John Doerner, Little Bighorn Battlefield National Monument, Crow Agency, Montana; Dr. William Farr, University of Montana, Missoula; Jerome A. Greene, National Park Service, Denver; Eric Halvorron, Hardin, Wyoming, Public Library; Nicole M. Hayes, Baker Library, Harvard Business School, Cambridge, Massachusetts; George H. LaBarre, LaBarre Galleries in Hollis, New Hampshire, who has attempted to educate me about nineteenth-century railroad stocks and bonds; Patricia Mauss, Northeast Minnesota Historical Center, Duluth; David Miller, recent author of a biography of General Montgomery Meigs, Alexandria, Va.; Mary Lou Moudry, Crow Wing County Historical Society, Brainerd; the late Brian Pohanka, well-known author of numerous Civil War books; Lewis T. Renz, author of *History of the Northern Pacific Railroad* (1980), Roseville, California; Tim Schandal, director, Union Depot and Lake Superior Museum, Duluth; Kim A. Scott, Montana State University Library, Bozeman; and Marjorie Strong, Vermont Historical Society, Montpelier.

Help was received from almost two hundred people at various libraries, historical associations, and sites, especially Susan Bleistein and Karen Moore of the Fairfax County, Virginia, Public Library system. Special note should also be made of the 42nd Street New York Public Library, where the staff's professionalism and courtesy remain as high as when I first used the library, in the late 1950s. I would also like to thank the Small Special Collections Library, University of Virginia–Charlottesville; Arlington County Public Library, Arlington, Virginia; Big Horn County Public Library, Hardin, Montana; Billings Public Library (Montana Room), Billings, Montana; Burlingame Special Collections Library, Montana State University–Bozeman; Crow Wing County Historical Society, Brainerd, Minnesota; Cumberland County Historical Society, Carlisle, Pennsylvania; Denver Public Library, Denver, Colorado; Duluth Public Library, Duluth, Minnesota; James J. Hill Library, St. Paul, Minnesota; the Library of Congress and National Archives, Washington, D.C., and Bladensburg, Maryland; McCracken Public Library, Buffalo Bill Historical Center, Cody, Wyoming; Minnesota Historical Society, St. Paul; Monroe County Historical Society, Monroe, Michigan; Montana State Historic Society, Helena; North Dakota State Historic Society, Bismarck; North Dakota State University—Institute for Regional Studies, Fargo; St. Louis County Historic Society, Duluth, Minnesota; Sandusky Public Library, Sandusky, Ohio; South Dakota State Historical Society, Pierre; U.S. Army Military Academy, Archives and Special Collections Department, West Point; U.S. Army Military History Institute, Carlisle, Pennsylvania; University of Minnesota–Duluth, Northeast Minnesota Historical Center; University of North Dakota, Grand Forks; and University of Wyoming, American Heritage Center, Cheyenne.

Numerous state and regional historic societies and centers have been helpful, including Buffalo and Erie County Historical Society, Buffalo, New York; Baker Library, Harvard Business School, Cambridge, Massachusetts; Historical Society of Pennsylvania, Philadelphia; Indiana Historical Society, Indianapolis; Maine Historical Society, Portland; Miles City Preservation Commission, Miles City, Montana; Nebraska State Historical Society, Lincoln; State Historical Society of Iowa, Des Moines; Tennessee State Library and Archives, Nashville; University of Montana, Missoula; Vermont Historical Society, Montpelier; and Wisconsin Historical Society, Madison.

Invaluable support has also been provided by many members of both the Little Big Horn Associates and the Northern Pacific Railway Historical Association (see their websites: www.nprha.org and www.lbha.org). Both organizations hold annual conferences, publish high-quality magazines, and are composed of innumerable intelligent, informed, and friendly individuals. Besides just being fun to be with, they have gone out of their way to answer questions and offer encouragement and support. Special note should be taken of the late Lawrence A. Frost's herculean efforts in documenting the 1873 survey. Whatever disagreements I might have had with him, particularly in regard to his depiction of David Stanley, part of this book would not have been possible without his effort and the well-documented research trail that he blazed.

Portions of chapter 7 are revised from passages in my article "The Forgotten Yellowstone Surveying Expeditions of 1871: W. Milnor Roberts and the Northern Pacific Railroad in Montana," published in the winter 2002 issue of *Montana The Magazine of Western History*. Portions of chapter 9 are revised from passages in my article "An Ambush That Changed History: Thomas L. Rosser, David S. Stanley, Gall, and the 1872 Eastern Yellowstone Expedition," published in the winter 2004 issue of *Journal of the West*. And portions of chapters 15 and 16 are revised from passages in my article "Clash on the Yellowstone: Monday, August 4, 1873," published in the summer 2003 issue of *Research Review: The Journal of the Little Big Horn Associates*.

I cannot begin to say how often I am frustrated by good books with bad maps or none at all. While maps are highly subjective, I have tried to provide easy-to-read maps, leaving the reader with an overall feeling for what happened and approximately where. I am very appreciative of the work of Vicki Trego Hill, El Paso, Texas, who has taken period maps and my rough sketches and turned them into something first rate.

In ancient times, the Greeks had enough sense to know that they did not know everything; to cover their bases, they built a temple to the "unknown" gods. In a similar vein, I have undoubtedly omitted some individuals, and I trust they will accept my sincere apologies.

INDEX